WILL THE
REAL
ALBERTA
PLEASE
STAND UP?

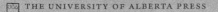 THE UNIVERSITY OF ALBERTA PRESS

WILL THE
REAL
ALBERTA
PLEASE
STAND UP?

GEO TAKACH

Published by
The University of Alberta Press
Ring House 2
Edmonton, Alberta, Canada   T6G 2E1

LIBRARY AND ARCHIVES CANADA
CATALOGUING IN PUBLICATION

Takach, George Francis, 1960–
     Will the real Alberta please stand up? /
Geo Takach.

Includes bibliographical references and index.
ISBN 978-0-88864-543-2

     1. Alberta. 2. Alberta—History. 3. Alberta—
Civilization. I. Title.

FC3661.T35 2010   971.23   C2010-905512-8

The University of Alberta Press is committed to
protecting our natural environment. As part of
our efforts, this book is printed on Enviro Paper:
it contains 100 per cent post-consumer recycled
fibres and is acid- and chlorine-free.

The University of Alberta Press gratefully
acknowledges the support received for its
publishing program from The Canada Council
for the Arts. The University of Alberta Press also
gratefully acknowledges the financial support of
the Government of Canada through the Book
Publishing Industry Development Program
(BPIDP) and from the Alberta Foundation for
the Arts for its publishing activities.

The author gratefully acknowledges the generous
support of the Alberta Foundation for the Arts
through its Grants to Individuals/Literary
Arts Project Grant program, and of the Faculty
Scholarly Activity and Research Fund at Grant
MacEwan University.

Lyrics to "The Toronto Song" quoted by permission
     of Wesley Q. Borg, Esq.
Lyrics to "Ole Buffalo" quoted by permission of
     Bill Bourne.
Lyrics to "Always Keep an Edge On Your Knife"
     quoted by permission of Corb Lund.

For the Bonnie wild rose

But as the province grows older, so does a provincial nationality become more in evidence.

—ALWYN BRAMLEY-MOORE,

Canada and Her Colonies, Or Home Rule for Alberta, 1911

Contents

Foreword

YOU MIGHT WONDER what possessed me to reprise my love affair
with the written word after a respite approaching a century. As a tenant
of Calgary's scenic Union Cemetery with little hope of tearing up the
lease, it's too late for me to be possessed, at least in the supernatural
sense. But I take this opportunity to rake muck with my rental agreement for a reason, and it's a darned good one. This book is enough to
wake the dead.

   When the author of this little tome approached my gatekeepers for
an interview, he was rebuffed with the traditional silence. (Modesty
prohibits revealing whether my keepers' apparel is impervious to fire.)
I mean, if I stiffed my biographer, the greatest Albertan to inhabit the
twentieth century, then why bother for some no-account from the
twenty-first? When pressed with this rejoinder from my keepers, our
author replied by betting that my biographer, J.W. Grant MacEwan,
never requested an interview. This, we admit here, is true. Nor, it
must also be acknowledged, did the distinguished Dr. M. dangle the

Bob Edwards with the lady who ended his bachelorhood after almost six decades.

[Glenbow Archives, NA–5688–1]

tantalizing invitation to write a foreword to any of *his* books. As he has since joined me here at Union, I am moved to broach the subject at the next tenants' meeting. But I digress.

In the January 24, 1919, edition of the *Eye Opener*, I opined that while a man's good deeds are limited, there is no limit to the mischief that he can accomplish. Tilting at the immense wagon wheels of irrelevance that ultimately grind us all to dust, this Takach laddie has combed library shelves, haunted archives, consulted prominent Albertans and interviewed Canadians of diverse walks, stripes and rates of decay, from sea to sea, all in a quest to define the identity of the province that I called home during my breathing years. I hesitate to add that he has left no turn unstoned, because, like he, I have too much respect for his subject to leave the final word on it to *anyone*. I leave to posterity the question of whether anyone should care.

Like the people who live in it, a place is never ridiculous for what it is, but for assuming to be what it isn't. Alberta may be many things to many people, but is she ridiculous? It's a fine question. Enjoy this book, gentle reader, and decide for yourself.

Ever forward, I remain yours formerly,

ROBERT CHAMBERS "Eye Opener Bob" EDWARDS, 1859–1922

Acknowledgements

I AM PROFOUNDLY GRATEFUL to the Alberta Foundation for the Arts and its sainted peer jury for supporting this project with a generous subsistence grant. Similar huzzahs go out to the Faculty Scholarly Activity and Research Fund at Grant MacEwan University for contributing munificently to the costs of my research, and to the excellent Coreen Selsky for helping with some directed pieces of that research.

Snappy salutes to the marvellous archivists and librarians at treasure troves like the Glenbow Archives, the Provincial Archives of Alberta, the City of Edmonton Archives and the Edmonton Public Library. All hail the able scholars, journalists and creators whose work makes adventures like this possible; their names grace the bibliography and the endnotes.

Many of my interviews were part of a parallel project, a one-hour documentary film titled *Will the Real Alberta Please Stand Up?* that I conceived, wrote, hosted, directed and co-produced for City TV.

The film premiered at the Royal Alberta Museum in Edmonton; was subsequently screened at the Glenbow Museum in Calgary; was first broadcast in 2009; and is available on DVD from our non-theatrical distributor, www.mcnabbconnolly.ca. Thanks to Reel Girls Media and everyone involved in that grand adventure, and to Ava Karvonen for the Ferbey and boot photos.

My first choice for this book was the University of Alberta Press, as I have admired its oeuvre for years. My thanks to Michael Luski and especially his doctorally enhanced successor, Sir Peter Midgley, as well as Linda Cameron, Alan Brownoff, Cathie Crooks, Jeff Carpenter, Mary Lou Roy, Sharon Wilson, Mike Anderson and Tony Buchanan, a team with which it is an honour and a delight to work. Much appreciation to the anonymous but eminent peer reviewers for their suggestions, to the Press Committee for green-lighting this work, to Meaghan Craven for editorial wisdom and to Team T and Jeananne Kathol Kirwin for help and shoulders.

Finally a deep bow to the accomplished and amazing Albertans quoted in this work (many of them longstanding personal heroes) for sharing their insights about our province. Ditto to the legendary comedy czar, Mark Breslin, who graciously ignored my sweating all over his office carpet on a sweltering summer's day. (In Toronto, as in life, it's not the heat, it's the stupidity.) A hearty high-five and blessings to the generous Canucks from left coast to right who stopped to talk with a stranger on the street. As I trust you shall see, they don't come much stranger than from Alberta.

Opening Questions[1]

Why a book exploring the soul of Alberta?

A legacy of our recent provincial centennial is a burst of worthy work studying and celebrating Alberta's land, her history and her people in everything from print, music and visual art to community projects and bewildered epithets. But little of it was foolish enough to focus directly on the question of what defines the essence of our province and her people.

There are several reasons not to try such a quest at home.

First, how do we define the soul of a place? Do we consider (1) her citizens' self-image or (2) the perceptions of others, which may mix like oil sands and water? In *Alberta Politics Uncovered*, the journalist, Mark Lisac, suggested that Albertans are soaked in self-deception and that popular perceptions of Alberta are a façade. Even the central Canadian media might begin to suspect this duality: in 2006, a *Toronto Star* headline blared, "Not Your Dad's Alberta: Never Mind That 'Aw Shucks' and 'Howdy' Stuff. Today, the Province is

The real Alberta is larger than life.

Affluent, Sophisticated and Cosmopolitan." Albertans are so steeped in the brew of their own lore that the stain can't be scoured off. So how can we separate the reality from the myth? And should we even bother to try?

A second reason to avoid this quest involves asking whether it is even possible for a province to have an identity in a country that has made self-definition a national obsession rivalling the post-centennial Toronto Maple Leafs for outright futility. For years, the subject of what makes us Canadian has been hotly debated in academic circles and coldly debated in arctic circles. A recent book called *What Is a*

Canadian? Forty-Three Thought-Provoking Responses concludes,
"A Canadian is a citizen of the Canadian state" as there is "no soul,
language or belief peculiar to most of its citizens."[2] This is hardly
inspiring to soul-searching in a province with just over 10 per cent of
the national population—and a much heftier share of the attitude.

Third, isn't it somewhat artificial to pigeonhole a populace according
to mostly man-made borders? (I know what you're thinking. If women
had drawn up the borders, the province might have made more sense.)
Are Albertans really *that* different from Canadians north of 60, west of
the Rockies, east of the 110th meridian of latitude (the final frontier in
our matchless jihad on rats) or even south of the 49th parallel?

Fourth, since much of Alberta's population was not born here, how
could we all possibly be homogenous or share an identity?

Fifth, the question of what is the essence of Alberta seems to beg
subjectivity. How can you distill countless and often dramatically
diverse statistics, statements and opinions into a coherent response?
The inquiry seems more massive and complex than any single adventure can answer—especially without a doctorate in stuff like history,
sociology or statistics. Leaving sensible questions of how one ultimately determines the essence of a society, as well as strict qualitative
and quantitative research methods, to experts in the academy, I have
donned my journalist's deerstalker to survey what people have written
on our province and her place in Canada. I have interviewed Albertans
who have achieved distinction in their fields, as well as locals, other
Canadians and tourists corralled in curbside conversations from the
wharves of Vancouver to the wilds of northern Newfoundland. And
I have harnessed decades of first-hand observation. While I don't
propose to do justice to every aspect of Wild Rose Country or represent the mesmerizing kaleidoscope of viewpoints that find expression
here, I have tried to present as objective and insightful a portrait of the
soul of Alberta as personal resources, publication realities and sanity
permit. Rather than attempt definitiveness, I seek to start a conversation by posing questions. Who are we as Albertans? What is our role

in Canada? And most critically, where do we want to go as a province and a people?

On the nuances of such a quest in self-analysis, Alberta's Heritage Community Foundation pronounced, "A unique Albertan identity is extremely difficult to describe, as there is no singular 'Albertan.' Rather, the difficult-to-define Albertan is made up of a rich mix of peoples which all contribute valuable characteristics and give meaning to the Albertan identity at large."[3] The word "large" is important because Alberta is large writ large. As an anonymous twenty-year expat from Ontario tells me in a street interview, "Per capita, Alberta is pretty much the extreme in every category you can think of." If you accept that an eight-hundred-pound gorilla like Alberta is best left alone, then that brings us to six solid roadblocks to our quest to define the real Alberta. Perhaps it is best to let sleeping doghouses lie.

The problem is that Albertans *won't* lie down. Only we would elevate a largely negative term like "doghouse" into a symbol of authority—at least in the oil patch, where it has become known both figuratively and literally as an office for higher-ups. Allied with this heightened consciousness is Alberta's economic and political profile, which has been rising on the national and global stages of late with a force normally reserved for statistics on childhood obesity.

Ironically, while the last economic boom cycle and the planet's rising environmental conscience tilted the spotlight on Alberta more than ever, she may well be Canada's most misunderstood province. Interviewing Albertans here at home and Canadians and foreign visitors from the country's left coast to the right has yielded a pile of perceptions to rival the eleven metres of bone deposits lining the business end of Head-Smashed-In Buffalo Jump.

To many, Alberta still represents the "Last Best West" of azure skies, soaring mountain peaks and golden grain fields. A land of incurable rednecks, cowboys, Bible thumpers and dung disturbers. The home of Western hospitality and four-wheel-drive optimism, typified by the memorable bumper sticker that played the byways after the bust in the

1980s, "Please, Lord, let there be another oil boom—I promise not to piss it away this time." Is there truth to these icons? Hell, yes! But as the last century shows, they're not even the tip of the grain elevator.

The real Alberta shocks most non-Albertans. It even floors people who live here. Nowhere else in Canada, if not Western civilization, do all of the majesty and the mayhem of the natural and human worlds converge, collude and collide more spectacularly. Yet after more than a hundred years of provincehood, the true Alberta, the lady behind the Stetson, the rigger's overalls and the latest designer footwear, remains a riddle wrapped in a saucy donair—classically beef but not always—and still largely distant to most outsiders.

For openers, many see the province as mountain or prairie. This is accurate, of course. But an amazing number of major biophysical regions meet here, making the province's landscape as rich in diversity as it is in weirdness. The mighty snow-eater, the chinook, blows in off the Rockies to turn a parka-dotted deep-freeze into a barefoot Frisbee-fest within hours. Eerie, eroded slabs of shale and sandstone, the hoodoos, haunt the badlands like Stonehenge fungi. Ghostly, alpine Medicine Lake drains like a clawfoot tub every autumn. Strange. And that's just a smattering of the *physical* landscape.

The human landscape is even more bizarre. And unpredictable. How else could you describe a province that revels in its macho rep while rocking the cradle of feminism in this country? Testosterone-choked ranges and rigs, sure. This is, after all, where an entire town (Devon) sprang up from oil workers ("rig pigs") being exiled by the irate fathers of pregnant girls. But it has also harboured the first double-x-chromosome chief justice and big-city police chief in Canada, the first female magistrate, the first female MLAs and the second female cabinet minister in the British Empire, as well as some reasonably outrageous drag queens. And incidentally, isn't it the only Canadian province named after a woman?

People love to pigeonhole and dismiss this place as a monolithic, predictable bastion of conservatism. As if the soul of a province can be defined by an electoral system running on the principles of winner-take-all and gerrymandering. It may surprise you, as it did me, to discover that Alberta remains a hotbed of political non-partisanship, apathy and even radicalism. The province exudes variety as much as the land oozes oil and monster houses during the booms—and exoduses and foreclosure proceedings during the inevitable busts.

Scan through the squares knitted into our family quilt over the last century and you'll find some enduring common threads. Ask an Albertan and you'll hear about a fierce independent streak, the legacy of pioneers who gave their lives to carve a living out of bush and dirt. A healthy mistrust of eastern muckamucks whom, Albertans perceive, never seem to run out of ways to bleed the Last Best West of staples like furs, oil and Stanley Cups. A vision for the future as wide as a prairie sky. A work ethic as hardy and steadfast as a prairie thistle. And a headlong rush through life as animated as a prairie chicken. Our motto, "Strong and free," aptly captures both our appetite for shopping and our singular and beloved lack of a provincial sales tax. These are some of the self-portraits that we like to paint.

But these initial impressions are just generalities. The reality is vastly more nuanced, more complex and more ridiculous. The last century shows that Albertans dearly believe that rules, like bucking broncos, are made to be broken. They seem to have a winking tolerance, if not outright admiration, for those who buck the herd—*any* herd.

We have Bob Edwards, a colourful frontier newsman who made his name skewering the hypocrisies of the rich, pious and powerful, undaunted by personal paradoxes like supporting Prohibition while drinking like a skunk and bashing politicians while standing for office himself.

We have Emily Murphy, a groundbreaking judge, women's-rights advocate and social reformer, whose pronouncements on eugenics and immigrants would keep today's human rights commissions in paperwork for Alberta's next hundred years.

And we have gentlemen who preside over payola, seduce a housemaid (or so the jury said), print their own money, trample on freedom of speech and proffer provocative pronouncements on foreign dictatorships from correspondence-school homework cribbed from the Internet. And these are just our premiers!

As then-Prime Minister Jean Chrétien quipped about Albertans, "They are a different type." That he later apologized for this probably offended more of us than his original quip did.

Alberta is eclectic, as tough to pin down in words as "Hitman" Hart was in the ring. Where else could the frontier priest, Albert Lacombe; the comedian and healer, Don Burnstick; and the beef-eschewing chanteuse, k.d. lang share a history with the cattle baron, Pat Burns; the basketball titans, the Edmonton Grads; and the defrocked Holocaust denier, Jimbo Keegstra? Where else could a capital city host a summer festival that's tawdry, anachronistic and dubiously appropriate historically (Klondike Days, recently rebranded as "Capital Ex" in a concession to modernity, if not to grandly failed marriages or maybe even laxatives), along with some the most progressive theatre this side of the Great White Way? Where else do people drag out debates on homosexuals' rights while creating one of Canada's first provincial human rights commissions—or burn crosses while hosting what's billed as the largest known, single-venue festival of multiculturalism? Where else do taxpayers offer relatively miserly public support for the poor while racking up volunteer rates that would outrun a pronghorn antelope? Where else does the government flame ahead with pioneering environmental legislation while getting barbecued by scientists and eco-groups for pimping our grandchildren's health to industrial polluters? Only in Alberta would a premier muse about a hazardous waste treatment plant doubling as a tourist attraction.

In other parts of Canada, these could be critical and even absurd contradictions. Out here, they fit right in. These, along with the six reasons raised earlier, should be enough to halt our quest to define the

Wild Rose Province and nip it at the bud. But that's hardly the way in Alberta, where roadblocks are viewed as invitations as much as obstacles—merely barriers to be hurdled and preferably on an Olympic scale. Or so we say. So...

Are Albertans down to earth or are we destroying it?

Are we rednecks or radicals?

Are we mavericks or are we more like sheep?

Is Alberta a cultural backwater or a flowing fountain of knowledge and the arts?

And just what does Alberta bring to Confederation besides federal transfer-payment fodder, a tradition of opposition Members of Parliament and the odd case of mad cow disease?

These are the main themes that we will mine here, chosen out of subjective interest rather than scholarly methodology. This book aims to explore Alberta's lesser known and often stunning contradictions, highlight her memories and myths, distill it all to an essence and begin to explain just why she is the way we find her today.

If you're wondering what would motivate such a quest or where its perpetrator is coming from, your host confesses to a near-life-long fascination and frustration with the province he has called home since the glory days of disco. Like many Albertans, I escaped to here from somewhere else. My arrival came after a 3,000-kilo-metre slog in winter-whiteout conditions, cramped in the back of the family Buick. My brave parents hailed from neither of the two ruling cultures in Québec, where they docked as political refugees after fleeing then-Communist Hungary and eventually produced me as a weekend freedom project. The folks noticed that the French and the English didn't always get along (the Front de Libération de Québec's mail bombs may have been a good clue) and that members of the "two founding nations" club liked outsiders about as much as they liked each other. So we packed up and pointed the hood ornament westward. Ever-sensitive to prejudice at an early age, I remember lumbering into Edmonton through refinery row and fearing that my own notions of Alberta as an oil-rigger's wasteland—pre-installed at the plant back in central Canada—were correct. In my first week at school here, a prescient social studies teacher anointed me as an Albertan MP in a parliamentary simulation, and I watched in dismay as my efforts to serve local interests were crushed by classmates representing (you guessed it) Ontario and Québec. Revelling in the righteousness of teenaged rebellion and freedom from the colonial bondage of biculturalism, I embraced our new home with the zeal of a revivalist rally. My embarrassment at how little I understood this part of the country segued to appreciation and pride as I came to know it better, then to frustration whenever Alberta was depicted as some kind of backwater. Frustration turned to fury when *Albertans* did the depicting.

These sentiments have resurfaced throughout my work as a professional writer for almost two decades. I have celebrated the province's feats and foibles in print, speeches, films, comedy performances and music, and on television, the Web and garage pads. The place seeps into your soul to such an extent that the tail end of a cross-country driving trip with my family turned into a white-knuckled race to shed the shackles of the Canadian Shield and hit the soothing openness of the prairie. There's no zealot quite like a convert; if I had been born here, I'd have less to shudder at by way of comparison. I don't fault folks for perpetuating prejudices and stereotypes—after all, they're ubiquitous and sometimes spot-on—but I do hope that they're open to revisiting them with a fresh eye, an inquiring mind and a strong stomach.

That's my motivation for this quest to explore the elusive essence of Wild Rose Country. My primary qualification is no more than curiosity. And my focus is mostly on the recent past, highlighting Alberta's century-plus of provincehood while leaving the bulk of her rich, earlier history to smarter sorts with longer attention spans.

Again, I won't pretend to present the sole, definitive answer, but I hope to raise the right questions. We need to ask these questions now more than ever, given the formidable and dangerous opportunities that Mother Nature has deposited under our doorstep, and the world's deepening addiction to viscous, black goo. In an age in which oil reigns supreme (some say rampant), Alberta is at a crossroads socially, culturally, economically and environmentally. For better or worse, the impact of Albertans' decisions will spill far beyond her borders and this week's headlines.

This book asks just who Albertans are today. To Albertans and their aficionados, I leave the more substantial and pressing issue of for what we want to be remembered tomorrow. That one is up to you.

1

Down to Earth?

Here veils of Northern Light are drawn
On high as winter closes,
And hoary dews at summer dawn
Adorn the wild red roses.
Sometimes the swelling clouds of rain
Repress the sun's caresses;
But soon the mountains smile again
And shake their icy tresses.

— STEPHAN G. STEPHANSSON, "Toast to Alberta," 1893

Born of the Land

KNOWING ALBERTA and her people requires knowing the land. Beyond unflattering comparisons between today's Albertans and the paleontological delights that once roamed Earth, Alberta houses among the most remarkable fossil records on record. She has perhaps the world's richest collection of Cretaceous treasures, giving us an electron-microscope's-eye view of dinosaurs, crocodiles, fish, insects and plants from 75 million years ago. The paleontologist, Dr. Philip Currie, sees Alberta as the best venue for his discipline, since the province hosts about 8 per cent of the world's known dinosaur species. He calls Dinosaur Provincial Park a perfect laboratory, with the highest known diversity of dinosaurs in a single site on Earth. Dinosaur bones have also been found around Grande Prairie, and marine reptile fossils have been discovered around Fort McMurray. Sites around Drumheller and elsewhere in southern Alberta are almost as rich. Museums in the United States, South America, Australia and Europe display fossils from Alberta, reflecting what some see as the glacial pace at which Albertans moved to preserve their resources after eye-popping finds such as the Albertosaurus, unearthed by Dr. Joseph Tyrrell in 1884. It took more than four decades to create Dinosaur Provincial Park in 1955, and until 1978 anyone could collect, sell or otherwise defile fossils found in Alberta.

Just why was this tract of land blessed with the grandest dinosaur boneyard on Earth? In an earlier age, Alberta was a vast, flat, coastal flood plain, wet, tropical, brimming with lush vegetation and ideal for animal life. Large rivers crossed this plain, depositing sediment rapidly, so animals caught in the muck were buried relatively shortly after perishing and embalmed with an efficacy that would stun a pharaoh's undertaker.

Alberta boasts a rich human legacy, too. About 18,000 years ago, the area was buried under a gargantuan sheet of ice radiating from the present Hudson Bay. Some, like archaeological curators Susan Berry and Jack Brink, suggest that the thaw that occurred about 12,000 years ago created an ice-free corridor through the eastern foothills of the Rockies between the glaciers covering most of British Columbia and a glacier centred at Hudson Bay. This cut-through just may have brought the first immigrants from Asia to the Americas, even though the trail from the Bering Land Bridge along the Pacific coastline might have been easier due to lower sea levels exposing more land along the coast. These immigration theories are disputed by Native advocates who interpret the term "Aboriginal" more literally. In any case, there is evidence that Aboriginal people have been in Albertan territory for at least 12,000 years. The oldest known human-built shelter in Canada, 10,000 years old, was discovered at Vermilion Lakes west of Banff. The oldest archaeological sites in the province, on the eastern slopes of Rockies, date from 9,000–11,000 years ago. These sites establish Alberta as a hotbed of the ingenuity that its administrations strive to harness through efforts like Canada's oldest provincial research council, a $1-billion Ingenuity Fund and random pleas for Albertans to smarten up already.

Illustrative of Aboriginal peoples' genius for survival are two remarkable hunting sites. The first is found about fifteen kilometres south of Taber at Fletcher, by a former lake where bison came to drink and hunters hid behind a ridge. The second and better known is Head-Smashed-In Buffalo Jump, found in the Porcupine Hills near Fort Macleod and excavated by an American archaeologist in 1938. There, about 5,800–10,000 years ago, the Kainai and Piikani first disguised themselves as their quarry by donning calf hides and bleating, to lure bison into an elaborate network of gathering basin, driving lanes and cairns that ultimately led straight off an eighteen-metre sandstone cliff. Remarking on an Assiniboine bison hunt in 1776, Alexander Henry the Elder observed, "Their gestures so resembled those of the animals themselves that had I not been in on the secret, I should have been as much deceived as the buffalo."[1]

Native tribes lived across Alberta, including, from roughly north to south, the Slavey, Beaver, Woodland Cree, Chipewyan, Plains Cree, Stoney and Blackfoot (whose nation comprises the Blood, Peigan and Blackfoot). To Jack Brink, curator of archaeology at the Royal Alberta Museum, Alberta's first peoples were as different from others as they were ingenious. "There was an awe-inspiring adaptability to land, mastered at every corner, altitude and temperature," he tells me. "What's distinctive about early peoples in Alberta is that they were always hunters and gatherers; never domestic, agriculture-based settlers as in the American southwest. This is partly why the archaeological record here is not as earth-shaking: we had none of the waste of resources or the lives that built monuments to crackpot rulers in other parts of the world." Mr. Brink calls the first peoples sophisticated, ingenious and the equal of other civilizations: "For example, the buffalo jump was incredibly choreographed, orchestrated, engineered, manipulated and spiritually connected. It's almost like they had the power of levitation to see the landscape from the air, like ancient mapmakers laying out a complex system of lanes. We're barely understanding how they did it today." While aspects of the buffalo hunt were practised in places like Saskatchewan, Wyoming and the Dakotas, Mr. Brink sees Head-Smashed-In as perhaps the most spectacular site.

Continuing Alberta's honour roll of internationally lauded treasures of antiquity, Writing-on-Stone Provincial Park, also in south-central Alberta, features the largest concentration of Aboriginal rock art in North America. The eroding Milk River produced a massive array of sandstone rock canvases on which the first peoples chose to record their stories and way of life. Unfettered by a written language, they devised two ways to create a visual legacy. The first and more common was to use rock, bone or wood to etch outlines of humans, animals, tools and shapes into carvings called petroglyphs. The second, found mostly in sheltered locations, was to paint images called pictographs onto the rock surface, applying charcoal and red ochre using human fingers or brushes made from bison bones. The images include what are believed to be round-bodied warriors poised behind large shields; square-bodied or hourglass-figured people with heart lines and sexual organs; bison, bears, elk, deer, antelope, sheep, dogs, skunks and snakes; bison kills, battle scenes and more. Some glyphs and graphs may be thousands of years old, while others, depicting European imports such as horses, firearms and lynchings, date from the early eighteenth century. The earliest petroglyphs are attributed to the Shoshoni, who migrated from the United States about seven centuries ago, while later, more active and naturalistic petroglyphs and picto graphs are considered the work of Blackfoot, Cree or Gros Ventres artists. Demonstrating the cultural sensitivity characterizing white contact, nineteenth-century North West Mounted Police (NWMP) officers used these artworks for target practice.[2] Of course, the last word always belongs to time itself: these probably sacred petroglyphs and pictographs are now wearing away from erosion.

Reflecting its long-perceived place as beyond the beaten track, Alberta did not earn a formal archaeological exploration until 1935. A University of New Mexico team dug a test pit at Head-Smashed-In, and within twenty-two years, the province had established an archaeological branch and a lab. Calling it one of the last frontiers of archaeological study, one author, D.R. King, noted Alberta's barely touched archaeological wealth, the limited resources available to find it and the danger wrought by the steady construction of infrastructure; he called on enlightened amateurs to step up and document the thousands of unrecorded sites.[3]

Despite the detritus of the postmodern world, a primeval spirit still permeates the province. It just takes an artist to see it. The Albertan literary lion, Rudy Wiebe, tells me, "Alberta is the only province where we have the prairie rising to the mountains. There's something profoundly spiritual about the mountains, reaching up to the divine. For the natives, it's the same thing: 'These mountains are our sacred places.' You don't get to know us too well, or you'd realize what kind of spiritual people we are."

Medicine wheels are circular arrangements of stones, often dozens of metres in diameter, with several rows of stones radiating from the outer circle like spokes, to an array of stones at the centre or hub of the wheel. They were likely used for ceremonial purposes. Of the seventy medicine wheels known to remain in North America, fifty of them lie in Alberta. To the veteran folk musician, Bill Bourne, this makes sense. "Alberta's a pretty magical place," he observes. "I always viewed this place as First Nations territory, and in that regard it seems to be a very spiritual place." His song, "Ole Buffalo," captures a quiet, shaggy and lonely soul whose head hangs low, "Oh, but his dreams fly high as the sky all right / And he'll join them by and by, he knows."

The buffalo remains an enduring part of Alberta's lore, memorialized by Wood Buffalo National Park in the northeast (an area larger than Switzerland but with more limited banking), where bison bordered on extinction a century ago, and in Elk Island National Park, home to about a thousand head of plains bison. Less legendary is the distinction between buffalo and bison, which are different species even though their names are used interchangeably. True buffalo are found in Africa and Asia, while the bison, native to Alberta, enjoys a more pronounced hump, a heftier head and a closer association with the barbecue. The terms are confused because Europeans who had seen actual buffalo in Asia and Africa so christened the bison based on a perceived resemblance.

This noble beast, the largest land mammal on the continent, was essential to life in the West. For several millennia, Aboriginal people hunted and used bison for everything from food, clothing, shelter and bedding to tools, weapons, fuel for fire, pots, cutlery, brushes, string and more. Horses, which ancient, blood-tipped spear points tell us were indigenous to North America, were reintroduced by tribes from the south to the prairie grasslands around 1730. This was bad news for the bison, as were the new convenience of firearms and the efforts of American authorities to undermine the survival of first peoples by eradicating herds. People shot bison from on foot, horseback and even trains to the point of near-extinction by 1880. Meanwhile, the mighty fur trade—history's first "Bay Days" led by the world's oldest company, chartered in 1670—had blanketed the prairies like bison dung, overrunning traditional Cree, Nakoda and Dene trading routes in the interest of fitting transatlantic fashionistas with fur coats, beaver hats and presumably further smugness. The Hudson's Bay Company and its archrival and later merger partner, the North West Company, built trading forts along the Saskatchewan, Athabasca and Peace rivers, extending as far west as Rocky Mountain House and making what is now Alberta the final frontier of the fur trade. Some say that the arrival of Europeans ended the traditional way of life for Alberta's Aboriginal people and brought them nothing but heartbreak. This is patently untrue: whites also brought unfair trading practices, measles, smallpox and whisky.

Although the new Dominion government knew about these activities, it was the alcohol that really fired up Sir John A. Macdonald: specifically, the corruption and debauchery at the aptly named Fort Whoop-Up, established as Fort Hamilton in 1869 by enterprising émigrés from Montana. In 1874 the PM dispatched the newly formed

NWMP westward in a pioneering exercise in peacekeeping. Forming a four-kilometre line, the force featured 275 armed men, 114 Red River carts with Métis drivers, kitchens, mowing machines, ploughs, 339 horses, 142 oxen and 93 beef cattle. Although the legendary westward march itself proved to be more disastrous than romantic, the great Blackfoot chief, Issapomahksika—better known to whites as Crowfoot—believed that the NWMP saved his people from both bad men and whisky. He declared, "The police have protected us as the feathers of a bird protect it from the frosts of winter."[4]

So law and order reached the West thanks to a motley band of American firewater pirates setting up in what would become the avowedly less ribald Lethbridge. The inevitable paperwork followed with Treaty 6 in 1876, Treaty 7 in 1877 and Treaty 8 in 1899.

When the writer, Myrna Kostash, reread *The Temptations of Big Bear* by Rudy Wiebe, she realized the extent to which she—and by extension, Albertan mythology as a whole—failed to account for the First Nations in the narrative of Western settlement. "In my book [the iconoclastic *All of Baba's Children*], I had swallowed hook, line and sinker the Ukrainian-Canadian myth that my ancestors were the first—this heroic narrative of breaking the land," she recalls. "When I discovered what that looked like from the native point of view, I was horrified. Don't just take what white folks tell you at face value!"

✳ The cartographic face of Alberta is roughly the size of the United Kingdom and California combined. She is 43 per cent larger than Japan, 17 per cent larger than France and only 3 per cent smaller than Texas, to which she has been compared on other fronts.

My first impression of Alberta on an elementary-school map of Canada was anger. Steeped in the mapmaking tragedies at Versailles which ravaged my ancestral Hungary in 1919, I have an indelible memory of discovering the jagged incision along the province's southwestern flank. My first reaction was to stand up at my desk and spew schoolyard epithets at the injustice of carving out part of Alberta's birthright in favour of neighbouring British Columbia. My second reaction was to sit back down and shut up as the preferred alternative to my teacher's invitation to visit the principal. Years later, I learned that the jagged line on Alberta's southwestern flank was not cartographic surgery but deference to the Continental Divide, which places the continent's high-water mark at our doorstep. As one of the grandest accumulations of ice and snow south of the Arctic, the Columbia Icefield is up to 365 metres deep, covering 230 square kilometres across the Alberta–BC border and marking the "geographic apex of North America, the point from which all land falls away."[5] This powwow of the Athabasca, Columbia and Saskatchewan glaciers provides meltwaters that flow to the Arctic Ocean, Hudson Bay and the Gulf of Mexico.

Rather than vent my anger at a real or imagined slight of the province—a quintessential Albertan habit—I should have rejoiced. Only recently, when Myrna Kostash wrote *Reading the River*, her exploration of the North Saskatchewan as the great river of the fur trade, did she identify herself for the first time as Albertan. She observes: "In fact, Alberta belongs to the rest of Canada a lot more than we belong to Montana. Our water starts from not only glaciers, but from Lake Winnipeg, the Great Lakes and eastern Canada. Water as our first line of communication reminds us of our connectedness with central Canada as opposed to this neo-conservative fabrication of needing a firewall in Alberta."

With the walls of provincehood drawn by 1905, Albertans turned to an image to project to the world.

Coats of arms were first developed over a thousand years ago to identify armoured warriors in battle, like medieval sports crests. In 1907 Premier Alexander Rutherford noticed that the other provinces had received armourial bearings from the British Crown, so he petitioned the eldest brother of the lady for whom the province was named—the briefly kingly Edward VII—to grant Alberta a coat of arms of "azure in front of range of snow mountains with the blue green coloured foothills, to a lighter green prairie into a golden wheat belt." His request was based on the design of an artist from Lacombe, Mrs. McCully, who was paid $3 for her trouble. Back in London, the College of Heralds rebuked the premier's request, calling it "of the poorest class of heraldry," sniffing at his "necessarily inadmissible" and "absolutely unintelligible" description, and demanding a less abstract representation of a wheat field than "a mere wash of yellow." But it took more than imperial paper-pushers to pummel the persevering prairie spirit, and Alberta eventually received a royal warrant for a coat of arms representing "azure in front of a range of snow moun-tains proper a range of hills vert, in base a wheat field surmounted by a prairie both also proper, on a chief argent of a St. George's Cross."

In 1910 the Alberta government was asked to explain its choice of coat of arms. Responding in the florid vernacular of the day, a corre-spondent noted that the arms reflected a view of the province from the east, citing "the almost limitless wheat field…rougher prairie land… the foothills…and finally, the noble and awe-inspiring Rockies." One can only applaud the ingenuity of a choice that could double as a tourist brochure and a recruiting poster for sodbusters. It is also telling that the government added the Cross of St. George. The red cross on a white shield echoes the official flag of an earlier tenant of the area, the Hudson's Bay Company, but it may also mark the province's battle to slay the "proper" dragons at the College of Heralds and to send a subtle warning to anyone considering messing with Alberta again, whether properly or otherwise.

Since then, Alberta's coat of arms has acquired some fashionable accessories, all of which reflect the landscape or its products. During the Depression, students selected *Rosa acicularis*—a product of not a flamenco dance floor, but a bushy shrub—as their official provincial flower. Found across the province, the wild rose may be an apt reflec-tion of her character: hardy, prolific, useful (its red berries or hips feed birds and flavour teas and preserves), circumpolar, sun-loving, nice to look at and, lest we forget the adjective that sometimes prefaces the

As Alberta's provincial fish, the mighty bull trout has been officially classified as a threatened species. Some of us find this ironic. [Geo Takach]

flower's name, prickly. A bevy of further accessorizing occurred from 1961–2003.

The flower teams up with the fleur-de-lys in the blue and white Franco-Albertan flag and reappears symbolically in the colours of Alberta's official tartan, designed by the Edmonton Rehabilitation Society. The tartan also includes green for Alberta's forests, gold for her wheat fields, blue for her skies and lakes, black for her coal and oil resources, and white for her clean, bright and occasionally snowy days. A dressy version was added recently for dancing and other festivities.

Students voted in the great horned owl as the official bird, apparently for its resourcefulness and resiliency, but perhaps also for such quintessentially Albertan attributes as a wide range, farsightedness and early breeding. Likewise, the Rocky Mountain bighorn sheep makes a suitable official mammal, with its notable preference for alpine road-ways and high-speed head-butting. The grandly named bull trout, Alberta's official fish, has earned catch-and-release rules to avoid another official designation: endangered.

The Prairie Conservation Forum gave Alberta the distinction of having an official grass, rough fescue, to mirror the province's honour as the sole host to that vegetation in North America. The Alberta Federation of Rock Clubs chipped in with petrified wood as the offi-cial stone. And the Junior Forest Warden Association of Alberta chose the lodgepole pine, an old favourite of tipi-builders, navvies and the lumber industry, as the official tree. Notably, our national counterpart, the maple, is *not* native to Alberta.

As a national centennial project, the Alberta government proclaimed an official flag, settling on the coat of arms against a background of royal ultramarine blue, which was said to represent our unpolluted skies. (Remember now, this was in 1967.) For Alberta's diamond jubilee thirteen years later, the government resumed its heraldry-heightening by beefing up the coat of arms. Joining the fun were the fair *Rosa acicularis*, the British lion and a pronghorn antelope (Manitoba having dibs on the bison) supporting a crest featuring a beaver, which recalled Alberta's two centuries at the outer limits of the fur trade. Rounding out the show was the motto, *fortis et liber* ("strong and free"), conceivably to reflect Alberta's periodically booming economy and our singular absence of a provincial sales tax, respectively. Besides sounding good, the use of a dead language prudently squashed any suits for discrimination brought by linguistic lobby groups. However, all of these armourial rookies were omitted from the flag, not out of animosity for these fine flora, fauna and Latinisms, but because people in responsible positions believed that children would have difficulty drawing them. This is about as grassroots as democracy can get.[6]

In 2008, in a parting shot at a legacy project—if not a naked plea for the rural vote eluding his opposition Liberals for almost a century— the outgoing leader, Kevin Taft, led an all-party motion to recognize rodeo as the provincial sport, but the minister of culture bucked it off the order paper. And in 2009 legislators approved the *Leccinum boreale*, the red cap mushroom, as our provincial fungus, though that designation had not sprouted into law as of mid-2010.

At the end of the day, Alberta's official symbols and her place on the map are rooted firmly in the land, reflecting her geography, her history and perhaps even her sense of self.

Stranger than a Strange Land

"Alberta boasts some of the most dramatic landscapes on earth," wrote Tanya Lloyd Kyi. "Nothing here was made in moderation—this is a world of towering cliffs, giant rivers, and infinite prairie."[7] Lauded by Canadians in my street interviews from coast to coast for the beauty of her mountains and the bounty of her prairie, Alberta has bushels of secrets when it comes to her natural attractions.

Of course, Alberta differs from her prairie siblings by dint of the Rockies and from her coastal neighbour due to the prairie. But on a deeper level, the province is one of the world's greatest hotbeds of biodiversity, defined as the variety of all living things and the ecosystems that sustain them. Alberta is the only place in North America where the prairie, boreal forest and mountain ecosystems meet. Canada has twenty terrestrial and marine ecozones, and of all the provinces and territories Alberta ties British Columbia for the top spot with six: Taiga Plains, Taiga Shield, Boreal Shield, Boreal Plains, Montane Cordillera and Prairie.[8] The province boasts a bevy of mountains; forested hills, rolling grasslands and broad river valleys in the foothills; low rocky hills, forests, lakes, swampy areas and low marshy muskeg in our little corner of the Canadian Shield; flat and hilly areas in the parkland; low flatlands, meadows, hilly areas and moraines in the boreal forest; and grasslands on the prairie.

Roxy Hastings, the curator of botany at the Royal Alberta Museum, declares, "Alberta is diverse, near the top of anywhere in the world. No matter how you cut it in terms of classifying biological systems, we do have a lot here. There are not many places in the world as diverse ecologically and geologically—maybe Colorado." Mr. Hastings cites volcanic rock in the southwest and advises that tropical vegetation at the Oldman Falls includes tree mosses, the closest living relatives of which are in Mexico. He finds new species of mosses and lichens every time he visits north of Waterton from the Oldman River south, where nine-tenths of the province's diverse organisms live.

When it comes to elevation, Wild Rose Country runs the gamut from the predictable vertigo of 3,747 metres atop Mt. Columbia along the BC border in Jasper National Park down to 152 metres above sea level at Slave River toward the province's northeast corner. That corner is home to both a scrap of the Canadian Shield and the most northerly North American nesting haunt of the mighty American white pelican.

For Bruce McGillivray, the biologist and executive director of the Royal Alberta Museum (since retired), the province is best summed up by the diversity of the land: "I can jump in my car and drive an hour in almost every direction and be in a totally different world," he states, standing before one of the popular natural dioramas in the museum's permanent "Wild Alberta" exhibit. "We've got mountains and grasslands meeting. You've got boreal forests butting up against the Aspen parkland. You can't do that anywhere else that I'm aware of that easily—maybe South Africa, but that's a long way."

This diversity translates into a strong affinity, as the retired oilman, Joe Dundas, explains in an interview: "We can see the wagon tracks from the old Fort Benton Trail. A hundred-some-odd years ago and you can still feel a sense of being. We're totally connected with the land."

Alberta's landscape is reflected in some of its most notable architecture, among other art forms. The architectural revolutionary,

Douglas Cardinal, created a distinctive, curved, organic style in land-marks like St. Mary's Church in Red Deer, Grande Prairie Regional College, St. Albert Place and the spaceship-shaped Edmonton Space and Sciences Centre (since renamed the TELUS World of Science in a sacrifice on the corporate funding altar). For Mr. Cardinal, Alberta is dramatic landscapes in which people are dictated to by forces of nature. That outlook shows in his design for the Canadian Museum of Civilization in Gatineau, the curvilinear walls of which he likens to the Rocky Mountains forming the backbone of the continent, and wind and water eroding and shaping the land forms that became the Americas. "So the message of this giant piece of sculpture is that our future depends on us being at one with nature," he tells me outside those distinctive walls. When American architects gave Mr. Cardinal an international award and made him an honorary member of their institute, they noted that the focus of his achievements was the envi-ronment in which he grew up: Alberta.

Mr. Cardinal's buildings are far from the only distinctive features on the landscape. The province boasts a dazzling array of weird geog-raphy and unusual or little-known features. For example, at the Red Rock Coulee Natural Area southwest of Medicine Hat, sandstone boulders emerge slowly from the ground as powerful winds blow away the surrounding soil. Red Rock Canyon in Waterton Lakes National Park is a monument to oxidized iron. And if you can picture a rock 41 metres wide, 18 metres long, 9 metres high and weighing 16,500 tonnes, your vision comes to life at Okotoks, north of Calgary. Carried from Mt. Edith Cavell in Jasper by a glacier and broken in two, it's called *Ohkotokiksi* by the Siksika (Blackfoot), an "erratic" by the glacial cogno-scenti and simply the "Big Rock" by locals. According to Blackfoot legend, the trickster, Napi, offered his robe to the rock, but took it back when it got cold. The rock took exception to this and gave chase until nightingales dive-bombed it with droppings, causing it to break in two. The Big Rock received what may be Canada's highest accolade: having not only a local beer but an entire brewery named after it.

Staying with rocks, you can drive through Alberta's version of Stonehenge gone bad at Frank in the Crowsnest Pass, site of the most disastrous rockslide in Canadian history. Before dawn on a spring day in 1903, in a hundred seconds, the slide devoured three square kilometres, killing at least seventy-six people and many trusted workhorses. The culprit, Turtle Mountain, also looms over the province's two other worst disasters (not including the Wayne Gretzky trade): the Bellevue Mine explosion in 1910, killing thirty people, and the Hillcrest Mine explosion in 1914, killing almost two hundred men in Canada's worst mining accident. For some, the Crowsnest Pass also claims a fourth calamity: the Crow Rate, launched in 1897 to help Western farmers by keeping the Canadian Pacific Railway's freight rates low on eastbound shipments of grain and flour in return for a federal government subsidy to the CPR of $3.3 million, plus the free passage of goods through to British Columbia. This Crow's Nest Pass Agreement never satisfied everyone, enduring alterations by the feds and ultimately getting derailed after almost a century of controversy. Behind the politics, geography still reigns.

In the southeast, the Cypress Hills—which straddle Alberta and Saskatchewan and are contained in Canada's first interprovincial park—claim two distinctions. At 1,500 metres, they are the highest point between the Rockies and central Canada, and their lush woods and grasslands present a green oasis tucked into the surrounding plains. On the less lush side, the legendary badlands are home to not only the world's largest bed of dinosaur bones, but intense, dry heat and notoriously voracious insects. The badlands are said to be named by French explorers for the steep, winding canyons that were hard to traverse and remarkably barren, otherworldly and foreboding. The weirdness is accented by the erosion of weaker sedimentary stuff like shale and sandstone, leaving harder stone exposed. The poster children for erosion are the colossal, mushroom-shaped pillars of rock, the supporting, softer "stems" of which have been worn down by wind and rain, leaving harder material like ironstone to form capstones.

Alberta's topographic weirdness mushrooms with the hoodoos in the badlands near Drumheller. [Geo Takach]

Astonished Europeans found these sinister and named them "hoodoos," a word from African voodoo culture (connoting witch-craft lore in which humans are turned into pillars of earth), translated loosely as "rotten luck." First Nations folks believed the hoodoos to be petrified giants or tipis housing evil spirits. In keeping with Alberta's democratic penchant of spreading the weirdness around, hoodoos also turn up along Cavell Road in Jasper National Park, at Tunnel Mountain near Banff, southeast of Lethbridge and at Writing-on-Stone Provincial Park, also in the province's southeastern corner.

Although the northern part of the province is covered in boreal forest, its native trees, to echo our best-known conservationist, Grant

MacEwan, are not distinguished for long living.[9] Fittingly, the two best-known trees in the province are both dead. With its gnarled limbs and solitary, windswept location evoking Alfred Hitchcock and Tim Burton, the Burmis Tree, a limber pine that died in the late 1970s, in the Crowsnest Pass is probably the most photographed tree in Alberta. Our other dead tree celebrity is housed at the Royal Alberta Museum as an impressive exception to the short-life rule. An almost-two-metre cross-section of the trunk of a 381-year-old Douglas fir felled in the province in 1965, this artifact is used to trace major events in global history and remind us of our spectacular impermanence.

Alberta features a kaleidoscope of almost surreal colours. Canola fields across the province are a blinding, neon, greenish yellow. For the green set, the twenty-two parks and connecting green spaces along the valley of the North Saskatchewan River comprise the largest urban parkland system in North America. The Athabasca Glacier along the Icefields Parkway offers a stroll on the edge of a 325-square-kilometre sheet of silver ice, receding faster than Kurt Browning's hairline. Also in the Rockies, Peyto Lake and Moraine Lake display a deep, icy cerulean blue.

The province can claim the driest, bluest and sunniest skies in Canada, or close enough to it. Dry, clear air blows in from the Arctic and from the Pacific Ocean through the Rockies, which wring out the moisture and dissuade clouds. Mellow Pacific air makes cold temperatures less brutal or prolonged than in Saskatchewan. Alberta leads the country in sunny days year-round; places second in fewest snow and fog days; and attracts the lowest annual snowfall in the land.[10]

The province's affiliation with the sun and its associated outlook appeared on her first day of provincehood, when a press report gushed about the "glorious Alberta sunshine" ushering in the new province.[11] Medicine Hat advertises itself as the sunniest city in Canada, but there is more than statistics at work here; there is defiance. (For years, the Hat hosted the most northerly weather station on the continent, and it became "a sort of parlour entertainment"[12] for others to blame bad

Alberta's mercurial, tempestuous weather, captured over the North Saskatchewan River valley, eerily reflects her relationship with Ottawa. [David Roles]

weather on the place, as did the American writer, Carl Sandburg, in his 1918 poem, "Prairie": "You at a sod house door reading the blizzards and chinooks let loose from Medicine Hat."[13]) The peak of summer delivers more than seventeen hours of sunlight a day in the capital city, from about 5:00 A.M. to about 10:00 P.M., perhaps to compensate for springs and autumns that can pass through Alberta in as little as a month. Winters are a crapshoot owing to the north–south showdown between frigid blasts from the Arctic Ocean and warm gusts from the Pacific or the American southwest, which end in wild shifts in temperature and precipitation year-round.

More frequent in the south than the north, the mighty chinook wind, the snow-eater, starts off at the Pacific coast, cools as it climbs the western slopes then warms swiftly on its way down the eastern slopes of the Rockies. The result is some of the most dramatic change in weather imaginable. In January 1935, the temperature plummeted by 42°F in just over a day in Edmonton. In January 1983, the temperature in Calgary rose from -17°C to 13°C in just four hours. And during that city's Winter Olympics five years later, a chinook melted enough ice to delay the bobsled and luge races until everything could freeze again. "An Albertan senses the chinook," observes the cowboy poet, Doris Daley, "and speaks its language."

Many enjoy a love-hate relationship with the weather, but Alberta offers a characteristically extreme experience. From 1983–1991, half of Canada's twenty-eight insurance "events"—defined as a thousand or more weather-related claims for building and contents damage— occurred here. The drought that swept Alberta in 1931, 1933–34 and 1936–38 saw black blizzards of drifting soil and dust block out the sun for days at a time. Hailstorm Alley, a one-hundred-kilometre belt of doom running from Calgary to west of Edmonton, once killed twelve people, injured 130 and left $13 million in reported damage in less than an hour. And until central Canada's ice storm of 1998, a half-hour hailstorm in Calgary was the costliest natural disaster in the annals of Canadian insurance, racking up 116,000 claims that totalled $400 million.[14]

Statistics Canada's numbers may say that other Canucks have it tougher than Albertans, but the province's Caucasian history, deeply rooted in the soil and in the folklore of frontier hardship, combined with more recent extremes and disasters, have elevated the weather to a topic of conversation approaching the exalted status of hockey, energy prices and the latest federal conspiracy. When the Royal Alberta Museum planned a major project to present Alberta at the Smithsonian in Washington, DC (the first province so featured, in 2006), people couldn't agree on the essence of the province, but they almost considered bringing a trailer set at -40°C to the National Mall. As Bruce McGillivray recalls, "It was 100°F there, 100 per cent humidity, and we thought, 'We've got to bring them ice or they'll never understand Alberta.'"

Openness

There is something about Alberta that is written in the sky.
[…] Under that sky and within the protection of that crest live
people who come from all races but who now share a family tree
that has stout-hearted roots in the courage of the explorers,
police, traders and missionaries and its heritage in the great
open-heartedness of the west.

—KEN LIDDELL, *This is Alberta*, 1953

Albertans are known across the country for their friendliness. A
bandleader in a restaurant in Vieux-Montréal calls us kind and
generous, a sentiment shared by, for example, pedestrians in that
city and in downtown Toronto, seniors and an Asian tourist aboard
a ferry to Labrador and working people in rural Newfoundland.
These impressions are not new. Leo Thwaite, a writer who visited
the province before World War I, noted "the delightful friendliness
and kindness of all classes of residents"; an "unfailing optimism…no
doubt partly attributable to the climate—the clear dry, sunny atmosphere in which the people work"; and that "a spirit of goodwill and
tolerance, which would be amazing in older and more congested countries, prevails everywhere."[15]

But does this popular image hold up to professional scrutiny? The
sociologist, Reginald Bibby, observed that Albertan pedestrians are
known to nod at people, "a practice that is rare and even dangerous in
many other parts of the country." His surveys dating back to the mid-
1970s show that Albertans are slightly more likely than other Canucks
to value friendliness highly; that about 52 per cent of us report getting
high levels of enjoyment from neighbours, compared to 44 per cent
nationally; that Albertans are less likely than others to be suspicious
of strangers; and that teenagers here are more inclined than other
young Canadians to value politeness and concern for others, and more
likely to aspire to take part in community life. The latter, Dr. Bibby

wrote, is consistent with the teens' parents' greater inclination to value community involvement and good citizenship. "So it is," he concluded, "that Alberta has developed an unrivalled reputation for being able to rally its people in hosting successful events that require extensive community support, be they the Commonwealth Games, the Winter Olympics, or Grey Cup games."[16]

There must be reasons for this. And they just may relate to the land and the sunny weather. Don Brinkman, the director of research programs at the Royal Tyrrell Museum in Drumheller, sums up Alberta as open, not only geographically, but in terms of her people, who are open to new ideas, new experiences and interacting with others. "It's a welcoming community," he declares in the back forty outside the museum. From a bench in downtown Edmonton, the filmmaker, Anne Wheeler, adds, "The people are very friendly and they take risks and they have a perspective on things because you're so small when you're out in the big, big, prairies. You have a sense of being just a tiny, little entity under this huge sky. But I think you have a very healthy perspective. You don't take yourself too seriously and you really value the people around you because you can't survive without them. So it's that genuine love of people and an enthusiastic approach to life." For another filmmaker, Lorna Thomas, the open vistas of the prairies are an inspiration. "You can see past, present and future all in one glance," she sighs.

To Preston Manning, the founder of the Reform Party and former leader of the federal opposition in Parliament, that openness became more apparent when he and his colleagues first got themselves elected in 1993. "When some of our MPs from Alberta get to Ottawa, they like to get up high somewhere, go up on the Peace Tower, so you can see like you could back home. So that's one of our distinguishing characteristics." Speaking from his office high atop a tower in downtown Calgary, Mr. Manning, of course, is the son of Alberta's longest-serving and first homegrown premier. But his sentiment is shared by Anne Chandler, a modern-day pioneer whose family farmed in England for five centuries. Reflecting on the impression that brought her family to the Camrose area in 1997 to farm, she rhapsodizes, "It was a feeling of liberation to get here, because there's just nothing to weigh a person down. It was just so open everywhere, and people smile. There's a real feeling of freedom, that you can enjoy your own space." Her reverie is interrupted, in a very Albertan way, that early October morning by the season's first flutter of snowflakes in her farmyard.

The notion of space as a core component of Alberta's soul finds support in some numbers. Three out of four Albertans live in a twenty-kilometre strip straddling the original railway lines.[17] Alberta has the fourth-lowest population density among the provinces, at 5.1 people per square kilometre, closer to Newfoundland and Labrador's low of 1.4 than Prince Edward Island's high of 23.9 in 2006.[18]

Echoing a phenomenon felt by some Albertans who visit central Canada—a practice that doesn't seem to be reciprocated as much by folks from there—the paleontologist, Philip Currie, an Ontarian expat, recalls, "On returning to Ontario, we felt so claustrophobic when we drove around. We missed the West. It's not like northern Ontario, where people are separated by large forests and isolated."

This idea of vastness may be difficult for others to appreciate, but it gets in your soul. Once you've lived with the freedom of that immense sky, shortening your horizon can make you do strange things, whether it's taking the elevator up the Peace Tower in Ottawa, or desperately counting westward kilometres until returning to the prairie after the Manitoba border. The American reporter, Leo Thwaite, wrote, "The lingering, undying memory is prairie" and found "a strange magic in its lure."[19]

That lure has its hardships, too. The journey westward does not end gloriously for everyone. Some settlers' diaries ache with emptiness, loneliness and despair. It is not a joyous place for agoraphobics. But for those who overcame the formidable challenges of the landscape or who were born in later, less arduous times, the lure remains.

When asked whether there is a discernible difference between Alberta and other parts of Canada, the acclaimed visual artist, Jane Ash Poitras, states, "The air smells cleaner. And you have that beautiful light in the winter. And the openness of it—people aren't as uptight here as they are in the east. They're less anal. There's less stress here. I think that we have more freedom here than we do in other places in Canada. It allows you to have the vision. It allows you to transcend." Ian Tyson's first career in the musical business had bottomed out when he heeded the advice of his own masterpiece, "Four Strong Winds," and went out to Alberta, where he ran wild cattle and rekindled his muse. "I remember waking up and seeing the Rockies, with snow on them," he wrote. "I said, 'Screw it, I'd rather starve here than live in Toronto.' The Rocks have been doing that to people for 150 years."[20]

The landscape also inspires Leslie Takach, a painter and my father, who followed the call of the West from Québec in the mid-1970s, after an earlier escape from Soviet-stained Hungary. While he found a similar sense of liberation on entering friendlier Alberta, the vastness also made him feel more vulnerable and exposed than before. "The sky is different, the horizon is wider, the colours are clean," he enthuses. "So this is a paradise for an artist, to create and copy the land. It is like a dream of Walt Disney, a super-production. This is the land I was searching for throughout my life."

Alberta has always been a magnet for immigrants, be they political, economic or claustrophobic, and it has also shaped the province's ethos. Melissa Blake, the mayor of the Municipality of Wood Buffalo, which includes the prototypical boomtown of Fort McMurray (dubbed "Fort McMoney" by legions of job-seekers from eastern Canada who now live there), suggests that these arrivals bring some common attitudes to their new home. "When you leave places of comfort for a place where you don't know a soul, you have to make up for that," she reasons while seated atop a picnic table outside Emily Murphy House in Edmonton. "People who come here leave behind everything. But they have courage and they come with the idea of making a good life for themselves. Because the social structures have changed a bit when they get here, they're much more able to make friends with their neighbours and share in ways that may take longer in other places. It's a very refreshing feeling in a new place. It doesn't take long to meet everybody in the room." Dr. James Shapiro, a British immigrant who led the development of the Edmonton Protocol treatment for type-1 diabetes in the 1990s, concurs. "The people are easy to interact with," he says.

Certainly, Alberta has a reputation as a place offering smiles as bright as a prairie sunset and as broad as the horizon on which it occurs. But this runs afoul of her parallel and carefully cultivated image as a maverick place where people say and do what they want, regardless of the niceties. Against a panoramic backdrop of the Calgary skyline, Aritha van Herk, the author of the delightful *Mavericks: An Incorrigible History of Alberta*, tells me, "Albertans are rude, rambunctious and raucous. I don't think that there's an inclination in this province to be politically correct, but I do think that behind all that rude raucousness, there's a tenderness that only becomes evident when you get to know them." She states that while the province neither looks very proper nor behaves that way, there is more to Alberta than that. "I know that doesn't seem evident always to the rest of the country," she admits, "but beneath it all there's a very fierce sense of caring, both for this place and for other people." So although people may differ on whether Albertans wear their welcoming qualities on their sleeves or in their vest pockets next to their shootin' iron, the consensus in my experience leans toward the view that Alberta is open in terms of hospitality as well as topography.

As for loyalty to place, Alberta has her share of homegrown patriotism, but she also tends to earn the unbridled loyalty of people who have chosen to come here. The intensity of this adoptive boosterism echoes ex-smokers leading the parade against tobacco. The journalist, Ted Byfield, renowned for proudly conservative and loudly pro-Albertan views perceived by many Canadians to represent the entire province, moved here in 1970. Leaning on a fence overlooking the North Saskatchewan River valley, he proclaims, "I have a very deepening loyalty to this tract of land they call Alberta, far more than I would to a tract of land they call Canada. I'm talking not about thoughts, just emotions. You have a sense of belonging that runs very deep in this province. Albertans are not separatists, but they are far more attached to where they were brought up." In a study of more than 2,000 Canadians aged 12–30 in 2004 by the Carleton University Survey Centre and the Department of Canadian Heritage, Albertans showed the strongest sense of attachment to their province and to their town or city. We scored over 85 per cent on provincial attachment (national average: 78 per cent) and 78 per cent on local attachment (72 per cent nationally). More than 87 per cent also felt close to Canada, though that figure was just 2 per cent above the national average and the second lowest after Québec.[21]

Good Sports
Interview with the Ferbey Four

As the curling wizard, David Nedohin, points out, every town in Alberta has a church, a Chinese restaurant, a hockey rink, rodeo grounds and a curling rink. With the latter in mind, we take our quest to define the soul of the province to his team, the Ferbey Four, found at the Saville Sports Centre in Edmonton in 2006 (since retired in 2010). Winners of three world titles and four Brier championships, and arguably the greatest rink ever assembled despite recent losses to their archrivals in Kevin Martin's rink, these affable curlers are Marcel Rocque (lead), Scott Pfeifer (second), Randy Ferbey (third, skip) and David Nedohin (fourth).

✳ *How would you describe Albertans to people who have never been here?*

RANDY: Most Albertans that we've run into have been some of the friendliest people we've seen in the world. They're passionate

The Ferbey Four, (left to right) Scott Pfeifer, David Nedohin, Randy Ferbey and Marcel Rocque.

about their province. And anytime they recognize an athlete or a celebrity being from there, they really welcome them, more than in any place we've ever been.

DAVID: When you talk about the Maritime hospitality, I think that is very similar in Alberta. We don't put ourselves in a class above other parts of the country or the world. And yet we still have this drive and this desire to prove that we're absolutely the best at everything that we do. That's in every walk of life and I think it's sort of rampant. It starts in one generation. You keep being told you can do anything. And it really does show in the success of Alberta.

✳ *What makes you most proud to be an Albertan?*

MARCEL: I think a lot of pride comes from how the province has done in terms of economics. Alberta's always flourished, largely due the natural resources here. But the spin-off is that gives your population a lot of pride and a lot of confidence. You never hear a bunch of Albertans doing a lot of complaining because things have always been pretty good here. I think pride in the province gives pride to the people and that carries forward.

DAVID: Alberta has that Western Canadian feel, that down-home-roots sort of thing. And yet we're very proud of the success that we have, and when somebody does very well, we don't try and drag them down because they're successful. We try and boost them up. That's a unique trait of this province.

SCOTT: The reason I'm most proud to be an Albertan is the resiliency of the province. We do have some good times but we also have some down times. And that's when everyone bears down, and it almost feels like being an Albertan, you're part of a big family. And right now we're doing great, but in a little while, you never know where you're going to be. At least we'll have the support of all the other Albertans.

✳ *What makes you most embarrassed to be an Albertan?*

RANDY: Most Albertans are proud to be Albertans. Of course we have our little quirks like everybody else, but we don't dwell on those. Generally speaking, I'm not embarrassed about too many things around here.

SCOTT: Every time I'm on the ice at the Brier and I've got the Alberta jacket on, I'm totally proud to be wearing the blue and yellow. There's nothing I'm embarrassed about at all about being an Albertan.

DAVID: For me, growing up in Manitoba, you always wanted to have that buffalo on your back. But I'm true blue and yellow Albertan now.

RANDY: That's not true. He's still got about 10 per cent Manitoba in him. Slowly, we're converting him to 100 per cent Albertan.

SCOTT: It's a work in progress.

✳ *Are Albertans good sports, good team players?*

RANDY: Well, these three guys are.

DAVID: You might want to ask other teams about that.

SCOTT: We have to be team players to be able to play with him. *(indicating Randy)*

MARCEL: I do believe they are. You look at how we interact with the rest of our provincial neighbours, and we're there, we're giving our share of what we've got. We're always going to support our fellow provinces and Canada. So generally speaking, Albertans are very generous and very much team players.

✳ *If you had to explain Alberta to a Martian and sum it up in one word—one word that captures how you feel about your province—what would that word be?*

RANDY: Outstanding.

DAVID: I think passion. Because it doesn't matter what we do in Alberta, it seems that every Albertan has passion about what they believe in.

RANDY: That's about twenty-five words, David.

DAVID: Passion is the word.

RANDY: I didn't talk about my "outstanding" that long.

SCOTT: I said it earlier. Albertans are really resilient.

MARCEL: We're strong. Albertans are strong.

RANDY: Yes, we are married.

Rural Roots, Urban Shoots

What makes me proud to be Albertan are really the things that you find in small-town Alberta. The sense of community, the sense of wanting to get things done, the sense of helping one another, the sense of not asking a government to do everything for them. So really, the people of this province make me the proudest.

—PREMIER RALPH KLEIN, 2006

As we have seen, so much of Alberta's ethos and sense of place are rooted in the land, from the stories told in the rock art at Writing-on-Stone to the images of rural communities evoked by a different kind of rock artist, David Nedohin. Alberta continues to cultivate a character that retains elements that are powerfully and inescapably rural. To clarify what that means, we turn to sociology. In the 1930s, Louis Wirth defined the urban way of life as having three features in large quantities: population, population density and cultural diversity.[22] Applying the converse, let's define the rural lifestyle as having a population that's relatively low in number and density, with a relatively homogenous culture. This low density could also refer to those who are smart enough not to live in sooty, snooty cities.

Take Brian McGaffigan, the mayor of Strome (population 252) in east-central Alberta. Born in London, England, an ex-Torontonian, an engineer, the holder of three degrees, a retired minister and a world traveller, he calls rural Alberta "the last bastion of freedom and independent thinkers," a place where people may have more time and space to think. His wife, Pat McGaffigan, a retired nurse who worked in Nepal for six years and lived in both Ontario and BC, praises the deep sense of space, history, friendliness, peace and safety in their small, prairie community. Noting the chaos in the world and the growing gulf between haves and have-nots in Alberta and elsewhere, she speculates that maybe people will want to come back to the country, where they can grow their own food and regain a sense of place and independence.

"Do you know where the real Alberta is?" beams Andy Donnelly, a popular announcer on Alberta's CKUA Radio whose travels take him across the province. "The real Alberta is rural Alberta. If you go out there, it will put its arms around you and embrace you. That's what Alberta does!"

The rural ethic is harnessed evocatively by Doris Daley, a North American champion cowboy poet, from the porch of her century-old farmhouse near Turner Valley. Reflecting on an earlier extended absence from Alberta, she defines her province by what she missed: "It wasn't hustle, bustle, rush, high-rises and oil booms. I was homesick for a chinook arch in the sky...for waves and oceans of grass in the Porcupine Hills...for going to family dances in the Elks' Hall in town. Homesick to watch the chuckwagon races on TV with Joe Carbury calling the race."

The theatre artist, Pat Darbasie, finds the province's soul in the need for people to work together. "What makes me most proud to be an Albertan is the sense of community," she tells me. "There's a sense of folk who relate to one another and that's huge. It has to do with the weather and our isolation; there's a need to reach out to other people. Even though we've become an urban centre, that need to connect is still there. And that's what makes theatre vibrant in this part of the world, too."

Apparently, this perception of a community focus in Alberta extends beyond the province. Geoff Poapst, a writer and consultant interviewed on his bicycle in Ottawa, comments, "There's this communitarian aspect that's good about Alberta, where people pull together to make it a better place, and that's something you don't see. I just wish it didn't end at the provincial boundaries, because it really would be neat to apply that kind of spirit, entrepreneurialism and energy to building the country. It's sad that doesn't happen."

Tamara Palmer Seiler, a University of Calgary professor and the co-author of a leading history on Alberta, anchors this community spirit firmly in the rural roots of the province. Interviewed for a film camera before a diorama of an oncoming train in Fort Calgary, she notes that Alberta's traditional character emerged from the period of agrarian settlement, characterized by farm life, small-town life and a strong sense of community. While small towns and settlements remain in Alberta, many are under siege economically. She feels that old notions of neighbourliness and small-town life have faded considerably here since the wave of urbanization after World War II. "It's an urban place and a boom-and-bust place," she observes. "That's a very important theme in Alberta's history, and that atmosphere doesn't always create the sort of sense of neighbourliness that we tend to think of when we think of the traditional Alberta."

The notion that the province's rural ethic is being pushed into the substratum is echoed by the author and journalist, Mark Lisac. Bravely ignoring the rainfall outside his perennial haunt, the beaux-arts Legislature building, he sees an interesting tension at work: on the one hand, Albertans outside large centres retain both a deeply felt need to act as a community and a constant sense of being threatened by the outside world, be it market forces, the federal government or even the weather; but on the other hand, they place considerable value on individualism and acting on one's own. "And so you have these really sharp conflicts where people feel they have to go out and achieve things on their own," he explains. "But at the same time they know that really, the only way they're going to stand a chance in a lot of circumstances is to act together. And it's really tough bringing those two sides together sometimes."

There are at least two reasons why the rural ethic remains a force in Alberta.

An obvious answer is that the provincial electoral map looks like a holdover from the days of the Bennett buggy, if not the Red River cart. Rural MLAs continue to dominate the Legislature, a situation that the ruling Tories are loath to update for fear of undercutting their electoral juggernaut. Mark Lisac wrote that if there is any genuine alienation in Alberta, much or all of it "centres on rural fears of lost livelihood and a lost way of life" and that "[i]nstead of dealing with those fears directly, people and politicians try to maintain an ultimately impossible rural control of politics."[23] As the venerable author, Robert Kroetsch, wrote, "The notion that rural virtues are superior to urban virtues is taken for granted in Alberta," and, regarding rural strength in the Legislature, "[i]t is agreed that farmers have steadier judgement and sounder principles."[24]

A subtler reason is that Alberta took longer to urbanize than much of the rest of Canada. At Confederation, of course, the population was overwhelmingly rural. Federally, the urban crowd didn't reach parity until shortly after the 1921 census, when the country was still 51 per cent rural. But Alberta's balance did not turn from rural to urban until a generation later in the 1950s.[25] As Karen Lynch, the executive director of Volunteer Alberta, the umbrella organization for the province's pitch-in people, points out, "Albertans are more outspoken and take larger risks because we're only one or two generations removed from our origins on the farm, when people solved problems together, community by community. That's quite different than other urban provinces."

Urbanization is a national issue—some would say epidemic—with urbanity devouring 12,250 square kilometres, an area twice the size of Prince Edward Island, from 1971–1995.[26] But as in so many areas, Albertans excel to the point of the extreme, with the city overrunning the countryside faster than anywhere else in Canada. Between 1941–1971, the urban population bulldozed from 32 per cent to 73 per cent.[27]

Marie Dobbs, a retired farmer, at home in Heisler, 1982. [Louise Asselstine]

In 2006 Alberta was 82 per cent urban and 18 per cent rural, compa-rable to the federal urban–rural split of 80–20 per cent.[28] But you can use numbers to say anything you want. If you draw the line at a census metropolitan area of 500,000 in 2001, then Alberta becomes the most urbanized province in Canada, with 63 per cent of Albertans living in such centres (i.e., Calgary and Edmonton).[29] If you draw it at a more modest 100,000, then we slip behind Ontario, Québec and British Columbia. Also, apart from the Northwest Territories and Nunavut, Alberta experienced the fastest-growing *rural* popula-tion between 2001–2006 at 3.8 per cent. But this rate of growth was still below the overall national average growth of 5.4 per cent, and often rural growth is linked to bedroom communities, a proximity to large urban centres with more than 30 per cent of the labour force commuting to work in the urban centre.[30] In more remote areas, which may be more rural in lifestyle, Alberta's population dropped by 0.1 per cent from 2001–2006.[31]

On the numbers, the rural way of life seems to be losing ground in our headlong oxcart ride toward somebody's vision of progress. Though the agricultural industry remains a strong force in Alberta, there are fewer farmers, working increasingly larger farms to remain financially viable. Devastated by droughts and sporadic but well-publicized cattle ailments from 2001–2004 along with global competition and rising operating costs, the number of farms in the province fell from 53,652 to 49,431 (a drop of 8 per cent) by 2006, less of a tumble than in Saskatchewan and Manitoba. But Albertan farmers' expense-to-receipts ratio was $0.89 to $1, the second-highest after BC and PEI.[32]

Ken Lewis is a third-generation farmer whose operation includes grain, cattle and potatoes. His family has been working the land in Parkland County west of Edmonton since 1932. Against the backdrop of a towering silo, he offers this advice for Albertans interested in taking up farming today: "In agriculture, you move out of this province. Saskatchewan is going to be the cow-calf capital of Canada. Alberta will continue to be more on the value-adding side, and on the small-seed grains, what have you, we'll stay really diverse. But I see a big shift on the cattle end out of the province. The young people getting into agriculture are very small in numbers. Our high land costs are moving industry out to Saskatchewan, but the feeding industry will stay here."

The gulf is widening between Alberta's bulging burgs and the ever-thinning rural regions. "Beyond Alberta's gleaming and robust cities, life is often bleak, even desperate," wrote the political scientist, David Taras, noting, "The irony is that industrialization of farm life, with its giant feedlots and mammoth slaughter operations, has left small operators living on the edge."[33] As Oliver Wendell Holmes, the American jurist, writer and non-mathematician reminded us, life is painting a picture, not doing a sum. And a recurring image of rural Alberta today, cropping up between perfectly successful farmsteads, is deserted barns and crumbling farm buildings—an image that Grant MacEwan likened to "neglected headstones in a cemetery…trying to tell something of the glories of other years which are so quickly forgotten."[34] Myrna Kostash regales me about visiting her baba's farm near Vegreville: "There was a curve along Highway 16, and the little dirt road was overgrown with willows and aspen and wild roses in the ditch. All that's gone now. They've twinned the highway, taken down the grain elevators. They've lifted up the railway tracks. I got lost trying to find my grandparents' home." She observes that from the time her grandfather was born on that land in 1906 until he died in 1994, that part of Alberta went from homesteads to its peak moment with asphalt highways and consolidated school districts to deserted farms, disappeared railroads, tumbledown schools and empty churches. "In one lifetime, from one kind of frontier to another," she observes, "the circularity of it is striking. That communal life is gone."

As a journalist and a documentary filmmaker, Garth Pritchard has seen everything from Pierre Laporte's corpse left in a trunk by Québecois terrorists to larger-scale horrors in Somalia, Kosovo and Afghanistan. Perched atop a corral fence on an acreage in the foothills, he lets loose on the state of rural Alberta in a boom economy. "Look behind me," he thunders. "It's where we graze our horses. Some real-estate person has turned this into a $1.5-million piece of land. I don't know how you take a $1.5-million piece of hay land and ever allow a cow or a horse back on it. Great for the landowner, okay. But can we afford to live here? That's truly sad. Go to Priddis, Jenner, Cereal, Manning. These are all little towns in Alberta being destroyed systematically. Rural Alberta is a disaster!"

In this light, the trend in Alberta to pave over first-class farmland and construct sprawling, car-compulsory, bedroom communities in the style of cozy, old-fashioned small towns is not merely ironic.

It pays homage more to American mythology than real life on the Canadian prairies.[35] And as the rural-affairs scholar, Roger Epp, wrote, there's an eerie "imperialist nostalgia" in a dominant culture's co-opting the imagery of subordinated groups for its own purposes, whether it's politicians receiving ceremonial Aboriginal headwear or urban ad campaigns evoking "rugged individualists hard at work in wide-open spaces."[36]

Land and space may be the foundation of Alberta's psyche, but it doesn't hurt when they also let you earn a living.

Riches

Anyway you subdivide it, Alberta's fortunes have always been tied fiercely to the land. The First Nations peoples knew this intimately, of course. But until the nineteenth century, few others knew what Alberta and the West actually looked like. In 1751 French voyageurs who followed the Saskatchewan and Bow rivers founded Fort Jonquiere a few miles west of Calgary. Anthony Henday followed in 1754, and the North West Company established a trading post east of Edmonton in 1795. The explorers, voyageurs and fur traders were more interested in rivers and portage routes than the quality of the soil, the level of rainfall or the length of the growing seasons. The mid-eighteenth century pit the Hudson's Bay Company against the North West Company in a furry, frontier version of the Montagues and the Capulets. Unlike the Bard's famous feud, they would kiss, make up and get married by 1821—only it was the poor *bison* that died in the end. By the mid-nineteenth century, the battle shifted from trapping furs to saving souls. Catholic and Protestant missionaries arrived in earnest efforts to rescue Alberta's indigenous peoples from a Christian hell that they never fathomed, only to lead them to another hell that they would come to know all too well.

In 1857 Britain's Royal Geographic Society, backed by the British government, sent Captain John Palliser on a three-year expedition to determine whether the West offered any further use to the empire beyond fur-bearing animals. Reporting on a swath of land extending across southern Saskatchewan and southeastern Alberta—an area now drily remembered as the Palliser Triangle—the captain saw the sandy soil, extensive grass cover and the odd cactus, and likened the growing conditions to a desert, "ill-suited to civilization," though the outlying fertile belt surrounding that area was deemed more suitable for ranching and agriculture. On the other hand, accounts from 1872 onward by Canada's leading field naturalist, John Macoun, suggested that the West was a lush land, screaming to be farmed. That these two gents travelled during different decades and weather conditions and did not cover exactly the same terrain would not hinder Sir John A. Macdonald's national dream or its umbilical ribbon of steel. When it came time for the feds to build a railroad through the dry belt and encourage settlement in the West, it's not rocket science—alas, nor even soil science—to guess which vision they adopted. They could never have sold folks on earth as dry as toast, bone-chilling cold or a growing season not appreciably longer than a decent coughing fit. Pamphlets from federal agriculture officials trumpeted southern Alberta as a farmer's paradise, advising that the lack of trees advantageously saved farmers the trouble of clearing their land. Eventually, settlers would discover the truth behind the recruitment posters, which never featured voracious, crop-eating pests, swarms of flies and mosquitoes, hail as big as kidney stones, or prodigious potential for cabin fever. Many homesteaders gave up.[37]

With the bison gone and much of the remaining Aboriginal population consigned to reserves, poverty or both, the stage was set for the province's first great Caucasian industry. From its beginnings in the interior of neighbouring British Columbia in the mid-nineteenth century, ranching spread to the Rocky Mountain foothills and eventually to the plains of southeastern Alberta and beyond. The first breeding herd of eleven cows and a bull was spirited to the banks of the Bow River at Morleyville in 1873 by a Methodist missionary, John

McDougall, from Fort Edmonton. Other herds were imported from
Montana.

The industry was boosted in 1874 by the arrival of the North West
Mounted Police, which offered protection against cattle rustlers, plus
a local market for beef and milk. The first Mounties reported that
cattle lived well on prairie grass. They established government-owned
ranches at Fish Creek and Pincher Creek in an effort to feed the
starving Native people and get them hooked on agriculture. The sweet
spot was southwestern Alberta, where sheltered valleys and snow-
clearing chinooks proved ideal for raising cattle. It was a precarious
lifestyle, setting the tone that subsists to this day. As the writer, Sid
Marty, pointed out, "the precious soil that makes ranching possible is
under the constant rule of the wind, and fortunes are tied to the thin-
nest of all mooring lines, to the roots of a single blade of grass."[38]

Alberta's golden age of ranching was the 1880s, when the federal
government's early efforts at recruiting farmers turned up almost as
dry as the Palliser Triangle itself. Southern Alberta proved to be more
conducive to ranching than to farming, with businesses, suppliers and
investors from Montana doing particularly well. The feds wanted a
homegrown cattle industry because the primary customers for beef at
that point were the Aboriginal population and the Mounties; as both
of these groups were Ottawa's responsibility, the feds were essentially
sending scarce public funds stateside. So when investors from Britain
and Ontario (led by Senator Matthew Cochrane, friend and neighbour to the federal minister of agriculture)[39] got wind of the Mounties'
reports and lobbied the government for a sweet deal for large-scale
ranching, Sir John A.'s arm didn't need much twisting, irrespective
of how bent his elbow might have been. In 1881 the feds let ranchers
lease up to 100,000 acres (more than 40,000 hectares and almost that
number of times the area of the new turf at Edmonton's Commonwealth
Stadium) of land at the low, low rate of one cent per acre per year for
up to twenty-one years. Pursuing Sir John A.'s national dream of a
transcontinental railway, the government encouraged ranchers from

Britain and Ontario to come west to keep Canada loyal to the empire. (Maybe this is what prompted the visiting Marquis of Lorne, Britain's most upscale remittance man, to declare, "If I were not Governor General of Canada, I would be a cattle rancher in Alberta.")

But the feds also wanted settlers. To that end, they divided the prairies into townships, each split into 36-square-mile (9,300-hectare) sections, with 16 sections reserved for the new Canadian Pacific Railway along its route, a pair of sections set aside for each of schools and the Hudson's Bay Company. Settlers could get a homestead quarter-section of 160 acres (65 hectares), big enough to grow crops to feed a family. If they lived on the land for 3 years, ploughed 30 acres (of which two-thirds were cropped) and built a habitable house worth at least $300 within 6 months of entry, they could apply for title to that land. They could buy more land for $3 per acre. Applicants had to be British subjects (or declare their intention to become so), the sole head of a family and either male and over eighteen or a widow with minor children.[40]

The province's ranching interests—a small cadre of mostly very well-heeled, educated and powerful men from Britain and Ontario—fought the government's settlement policy, aided by a less than enthusiastic response to Ottawa's recruiting drives. But by 1896 the American frontier had been settled, and both Yanks and Canucks who had settled stateside hit the trail north for a piece of the feds' "Last Best West." Meanwhile, Ottawa cranked out the posters, leaflets and immigration agents (describing the winters as "sunny, clear and bracing" rather than, say, "Siberian"), to attract the labour required to load the breadbasket that was supposed to feed the empire. As a result, the open range was overrun by homesteaders. As if that wasn't bad enough for the ranching barons, the winter of 1906–1907 was worse. When the friendly chinook winds failed to sweep in to melt the snow, umpteen thousands of unfortunate cattle were cut off from those single blades of grass. That and some cattlemen's failure to cut hay for them transformed the range into the world's first frozen-steak stand. While the ranching industry manages to brave on to this day, its heyday was already in the rear-view mirror by 1912 when the Calgary Stampede debuted as an exercise in frontier nostalgia. That the industry endures in the public's consciousness is born out in my street interviews, in which a common, coast-to-coast response to images of Alberta was "beef," often followed by an exclamation point and accompanied by a reference to the Stampede.

Stereotypical or not, the beef factor is huge here. Ken Lewis, a third-generation mixed farmer whose work includes cattle, explains, "Promotion is one thing, but probably 75 per cent of the fat-kill cattle in Canada come out of Alberta, whether done here or exported to the US, so the beef business in Canada revolves around Alberta." Indeed, there are almost twice as many head of cattle in the province as people. Alberta is by far the largest cattle-producer in Canada, leading the herd with almost 6.5 million head in 2007, or 41 per cent of the national total. That year, Alberta produced 720,125 tonnes of carcass and boxed beef, the weight of almost 60,000 standard city buses. With admirable self-restraint, Albertans only consumed about 17 per cent of that (the beef, not the buses), shipping almost half of it to the rest of Canada, slightly over a quarter of it stateside and the rest abroad. Ranchers in Alberta remain a hardy lot. With 7 million hectares of rangeland, they raise not only cattle, but also livestock like sheep, llamas and emus. The province leads the nation in the burgeoning bison industry: of the nearly 2,000 farms and 195,728 head reported federally in 2006 (up more than one-third in five years), Alberta harboured almost half of both the farms and the herd.[41]

As open-range ranching gave way to settler's fences—1,000 settlers in 1881 multiplied to 73,000 by 1901 and then almost fivefold by 1910— Alberta's agricultural industry took root, fuelled by federal recruitment drives, poor economic conditions in parts of Europe, advances in farm machinery and the rising price of wheat after an agricultural depression. The soil was of famously fabulous fecundity. What made it so? Leo Thwaite credited the province's earthy delights to a confluence of

Skyscrapers of the Prairie *by Leslie Takach, 1995. Oil on canvas.* Reproduced with the kind permission of the artist.

prolific soil, decaying vegetation, nitrogen, potash and especially phosphoric acid, with enough lime to free the nitrogen for absorption.[42]

The early and obvious leader here was King Wheat, boosted in 1911 by the commercialization of Marquis wheat, which ripened a week earlier than other varieties, and later by improvements such as the Noble Blade for weeding, developed in the province. Thanks to moist air blowing in from British Columbia, the Peace River region, 560 kilometres northwest of Edmonton, became the most northerly spot on the continent to grow grain. (This happy combination of moisture, sunshine and fertile soil also helps grow alfalfa and clover for honey production in northern communities like Falher, which stages bee-beard contests and claims the world's largest bee.) Until the 1950s,

Alberta's economic fortunes perked up or blew away with her wheat crop and its market price. Wheat still led the provincial field in agricultural exports in 2006, followed by beef, canola seed, live cattle and pork. The province is the second-largest exporter of primary and processed agricultural and food products in Canada, after Ontario, shipping half of her exports to the US and notable volumes to Japan, Mexico and China. Over roughly the past decade, with 6 per cent of the country's land area and about 10 per cent of the population, Albertans produced 29 per cent of Canada's wheat crop, 34 per cent of the canola, 44 per cent of the barley and 20 per cent of the oats. The province claims to produce all of the country's sugar beets, 28 per cent of the hay and clover, 23 per cent of the honey and 22 per cent of the dry peas. Alberta is also the irrigation capital of Canada, with almost two-thirds of its irrigated farmland, though no figures are available on our share of the nation's famous dry humour.[43]

Almost one-third of Alberta is agricultural land. Forests cover more than half of the province (including 1.9 billion cubic metres of softwood and 1.2 billion cubic metres of hardwood) and provide the main source of employment in 50 communities.[44] Water makes up less than 3 per cent of Alberta's surface, which leaves less than 10 per cent of the surface for mountains and whatever else Statistics Canada calls "Other."[45]

Alberta's astonishing good fortune doesn't stop at ground level. She has almost 34 billion tonnes of coal (70 per cent of Canada's reserves); 97 trillion cubic feet of natural gas (80 per cent of Canada's production and the source of Rudyard Kipling's famous admiring quote, "This part of the country seems to have all hell for a basement, and the only trap door appears to be in Medicine Hat"),[46] and about 5.5 billion barrels of conventional crude oil and 1.7 trillion barrels of synthetic crude produced from oil sands (70 per cent of national and 5 per cent of North American oil production). She is the world's ninth-largest producer of oil and the third-largest producer of natural gas. The tar sands or oil sands—some Albertans prefer the latter term, which apparently sounds cleaner—occupy an estimated 140,200 square kilometres in the northeast, an area twice the size of New Brunswick and almost five times as large as Vancouver Island. Also present in less spectacular doses are sand, gravel, salt and the odd mineral and precious stone.[47]

This basement bonanza began in the distant mists of the Paleozoic era (250–544 million years ago) when two mountain ranges, one sweeping from what is now central Canada to Montana, and the other moving north into the Northwest Territories, formed a channel for the Pacific Ocean to travel east toward Manitoba. This created an inland sea covering what we call Alberta, complete with shellfish to populate her shallow shoreline. During the cycles of dry land and sea, a returning rush of water from the Pacific had to detour north when it came up against some newer mountains that had cropped up in British Columbia. The result was a network of coral reefs that started the inexorable march of evolution from your basic sea-based flora and fauna to more complex landlubber life, which was mummified in porous marine rocks during the Devonian period about 353–410 million years ago and covered by layers of rock and other debris. This decaying treasure lies 1,500 metres underground in a path 320 kilometres wide, extending from the northeast corner of Alberta down to Drumheller in the southeast and to the border with southern Saskatchewan.

An early report of oil in Alberta came from a Cree named Wa-Pa-Su ("the Swan"), who brought samples from the Athabasca River valley to the Hudson's Bay Company's Fort Churchill in 1719.[48] Natives used the stuff to waterproof their canoes. By the late nineteenth century, driven by the railway companies, coal-mining towns began dotting the landscape around Lethbridge, the Crowsnest Pass and the Rockies, attracting labour from parts of the world in which backbreaking work down a dark, dirty, shaft in among the most dangerous mines in the world, with little freedom to leave, all for $1.75 a day—less deductions for food, shelter if you could get it, mail delivery and medical care— was a step up.[49]

The Bow Valley view from the Banff Springs Hotel, featuring Tunnel Mountain (left), Mt. Rundle (right) and a posh golf course attracting more than its share of duffers, carts and rutting elk. [Geo Takach]

Natural gas reserves were discovered by Canadian Pacific Railway water-drillers in 1883 at Langevin siding (now Alderson), about thirty-five kilometres west of Medicine Hat. A local paper reported that the drillers would keep digging for water, but gave up working at night for reasons of safety, and that within a year gas was being piped into the railway workers' building for heating and cooking stoves.[50] The Hat rated a nod in the syndicated newspaper cartoon, *Ripley's Believe it or Not*, when even during the Depression it was cheaper to leave gas-burning streetlights lit than to turn them off each day.[51]

That discovery parallels the founding of Canada's national parks system. Just a few weeks before drillers seeking water found natural gas at Langevin, three off-duty railway construction workers seeking gold in the eastern slopes of the Rockies found water when one of them tumbled down a hole into a cave, landing in a naturally hot sulphur spring. In an early display of that Albertan entrepreneurial spirit, the trio tried to build a tourist business, only to become nationalized when the federal government created Banff National Park in 1885. As the workers' boss, the railway's general manager, William Cornelius Van Horne, famously boomed, "If we can't export the scenery, we'll import the tourists." Later, Banff was expanded and joined by four other national parks. Elk Island northeast of Edmonton is a refuge for wildlife like elk, bison, moose, deer, 250 species of birds and the aspen parkland itself. Jasper is northwest of Banff and somewhat like its sister mountain park, but with less shopping. Waterton Lakes joins with Glacier in Montana to connect prairies and mountains in the world's first International Peace Park. And Wood Buffalo in the province's northeastern corner hosts rare and endangered residents like bison, whooping cranes and salt plains, along with two internationally significant wetlands, all in the world's second-largest national park.[52]

On top of this homage to what's left of nature, Wild Rose Country claims more than 27,500 square kilometres of provincial parks and protected areas, including ecological reserves, wilderness, natural areas, recreation areas and rangelands. Statistics buffs may note that this equals the irrigated land area of Italy, the land area of the Solomon Islands in the South Pacific and possibly even the area of retail developments in the province.

Wild Rose Country has always enjoyed natural advantages, but enjoying them has taken some work. Three weeks after Alberta became a province, the *Calgary Herald* raged, "Square mile for square mile, Alberta is richer in natural resources than any other part of the dominion. [...] The prairie provinces are robbed of their chief source of revenue, not for the benefit of the federal treasury, nor of the Dominion at large, but for the benefit of the horde of grafters who stand in with the Liberal machine. And we are asked to say that this is 'wise and just.'"[53] Battles over Alberta's natural bounty, whether the threat is actual or perceived, are as much a part of the province as the resources themselves.

Resource Battles

Having begun her constitutional life as the far-flung flank of a private fur farm, Alberta moved turbulently through district, territorial and provincial status. At Alberta's sunlit provincial inauguration ceremony in Edmonton on September 1, 1905, the governor general, the fourth Earl Grey—best remembered for donating a silver cup symbolizing supremacy of football north of the 49th parallel—declared that Albertans enjoyed perhaps unprecedented opportunity, "within the reach of all who can pay their way here, of making for themselves a happy and comfortable home, amid pleasant surroundings, with the inspiring feeling of independence which comes with the full ownership of the land you till..." His Excellency predicted a steady flow of incoming settlers seeking to improve their lot by securing a piece of Alberta's abundant riches, a "certain and liberal reward for all who are ready to give honest, preserving and intelligent industry to the cultivation of your land." Next up was Prime Minister Laurier, who compared Canada to the kingdom of heaven, with the words, "Those who come at the eleventh hour will receive as fair treatment as those who have been in the fold for a long time."[54] These florid phrases are remarkably prescient, capturing recurring values that remain associated with Alberta—whether in truth, mythology or both—more than a century later: opportunity, self-reliance, independence, immigration, riches, industry and fairness. But most important, the statements of Messrs. Grey and Laurier suggest a deep wound that haunts the province still.

Barely had the federal dignitaries' coattails fluttered back east and the bunting been put away when the sabres rattled anew. Provincial control of public lands was constitutionally entrenched in 1867, back before income and sales taxes, meaning that the provinces could levy only direct taxes, rather than the more lucrative customs and excise taxes. Except for fees, licences and transfers, the main sources of provincial revenue were resource royalties, property taxes and the sale and lease of public land. So yes, the fledgling province had won her own government, but like her eight siblings, she was subservient to the dominant federal power, conceived under the vision of Sir John A. Macdonald at Confederation. And unlike every other province except Manitoba and Saskatchewan, Alberta lacked control over public land, timber and mineral resources within her borders. Such was the importance of this control that in 1880, for example, Nova Scotia earned 80 per cent of its income from its public lands, while New Brunswick's figure was 75 per cent.[55] Prime Minister Laurier justified this exception "on the highest grounds of policy" to continue the federal practice of giving out free homestead land as incentive for immigration. This echoed his predecessor, Sir John A., who also needed title to Western public lands and natural resources to build his railway, fulfill treaty obligations to Aboriginal peoples and recoup the £300,000 spent to buy Rupert's Land from the Hudson's Bay Company. But there were many other issues at work, such as the PM's unwillingness to grant more power to the new provinces (led in territorial days by Frederick Haultain, who had the further handicap during Mr. Laurier's administration of sporting Conservative colours in his off-hours) and the nasty, national squabble over the rights of Catholics to publicly funded schooling in Saskatchewan and Alberta.[56]

In lieu of title to her natural resources, Alberta received an annual grant starting at $375,000. With expenses for public buildings and a grant in lieu of debt liquidation because she was debt-free when she became a province, Alberta received about half of her $2.2 million in revenue from the federal government.[57] Alberta's new premier, Alexander Rutherford, called the grant in lieu of natural resources an "excellent subsidy."[58] He might have taken up the fight for control over public land had he not been a Liberal premier appointed by the federal Liberals and a generally agreeable sort. One of his MLAs in

A fateful moment: Prime Minister Mackenzie King (seated third from left) stops talking to his late dog, Pat, to transfer public land and natural resources in Alberta to the province, led by Premier John Brownlee (seated fourth from left), 1929.

[Library and Archives Canada, PA–188951, photo: J.J. Hisgrove]

the second Alberta Legislature, Alwyn Bramley-Moore, published a book advocating "home rule" for Alberta; after he went off to fight and die in the Great War, all was quiet on at least that front, but the issue never stopped simmering. When Premier Charles Stewart returned from a conference in Ottawa in 1917, one of his own backbenchers attacked him for not pushing for Alberta's control of her own natural resources.[59]

The battle was left for the United Farmers of Alberta, who took office in 1921, in time for the minor oil boom at Turner Valley in 1924. After years of work on the file, Attorney General and later Premier

John Brownlee skillfully negotiated the rights from Prime Minister Mackenzie King, and an agreement of transfer was signed just seven weeks after Black Thursday in 1929. Not much happened on the resource front during the Dirty Thirties beyond the irony of the first provincial Conservative leader, R.B. Bennett—who in 1905 had protested Ottawa's retaining control over natural resources—assuming the prime minister's chair in time to have his name lent to vehicles for which people could not afford to buy gas. (You simply removed the engine, hooked up a horse in harness to the car and voila, a Bennett buggy!) After the modern oil industry began at Leduc in 1947, there were rumblings about the spectre of the feds grabbing the province's resource wealth by taxing personal and business income; that didn't happen, but the underlying suspicion remained.

Postwar prosperity, the rising demand for energy and the building of pipelines forced Ottawa to confront the same issue that it had faced with coal in the days of Sir John A.'s National Policy: how to best protect domestic producers and consumers in a country so vast that in some regions, imports from a closer foreign market make economic sense. Historically, for example, Ontario got its coal from the US, while Nova Scotia supplied the eastern part of the country and Alberta supplied the western part. In the early 1960s, the National Oil Policy similarly split the land, giving Albertan energy producers protected access to the market west of the Ottawa River valley, while Québec and the Atlantic provinces kept buying imports. So there was a time when Canadians (notably Ontarians) had to pay higher than the world price for Alberta oil, but few Albertans mention this today.

Then came the OPEC cartel's hiking of oil prices in 1973 and the ultimate bogeyman in Albertan lore, the National Energy Program (NEP), unleashed by Prime Minister Pierre Trudeau. The feds wanted Canada to be self-sufficient energy-wise, to own its domestic industry and to give Ottawa and consumers a bigger share of the growing energy wealth. The NEP followed a 160 per cent hike in world oil prices in 1979–1980 and a two-year standoff between Ottawa

and Alberta over energy pricing and revenue sharing. While establishing grants to promote drilling in remote areas and to encourage
consumers to conserve and to convert to gas or electric heating hardly
inspired rioting, measures like new taxes slapped on the oil industry
and a beefed-up, government-owned Petro Canada incensed many
Albertans. To sprinkle more oil on the fire, Mr. Trudeau's full-scale
interventionism occurred without consulting the affected provinces or
industries. While Saskatchewan and British Columbia made do with
protests, Alberta cut back her oil production (twice), put the brakes
on two huge heavy-oil and tar-sands projects and challenged the
constitutionality of the proposed federal tax on gas exports. The province won the court case and used that as leverage in negotiations with
the feds, who eventually shrunk the gap between domestic and world
oil prices, while tinkering further as oil prices, gas exports and the
economy went south.[60] The NEP is said to have siphoned $68 billion
in differential pricing alone from Albertan coffers from 1973 to 1985,
when a newly elected Conservative federal government abandoned
both the NEP and its goals.[61] As probably the foulest federal-provincial feud in Canadian history, the NEP gave Albertans their own Louis
Riel to remember and invoke when it became politically advantageous.

On the question of owning natural resources, some Albertans
adopt a more charitable approach, like when the late lieutenant-
governor, Lois Hole, admitted, "We didn't put the oil in the ground. It
wouldn't hurt to share with some of the others."[62] For other Albertans,
resentment and perceived threats linger like a commissioned sales-
person. And that is precisely the perception that I encountered in
my street interviews, albeit in mild and politely Canadian ways. In an
open-air restaurant in Vieux-Montréal, the house bandleader, Robert
O'Callaghan, says, "When I think of Alberta, I think of very sweet,
very friendly people. But then also at the same time I think of Ralph
Klein and I'm confused. Because he's probably a very nice man, but
the things that he says and the way that he presents Alberta seem to
me to contradict the image of beautiful landscapes and sweet, friendly,

generous people." Aboard the ferry from St. Barbe, Newfoundland, to Blanc Sablon on the border of Québec and Labrador, a ballcapped fisherman, Gary Martin, also invoking then-Premier Klein, notes, "He's got so much money in Alberta, he figures he can buy Ottawa. So I guess him and the attitude that he has sometimes, I find a little bit unusual." And across the country, at Canada Place on the Vancouver shore, I meet two young Saskatchewanians, Anita Radmacher and Judd Bakken, who call Albertans "a little more hoity-toity" people who "flaunt their wealth a bit, nothing too extreme"—a perception that Albertans are too big for their britches sometimes. As Robert O'Callaghan explains, "The danger is when a province or a country or an individual who's doing too well has a tendency to say, 'The hell with everybody else.' Probably most people from Alberta don't really feel like that, but there's a little bit of that image being projected in the public forum now. Like, 'We're doing very well, so don't bother us.'"

These impressions give us a glimpse of competing perceptions of Albertans in the court of public opinion. But in the popular media, where conflict is infinitely more interesting than harmony—when it comes to natural resources (especially oil)—Albertans are modern-day minutemen, ready to grab, figuratively or maybe even literally, the old .22 rifle—if not the new AK-47—and open fire on whatever threatens our cherished land.

2 Rednecks or Radicals?

In general, Alberta is seen probably as the bad boy of Confederation,

and I say "boy" quite deliberately. It's also probably seen as kind of

a wild place, a place of little culture, a place of right-wing politics.

Those images have some basis in fact, but they aren't the whole story.

—TAMARA PALMER SEILER, 2005

Overleaf: Premier William Aberhart (front row, third from left), his young protégé Ernest Manning (viewed to right of premier, as it were) and the rest of their gang of eight freshly minted cabinet ministers in 1935. [Glenbow Archives, ND-3-37103a]

By Any Other Name

LABELS ARE TERRIFIC, TIMESAVING POINTERS. Ideal for the temporally challenged and the deeply superficial, they offer short-hand conclusions to everything from garden produce to vegetation of a more political nature. Inconveniently, the nuances of politics don't always lend themselves to one-word solutions any more than allegedly organic growing practices. Nor, as it turns out, do ideological labels as they are used in popular parlance fit all of their actual meanings. This contradiction thrives in Alberta.

In my cross-country quest, interviewees readily identified Alberta as "conservative," "really conservative" and so conservative that it's "eerie and bizarre." "Conservative" is a name given to one of the nation's oldest political parties, but what does it really mean? Philosophically, conservatism is based on the idea that people are imperfect. True conservatives respect authority, order, stability and hierarchy. They value community. They believe that the public interest requires regulating capitalism and they favour the protection of tariffs over outright free trade. Like liberals, they are partial to citizens' right to property, but more than liberals, conservatives recognize that individual rights must occasionally give way to the greater rights of the community.[1] That's probably not what most Canadians today would call conservative.

In contrast, liberalism is rooted in the primacy of liberty and equality for individuals, subject to limited checks and balances from a representative government. True liberals believe that economies run best when people act in their own interest and that governments should be restricted to protecting fundamental freedoms and delivering essential services that citizens cannot deliver by themselves. Social or modern liberalism has come to endorse the welfare state as providing equal opportunity for all.[2]

So a vital distinction between the two schools of thought is over the role of government: conservatives see a larger role for it while liberals aim to curb it. Political parties bearing those labels emerged in Victorian England. Early Conservatives were United Empire Loyalists, Anglicans and anti-Americans, while Liberals grew out of the Reform movement, rebelling against the Family Compact and Chateau Clique of Upper and Lower Canada, respectively. When the Tory titan, Sir John A. Macdonald, produced his National Policy of protective tariffs in 1879, the Liberals countered by embracing free trade with the United States. This key divisive point came to a head in the 1911 federal election, when Western farmers clamoured for cheaper machinery from the Americans under free trade rather than having to buy more costly products from central Canada. Upholding what would become a predictable tradition, these Western interests lost at the ballot box, then to the Conservatives. After the Liberals returned to what would become *their* traditional role in the twentieth century—forming the federal government—the distinction between the two political parties blurred in a flurry of duelling spending promises.

These political labels seem to have passed their best-before date. Three-quarters of a century after the Tories won on a platform against free trade, the federal election of 1988 saw Sir John A.'s party return to power, this time in *support* of free trade with the US, which the

Liberals opposed. Labels seem to mean even less in Alberta, where governments have preferred the pragmatism of pleasing voters to the vagaries of ideological purity. Both small- and large-c conservative governments have spent like Caligula, with more recent administrations being accused of an apparently contradictory, laissez-faire attitude to issues like poverty, industrial development and saving money for a rainy day.

Senator Tommy Banks sees contradictions between Albertans' conservative reputation and their practices. Interviewed on the lawn of Parliament Hill, he says, "Much of the rest of the country and ourselves to a degree are under self-delusions. We have this monolithic view of Alberta, and it's anything but a monolith. Without referring to liberals or conservatives in any of the political-party senses, we have a view—which I shared for a long time—that Alberta's a pretty conservative place. But it has done enormously liberal things in its history, way in advance of many other people." He points to a nearby statue of the Famous Five, women from Alberta who caused the Privy Council in England to determine that women were in fact persons and could therefore be admitted, for example, to the Senate. Citing further Canadian firsts that rank Alberta at the cutting edge of what one would ordinarily call liberal, Senator Banks concludes, "So even Alberta conservatives have very liberal tendencies when it comes to things like human rights and advancing the interest of individuals. And we do things that are pretty liberal politically because we're extremely tolerant in Alberta, far more than we think we are and far more than certainly most other people give us credit for."

The last twenty years have muddied the differences between liberals and conservatives further. On the one hand, "neo-conservatism" is said to espouse not only tradition, religion and family values in the style of Preston Manning (not to mention Ernest Manning), but deference to the freedom of markets and individuals from government intervention. The appeal to order, stability and authority in the name of traditional values fits the classical definition of conservatism. But the assault that Ralph Klein notoriously declared on public spending and red tape clearly falls under the banner of neo-liberalism. Reducing people's reliance on government, trying to run it like a business and calling for individuals to take more responsibility for themselves are fundamentally liberal concepts. The notion of cutting public services and expectations of government (the height of chic in the provincial election of 1993, when the incumbent Klein-led Conservatives promised Albertans "drastic cuts" while the Liberal opposition offered "brutal cuts") appealed to Alberta's deep-rooted, pioneering, do-it-yourself ethos but it was embraced less enthusiastically by the providers and most needy consumers of those services. At its core, the Klein Revolution was both neo-conservative and neo-liberal. But such is the power of labels that in many parts of Alberta, anything "liberal" has become as politically palatable as pedophilia.

So is Alberta truly conservative? On this, Ted Byfield, an icon of that label in current popular usage, might seem more equivocal than his decades of writings in books, magazines and newspapers might suggest. "Yes and no," he replies, noting Albertans' instinct to conserve their magnificent natural resources and the culture that emerged from developing them. "But when conservatism comes to mean following a party line that says, 'less government spending' and all the rest of that, Albertans would shrink a bit from that," he adds. "For instance, I could imagine a time when Alberta was regarded as distinctly left-wing. Many people accused us of that in the thirties. But it really meant that we could see ourselves losing the thing that we had been bequeathed, and that's what caused the resistance to the rest of the country then and still does."

The theatre artist, Pat Darbasie, sees forces of inertia at work in the province, observing that Albertans tend to maintain the status quo at times. "There are pockets of liberalism and radicalism that jostle it a bit, but the status quo is conservative," she tells me. "There's a sense, especially in a boom time, that if it ain't broke, don't mess with it. So even though there might be some dissatisfaction among some Albertans, there isn't a big push to change." In more than a century of provincehood, Alberta has had all of three changes in government. But what really makes this voting history noteworthy is that no defeated party in the province has ever reassumed the reins of power. When Albertans are done with a political party, they don't just throw it out of office; they consign it to electoral oblivion forever. As the journalist, commentator and elected senator-in-waiting, Link Byfield, observes, every one of Alberta's four governing parties came in with a defining agenda: "The Liberals encouraged settlement and homesteaders," he notes. "The United Farmers of Alberta promoted cooperativism, progressivism, the proto-feminist movement, Prohibition and the wheat pool. Social Credit was defined by the Depression; their inspiration was social and community stability; and they encouraged an aggressive oil industry after Leduc 1947. The Progressive Conservatives espoused development in a larger, more systematic way." He sees a weird pattern to Alberta politics, as well as an inability to change the basic inspiration once a party is in power. "This is typical of the Alberta mindset," he explains. "We always think of progression rather than permanence. If there's an Alberta psychology, that's it and it hasn't changed one iota since 1905."

It's not just the infrequency of the change in governments that's remarkable, but the strength of the majorities. In no other province does any party do as well at the polls as the Conservatives in Wild Rose Country. In provincial elections held from 1993–2005, Albertans voted 50 per cent Tory (edging PEI for first place nationally), just under 33 per cent Liberal (ranking eighth in Canada) and 10 per cent New Democratic Party (tied for fifth).[3]

As politically monolithic as this all seems, it was not always that way.

Non-partisan

Party is merely a struggle for office, the madness of many for the gain of a few.

—JOHN A. MACDONALD, 1867[4]

After Europeans hit the great northwest, the Hudson's Bay Company ran the sprawling wilderness as its own fur harvest. Authority was rough and rudimentary, and Natives or fur traders needed regulations or governments like a hole in the canoe. By the time the Legislature of the North-West Territories started business in 1888, the major issues of the day were building roads, hospitals and schools. The territorial premier, Frederick Haultain, believed that he spoke for the entire House in condemning party politics in the territorial Legislature as "undesirable, unintelligent and unnecessary."[5]

Other members tended to agree, irrespective of their personal party preferences. Ironically, Premier Haultain was consigned to historical obscurity by the very party system that he eschewed. In a marathon speech in the Legislature in 1900, he launched what became a five-year crusade for provincehood for the territories, seeking all of the political autonomy and fiscal power that came with it. Unsurprisingly, this rejection of established political parties did little to move Prime Minister Wilfrid Laurier or his Liberal government. Defiantly, Mr. Haultain campaigned against the Liberals and supported the Conservatives in the 1904 federal election; Team Laurier tossed him a judicial appointment to buy him off but he refused. When provincehood became inevitable, the feds named Liberal friends as interim lieutenant-governors of the new provinces of Saskatchewan and Alberta, despite Mr. Haultain's eight years of distinguished service as premier. By late 1905 and the first provincial election in Alberta, talk of non-partisanship was crushed by the Liberals and then the Conservatives holding conventions to nominate candidates to run under their respective party banners.

Despite the introduction of old-school political parties and their federal apron strings, the non-partisan tradition did not go gentle into the good Albertan night. The primary opposition to Alberta's first two landslide governments (manned by Liberals) came from their own caucus. Their leader, A.C. Rutherford, was a remarkable visionary, a prodigious worker and an upstanding bloke, but he was done in by his passive demeanour, unremarkable oratorical skills and reluctance to delegate authority, all crowned by political naïveté and a fundamental distaste for partisan gamesmanship. As a "provincial nationalist," he found himself at odds with the arch-partisan and centralist Laurier crew. During Alberta's second provincial election campaign in 1909, Mr. Rutherford declared, "I appeal to you for the elimination of selfish and partisan considerations. I appeal to you not as Liberals or Conservatives, but as Albertans. The Province must stand before the party."[6] During that same election campaign, one of Alberta's two opposition MLAs quit the Conservative caucus. Pillorying political parties as an unnecessary evil imported from central Canada, the dissident, Cornelius Hiebert, ran as an independent in Red Deer after his own riding was wiped out by governmental gerrymandering. He fared poorly, lost his $100 deposit and was labelled "despised" and "arrogant"[7] by the Calgary Herald, which pilloried "political acrobats"—especially when they leaped from the Tory party that the newssheet supported.

Premier Rutherford was forced out of office by a railway scandal in 1910, though he was almost certainly guiltier of naïveté and negligence than any malevolence, and he had not profited personally from the controversial government guarantees issued to defaulting railway interests. He tried unsuccessfully to regain his seat in 1913 and the sting must have stayed with him. In a remarkable turnabout eight years later, he campaigned for Conservative candidates against what he called the "rotten" administration of his former party, singling out the man who had defeated him for the nomination in 1913 and the Liberal leader for good measure. This moved the Edmonton Journal to comment that old party politics in Alberta were passé.[8]

Alberta's non-partisan streak did not find as strong a voice in the other Prairie provinces, even though they all came from the same primordial, territorial swamp. After electoral success in North Dakota, an organization called the Non-Partisan League migrated to the province in 1916, the year that women got the vote on the prairies. The league fired lively volleys at time-honoured political games and the economic woes and social inequality that resulted from middlemen—bankers, grain elevator operators, mill owners and speculators—fattening their wallets at the expense of producers by manipulating prices, overcharging on dockage fees, weighing unfairly, under-grading grain and generally behaving like pirates. In the provincial election in 1917, two league candidates were elected, Louise McKinney and James Weir. The league faded due to organizational challenges and the lack of a quick thumbs-up from the rising United Grain Growers.

The torch of political non-partisanship was taken up by the United Farmers of Alberta (UFA), born in 1909 of the union of two farm organizations in competition for control of grain marketing. The UFA's leader, a formidable Midwestern import poetically named Henry Wise Wood, believed that the marketplace should be governed not by forces of competition but by co-operation. Loathing the notion of opposition for its own sake, he called for occupational groups to take control over their elected representatives to ensure that the wishes of the people prevailed. And he resisted what he saw as the tyrannical trappings of partisan politics. After a rumbling groundswell of farmers' protests for direct political action, the UFA morphed from a vocational group into a political party, absorbed the Non-Partisan League and fielded candidates in the provincial election of 1921, more interested in presenting the farmer's voice in the Legislature than in wielding governmental power. The fledgling party was so ardently opposed to political backroom dealings that it fought its four elections exclusively on $2 constituency memberships and silver collections at campaign meetings.[9]

The UFA advocated government by consensus rather than party affiliation and it adopted the perspective, rooted in the western US and enshrined in several state constitutions, of the supremacy of the ultimate voter over parliamentary procedure through initiative, referendum and recall. Respectively, these three measures allowed citizens to initiate legislation themselves by collecting a prescribed number of signatures to force a vote, typically called a proposition; vote to adopt or repeal specific legislation and thus bind their legislature to comply; and collect a prescribed number of signatures to sack their elected representative. When the UFA won the election, it was stunned and unprepared to govern. The leaderless UFA's natural choice for premier, Henry Wise Wood, refused the job. Once ensconced in the Legislature with a formally chosen leader, the aptly christened Herbert Greenfield, the UFA took up grassroots democracy. Government members took their lead from constituency associations and policy conventions, effectively bypassing the primacy of the ballot box. Imagine the surprise of these parliamentary greenhorns when some hardliner non-partisans from the backbenches sought to take down "partyism" by voting against a dairy-related bill and almost took down their own government, which had to be rescued by MLAs from the Labour opposition.

Alberta's penchant for political non-partisanship was echoed at the federal level by the Progressive Party, which boasted two strains. The Manitoban school was rooted in economic protest, seeking improvements through political action. But the Albertan school took Henry Wise Wood's approach of pushing for co-operation over competition in all things and a more radical stance toward overhauling the entire political system.[10] Protesting the strictures of the political party system perceived to inhibit their ability to represent their constituents in Parliament, Albertan MPs from the Progressive Party broke away in 1924 to form the "Ginger Group" with Labour MPs J.S. Woodsworth and William Irvine. In the finest non-partisan tradition, Progressives refused to call themselves an actual political party and declined to serve as the loyal opposition despite winning the second-highest number of seats in 1926.[11] Not even the Depression dimmed this sentiment. Some Albertan MLAs took to calling parliamentary government "limited state dictatorship." Not content with mere epithet-tossing, the UFA government boycotted the Royal Commission on Dominion-

Provincial Relations, directing its comments to "the Sover
of Canada."[12]

Like the United Farmers of Alberta, a teacher-turned-
turned-activist named William Aberhart had a dream to i
lot of common folk in Alberta. Like the UFA, he tried to
existing political parties to adopt his idea of a solution: in his case, to
boost Depression-wracked Albertans' purchasing power through an
unproven economic theory called social credit. Like the UFA, he
found that co-operation and non-partisanship got him nowhere: the
UFA was no more serious about implementing his vision of social
credit than the Liberals had been about adopting co-operativism at
the behest of the UFA. Yet he, too, resisted calls from his supporters to
take direct political action. Finally, he declared that none of the established parties could cure the Depression and invited candidates to
form a new party. He set only two criteria: candidates had to be "reli-
able, honourable, bribe-proof businessmen" and they had to renounce
any affiliation with political parties.[13] In Albertan elections, political
inexperience is considered a selling point.

Citizen Aberhart pledged a non-partisan spirit, free of fealty to
central Canadian interests, which he vilified with venomous and
dazzling success. After his landslide victory in 1935—just nine months
after starting his political party—he had to go to the trouble of getting
elected himself in an unopposed by-election (being too busy master-
minding and campaigning before), although he didn't bother making a
speech in the Legislature until 1939. Among his first steps was to pass a
law empowering constituents to recall their MLA by presenting a peti-
tion to the Legislature. This small step for grassroots democracy
landed with a squish. When his own constituents took him up on it
(he claimed it was an opposition plot), he repealed the *Recall Act* and
kept his seat. In another sacrifice of the people's voice, he did not call
on the 1,600 grassroots Social Credit study groups to implement social
credit but left it to a cabal of "experts." Even in Alberta, grassroots
democracy and non-partisanship can only go so far.

If anything, Alberta's tradition of political leadership is based more on practicality than ideology. When Premier Aberhart died in office in 1943, his protégé, the provincial secretary, Ernest Manning, quietly took his boss's desk and stayed for a quarter-century. Like his predecessor, a school principal and a radio evangelist, Mr. Manning did not see himself as a politician. The first premier of the present Conservative dynasty—and perhaps the first premier of Alberta ever to really want the job—Peter Lougheed, once admitted, "The more non-political, the more apolitical a person is, the better chance he has of winning."[14]

So, why is a province renowned in recent decades for its small- and large-C conservatism so steeped in anti-political sentiment?

The tradition began with Premier Haultain's struggle for province-hood and a deep-rooted desire to start anew in Alberta, rather than import what some saw as deficient, morally bankrupt, political and economic regimes from central Canada. Then the Rutherford Liberals were divided by the Great Waterways Railway Scandal, reinforcing the perceived fusion of partisan politics and moral turpitude. Albertan leaders have fuelled their stays in power by appealing to these non-partisan leanings while assuming the mantle of defending Albertans' rights against the federal government—with the added benefit of painting their opposition as redundant. Also, the relatively heavy influx of American and other settlers cultivated a predisposition to support political *ideas* rather than political *parties* established in older parts of the country from roots in Victorian England.[15]

Certainly, Alberta's position as the Last Best West cultivated hostility to Ottawa and other symbols of a Bytown era. The notions of starting afresh on the frontier and struggling to survive unleashed a bias against entrenched power, inherited privilege and the haughty attitudes that went with them. Irene Parlby declared, "We must work for a higher standard of business and political morality, which will never be achieved until we destroy, root and branch, the whole system of patronage which spreads its malignant tentacles through every fibre of our national life."[16] And she ought to have known, not merely as a trailblazing female legislator but because she swapped a posh British pedigree for life on a farm near Alix, Alberta.

Nowhere is Alberta's aversion for partisan politics more apparent than at its highest altar, the ballot box. Depending on your outlook, the province's abysmal voter turnouts are either a hearty nose-thumbing at perceived political elites or a disgraceful abrogation of a right for which zillions have perished through the ages. But a turnout of 41 per cent in the provincial election of 2008—well under the 68 per cent averaged in the previous other provincial and territorial elections across Canada[17]—sets the bar low enough to retire the most zealous limbo dancer. Near the end of his undefeated, quarter-century parade through the polls, Premier Klein boasted outright of running boring election campaigns. He preferred to ignore opposition parties, perhaps to avoid the suggestion that they were necessary.

So despite a reputation for arch-conservatism, Alberta has maintained a hardy and singular tradition of non-partisanship since her earliest days. And it makes sense; after all, Aboriginal people survived in the area without political parties for over 10,000 years. As the writer, Gordon Laird, put it, the "pre-fab settler utopia" of the early Canadian West was not designed to include politics: "This was the fantasy of 'Minimal Government'—civil society built around property, happy consumers and family values—a fantasy that would be echoed by neo-conservatives in the 1990s."[18] Apparently, a good fantasy is hard to forget. But Alberta's myth-making machine has done a solid job of not only trimming the sails of non-partisanship but also sinking a political tradition rooted far from the right of the spectrum.

Left to Right

The powerful image of carving out a living on the frontier lingers like the scent of cinnamon simmering on a wood-burning stove. In this sepia scenario, exemplified by poetic paeans to the open range, you could graze your cattle and walk for a thousand miles without seeing a fence or anything with which to scrape off your boots. Purveyors of this ethos, typically but not exclusively found in momentary repose at the swank Ranchmen's Club in Calgary, would avow that it forged an unflinching, squinting Social Darwinism. That's a natural response to a world where fortunes are won and lost from betting, whether it's on weather, commodity prices, freight rates, tariffs or that single blade of grass rooting the cattle industry.

Alberta is perceived as American in flavour, not only by professional cognoscenti but by Canadians interviewed on my investigations. The American populist strain dominated rural Alberta in the province's early years. More than 30 per cent of the homestead applications granted in 1909 went to Americans,[19] and transplanted Yankees made up a quarter of the population by 1911, outnumbering British-born Albertans and both absorbing and overshadowing the early sway of liberalism from Ontario.[20] The American influence was particularly prominent in Calgary, where the American Women's Club held social and charitable sway from 1912–2007 and where the tony suburb of Mount Royal was originally called American Hill. While folks are correct about Uncle Sam's important imprimatur on Wild Rose Country, there's another wing involved. This isn't necessarily a bad thing when you consider the observation by the comedian, Pat Paulsen, that putting either the right wing or the left wing in charge will leave the country flying around in circles.[21]

The first of two great American migrations to Alberta came with the evaporation of the American frontier near the end of the nineteenth century. As homestead land in the American West filled up, settlers from places like Nebraska and the Dakotas poured into western Saskatchewan, Peace River Country and especially southern Alberta. Many of these economic immigrants belonged to the American Society of Equity, a unionist group embracing farmers' causes and sporting radical ideas about monetary theory and direct democracy—ideas that would gain wider currency in

Alberta in ensuing decades. These settlers established organizations that promoted their two favourite pastimes: (1) surviving, and (2) farming as a means to achieve pastime number (1). These groups included the Canadian Society for Equity (a branch of the American mother ship, which embraced co-operatives) and the Alberta Farmers' Organization (which promoted local strength in crop-growing); eventually these folded into the anti-party, collectivist United Farmers of Alberta. While this unionist, co-operative ethos leans more to the left than to the right, the notion of individuals yielding to the common good is, on the classical definition, conservative, though most folks today would call it liberal. In any case, the first great wave of American immigration into Alberta hardly infused the province with mouth-breathing, knuckle-dragging, rifle-toting right-wingers. This clash of incoming progressives with traditional, Canadian conservatives is said to ground the province's singular political culture.[22]

The farmer's agenda dominated Alberta. In 1901, for example, three-quarters of Alberta's population was rural—compared to less than two-thirds for all of Canada—and most people worked on family farms as small businesses, with their efforts not only feeding others but greasing the wheels of distributors, railways and governments alike.[23] Conditions were ripe for radical action, and Alberta's remoteness did not dam the tide of socialism that swept the land after World War I. Canada's One Big Union movement was born in 1919 at the Western Labour Conference held in Calgary, of all places. Hosted by the Socialist Party of Canada, the powwow declared support for the new Bolshevik regime in Russia and even dispatched collegial greetings. More significantly, the gathering launched a referendum on withdrawing from both the Trades and Labour Congress of Canada and the American Federation of Labour to form (you guessed it) One Big Union of workers from all industries, with the goal of achieving fairness for workers through full-scale strikes. The vote passed, appropriately, during the Winnipeg General Strike. (Apparently, *someone* was around to count the ballots.) Ultimately, membership dwindled and the organization joined the Canadian Labour Congress. That same year, Alberta and Saskatchewan led the push for what became the Canadian Wheat Board. Calgary elected two of the three successful Labour MPs in the 1921 federal election.

Meanwhile, the ties between organized labour and the governing United Farmers of Alberta were fraying, as Premier John Brownlee failed to appoint a Labour MLA to cabinet after the 1926 election as the government had in 1921. And he dealt with coal-mine workers' grievances by summoning the provincial police—to help the mining companies. He further antagonized proponents of progressivism by selling off the publicly owned northern railways that had taken down Premier Rutherford and by dragging his heels on implementing a national old-age pension even though it was proposed by federal members of his own party.

In 1932, with dusty farms blowing away in the wind and desperate people starving during the Great Depression, everyone's favourite hotbed of radicalism, Calgary, hosted a gathering of farmers, labour advocates and socialists at a labour conference at the local Legion Hall. The event ended in a public meeting with 1,300 people jammed into the sweltering building and 300 more turned away. Led by the cry of the Labour MP, J.S. Woodsworth, reiterating the incompatibility of profits and human welfare, they committed to holding a national convention in Regina in the next year, where they would produce a manifesto calling for radical changes in the Canadian economy. For the moment, though, they declared their goals: a centrally planned economy, secure land for farmers, state-controlled banking and health care, publicly owned utilities and natural resources, insurance (against crop failure, illness, old age, poverty and unemployment) and equal opportunity for all, regardless of sex, race or religion.[24] The follow-up meeting in Regina in 1933 led to the birth of the Co-operative Commonwealth Federation (CCF), the forerunner of the New Democratic Party (NDP). The CCF's original mission was to have government nationalize or regulate Canada's banking, credit and financial systems—an unabashedly leftist idea that, again, most would not trace back to Wild Rose Country, let alone this apparently most American of Canadian cities. While one could argue that a good economic catastrophe would be enough to turn a lot of people to the left, especially back then, events like these show Albertans not so much turning as leaping.

Which brings us back to perhaps the province's most notorious contribution to Canadian political history, the arrival of William "Bible Bill" Aberhart. As a preacher, educator and semi-reluctant politician, he has been called many things, but right-wing won't top the list. His biographer, David Elliott, suggests that the great man's economic and social thought had more in common with the political left than the right; that he mixed "quasi social gospel theology and left-leaning fascist tendencies"; and that his agenda owed more to the Communist Manifesto and to the Victorian utopian novelist, Edward Bellamy, than to the social credit dogma which he espoused.[25]

Social credit itself was a relatively obscure monetary theory propagated by Major C.H. Douglas, a Scottish engineer with questionable qualifications in economics and a mania for what he saw as an international financial conspiracy. His work would probably have remained tucked away in the tickle-trunk of history had Mr. Aberhart not invoked it in a desperate crusade to alleviate Albertans' suffering during the Dirty Thirties. His home-brewed adaptation, set out in his famous Yellow Pamphlet and attacked for inaccuracy by Mr. Douglas himself, called for citizens to receive food, clothing and shelter through a $25 credit from the government (the social credit angle); the abolition of conventional money, banks, life insurance, inheritances and other capitalist trappings (the old farming protest ideal); equality of the sexes, free education and health care (the communist angle, at least in theory); and the incarceration and suspension of civil rights of citizens who buck the new order (the communist angle in practice, blended with Victorian utopianism). In drumming up support for his revolution, Mr. Aberhart headlined meetings of groups like the League for Social Reconstruction and the Canadian Labour Party, as well as locals of the UFA, which still held power. He teamed up with federal and provincial leaders of the CCF to promote social and economic solutions to the Depression. Neither his approach nor his allies hounded the right of the political spectrum.

And let's not forget the social gospel aspect of Bible Bill's platform. Harnessing all his skills as a preacher, he figuratively and relentlessly crucified the "fifty big shots in Canada"—the personification of all the poverty, suffering and despair visited on Albertans by the Great Depression. The religious fervor and language in which he cloaked his appeals spread his following like a prairie fire. Every good advocate needs a good scapegoat, and the grand orator found a blue-ribbon special in the banks, loathed across the prairies but demonized with singular fervour in Wild Rose Country. Controlled by more powerful forces in places like Toronto and Montréal, banks had refused to return Alberta government bonds during the scandal that railroaded Premier Rutherford from office. They had foreclosed mercilessly on farmers, especially in the province's southeast during the drought of the late 1920s and early 1930s, leading to a massive abandonment of farms. Small wonder that the Socreds hatched the only government-owned bank in Canada and the United States. Alberta Treasury Branches were created in 1938 as a vehicle to implement social credit and to provide credit to desperate Albertans not served by the steady stream of central-based banks that pulled up stakes and went home during the Depression. The institution lives on as ATB Financial, an arm's-length David battling competing banking Goliaths from Toronto and beyond.

Yet despite this and all of his other adventures in small-s socialism, Mr. Aberhart was careful not to lean far enough to the left to fall over. When the *Financial Post* called Alberta's brand of Social Credit a "thin disguise for Communism," he responded with mass rallies, radio rebuttals and a propaganda campaign that notoriously skewered "bankers' toadies."[26] Adding to the ideological confusion was that

Major Douglas was a raving anti-Semite whose views, like the ambiance of sullied diapers, grew more insistent over time. Social Credit theory blamed the world's economic woes on an international conspiracy of bankers, whom, in the tradition of *The Merchant of Venice*, were perceived to be Semitically enhanced. This theory was swallowed hook, line and swastika by some Social Credit MPs, the editors of the party's national newspaper and hardliners on the Social Credit Board established by Premier Aberhart to implement the major's theories. (The board was an early version of the delegated administrative organizations that arose during the Klein era, but without the charm.) Unsurprisingly, all of this invited accusations of Alberta's flying on the arch-*right* wing. Although the premier never bashed Jews, the stench of that practice tainted the province. Ultimately, the legacy of William Aberhart has little to do with social credit, which was fading as early as 1940, a victim of economics, logistics and an overriding federal constitutional power over banking. Rather, history may look more kindly on his reforms in education, health care, and oil and gas resource management.

Two key events over the next decade had profound consequences for the province's political culture. The first event started with Premier Aberhart's death in office in 1943—not a bad career move, considering his battles against exhaustion, dejection and torrential flack from an increasingly dubious public on one hand and the dogmatic hardliners on his Social Credit Board on the other. Under his successor, Ernest Manning, the government launched its last effort to bring in social credit in 1946 by passing the *Alberta Bill of Rights Act*. Mindful of the battery of Social Credit legislation that had been disallowed by the Supreme Court of Canada as beyond provincial jurisdiction, the government made its proposed law subject to a finding of constitutional validity by the courts. The new law obligated the province to guarantee education, medical care and the "necessaries of life" to Albertans under age nineteen; the opportunity to work or a social security pension to those aged nineteen to sixty; and retirement pension and medical benefits to those over sixty. This radical, pioneering attempt to build a comprehensive social safety net came around the time Tommy Douglas's reforms put neighbouring Saskatchewan at the forefront of the road to national Medicare, but Alberta's attempt would have gone further. The problem, of course, was money. Premier Manning's scheme would have been financed by changes in the monetary system, overseen by a board of Credit Commissioners; the board would issue Alberta Credit certificates to banks as reserves for them to generate new loans, both to the government and to citizens. When this part of the scheme didn't make it up the judicial/constitutional flagpole, and the Social Credit Board produced a publicly funded annual report that drew public outrage at its unvarnished anti-Semitism, the premier gave the government a Douglas enema, forcing resignations from the overzealous scions of the Socreds' national rag and flushing the Social Credit Board down the commode of history.

While lacking the drama of the great Stalinist purge in Russia a decade earlier, the delousing of Social Credit launched a seismic shift in Alberta's political culture. After primarily non-partisan beginnings and an agrarian, social-gospel-tinged veer to the left, Premier Manning steered the ship on a leisurely timed but methodical course to the right. Like his predecessor, he was a fervent Christian, continuing with his mentor's evangelical radio broadcasts while occupying the premier's desk. Unlike his predecessor, he presided during the birth and heyday of the Cold War, when Communism was seen to rival Mephistopheles and Bible Bill's fifty big shots in the east for sheer demonic value. Aiding this shift was the miraculous discovery of oil at Leduc, celebrated with a geyser before five hundred shivering onlookers on the morning of February 13, 1947. The arrival of black gold cemented Mr. Manning's marrying fundamentalist Christianity and rightist free enterprise, along with his views of individual struggle, as the highway to salvation and the private sector as the anointed drivers.

"What is it about oil that fails to produce the kind of proletarian and social consciousness of mining and forestry?" asks Myrna Kostash. "BC and Saskatchewan have powerful unions. What is it about the extraction of oil that privatized us? There's something about the extraction of oil that has gone against our social consciousness." According to the economist, Robert Mansell, the capital intensity of the agriculture and oil industries tilted the balance of power to market forces rather than organized labour or related values.[27]

Although Social Credit enjoyed another massive majority in the Legislature in 1944 with fifty-one of fifty-seven seats, those numbers don't tell the whole tale. The governing party won just over half of the popular vote, but the CCF, with its two seats, earned one-quarter of the votes, with Labour-friendly parties earning another 5 per cent of the tally.[28] Both Social Credit and the CCF matched their respective seat totals in the 1948 election, so it's not like the left wing evaporated in the fumes of the sacred well christened Leduc No. 1. That would come later, at least at the electoral level, as the socialist vote fell and its representation dwindled to zero by 1959. Except for two odd-duck elections in the 1980s earning the capital city the enchanting sobriquet of "Redmonton" and Ralph Klein's final electoral foray in 2004, the CCF–NDP battery of MLAS has never topped two. And despite his impregnable power base, Premier Manning persisted in making bogeymen out of socialists and communists, having apparently exhausted Alberta's tradition of castigating eastern financial conspirators as the principal architects of latter-day evil. (This would help in his dotage, when he accepted a directorship at the Canadian Imperial Bank of Commerce.) Yet he never abandoned Social Credit's original humanitarian streak. In an undated monograph published by the Alberta Social Credit League, Premier Manning wrote of society's obligation to help citizens earn enough money on their own to provide a decent living for themselves and their dependents, in default of which society had to step in collectively to cover the cost of providing an acceptable standard of social services that everyone could afford.[29] He added to this remarkably social-democratic outlook in a speech, declaring, "As long as my colleagues and I have anything to do with the government of this province, we will see to it that Alberta continues to lead the world in the great fight to secure for every man, woman and child complete and permanent freedom from fear and worry and from social and economic insecurity."[30]

Leduc No. 1 brought a fabulous boost to the government's coffers by way of royalties now that Albertans owned the natural resources found in the province. Thus, Premier Manning was able to pay down the provincial debt accumulated during the Depression and talk like Scrooge about personal responsibility, while spending like Santa on public services like schools, hospitals and roads. In 1957, for example, his government spent $90 for each Albertan, while the national average was $60.[31] Later, he justified his relatively lavish spending on humanitarian grounds, arguing that social concerns are not incongruent with encouraging free enterprise and private ownership.[32] Few would argue with a goal of bringing Albertans into something like modernity. But then again, not everyone noticed that government in Alberta was booming right along with the postwar economy. A study in 1960 revealed that Alberta harboured 123 agencies, boards and commissions[33] compared to eighty-six in Ontario, which enjoyed more than four times Alberta's population at the time.[34]

There is an obvious disconnect between chanting the right-wing mantra of minimalist government while building what the political scientist, Trevor Harrison, called "a larger, more integrated, pervasive, impenetrable and centralized state" in which "the immediate political body upon which citizens may have an influence through their vote […] has grown smaller, [and] the state […] has grown larger and more distant from popular control."[35] Yet this tactic continues to be used with glorious success in Alberta. The Conservative governments of Peter Lougheed and Don Getty banked actively on economic diversification to grow the provincial economy, investing heavily in businesses and racking up $2.4 billion in investment losses, which exceeded by far the debt accumulated by the Conservative government in Saskatchewan and even the NDP government in Manitoba.[36] Over the first quarter-century of the Conservative dynasty (1971–1994), subsidies to the private sector in the name of "resource conservation and industrial development" exceeded $1.4 billion (or $792 per capita each year, in 1994 dollars), totalling 367 per cent of the annual averages of the other provinces. In the last six years of that period, "conservative" Alberta is said to have subsidized the tourism industry to the tune of $251 million while the so-called "left coast"— British Columbia—spent $157 million, about 40 per cent less.[37]

Although the Alberta government preaches fiscal prudence and the benefits of saving money for the future, it spends record amounts each year. While critics cite the perils of public spending being either unsustainable or insufficient, the government finds itself having to keep up with Albertans' insatiable demands. The provincial auditor general estimated the province's infrastructure deficit at $6.1 billion in 2007,[38] and in its 2008 budget, the Alberta government allocated $2,500 per person to capital spending, which it pegged at three times the level spent by any other province.[39] Since the days of Ernest Manning, Alberta's governments have behaved like neo-liberals in embracing the notion of small government, spent liberally on the whole and called themselves conservative.

Another force unleashed by Leduc was the second major wave of American immigration into Alberta, brought about by the need for expertise in not only the oil industry but in pillars of community life like universities, medical facilities and golf clubs. This influx is much better remembered than the one during the first wave of agrarian settlement before World War I and the leftist leanings that came with it. The biggest ripples of this lesser, second wave were felt, again, in Calgary. Most of the brass at the major oil companies, which were mainly American-owned, came from California, Oklahoma, Texas and Louisiana, and nine of fifteen presidents of the posh Petroleum Club from 1955–1970 were Americans.[40] It is commonly thought that the postwar wave of Americans brought more of a right-wing outlook, though it would be hard to measure this without installing some kind of political voltmeter at every customs kiosk.

Setting aside ideological slants for a moment, two points stand out about the face of political leadership over the course of Alberta's history. The first is a reluctance to hold office: until the Conservative dynasty, just about every premier had to be cajoled into the job.[41] Secondly, It's remarkable how easily one can group Alberta's political leaders. If we consider territorial or provincial premiers and toss in a couple of Albertan-born prime ministers and a federal opposition leader, we get four personality types: (1) the farmer (Premiers Stewart, Greenfield, Reid, Strom and Stelmach); (2) the manager, whether a lawyer (Premiers Haultain, Rutherford, Sifton, Brownlee and Lougheed and Prime Minister Bennett), a quarterback/businessman (Premier Getty) or a policy wonk (Prime Minister Joe Clark, opposition leader Preston Manning); (3) the preacher (Premiers Aberhart and Manning); and finally, thus far in a class by himself, (4) the everyman (Premier Klein).

Handily the first Albertan identified by Canadians in my travels—often unflatteringly—Ralph Klein is a living embodiment of the pragmatism pervading Albertan politics since the collapse of Social Credit's ideological crusade. After a high-profile, dozen-year run as mayor of Calgary, Ralph brought his folksy, anti-political ethos to the provincial scene in the election of 1989. Though thought to be a Liberal, he followed the power, ran successfully as a Conservative and won the premiership in a party vote three years later. Faced with spiralling provincial deficits and debt, he campaigned on a remarkable platform that said, in essence, "We screwed up—vote for me and I'll fix it." In the 1993 election, in a higher-than-normal turnout of 60 per cent, the government got 45 per cent of the vote, beating the Liberals by less than 5 per cent. In Ralph's last campaign in 2004, he polled 47 per cent of the vote on a 45 per cent turnout—hardly a coronation in either case.[42] But those votes sandwiched two impressive majorities, and he never lost an election in twenty-six years of public life.

Ralph's appeal to his coined, iconic couple, "Martha and Henry," and to what he called "severely normal" Albertans came off as populist and down-to-earth. People loved his approachability, honesty and impulsiveness, not to mention his contriteness when he screwed up. "It's just Ralph," we'd shrug, whether he was dissing "Dome Syndrome" (his euphemism for life in the Legislature), battling the bottle or reaming out an occupant of a homeless shelter for not working. Depending on your perspective, the Klein Revolution, which saw the province's public spending slashed by 20 per cent, was either a courageous victory against bloated, invasive government and parasitic "special interests"; or a self-serving attack on society's most vulnerable members; or a triumph for efficient, open and accountable government; or a cynical sham devised to keep a tired government in power; or some unholy combination thereof. A definition on which Albertans might agree is that the effort was a remarkable public relations exercise, in which a new leader of a fading political dynasty campaigned against his own government's record and won.

Lionized in his prime by the likes of the *New York Times, Wall Street Journal, Barron's, The Globe and Mail* and bond agencies, Ralph was eviscerated by teachers, health-care workers, unions, self-styled raging grannies, authors, scholars and social activists—people who bore the brunt of his revolution. It would be simple to dismiss him as a puppet of the business elite that canonized him, were it not for one thing: rank-and-file Albertans, those mythical Marthas and Henrys sharing a whole-wheat muffin on the veranda—if not a more liquid grain product on the apartment patio—loved him. He was the product of a working-class, broken home; a tireless, self-made success; and most of all, a regular Joe. In a province that has elevated political mistrust to a way of life, Ralph was her perfect anti-politician and thus among the ablest politicians in her history. Interviewed on the morning after he left the dome for the last time as its headmaster in 2006, Premier Klein tells me, "It was deemed un-Canadian to eliminate the deficit, privatize liquor stores and franchise registries, but Albertans said, 'That's what we wanted,' and that's what we did. Albertans accepted those things because they're individualistic and they're prepared to think differently." When asked to define his legacy, he replies, "The legacy that I'm extremely proud of as premier is eliminating the deficit, during tough times when the price of oil was nowhere near what it is today, and then eliminating the net debt and the gross debt. That's the epitaph I would love to have on my gravestone."

More telling about Alberta than Ralph's folksy persona is his observation that it was easier to govern the province during a storm than when the economic sun shone. The furor over government overspending in the 1990s echoed William Aberhart's apocalyptic warning of the Rapture, the impending Second Coming that would lift up the righteous and heave the heathen into Satan's fire. And Ralph's appealing to Albertans to tighten their belts today so their children and grandchildren could live debt-free tomorrow harkened back to earlier struggles: if Albertans could survive drought and depression, then they could dial up those prairie, pioneering values once again and emerge in a debt-free paradise. Like Premier Aberhart, Ralph had to withstand excoriation as well as adulation. While the National Citizens Coalition awarded him a medal for transforming government in 1995, his critics lambasted him for cultivating a crisis atmosphere through intimidation, scapegoating and vigilantism; persecuting have-nots; gutting public health, education and welfare, along with the civil service and Alberta's economic infrastructure; scaring away thousands of young, well-educated Albertans; raping the environment; and claiming to listen to the people, while centralizing political control, curbing democracy and privatizing public life.[43]

In making the case for his revolution, Premier Klein likened running the provincial economy to a household, pointing out that continuing to live on credit would shift more of the monthly budget to interest payments. The subtext, of course, was that in a worst-case picture, the house itself could be lost to foreclosure—a nightmare carved into Alberta's consciousness. As the journalist, Catherine Ford, noted, this was accepted "in a province holding the vestiges of pioneer ethics— help yourself, help your neighbour, ask for nothing"—and by social conservatives, "who cling to the enduring belief that only those who have worked for it should share the wealth, even when the provincial coffers overflow."[44] The call for toughness both played to and added to Albertans' self-perception as pioneers, entrepreneurs and mavericks who dare to buck the herd, take risks and ask not what government can do for them, so long as government does not get in their way or raise their taxes. As the retired oilman, Joe Dundas, tells me in down-town Calgary, "We need government; let governments do what they're supposed to and let ourselves do the rest. But this Liberal idea—'We want you to depend on the government and the government will deliver everything you want'—means you have to be taxed, therefore you are totally dependent on the government." He believes that's absolutely opposite to how Albertans think. "We don't need you telling us what to do," he declares. "You can run the army and various things that you should look after, but stay out of our health care, stay out of our other stuff and we'll look after ourselves. Just get out of our face!"

In seeking to explain the political dominance of Alberta's right wing, the historians' tag-team of Howard and Tamara Palmer cited several factors: a pervasive, frontier mythology; the free-enterprise ethos of the oil patch, which boasts a large middle class and a small working class; relative economic prosperity; immigrants sharing an aversion to left-wing ideals from which they fled postwar Britain and Eastern and Central Europe; an economic, religious and social connection to the United States; the revolt against the Trudeau Liberals from 1968–1984, particularly the National Energy Program; a lingering fear of what will happen when Alberta's resources are depleted; and Albertans' longstanding status in opposition federally.[45]

The right-wing tradition permeates even quarters that are not famous for it. Albertans under thirty-five are more likely than their counterparts in other provinces to describe themselves as "somewhat or very right of centre." Of course, more Albertans under thirty-five identify themselves as "somewhat or very left of centre" than as right of centre, but this is still noteworthy.[46]

The perception that Alberta is a political monolith is perpetuated not only by entrenched political and financial interests that aim to keep it that way, but also by the media. Speaking of Alberta's potential annexation (along with British Columbia) by the US for military and economic purposes, the American commentator, Lawrence Solomon, called Alberta "Canada's most conservative province—anti-Kyoto, anti-gun control, hostile to national health care, receptive to plebiscites and Bible-belt Christians, free of provincial sales tax—is in some ways more American than Canadian. Prime Minister Jean Chrétien turned his back on President Bush's plan to invade Iraq; Alberta Premier Ralph Klein forthrightly embraced it."[47] Of course, there is some truth to this quick sketch of Alberta. Whether a more nuanced portrait would reveal other shades has been overshadowed by Marshall McLuhan's truth that the medium is the message—which many media outlets may not know comes from a man who was born in Alberta. Now let's see how the province measures up to the songs of the Solomons of the world.

Rednecks

I had a great time in Alberta. I went into a bar and I was having a couple of drinks with some people I didn't even know. They were so friendly, and I felt comfortable enough to ask them, you know, "Where do the Jews hang out?" And they pointed and they said, "From that tree." And that was great. So I really got to know what you'd call that Alberta hospitality.

—MARK BRESLIN, 2005

Second only to cattle in images of Alberta proffered by Canadians in my street interviews are allusions to her political and cultural orientation. From British Columbia to Newfoundland and Labrador, the same word rings out repeatedly in my interviews. "Je pense au 'redneck,' malheureusement," laughs Marie-Christine Trahan, a young mother in Montréal, "mais je ne les connais pas. Je ne sais pas." At least she admits her limited acquaintance with the province. "I hate to say this, but the word 'redneck' keeps coming up," confesses Lorne Shapiro, a ballcapped bloke in Dorval. "And I don't know if I'm just basing that on some stupid imagined myth or if it's actually true." In a more benign light, Adam Plenkiewicz, a student I interviewed in Vieux-Montréal on Canada Day, literally draped in the national flag, declares, "In any country you need a political balance from left wing to right wing. Alberta is the conservative homeland of Canada and basically we need Alberta." More bluntly, the American comedian, Bill Maher, called Alberta "a big redneck nothing."[48]

Like Alberta herself, the term "redneck" is a bit more complex than it appears. Born in the 1830s to denote rural, white labourers in the southern United States, the epithet is also a badge of honour for those who give it traditional qualities like a strong sense of duty, honour, family and place.[49] Some Albertans embrace the pejorative aspect in a fond rebellion against being pigeonholed by other Canadians. But by its most common and ugliest definition, a "redneck" might refer to a knuckle-dragging, drooling bigot—to quote a young Albertan small-business owner, Coba Veldkamp—"driving around in a pickup truck with a beer in one hand and a shotgun in the other."

To the sociologist, Tami Bereska, there is no doubt about what Alberta is. "Redneck in our attitude towards social issues like homosexuality, same-sex marriage, ethnic and cultural differences," she observes. "Social attitudes are very conservative here compared to other parts of the country. The premier [then Ralph Klein] caters to the redneck population and I'm related to many of them. Albertans are either more bigoted or more open about it. In Alberta, prejudice is more overt and up front. It's a place where there's still a lot of name-calling in the streets."

But others, like Joe Dundas, object strongly to the contemporary use of the term. "We don't push back hard enough on people, mainly the eastern media, who run us down and call us rednecks," he states. "But I'm proud to be a redneck because they don't even know what it means. It means you worked off the damn land, okay? And they say, 'Well, do you know what it means today?' And I say, 'No, that's what it meant before. You can't change the definition of it, mister.'"

"Are we rednecks?" inquires the filmmaker, Norm Fassbender. "That's a really loaded label. Sure there are rednecks here but there are rednecks everywhere. Go to Ontario, Nova Scotia, Texas, Oklahoma. But generally, speaking, no, Albertans aren't rednecks. There's a diversity of opinion here, and some are extreme on the right, some are extreme on the left. Overall, they're pretty regular." Indeed, Alberta is home to organizations with different tilts on the political spectrum, such as the Canada West Foundation, the National Citizens Coalition, the Manning Centre for Building Democracy, the Citizens Centre for Freedom and Democracy, and the Alberta Federation of Women United for Families, all perceived as leaning rightward; and the Parkland Institute, the Pembina Institute, Public Interest Alberta and *Alberta Views* magazine, which are seen as providing alternative perspectives and which might be considered centrist elsewhere but are painted by some Albertans as leftist simply because they are not avowedly rightist.

The architect, Douglas Cardinal, sees his home province in a philosophical context. "People consider that we're really right-wing people," he says. "But it's not being right-wing. It's just not relying on governments to solve our problems. We're used to being able to contribute our efforts and our talents. We're not interested in what we're going to get from government. We're more interested in what we can give to our community. We probably wonder why people don't just shape up, take responsibility and do something with their lives."

Like other provinces, Alberta was not immune to nativism, which combines racial, religious or ethnic prejudice with nationalism. Apart from southern ranchers, who hated the idea of homesteaders fencing in the open range, most early Albertans favoured further settlement in the province regardless of the newbies' nationality or religion. There was some grumbling about Chinese launderers, the polygamy of the Mormons and the unruliness of Hungarians and Ukrainians coming to work the mines, as well as hostility toward Doukhobors, Hutterites and Mennonites, who did not assimilate as apparently. But for the most part, especially in rural areas, the economic troubles preceding World War II prompted community solidarity over prejudice.

Spurred by incomers from neighbouring British Columbia in 1924, some Albertans took to wearing white sheets. When momentum sagged the next year, Klansmen from more triple-к-friendly Saskatchewan dropped in to help, joined by an export from Hamilton who had posed unsuccessfully as a priest and who became the Imperial Wizard of Alberta. In a departure from its customary motivation based on race, most of the Ku Klux Klan's forays in the province were motivated by fear and loathing of Catholics, French-speakers and immigrants.[50]

The group met popular resistance in Alberta, as it did elsewhere. Weekly papers like the *Drumheller Mail*, *High River Times*, *Vegreville Observer* and *Lacombe Western Globe* battled, ridiculed and exposed the Klan for its bigotry, mob rule and vigilantism. When the white-sheet set threatened the editor of the *Globe*, Charles "Barney" Halpin, he printed the threat. He also reported on the trial of the Imperial Wizard, who was convicted of the un-priestly crimes of breaking and entering and insurance fraud in 1932.[51] That pretty much short-sheeted the Klan in Alberta; nor did it help that its members' funds tended to disappear along with its organizers. It seems that on the prairie, at least some hate-mongers get their own vigilante justice.

Howard Palmer called the province "neither a haven of tolerance nor a den of prejudice." He felt that Albertans shared nativist sentiments held across the four Western provinces, though nativism in Wild Rose Country was less organized and less violent than in Manitoba or BC due to differences in economic base, population, size and ethnic concentration. Both the Liberal and the UFA governments in Alberta began with a more open attitude to non-Anglo-Saxon immigrants than the senior political parties from central Canada, but they grew more conservative with the evolution of their mandates and perhaps also their frustration at failing to meet their political and economic goals at the national level. Dr. Palmer concluded that Albertans' attitudes toward citizens who fell outside of the dominant, white, Anglo-Saxon Protestant class were similar to those of other Canadians and congruent with the rise and fall of nativism around the English-speaking world in the twentieth century.[52]

The province's record on the country's official languages is murkier. Since 1971 the government's attitude toward language issues has swerved from what Edmund Auger called "generalized repression to selective tolerance."[53] In 1990 the government was sued by a group of Franco-Albertan parents seeking to participate actively in the governance of their children's education and schools in one of our official languages: the Supreme Court of Canada ruled that the Canadian Charter of Rights and Freedoms, which requires provinces and territories to offer primary and secondary schooling to official-language minorities in their mother tongue where the numbers justify it, also gives said minorities the right to manage their own schools, a right breached by the Alberta government.[54] This ruling set a national precedent and led to a province-wide system of French minority schools managed by French school boards. Although Alberta has active French-speaking and Métis cultures, particularly in more northerly parts of the province, French is simply not a big-ticket item here. In 2001 almost one in four Canadians spoke French, and 7 per cent of Albertans speaking both official languages ranked Alberta eighth among the provinces and territories. Her total of native French-speakers, 2 per cent, ranks ninth. And 43 per cent of Albertan students were enrolled in French as a second language or French immersion programs, a figure that ranks second-last in the land, ahead of only Nova Scotia.[55] Does this mean that most Albertans don't accept la lingua franca? Probably not: the most common non-native language in the North-West Territories before 1870 was French. It's more likely that Albertans dismiss bilingualism as out of touch with life in our province. According to the Association for Canadian Studies, almost one in three Albertans believe that increasing multiculturalism best describes the story of Canada, the second-highest figure among the provinces.[56] Students in Alberta's primary and secondary schools can get instruction primarily in Blackfoot, Cree and French; bilingual programs in French, Ukrainian, German, Spanish and Chinese; and language and culture programs in Chinese, German, Italian, Japanese, Punjabi and Spanish.[57]

Canadian provincial politics have been shaped by five distinct waves of immigrants, the first three—French, United Empire Loyalist and British—of which grounded our national official-language policy and preceded white settlement of the West. Alberta became part of the fourth wave from the 1890s to the 1920s, which washed in British, American and Eastern European immigrants; their dominant political orientations were labour-socialist in the case of the British, populist-liberal for the Americans (fuelling the UFA governments) and deference to New-World systems for the continental Europeans. The next wave began after World War II and swept in overwhelmingly urban immigrants from those earlier origins and also from Asia, Southern Europe, the Caribbean and Latin America. The fifth wave continues today, bringing in a polyglot of political views, races and dining preferences.[58] There are no apparent cases of Albertans stomping on the fleur-de-lys in the fashion of anti-separatists in Brockville, Ontario. Most Albertans who oppose, say, bilingualism and biculturalism, don't hate Francophones or French. What we're more likely to detest is any kind of official directive from Ottawa, whether linguistic or otherwise.

When asked about whether Albertans are different from other Canadians, Ted Byfield tells me that our distaste for political correctness stems from resisting arbitrary efforts to control what people think. While recognizing that many of the aims of political correctness, like stopping bigotry, are good, making them law causes Albertans to question it. "I don't suppose they're questioned seriously anywhere else in Canada," he says, "particularly in Toronto, because that's where all that stuff comes from." He calls Alberta "probably the most tolerant province in the country" and notes, "We've got more women running companies here than any other province. We've made more efforts with Native peoples here than any other province. The whole Fort McMurray thing, when it began was an effort to try to bring the Native peoples into that business culture and that industrial culture there, and Syncrude made huge efforts to do this. So in terms of what we do, we are very, very politically correct, but we don't like being told to be politically correct."

While it may be unusual for people not known to champion socially conservative views as Ted Byfield does to agree with him outright on political affairs, his position on tolerance in Alberta finds support from folks like Fil Fraser, a film producer, broadcaster, author and human rights commissioner. Mr. Fraser comments, "I never faced a jot of racial discrimination in Alberta and my radar is pretty good. In very general terms, Albertans have never dealt with me as a black man, just as a guy. I know this would not have happened in my home province of Quebec and absolutely not in Ontario or the Maritimes, where racial hatred carries on to this day. Notwithstanding Ralph Klein and a little rump of throwbacks, Albertans are extraordinarily tolerant." Indeed, in a survey of Canadians' approval of marriages between blacks and whites conducted in 2005, Albertans emerged with the second-highest total at 93 per cent, trailing only BC's 96 per cent.[59] And in a poll in 2009, Alberta led the provinces in having a positive view of Hindus, Sikhs, Buddhists and Jews; in holding a moderate to favourable view of Muslims (38 per cent); and in believing Islam to be a mostly peaceful religion (44 per cent).[60]

Of course, no jurisdiction can stake a claim to complete tolerance, especially if you rewind the calendar. Back in 1911, the boards of trade of Calgary and Edmonton petitioned the federal government to keep black people out of Western Canada. But they were hardly alone in the diminished humanity of the era. While the feds avoided overt action, they sent a posse of minions to Oklahoma to discourage immigration by blacks. Yet three hundred undaunted pioneers of colour left that state for the harsher climes but friendlier soil of Pine Creek north of Edmonton. They had to clear a lot of trees to get to that soil but they stayed long enough to get title to their homesteads, at a much higher success rate than your average settler in Alberta. In 1931 they named their resilient community Amber Valley after the poplar leaves in autumn. Since then, it has declined to ghost-town status, but it remains a proud symbol of black settlement and racial tolerance in the province. The black population held at about a thousand until the mid-1960s, when it grew with immigration from the West Indies and Africa.[61] Two outstanding Albertans of this heritage are John Ware (1845–1905), a former American slave who became a legendary cowboy, and Violet King Henry (1930–1981), who became the first black female lawyer in Canada in 1954 and the first woman to serve on the American national executive of the YM-YWCA in 1976.[62]

Are Albertans racists at ground level? It depends on whom you ask. An anonymous African immigrant interviewed on a street corner in downtown Edmonton says, "There are really tolerant, caring people here. People from all walks of life come here and I think they do stay here. The weather is not good, but the people are extremely good." On the other hand, Nyambura Belcourt, the executive director of the Edmonton Multicultural Society and an immigrant from Kenya, says: "Alberta has almost the same level of racism as in Africa, but a little bit more. Albertans have a lower racial tolerance because they don't look at a broad enough horizon. Ninety-five per cent of our population has no clue about what's going on beyond their borders. Alberta is more racist than most because of ignorance and materialism. Albertans have money, but they're nervous because others don't know what's in their pocket and they are worried about others taking what they have." The internationally honoured and collected visual artist, Jane Ash Poitras, observes, "There's a tremendous amount of racism. If you go to emergency and you're a Native person, you don't get preferential treatment. If you're a nice, white person, you get preferential treatment, especially if you have blue eyes and blonde hair." Reflecting on Alberta's rich Aboriginal culture, she sees little in her home city of Edmonton celebrating Native people. "What about public art?" she asks. "Where is the Aboriginal art? There is no visible evidence of any Native person even living in Alberta, let alone even alive in Alberta, so let's get with it. In Toronto and Ottawa, I get treated like an angel. Here in Alberta nobody knows who I am," she laughs.

While there is a popular impression of Albertans as a redneck society that's intolerant of racial, religious or other characteristics, there is also a broad welcoming streak in our provincial personality. One example is on the gridiron. The Edmonton Eskimos' championship run in the 1950s was graced by two black football stars, Rollie Miles and Johnny Bright, who was the subject of a notoriously brutal racial attack on an American college field. (Lest we paint too rosy a picture of the era, "Sugarfoot" Anderson, an African-American who joined the Calgary Stampeders in 1949, was invited to join a local country club despite a policy precluding blacks or Jews. He declined due to that policy.) Warren Moon joined the Eskimos in 1978, before American pro football was ready for a non-white quarterback. And Norman Kwong entered the ranks of the Stamps, the Esks and later, the lieutenant-governor's office. "Being the only Chinese-Canadian in the league, I think it prompted people to be more on my side than against me," His Honour recalls. "When I first came into the league, back in early late forties, there were teams in Canada that would not take a black player, and Albertans were very different in that way. They allowed black players to come into the league, and we had some really great ones in Calgary and in Edmonton. We've led the way in that regard, and it's certainly improved our sport and our sporting teams."

The image of redneck Alberta persists in the rest of Canada, perpetuated by high-profile flash points like electorally anointing the only separatist in memory from outside Québec. (That nobody calls the more militant Québecois "nationalists" rednecks is another in a long conga-line of ironies gracing the nation.) After the re-election of Prime Minister Pierre Trudeau, every oilman's preferred candidate—for tarring and feathering—Western separatist rallies and political parties sprouted around Alberta, feeding off rage at the federal government's National Energy Program. Support for these parties tended to come from disenchanted conservatives who might typically be white, with perhaps some wrinkles and vociferous views on issues like abortion, immigration and voting privileges for homosexuals. In 1982 the good folks of Olds-Didsbury were handed a quintessential opportunity to protest and went to town with it. In a provincial by-election they elected a candidate for the newly formed, separatist Western Canada Concept (WCC) party with 42 per cent of the vote in a turnout of 69 per cent. That means 4,015 souls in a riding of almost 14,000 voters painted Albertans with the brush of separatism. Having made their point, the early adopters of the WCC turfed their man in the general election held a few months later. In the latter vote, Peter Lougheed's Conservatives returned to power with a King-Kong majority of 75 of 79 seats, leading to the curious sight of government backbenchers lining what would be the opposition's side of the house in most democratic jurisdictions. Meanwhile, Alberta's fringe separatist parties blew away with an airiness normally reserved for tumbleweeds. In this light, maybe this long line of Conservative majorities is less about being rednecks and more about wishing the gift of flight on the federal government—that is, giving Ottawa the bird.

You could make the same argument for Albertans' notorious distaste for the federal gun registry, perceived by some as yet another catastrophe gifted by the federal Liberals. One might be forgiven for concluding that Wild Rose Country is NRA North, with God-fearing locals in Smithbilts and spurs stampeding to the American border on horseback to pry the firearm from Charlton Heston's cold, dead hands. If guns themselves seem high in Albertans' sight-line, it's probably because of the province's leading the opposition—joined by other jurisdictions—to the federal gun registry in court. The National Firearms Association is headquartered in Edmonton and apparently dedicated to hunting and sport shooting only. Statistics cited by a gun-control lobby indicate Alberta as ranking third in firearm ownership and tied for fourth in firearm-related deaths among the provinces and territories from 1990–1998.[63] Also, the province ranked second to Saskatchewan in firearm-related homicides, fifth in gun-related robberies and sixth in victims of firearm-related crimes per capita among the provinces and territories in 2006.[64] However, according to a study by the sociologist, Timothy Hartnagel, "perception of violent crime as a problem is not a significant net predictor of support for gun registration" in Alberta, and respondents tended to disbelieve that gun control laws would reduce the incidence of violent crime.[65]

Again, maybe all the steam emanating from Alberta has more to do with visions of the latest incursions from Ottawa than arch-conservatism. And perhaps this mad-on for gun control is less about American-style arms-bearing and more about the proud, bald-ass prairie rite of having a rifle handy against predators that threaten your livestock and your livelihood. Almost a century ago, Leo Thwaite wrote of Alberta: "Second only to polo in the excitement which it creates and the favour in which it is held is the hunting of coyotes."[66]

For a howl (and a definitive statement on Albertans' politics), I hunted down Mark Breslin, the founder and CEO of Yuk Yuk's, the world's largest chain of comedy clubs. Resplendent in a snappy, white summer suit at his desk in downtown Toronto, he observes:

It's interesting that Alberta is kind of an entrepreneurial oasis in the middle of Canada, which tends to be kind of a semi-socialist country. In the future, Alberta will probably point the way for people to compete on a world market, which is something that Canada has always been very nervous about. I think Alberta's going to be the first, for instance, to rescind the notion of welfare. As time goes on and we realize that the poor are just dragging us down, Alberta's going to be a true leader in being able to say, "Enough of these lives. They're just being led without productivity." I don't know whether they're going to gas them or whether they're going to put them to sleep in some kind of gentle way. Being Albertans, it will be done in a gentle way, in a sensitive way. That's the kind of thing that Albertans are going to be first in. And of course, we're already seeing Albertans taking the fore-front of a two-tier health system, for instance. That's a lot better than the rest of Canada, which basically has a no-tier health system.

Proponents of the Alberta-as-redneck theory are quick to jerk a thumb at the province's take on the social safety net. How, they ask, can a province as wealthy as Alberta be so hard on those who are the least fortunate? How can a province that had horrible poverty and national humiliation seared into its soul during the Great Depression neglect fundamental needs when even Ernest Manning, the chap who captained her turn to the right, dedicated his government to leading the fight against fear, worry and social and economic insecurity?[67] And most chillingly of all, why do Albertans seem to enjoy being so nasty about it?

A study of Alberta's social services traces Alberta's tough love back to frontier days, when her territorial and provincial governments lacked the funds or the awareness to support public welfare. Citing the unprecedented discrimination against, and punishment of, low-income Albertans, whether "deserving" (widowed, disabled, elderly, families, children) or "less deserving" (unemployed but employ-able), under the Klein government's spending cuts in the 1990s, one study noted that "The notions of 'less eligibility' and 'deserving versus undeserving poor' are certainly not unique in Alberta alone, but the degree and length of punitive action through policy reform carries a made-in-Alberta label."[68] Is this nasty label deserved? Alberta's share of gross domestic product devoted to public spending was the lowest in Canada, at 13 per cent in 2003 compared to the next-lowest, Ontario's 18 per cent, the high in Nova Scotia of 34 per cent, a mean among provinces of 22 per cent and the federal figure of 17 per cent. In 1993, the maiden year of the Klein Revolution, the figures were both higher and closer, with Alberta at 22 per cent, the provincial mean at 27 per cent and the federal government at 25 per cent.[69]

Taxes remain a dirty word in the province. Some Albertans exult in having the lowest overall taxes in Canada. In 2000 the provincial government unhinged its taxes from the federal calculation and substituted a flat tax. Critics state that this shift offered relief for the working poor but shifted the burden from the wealthy to the middle class. In 2008 each Albertan and each business in the province paid roughly $3,000–$5,000 less in taxes than people in other provinces—a saving to taxpayers of $10–$18 billion every year.[70] There are various user fees and hidden or low-profile taxes on gasoline, tires, hotels, tobacco and insurance premiums, though the highest-profile tax, health care premiums, was axed in 2009 after years of protest.

The province is known for its singular lack of a provincial sales tax. (In desperation, the Aberhart government introduced a sales tax once, but it didn't work out.) So Albertans spring for half the sales tax paid in the province with the next lowest PST. Small wonder that the province led the charge to the Supreme Court of Canada against the imposition of the federal GST.[71] Alberta lost, of course, but she made her point about not liking the extra tax one damned bit. This carries huge political clout in a place that has elevated retail to a religious rite. Lest we forget, it was an Albertan business that launched the legal battle that led the country's highest court to kibosh restrictions on Sunday shopping in 1985.[72] Of course, one taxpayer's savings is another government's loss in revenue. But that doesn't come up so much in a province where the official ethic is self-reliance and low expectations from government. (Recent administrations have applied that ethic more flexibly in the case of industries like, say, oil.)

On the one hand, in 2001, Alberta's spending on health, education and social services of almost 11 per cent of GDP was tied with Ontario for the lowest in Canada. On the other hand, Alberta's spending on those areas relative to total spending was the third-highest in Canada at 65 per cent that year, rising to 71 per cent by 2008–2009.[73]

Numbers can say anything that you want them to say. But recalling Oliver Wendell Holmes, life is not doing a sum but painting a picture. And often, the portrait of Alberta painted in the mainstream media evokes the masterpiece of the Norwegian painter, Edvard Munsch, *The Scream*. It's hard enough for people to stay conscious of Alberta's early advances in areas like education and women's rights, and even her efforts to protect human rights and create a social safety net. But powerful imagery is an even fiercer eraser than Father Time, and the Klein government—still fresh in the public eye—left a deluxe photo album of harshness at the expense of its most vulnerable charges.

Alberta's attack on poverty lopped nearly 36,000 cases off the family and social service rolls in 1993–1994. This landed some people back at work, some in educational programs and most notoriously, some on a one-way bus trip to BC. This last option, dubbed "Greyhound therapy" by the media, raised eyebrows nationwide but was more apocryphal than actual. The research director of BC's Social Planning and Research Council, Michael Goldberg, called it largely a myth. "Some people got on the buses, but it was a teeny number," he said. "No one moves from place to place to get a few more welfare dollars."[74] Still, the image lingered, and other statistics tend to support the image of Alberta as a hard place to be physically, mentally or economically disadvantaged. Social services clients who did not or could not make sixty job applications per month would lose their welfare payments. In 2004 the National Council of Welfare cited Alberta's rate for welfare for a single mother with one child as the lowest in Canada at $11,638, compared to substantially less well-off Newfoundland at $15,056.[75]

The province is regularly reprimanded for its miserly support to those with severe disabilities. The government sunk to new depths in 1997 when it moved to force a settlement on victims of its former forced-sterilization program (more on this shortly) and thereby remove their right to sue for compensation. Although it backed off in the face of public outrage, another ugly image entered the public album. Despite the enormous wealth enjoyed by Albertans relative to the rest of the country, it has a significant and widening gap between the highest and lowest incomes. The Edmonton Food Bank has the distinction of being the first of its kind in Canada. Its executive director, Marjorie Bencz, sees a big dichotomy at work. "Alberta has some of the most regressive social policies in Canada, and yet we're the province with the most surpluses," she tells me, surrounded by elephantine boxes awaiting donations. She adds that Alberta has some of the most wealth and least unemployment in any province or country. "And at the same time, we still have people that are challenged by not having adequate housing and struggling with food insecurity as well. The community steps up to help people in need."

Certainly, the notion of the community assistance is steeped in provincial lore, a legacy of Aboriginal and white pioneering days, and a strong rural tradition. Edmonton's football fans helped raise 54,000 pounds (25,545 kilograms) of food in 2007, the largest amount raised in any Canadian Football League city to that point.[76] "Why food banks?" muses Link Byfield. "Because we prefer them to government solutions, which never work. There's an egalitarian streak here. We believe everyone should get a chance to help and do well." He illustrates this by citing a sign in a gas station near St. Paul: "If you need a penny, take a penny. If you need a nickel, get a job."

Albertans may be publicly frugal, but are we privately generous? Among the provinces, Albertans had the highest total incomes reported by Canadian taxpayers in 2005 at $50,300, compared to a low of

$34,400 for Newfoundland and Labrador and a national average of $45,400. That year, Alberta ranked fourth in the rate of donors at 25 per cent, just over the national average but first in donations per filer at $0.47, three pennies ahead of the runner-up, Ontario, and well above the national average of $0.34.[77] Whether this reflects on Albertans' generosity or merely the thickness of their wallets is anybody's guess.

Perhaps a better measure of generosity is volunteerism. "Albertans have a community spirit and invented huge-event volunteerism," observes Senator Tommy Banks. In a crowded field of sporting, cultural and other events, the Calgary Winter Olympics in 1988 remain a landmark and a model of grassroots involvement. In 2004, 48 per cent of Alberta residents volunteered, posting an average of 175 hours per person. These figures are slightly higher than the national averages of 45 per cent and 168 hours. In total, Albertans volunteered over 214 million hours in 2004, the equivalent of over 111,000 full-time jobs. While government is the major source of funding for volunteer and charitable organizations in most regions, Albertan groups claim the lowest share of revenue from public funds in Canada at 33 per cent, compared to 49 per cent for the rest of the land.[78]

The focus of these organizations is telling. Religious groups make up the majority of the volunteer sector across the country; although their share in Alberta—19 per cent of the groups—jives with the national average, the province's religious groups garnered more than double the gifts and donations of any other activity area and over one-third of all gifts and donations. The province harboured the nation's highest share of groups devoted primarily to sports and recreation (tied at 26 per cent with Québec); the fourth-highest share of arts and culture groups (10 per cent, but only 0.5 per cent behind the highest share); and the lowest share of not only groups devoted to the environment (1.7 per cent, just a point under the national average), but also business and professional associations and unions (3.3 per cent, two points under the national average). Organizations in Alberta are the most likely in Canada to have a local focus, serving their neighbourhood, city, town or rural municipality rather than a region or the entire province; almost three-quarters of Alberta's groups have that local constituency. Alberta's donor rate of 79 per cent in 2004 was six points below the national average, though Albertans' average annual donation of $500 was the highest in Canada. Despite claiming 12 per cent of the non-profit and voluntary groups in Canada—with about 10 per cent of the population at that time—Alberta logged almost 20 per cent of the total hours volunteered. She ranked seventh in the number of groups per capita, but perhaps the execution, measured by the commitment of hours, is more indicative than the structure, measured by the number of groups.[79]

The most fertile field of volunteer activity in Wild Rose Country is sports and recreation (20 per cent of all volunteer hours), followed by religion (15 per cent), social services (14 per cent) and education and research (13 per cent). The leading reasons given by Albertans for volunteering are to contribute positively to their community, to use their skills and expertise, and to act on a personal link to a cause supported by an organization.[80] Putting a face on all of these good works, the most typical Alberta volunteer is female, aged 35–54 and either married or living as a couple. She would likely have a university degree, attend religious services on a weekly basis, have school-aged children and live in a household with an annual income topping $60,000.[81]

This data on volunteerism reinforces the notions that compared to other Canadians, Albertans depend less on government; are more focused on donating time to local causes, sports and recreation; and are less devoted to more political causes, such as the environment, business and labour. This is congruent with factors noted earlier, such as the province's status as Canada's last frontier for white settlement, creating the need to band together to survive the harshness of both isolation and the weather; her strong rural roots; and her taking longer to urbanize than other parts of the country. It also reflects the fierce work ethic shared by everyone from the dominant, Protestant tradition to the hardy immigrants in sheepskin coats touted by Clifford Sifton during the first great wave of white settlement. If this is redneck behaviour, then it probably falls within the lesser known, but more positive, connotations of the term as embracing a strong sense of duty, honour, family and place.

Now let's turn to a few flashpoints for redneck-ness and how they play out in Alberta.

In Alberta's early years, labour had something resembling a voice through avenues like farmers' groups. But organized labour was overwhelmed by the capital intensity of the primary economic drivers in the province: agriculture and energy.[82] The province has posted the lowest unionization rate in Canada, and the government has an uneasy relationship with its own employee union. In 2006, Alberta was one of only three provinces to deny its employees the right to strike, and the credibility of the alternative, arbitration, took a beating in 1981 when the government tried to restrain the amount awardable.[83] In 2007, she was one of three provinces without first-contract arbitration, a situation that dissuades negotiations with workers and lets government favour employers over workers who choose to organize and demand fair wages and working conditions.[84] Alberta's tough stand on labour groups, especially in recent years, reinforces her image as a bastion of unsavoury redneck-ism.

Another source of Alberta's perceived intolerance is her government's stand on homosexuals. She dawdled on amending human rights legislation to prohibit discrimination based on sexual orientation, notwithstanding the Supreme Court of Canada's applying that prohibition in 1998 in a precedent born in Edmonton. Why the heel-dragging? Research from 2003, corroborated in 2006, indicated that 54 per cent of Canadians opposed same-sex marriage, with Alberta leading the nation at 67 per cent, followed by the Atlantic region (63 per cent) and Ontario (57 per cent). The researcher, Reginald Bibby, concluded, "Albertans are not wary of gay marriage because they are more religious or more right-wing than other Canadians.

What makes the difference is the provincial government's consternation."[85] He suggested that Premier Klein tipped the scales by influencing undecided Albertans with musings about family life being threatened. It's tough to tell whether the government's orneriness stems from fear and loathing of homosexuality, directives from Ottawa or directives from homosexuals in Ottawa. Meanwhile, Alberta's nine "affirming" churches—congregations of the United Church of Canada that actively welcome folks of all sexual orientations—are second only to Ontario.[86] Michael Phair, a former fifteen-year alderman in Edmonton and a longtime community advocate for gays, lesbians, immigrants and newcomers, believes that rhetoric from Alberta is long outdated. "I don't want to ignore that some do think that way, but it's reprehensible that Albertans are portrayed as *only* that," he tells me. "I see significant change, particularly when I work with eighteen- to thirty-year-olds. We've moved beyond tolerating to celebrating diversity, particularly in urban settings. There's a broadening of valuing who people are and how they live and act."

Public perceptions of Alberta's reputation for intolerance often come from MLAs playing to rural, "conservative" values. In one notorious example, three cabinet ministers protested an award made by a peer jury of the Alberta Foundation for the Arts on the ground that it offended public decency, but the award was upheld by the minister responsible for culture, Shirley McClellan, who not only represented an area outside of the province's two largest cities, but was also the deputy premier. Despite the antics of some government MLAs—such as countering the entrenchment of sexual orientation in human rights legislation in 2009 by elevating existing parental rights to remove students from classrooms during lessons on sexuality, sexual orientation and evolution to grounds for human-rights complaints—tolerance and sanity seem to prevail at least some of the time.

Anti-Semitism has not enjoyed particularly virulent support in Alberta, at least not openly. This may be because her Jewish population has never been as numerous as in, say, Montréal or Toronto.

For example, the province's professional schools did not limit Jewish enrollment, as did institutions in Ontario and Manitoba in the 1930s.[87] An Albertan volunteer chapter of the goodwill-promoting Canadian Council of Christians and Jews was formed in 1987, and the national group's Western regional office was in Calgary for many years. But two extended incidents in the last century left a lingering stench. The first was the anti-Semitic bent of the Scottish father of Social Credit, Major Douglas, and its propagation by Social Credit hardliners at provincial and national levels, though Premiers Aberhart and Manning disassociated themselves from this rump of the party and the latter expelled them outright. The second incident came from the town of Eckville, whose 872 residents in 1982 included a mom who was concerned by the Jewish conspiracy theories littering her son's social studies notes. The propagator, Jim Keegstra, had been teaching for a decade and was also serving as the town's mayor when exposed. He was suspended and convicted for spreading racial hatred—twice, in fact, over the decade that it took for the Supreme Court of Canada to deny his appeals. Voters in Eckville failed to impeach him but gave him a resounding boot from office in the next election, as did the national executive of the Social Credit Party, on which he had served. Again, while not representing anything approaching the mainstream of the province, these two events left an ugly stain.

Where Alberta really distinguishes herself is in the arena of eugenics, which literally means "good breeding stock," and comes to us from the British scientist, Sir Francis Galton, a half-cousin of Charles Darwin and apparently more than half-familiar with Darwinism. While compulsory sterilization by the state is viewed today as a monstrosity with Nazi overtones, it was favoured widely earlier in the last century by a wide array of political, medical and public interests as a way of ensuring that only those with desirable genetic backgrounds should have children. Voices like the National Council of Women, the Canadian Medical Association and at least three of Alberta's Famous Five (Emily Murphy, Nellie McClung and Irene Parlby) supported it.

They were concerned with preventing people from transmitting mental disabilities to their children or having children while being deemed incapable of intelligent parenting. Mrs. Murphy in particular shared heartbreaking stories of unfortunate souls who wound up pregnant and in her courtroom, while a president of the United Farm Women of Alberta declared, "Democracy was never intended for degenerates." On the other hand, the chapter of that group in Camrose (population 2,200 in 1925) passed a resolution that "sterilization constitutes a violent and drastic invasion of the most elementary human rights."[88]

In any case, Alberta was breaking new ground. The British had established a eugenics board in 1913, and the Americans raced to the vanguard by enacting sterilization laws in some thirty states, a practice upheld by the US Supreme Court in 1927. Although the initial impetus in Canada came from Ontario, Alberta's *Sexual Sterilization Act* became the first of its kind in the British Empire in 1928. Neighbouring British Columbia was the only other province to follow suit.[89] Fans of the redneck-Alberta theory love to remind people that the province beat the Nazis to eugenics by five years. That seems less impressive when you consider that history's favourite fascists didn't seize power until 1933, five years after the UFA government passed its law. At most, the Germans were quick to follow Alberta's lead.

Unlike BC, which destroyed all records of its estimated several hundred eugenics cases, Alberta saved about one-fifth of its paperwork on its more than 2,800 cases. In nearly two-thirds of those files, a researcher found no documented genetic conditions, although apparently the government was working with the best information available at the time.[90] One might think that Alberta's appetite for sterilization would have waned over time. Au contraire: the new Social Credit government actually expanded its scope in 1937 and again in 1942, and kept operating, following the leading medical thinking of the time. Strikingly, almost half of the sterilizations in the province were performed from 1955 until the practice was legislatively kiboshed by the Conservatives in 1972, shortly after taking office.[91] It's not a proud legacy. In 1998 the University of Alberta's philosophy department moved to stop granting awards in the name of its founder and the institution's first provost, Dr. John MacEachran. The department cited his role in the "unethical and unprofessional" conduct of the Eugenics Board, which he led from 1929–1965.[92]

No foray into Alberta's redneck label is complete without mentioning what many Canadians on my travels cited as the province's reputation as the Bible belt of Canada. "There is a Christian environment in Alberta, maybe because people are so solid in their beliefs," advises Fil Fraser, the producer, author and former president of Vision TV, a multi-faith media network. "There was always a discomfort in Alberta with the mix of religion and politics. Alberta is so sure of itself and so firm in its beliefs rooted in basic Christianity. It's not quite evangelical, though [Ernest] Manning did preach as an evangelist, and an evangelist can only convince others if he believes."

It's true that Alberta's political leadership was linked closely to Christian beliefs for a third of a century under Premiers Aberhart and Manning, and to a more historically distant but equally fervent extent to the social gospel that fuelled the earlier UFA movement. While the UFA aimed to accommodate secular values and elevated social justice to its prime directive, Social Credit took the separatist pressures exerted by evangelical sects on large national organizations like the Anglican and United churches, and transposed them into the secular realm to unite Alberta against the greedy, domineering, metropolitan mercenaries to the east that Mr. Aberhart personified as "the fifty big shots from Canada."[93] He earned the nickname Bible Bill for founding the Calgary Prophetic Bible Institute and building a massive following—some 300,000 listeners—through his radio program, *Back to the Bible Hour*. The first graduate of his institute was (wait for it) Ernest Manning, who came for the ministry and stayed to succeed him on the radio waves as well as in the premier's chair. Unlike his fiery predecessor, Mr. Manning was more reserved, cautious and pragmatic in his approach, living by a moral code so unimpeachable that even his political opposition couldn't smear him. The strength of some Albertans' faith in their longtime leader shone through when Grant MacEwan campaigned against him as leader of the opposition in the 1958 election. As Dr. MacEwan's son-in-law, Max Foran, tells it, "Grant went to Eckville and talked to a farmer. The farmer said he's going to vote for Mr. Manning because 'Look at all the good things Mr. Manning's done!' And Grant said, 'Well, don't you think a lot of that is because of all the oil and gas revenues?' And the farmer said, 'Yes, but the oil is only in the ground because Mr. Manning asked God to put it there!'" By the time the Conservatives reached the portals of power provincially in 1971, Church and state were substantially more separable in Canadian public life.

Ted Byfield, who is editing a twelve-volume history of Christianity and makes no secret of his faith, looks at Alberta's coming by its religious ethic honestly. He feels that "the Bible belt" is a weird way to describe us because "while we have probably more churches per square mile than any other province, we also have more porn outfits." He traces what we might call a depth of religion in Alberta to her leading industries. "Raising cattle, raising grain, finding oil, these are huge gambles," he explains. "And people take their livelihoods, they take everything they've got, their wealth and their own estate, and put it on this piece of land or that particular geological report, they base it all there. So they live on the edge all the time and they enjoy that, too. It's a province of gamblers. And gamblers tend to believe in God because that's their only hope. And that's what gives us our Bible belt reputation." He cites Albertans' faith, "not necessarily just in God but in our own capabilities and the ancient principle that there is justice in everything."

The impression of Alberta as the buckle on the nation's Bible belt was bolstered over the last three decades by Mr. Byfield and his son, Link, through their weekly newsmagazine, *Alberta Report* (1973–2003), and by defiantly "conservative" politicians from the province who have ascended (or descended, depending on your outlook) to the national scene. These include the former opposition leaders, Preston Manning and Stockwell Day; the prime minister at this writing, Stephen Harper; and a memorable gang of former Reform Party stalwarts like the motorcycle mama, Deborah Grey, and Stetson-sporting Myron Thompson. Of course, not every Albertan is Ted Byfield or Preston Manning. There are scores of Albertans of the Christian faith, different faiths, little faith or none at all, but they don't grab headlines like these gents do. For his part, Preston Manning singles out Alberta's difficult times as formative. "When the province was flat on its back during the Depression and war, a significant part of the province turned to a faith-based perspective for solace and strength," he observes. "That's still there and part of our heritage whether it's part of our consciousness or not."

"We're not more religious than most," laments Link Byfield. "I wish we were." In a street interview in Edmonton, Debbie Fenton comments, "I think of Alberta as a new-age place. Many of us are spiritual but don't go to worship in buildings." Given Alberta's reputation, it may come as a surprise that they are both correct. According to Statistics Canada, Alberta is the least religious province in the country except for neighbouring British Columbia. In 2001 Albertans claimed the third-highest incidence of no religious affiliation (24 per cent), behind only BC (36 per cent) and Yukon (39 per cent) and well above the national average (16 per cent). An earlier study echoed those rankings (if not the exact figures), adding that Albertans' religious attendance, measured by going to a place of worship at least once a month, was the second-lowest among the provinces (33 per cent), leading only BC (21 per cent) and below the national average (39 per cent). If these surveys can be said to pinpoint Canada's Bible belt, then it falls squarely in the Maritimes, not Alberta.[94]

Although it's not universally seen as an indication of redneckery, Alberta's perceived friendliness to business and unfriendliness to society's less fortunate have also painted her as arch-rightist. The provincial government claims the lowest overall personal and corporate income taxes in Canada, but the Parkland Institute has calculated that Albertans earning $30,000 or $60,000 a year pay more tax than people who earn the same incomes in British Columbia or Ontario, and that the so-called "Alberta Advantage" only exists for taxpayers earning $80,000 or more per year.[95]

In either case, it's a province that's easy on the well-to-do. But rank-and-file Albertans have a habit of confounding pollsters and pundits. In a study of 1,200 randomly selected Albertans in 1994, 86 per cent of them felt that big business had *too much* influence on government. This result cut across the province and party lines. Other sectors deemed to have too much influence included unions (67 per cent), environmentalists (45 per cent), Aboriginal groups (45 per cent), ethnic minorities (42 per cent) and women's groups (36 per cent). A similar study in 2003 singled out big business (79 per cent), the media (67 per cent), Aboriginal groups (42 per cent) and labour unions (39 per cent).[96] During the Klein Revolution, the term "special interests" became a neo-liberal put-down to depict dissenting groups as placing themselves ahead of the greater good. That respondents in these studies essentially distrusted business as well as unions is telling. Clearly, this is a province that does not like *anyone* telling her what to do, whether it's industry fat cats, union agitators, radical tree-huggers, greedy doctors, whining nurses and teachers, raging grannies, Toronto-controlled media or any other perceived bogeyperson with a cause.

The sociologist, Reginald Bibby, concluded that Albertans are almost evenly split on those who see themselves as conservative, moderate or liberal. He also suggested that the national media hub in Ontario spreads inaccurate views of Albertans in "seeing Alberta as an isolated and culturally backward, semi-southern state, complete with a large dose of fundamentalist religion." Summarizing the preliminary findings of his longstanding national surveys, Dr. Bibby wrote:

> We are just as likely as people elsewhere in the country to approve of interracial marriage, to believe immigrants are good for the country,

and affirm the equality of women. We are no more inclined than others to think discipline in the home is not strict enough, that our laws concerning young offenders should be toughened, or that we need to bring back the death penalty. We match the rest of the nation in our endorsement of the legalization of marijuana, our desire to see Quebec stay in Canada, and our belief that people who cannot afford it have a right to medical care and incomes adequate to live on.

Our sexual attitudes are very similar to other Canadians with the single exception of Quebec, where views tend to be more liberal than everywhere else.

That's not to say we don't have our differences. We break with the country as a whole in favouring a melting pot over a mosaic, opposing bilingualism, and having confidence in our provincial government. But these kinds of findings hardly point to Alberta being overpopulated with "rednecks."[97]

"Most of us are not rednecks," concludes Link Byfield, who has been accused of being one for decades. "Those that are rednecks are not admired. We sure don't act like we live in Georgia or the Ozarks or Arkansas." The Juno Award–winning folksinger and songwriter, Bill Bourne, tells me, "Some Albertans are rednecks, whatever that means. It's a perception of Alberta that's largely defined by the leadership. Albertans seem to be very trusting people and they really seem to trust their leaders, I think in some cases, maybe too much. I think people in Alberta would benefit from being a bit more politically active."

Separated at Birth

On the theory that one way to self-definition is comparing oneself to others, we turn to Alberta's special connection with her next-door neighbour, Saskatchewan, a link that stems from sharing geography, history, families, extreme weather and grain elevator demolitions. Emerging together from the primordial soup of Rupert's Land and eventually, separate districts in the North-West Territories, the two were envisioned by their guardian, Premier Frederick Haultain, as a single, super-province called Buffalo. But when they entered provincehood together in 1905, the constitutionally authorized obstetrician—the federal government—surgically severed them into two jurisdictions, more or less equal in size, population and economic clout. A century later, a popular metaphor is to imagine Saskatchewan and Alberta as prairie versions of Britain and the United States, respectively.[98] Even their provincial mottos reinforce this: The Land of Living Skies is "from many peoples, strength" while Wild Rose Country is "strong and free." On the good ship Canada, Saskatchewan is known across the land for tilting portside, and Alberta for leaning to the starboard. One may well ask, "Why?" or perhaps the even better question, "How come?" And what does that tell us about whether Albertans are radicals or rednecks?

If you run with Caucasian history and Canadiana, the Land of Living Skies was settled a generation before Wild Rose Country. This means that Saskatchewan bore the brunt of the trial and error that went with putting down colonial roots on the Canadian plains. White settlers bent on Alberta benefitted from their easterly neighbours' experiences in selecting land, tools and grains, and from advances in knowledge and technology. Through this lens, on the whole, Alberta was settled with less hardship than Saskatchewan.

Certainly the dominant economic group in the early decades of both provinces was the quintessential small producer, the farmer. In Saskatchewan, farmers went from a peak of almost two-thirds of the labour force in 1911 to just under half by 1951, with Alberta's corresponding figures at half in 1911 and one-third in 1951.[99] The next biggest group was blue-collar workers, then white-collar professional, managerial and other workers. One historian, John Archer, pointed to the treatment of that frontier staple, the hired man, as helpful in understanding the apparent ideological split between the two provinces. "In a hard-pressed frontier society like Saskatchewan, the hired man was usually a neighbour's son, and hence was treated as one of the family," he wrote, while in Alberta, the hired man was paid for his work and treated as an employee, rather than as an equal.[100]

Despite this subtle underpinning of a split over individualism versus collectivism, both provinces started with Liberals in charge. Not that people voted the Grits in then; rather, the first governments were appointed temporarily by the federal government, which was Liberal in 1905. But once in power, they were able to campaign for office with the advantage of incumbency, and in the case of at least Alberta, the further benefit of gerrymandering the electoral map to capture the most seats in the Legislature. In Saskatchewan, the Liberals had competent representation from leaders of farming groups and thereby preempted the popular revolt that swept the United Famers of Alberta to power next door. Also, rural ridings are not nearly as overrepresented in the Saskatchewan Legislature as they are in Alberta.

It's not that the seeds of a populist movement—a widespread sense of a common cause, often facing a threat—were not present in Saskatchewan as they were in Alberta, with farmers besieged by eastern banks, grain traders and railways. Rather, Liberals in Saskatchewan co-opted the grain growers in the 1920s and 1930s. In a bellwether election in 1938 after Social Credit broke through in Alberta, that party ran in Saskatchewan and won all of two seats. In considering the political differences between the sister provinces, Karman Kawchuk, a political scientist at the University of Saskatchewan, tells me, "Different kinds of people came to both provinces. For example, there were fewer ranchers, Mormons and Texas oil types in Saskatchewan than in Alberta. Also, economics are rooted in the land, and on the northern grain belt, farmers are poorer and more sympathetic to the Canadian Wheat Board, for example." Max Foran, a historian at the University of Calgary, adds other formative factors distinguishing the two neighbours. "It has a lot to do with Saskatchewan never having any experiment with a leftist government," he says, referencing Alberta's trying and ultimately rejecting the United Farmers, and the greater success of community pastures in Saskatchewan owing to its superior soil conditions and land opportunities.

Unlike Albertans, who spurned the Liberals after four provincial elections, Saskatchewan's voters kept electing Liberal governments by liberal majorities provincially, with one exception (a minority Conservative government in 1929, even though the Grits won four more seats), until 1944. That year, they launched their own popular uprising with the Co-operative Commonwealth Foundation (CCF), the forerunner of the NDP. In a twist that would surely thrill devotees of the *Chariots of the Gods* school, there is a capital "L"-shaped area in Saskatchewan, extending from Lloydminster down to the United States and then eastward along a southern strip along the border; the Labour or Progressive parties almost never won in that area. In the Land of Living Skies, Social Credit never did better than a fifth of the popular vote and three seats provincially (and less than that federally, topping out at two seats in 1935) until the party died off there in the 1960s, but the fragmentation of the right-wing vote kept the CCF and the Liberals in power. At times, the Liberals themselves leaned a bit to the right of centre and had an occasionally tense relationship with the federal mother ship.[101] Unlike Alberta, Saskatchewan never bought into the non-partisan movement and has enjoyed four different governing parties provincially since Alberta's Conservative dynasty took office in 1971. Saskatchewan has changed governments six times in its history, which is double Alberta's total, but still low for a span of more than a century. In Alberta, people turned away from the leftist, social-gospel-flavoured UFA to Social Credit, which was avowedly left wing in its early years. Although they were elected under different economic conditions—Social Credit in the bowels of the Depression and the CCF on the road to recovery late in World War II—both movements saw urban business and professional interests as their enemies.[102] By the time Social Credit turned right under

Ernest Manning, its underlying economic theory was long discredited and the CCF was securely in power, so Saskatchewanians never gave it a chance. In fact, Premier Manning's rightward tilt in Alberta came on the heels of the election of the country's first socialist government next door—and in the rising tide of the Cold War, his heightened fear and loathing of the Red Menace. In this light, Saskatchewan's sharp turn to the left was, arguably, at least partly the cause of Alberta's turn to the right.

Fil Fraser, in one of his many guises as a former director of alcoholism prevention for the governments of both provinces, sees a dramatic difference between Regina and Edmonton—apart from being paid 50 per cent more in Alberta to do the same job. Having met both Premier Manning and Saskatchewan's Premier Tommy Douglas and being curious about how men from similar rural, religious backgrounds could go on to lead their respective provinces down such different paths, Mr. Fraser tried to bring the two together for a discussion on a public affairs television program that he hosted in the early 1970s. Mr. Douglas eagerly embraced the opportunity but Mr. Manning neither refused nor committed to a date. Years later, Preston Manning told Mr. Fraser (in hushed tones) that maybe it was because his father "simply couldn't stand to be in the same room with 'that socialist.'"[103]

In wondering why two similar social units with common origins could react so differently, the historian, Peter Sinclair, observed that both the CCF in Saskatchewan and Social Credit in Alberta were populist movements. He listed these characteristics of both, with distinctive flavours in each province: stressing the virtue and the political supremacy of common people; rejecting intermediaries between people and their leaders; turning to direct protest against outsiders, specifically large interests to the east; and demanding the reform of capitalist structures rather than an outright revolution.[104] Yet, while Alberta attacked the financial system and Saskatchewan supported labour rights, co-operatives, state ownership and state welfare, neither province abandoned private property, private enterprise or private jokes.

Although the forces of agrarian populism that brought the UFA, Social Credit and the CCF to power have settled into the grain-dust of time, a healthy suspicion of central Canada lingers in both provinces. This is due to the political realities of a federal political system that subordinates the interests of the hinterland to those in areas that were settled earlier and more populously. In Alberta, the torch of political dissent passed from Premier Haultain's non-partisan vision to the economic protests of the UFA and Social Credit, which found a new bogeyman in socialism and passed that on to the Conservatives. Albertans talk a good game about free enterprise, while blessing the oil, gas and mining sectors with more than $5.6 billion in government subsidies from 1986–1993—contributing heavily to deficits that led to the lamented cuts in social spending during the Klein Revolution—while Saskatchewan's dowry to industrial interests was a relatively paltry $275 million.[105] Could fewer handouts to business be the real reason why Saskatchewan gets knocked for discouraging free enterprise?

So how did all this affect what happened to the two former co-districts? Saskatchewan had a larger population than Alberta as late as 1951 but lost ground steadily as Albertans outnumbered Saskatchewanians by three to one by 2003. After 1929 Alberta's gross domestic product declined relative to her neighbour despite the oil boom triggered at Leduc, and Saskatchewan continued to log gains until 1971, then fell and rose in inverse proportion to Alberta's fortunes with energy prices. Following the steady rise of those prices after 1996, Alberta's advantage widened, providing a longstanding lead in attracting private investment. This led two economists, Herbert Emery and Ronald Kneebone, to conclude that the policies of the two provinces bore few differences. They wrote, "While the perception exists that Saskatchewan socialism helped cause Alberta's eventual dominant position, ultimately, Saskatchewan's fate is really one of natural economic evolution in the presence of falling transport costs and agglomeration economies. Alberta's early lead in manufacturing development, and mineral endowments, were the seeds of its economic leadership."[106]

And yet Saskatchewan's fortunes are back on the rise at this writing, as it leads the world in uranium, kimberlite (diamond-bearing) fields, lentils and mustard seeds, while producing one-third of Canada's primary energy from coal, oil, natural gas, uranium, hydro-electricity, wind power and biofuels,[107] not to mention one of the land's finest TV series, *Corner Gas*. Saskatchewan has taken to actively and successfully recruiting Albertans who are weary of the higher cost and manic pace of living here—enjoying sufficient success to reverse a long trend of losing citizens to Alberta.

An Albertan's culture shock of moving to Saskatchewan may not be as great as one would think. Professor Kawchuk points to a further similarity between the sister provinces, evidence of converging political views (e.g., the 2007 provincial election in Saskatchewan); political similarities between rural Alberta and most of Saskatchewan—especially the west, south and rural areas—for at least a generation; and increasing similarities among the two largest cities in each province, due partly to migration, family ties and the role played by Edmonton and especially Calgary as cultural-athletic-consumer metropolii for Saskatoon and Regina people.

Yet my interviews across the country suggest (admittedly unscientifically) that the public perception of socialists leading Saskatchewan downhill lingers in parts of Alberta as much as the perception of rednecks wrecking Alberta may subsist elsewhere. The weight of public perception, bloated further by extending over time, is the spare tire that Alberta just can't shake. Fuelled by the mid-century crusades of the CCF, the Land of Living Skies remains known for compassion and a leftward tilt. But Alberta's early radicalism has been muted by decades of prosperity and replaced by a laissez-faire reputation, even as the province has been enormously, even exorbitantly, business-friendly at taxpayers' expense. Whether people in both provinces really are fundamentally different politically or are merely saddled with different political mythologies is debatable. But from what we've glimpsed here, one would be hard-pressed to conclude that Albertans are inherently conservative any more than Saskatchewanians are purebred socialists.

How Canadian?

I do not think I should be very wide of the mark, if I said that the older parts of Canada have for years regarded Alberta as a rather peculiar place, favorable to the breeding of extreme radicals and peculiar political phenomena, and let it go at that. One wonders if it ever occurs to them that there are always causes and conditions which breed these things.
—IRENE PARLBY[108]

Just how different from our fellow Canadians are we in Alberta?

There's politics, of course. Alberta's provincial electoral history is completely unique and runs afoul of the environmental troika of reduce, reuse and recycle in that once Albertans are done with a political dynasty, we send it to the landfill of history, from whence it will never return, except perhaps to leach into the groundwater supply. Max Foran traces this peculiar electoral behaviour back to Albertans' original desire to be different. "The Laurier Liberals shoved partisan government onto us," he comments. "We never really wanted partisan politics so if we've got to have it, let's just *mock* it in a way. I don't think it was conscious, but it's very interesting."

Certainly, there are distinct things about Alberta mentioned immediately by other Canadians in my interviews around the country: the beef, the oil, the mountains and the prairie, the conservative or redneck thing, the Calgary Stampede, West Edmonton Mall, Ralph, the Oilers or the Flames, money, jobs and the absence of a provincial sales tax—pretty much in that order, among other oddities highlighted later.

Although different provinces have their own quirks, there's less of a sense of whimsy here than in other places, observes Link Byfield: "Albertans are fairly serious people on the whole, especially compared to Newfies and people in Atlantic Canada, and the Québecois have their own bizarre sense of humour." But there is a definitely Albertan sense of humour, asserted the humorist, Will Ferguson: "It is not as florid or as richly layered as Newfoundland's, nor as gentle as that of the Maritimes, but it is every bit as effective. In Alberta, the humour—like the politics—is one based on ruthless common sense."[109]

Adding to the ability of Alberta and her fellow jurisdictions to express their differences is that provincial and territorial governments have more power and discretion than in almost any other federal system. They have been called almost sub-national governments, enjoying a higher overall share of public revenues and public spending than the feds since the 1990s.[110] Our earlier glance at some of the Alberta government's priorities and actions over the years reveals some differences. But how about the folks who live out from under the dome of the Legislature, especially those who, relative to our lawmakers and the demographic of the people that they tend to represent, are less chronologically challenged?

In 2004 the Carleton University Survey Centre and the Department of Canadian Heritage surveyed the attitudes of more than 2,000 Canadians aged 12–30 in every region except the three territories. Albertans were found to stand out in three respects. First, young Albertans had the strongest sense of attachment in Canada to both their province (85 per cent, 7 per cent above the national average) and to their town or city (78 per cent, 6 per cent above). That's distinctive. But it doesn't undercut Albertans' attachment to their country, as 87 per cent of the respondents felt close to Canada, though that figure was second-lowest to Québec's 64 per cent. Second, Albertans were most likely to cite Canada's geographic size as the country's principal challenge (35 per cent, 4 per cent above the national average). Again, that's distinctive. But other challenges cited by Albertans ranked closely with those raised by other Canucks: the diversity of Canadians (31 per cent, 1 per cent above), domination by other countries (15 per cent, matching the average), inequality of wealth and power among Canadians (10 per cent, 4 per cent below) and lack of entrepreneurial spirit (6 per cent, matching the average). And finally, more Albertans than any other province or region named granting the franchise to women federally in 1918 as the most significant event in Canadian history among the suggested options (26 per cent, 6 per cent above). That fits with Alberta's claim to rocking the cradle of feminism in this country. But again, other responses from Alberta were not out of whack with the rest. Nationally, the highest average response was the development of Medicare (21 per cent national average, but named by only 17 per cent of Albertans). The other events cited were the Charter of Rights and Freedoms (17 per cent of Albertans, 2 per cent below the average), Confederation (21 per cent of Albertans, 3 per cent above), the Battle of the Plains of Abraham (9 per cent of Albertans, 2 per cent below) and First Nations treaties (3 per cent of Albertans, 1 per cent below).

In areas in which Albertans did not rank ahead of other Canadians, that survey showed two notable things. First, about one-third of Albertans think that increasing multiculturalism best describes the story of Canada. That ranked them second among the provinces and above the national average of 27 per cent. The one-fifth of Albertans who mentioned the social safety net fell slightly below the national average (23 per cent), as did the 16 per cent who cited coming to terms with two languages and two cultures. We did rank modestly ahead of the national average in citing increasing political sovereignty or independence (17 per cent) and the increasing exploitation of the environment (8 per cent). Second, Albertans ranked second, just 2 per cent behind Ontarians (who scored 65 per cent) in naming knowledge of Canada as a whole as their most important historical topic. In other topics cited as important—family, community, ethnic group, region and church—Alberta came in a total of 6 per cent off the national average on those five topics combined.[111]

Much as one can learn a lot about people from their house pets, we can digest these views of young Canadians, and if they are even close to the views of their elders, we might suspect that Albertans don't differ profoundly from their compatriots on national issues. In fact, there's strong evidence (i.e., highly symbolic, anecdotal and above all, media-backed) that Albertans love their country. Political junkies and history buffs who salivate at the mere mention of the ill-fated Meech Lake Accord will remember that when one premier moved to walk out of the negotiations, it was Alberta's premier du jour, Don Getty (schooled by his decade quarterbacking the Edmonton Eskimos), who gently ushered him back to the table. Another successful team player, Marcel Rocque, the lead for the former Ferbey Four, says, "You look at how we interact with our provincial neighbours and you know we're there, we're giving our share of what we've got. We're always going to support our fellow provinces and the country." In a national poll, 78 per cent of Albertans acknowledged that our province put more into Confederation than she took out, compared to 55 per cent of respondents in BC and a national average of 46 per cent.[112] Generally, Albertans see a deep distinction between Canada, which they love, and getting marching orders from central Canada, which they loathe. Let's return to the shores of the Meech Lake era for another moment. In an exercise a bit like this book but a lot more expensive, the federal government hatched a document aimed at "constitutional renewal," which purports to set out "fundamental values and realities of Canada."[113] These seven values and realities, along with this Albertan's take on them, are as follows.

First came freedom, democracy and the rule of law. Apparently, Canada is based on civility and built on accommodation rather than revolution: "the frontiers would be harnessed largely by the rule of law, not the gun." Albertans buy into this, but only literally. Absent magpies or coyotes, most of us don't resort to gunplay to thwart perceived oppressors. However, as to revolutions, the province's last century is littered with radical economic ideas and political shock therapy, from voters' treatment of political parties to the slashing and burning of the provincial debt. Freedom is profoundly important here, and perceived incursions are met with defiance and what other Canadians would call political incorrectness. Albertans embrace democracy as a concept, even if they exercise their franchise less than people in any other province. They accept the rule of law, of course, but like it less when they believe it is rammed down their craw by Ottawa, be it by federal politicians (Liberals for most of the last century), bureaucrats or Supreme Court judges, over whom Albertans feel absolutely no influence.

The second value cited was federalism: Canadians are said to nurture a sense of community and diversity under our umbrella of unity, while recognizing the diversity and equality of provinces and accommodating special needs. This statement of motherhood and back-bacon pie gets no argument in Alberta—until the word "special," which is abhorrent to what other Canadians would call the right wing of the national bird. The frontier was a powerful leveller and any form of inherited or other unearned privilege does not play well here to this day. While many Albertans accepted the recognition of Québec as a "distinct society" within Canada under the Meech Lake Accord, it rankled enough people here (and elsewhere) to gripe about it.

Next came freedom and human rights: Canadians are said to believe in freedom, modified by a sense of justice, caring and compassion for others. These beliefs are echoed everywhere from the social gospel that fuelled the early farmer's movements in Alberta to statements of principle by her Social Credit governments. But in the eyes of many here and across Canada, the execution—from eugenics and attempts to limit freedom of the press to heel-dragging on Medicare (as proposed by the feds) and that recent assault on the provincial debt—leaves much to be desired.

The fourth value mentioned in the federal project was equality: Canadians are said to favour equal prospects and respect for the inherent worth and dignity of each individual. Again, this rings true in Alberta—with exceptions noted by her critics for people who are or seem to be mentally, physically, socially, economically or Conservatively challenged. But hey, nobody's perfect.

Next came community: Canadians are believed to have a sense of cohesion at the national, regional, local, religious and cultural levels. Certainly Albertans accept this. The ethic of community is a legacy of Aboriginal life, as well as white pioneering lore in the province. But on the other hand, Albertans pride themselves on "rugged individualism," a phrase so hoary around Wild Rose Country that it risks being neither rugged nor individualistic.

The sixth value was diversity: Canadians are said to be inclusive, sharing the aspirations of Aboriginal people and the Québecois. Albertans can claim a bright spot or two in the largely unhappy colonial history of Canada's first peoples. And they have shared connections around the constitutional bargaining table with Québec, mostly around the idea of wresting more power from Ottawa. As we'll see, the province has been a decent melting pot for Canadians and others of different races, creeds and hockey team preferences.

The last federally cited value was mutual support: Canadians are said to believe in helping those who need it through social programs. Albertans would agree in general, though the distinction between the deserving and the less deserving seems to be, to put it mildly, at least as pronounced here as anywhere else. As we have seen, some Albertans seem to prefer private charity to public largesse. Since the postwar prosperity ushered in by the gusher at Leduc, Alberta's governments have talked a good right-wing game while spending like uncaged shopaholics. Examples of substantial investments in support programs from the 2008 provincial budget are committing $666 million to Albertans with severe disabilities, $536 million to protect children through intervention and foster care, and $188 million to students' assistance and debt relief programs, which the government calls the most generous in Canada.[114] Alberta's per-capita spending is the highest in the nation.

✳ So does the federal government's statement of Canadian values and realities fit with Alberta? This cursory summary suggests mostly yes, with some notable nuances. On the one hand, Albertans believe in all seven precepts posited in the federal discussion paper, and the province's record reflects that, at least in recent years. In the last generation or so, the provinces have grown increasingly similar in policies and priorities, even if they are distinctive in areas such as their natural resources, geography, economy, mix of basic political values and political leadership, as well as their ethnic, cultural and linguistic diversity.[115] Canadians share similarities in their attitudes toward justice, fairness and good government; their provincial demographics; the nature of their economies; the relationships among their citizens; their occupational structures; and their respective urban-rural splits in population.[116] Albertans have the same attitudes as other Canadians on issues such as immigrants being good for the nation, women receiving equal pay for equal work, whites marrying Asians and blacks, legalizing the use of marijuana and keeping Québec in Canada, though Albertans have shown significant variances on favouring bilingualism (43 per cent; 63 per cent nationally) and the notion of the nation as a melting pot (40 per cent; 28 per cent nationally).[117] Typically, both significant differences in that study relate to equal rather than special treatment, always a hot button for an anti-elitist place like Alberta. This attitude resurfaces in Albertans' support for federal equalization payments, which, at 78 per cent in one survey, was 8 per cent below the national tally, although still a solid majority.[118]

Where dissonance sometimes arises is when opinions in Wild Rose Country on controversial topics are overblown or ignored by the provincial government for political reasons. Take the time Premier

Klein threatened to pull out of the federal equalization program rather than see it include oil and gas revenues—regardless of whether Alberta could actually pull out of a program administered federally through federal revenues or whether Albertans supported doing so.[119] Here are four further examples from 2003–2004. The provincial government refused to join the National Health Council even though a poll showed that 79 per cent of Albertans supported joining. The government refused to consider moving to a system of public auto insurance even though polls showed that almost 60 per cent of Albertans favoured it.[120] Premier Klein added a Senate election to the 2004 provincial election to placate proponents of a reformed upper house, although the almost 20 per cent rejected/spoiled ballot rate on that issue and the overall turnout of 45 per cent suggests that it was not even on Albertans' backburner and probably off the stove altogether.[121] And the premier's standing up for the war in Iraq received more media attention than about 15,000 Albertans marching in protest against that war at the Legislature—at least thrice the size of the rallies in Toronto and Ottawa that same day and likely the largest mass rally in provincial history.[122] Beyond these examples, most likely to isolate Albertans from our fellow Canucks and beyond is the provincial government's stand on environmental issues, notably the no-holds-barred approach to developing the oil sands and caps on greenhouse-gas emissions, the latter of which are an easier sell in less heavily contributing jurisdictions.

So Alberta's differences may be exaggerated by entrenched political and media channels with an interest in perpetuating an image of the province as conservative, different or just plain ornery. "Albertans are not that much different," states Paula Beauregard, who moved here from Québec. "Many of us are transplants from other provinces. People do come out here for work."

On the other hand, the province can legitimately claim that it *is* different politically from the rest of Canada in respects highlighted in this chapter and echoed by the sociologist, Harry Hiller, who, while noting that Albertans do not hold opinions radically different from other Canadians, found a "widely shared" perception that Albertans are distinctive politically.[123] Dominique Clift noted that through a cultural lens, Alberta and Québec seem to stand out as examples of the kind of regionalism that undermines national unity: "Yet their obsessive concern with community development reveals an underlying similarity founded on...a religious view of work as a source of personal identity and status," he wrote, "as well as a calling making one personally answerable to God. It is the secular equivalent of this that Canada still lacks."[124]

This notion of being different is echoed by Tami Bereska, a sociologist whose research interests include social deviance. So, I ask her, are Albertans deviants? She responds that deviance is subjective and that power is intertwined with how we see people and what we call them. "Albertans are sociologically the type that certain people see as deviant," she says. "Certainly people on the West Coast would label us as rednecks. Behaviour that I label as redneck might be labelled differently by others: 'wise,' 'fiscally responsible,' or 'true to family values.' We're certainly a province that's willing to speak our mind regardless of how unpopular it might be. Our elected figurehead, [then-Premier] Ralph Klein, doesn't care whether what he says might be perceived as fundamentally different from others' views. A willingness to speak up against what's popular is always seen as deviance."

At this point, there are plenty of arguments on both sides of the radical-or-redneck question. In either case, there is much to support the notion of Albertans as deviants. They have fiercely adopted the mantra of Western alienation and the mantles of mavericks, risk-takers and residents of a province unlike the others in Canada. So that's where we'll turn next.

3 Mavericks or Sheep?

What sets Alberta apart is that we are willing to try to do things differently. Albertans are ahead of the parade on this issue.

—PREMIER RALPH KLEIN, 2006

Overleaf: Voting patterns in Alberta eerily reflect her first large industry, lovingly captured in a an undated death-row photo. [City of Edmonton Archives, EA-122-52]

The Maverick Mantra

A COUNTRY WITH CANADA'S ARSENAL of distances, histories and cultures is fertile ground for diversity. Despite this, some people still feel that Alberta stands out. The political scientist, Michael Howlett, notes that all provinces have political economic myths, some of which were accurate once but virtually none of which reflect reality today; yet many cling to provincial myths, such as Newfoundland as the fishery, Ontario as smug and stable, Québec as defensively nationalistic, Saskatchewan as agrarian socialist and Alberta as "a province unlike the others."[1] Even beyond the obvious case of Québec, no other jurisdiction is singled out for being different as its distinguishing feature.

"Everybody in the world has to put up with stereotypes," admits Senator Tommy Banks. "A lot of stereotypes of Alberta are true. Albertans are fiercely independent people who think differently about politics than their fellow Canadians."

Certainly, the province has experienced its share of being singled out by journalists and politicians from central Canada. Premier Klein's ultimately harmless musings about a new, "third wave" of health care met with harsh words, cash penalties and attack ads from the federal Liberal government, while much more aggressive and tangible violations of the *Canada Health Act* in Québec—the Liberals' traditional power base—tended to get less attention. During the federal election campaign in 2000, Prime Minister Jean Chrétien told an audience in New Brunswick, apparently in jest, that he "likes to do politics with people from the East" rather than with people like Stockwell Day, then leader of the opposition, and Joe Clark, the unlucky ex-PM, then still toiling away for the opposition, whom, he said, "are from Alberta, they are a different type."[2] Although the PM later issued something perhaps resembling a middling partial apology of sorts (more or less), Albertans gnashed their teeth at this latest in a litany of real or perceived affronts from Ottawa.

Reflecting this notion of going at it alone, a popular self-image embraced by many Albertans is that of the maverick, a legacy of the ranching industry that held sway in southern Alberta in the late nineteenth century. While a dictionary might evoke images of unbranded calves, the Albertan brand of maverick is defined in the Glenbow Museum exhibit bearing that name as a unique character, a forward-looking, creative risk-taker who moves in new directions and makes a mark in a new social, cultural or political direction. Aritha van Herk, whose popular history titled (you guessed it) *Mavericks* inspired the exhibit, lyrically deploys adjectives like "adamant," "audacious," "acerbic," "adventurous" and "adversarial"—and these are just the "A" words.[3]

"Unless you're part of the Alberta experience, I don't think you understand what the word 'mavericks' means to us," ventures the Edmonton Food Bank's director, Marjorie Bencz, "and how it's an integral part of our underlying culture, even if we come from different backgrounds and experiences."

"In the wide-open world of ranching, the world looks different from the top of a horse," muses David Ward, a producer-announcer at CKUA Radio. "What does a blank space do to your imagination? Make you more entrepreneurial? There's more to imagine if you have to clear the land first. You need a community landscape to create context for the imagination to work differently and create different ways to solve problems, with different values."

Predating Alberta's provincehood, this singular devotion to difference attracted early attention. Writing before World War I, Leo Thwaite found that "there is some quality in the Alberta atmosphere which induces men and women from other lands to put forth the best of their energy and faculties." He noticed a "restless energy, quick perception, unbounded optimism," which he attributed to a special combination of hustle imported by Americans and "community steadiness and thoroughness," along with a love of law and order, brought by the British.[4]

The cowboy poet, Doris Daley, echoes this view of the province's maverick-hood being tied to the land. "There are lots of resources, but you also need a can-do attitude to figure out how to make those resources work for you. My family is a ranching family, and there were rolling hills of grass that could be turned into food to feed hungry people if you only said, 'Can do.'" Thirsty people get theirs here, too: while neighbouring BC may have the holy grail of paleontology, the Burgess Shale, it took Albertans to produce the world's only brew inspired by the trilobite fossils found there (Shale Ale).

Steeped in the provincial culture, this hustling ethos is exemplified by Nellie McClung's memorable creed, "Never retreat, never explain, never apologize. Get the thing done and let them howl,"[5] and Emily Murphy's wisdom that "The world loves a peaceful man, but gives way to a strenuous kicker."[6] The ethic also seems to surface when compared to other places. Mayor Melissa Blake of Wood Buffalo, Canada's largest municipality in terms of land area, sits atop a picnic table outside of Emily Murphy House in Edmonton, reflects on her more than twenty-five years in Fort McMurray and sees "a very distinct difference" between the province and her native Québec. "The difference is our can-do attitude. It's really engrained in the culture that is Alberta. And with that comes challenge, but I still think that it is the best place going for people to consider getting engaged and doing things that they may not have dreamt about doing elsewhere."

Exemplifying that credo, Jackie Flanagan started *Alberta Views* magazine in 1998 with a vision of presenting a different side of her province than the conservative, Christian image famously propagated by the Byfield family's *Alberta Report*. As Ms. Flanagan recalls, even though she is Alberta-born, she did not feel Albertan because she never supported the ruling party. Then she went to live in Québec and became frustrated by its bureaucracy, the formality of its culture, the tensions between federalists and separatists, unions and industrialists, and so on. "There's so much government, the rules and regulations and bureaucratic structures just weigh down on people," she tells me in a Calgary eatery. "In Alberta, we are relatively free of those polarizations and of bureaucratic limitations on our movements, on the fulfillment of dreams and creative possibilities. For someone who was so mad at Alberta and criticized Alberta for the last eleven years through my magazine, I am somewhat surprised to hear myself saying all these glowing things about Alberta!" She realizes that she bought fully into the same stereotypical notion of rugged individualism that she mocked, even though she would have identified herself as a socialist. "But it's true," she declares. "I feel a sense of individual responsibility. I feel as if it's up to me. If something's going to change, I've got to do it."

Part of how Albertans define themselves is in terms of their province's relationship to central Canada. Speaking outside the sweeping curves of St. Albert Place along the Sturgeon River on a golden autumn day, the comedian, Don Burnstick, states, "We're not like the other provinces. It's like a dysfunctional relationship in the east. They kind of suck the life out of each other, you know. Alberta is more independent. We're kind of like the bully of the schoolyard. They don't like us over there, but they'll never come over here and say that to our face. Because we've found our own identity, our own independence. We're very self-sufficient. We could split from Canada—Quebec tried—but we don't want to do that. We like being a part of Canada. We're like the muscle of Canada."

Across the country in Gatineau, by the Ottawa River and the Canadian Museum of Civilization—another building of his design—Douglas Cardinal says, "Alberta is considered by the east as almost their colony to plunder and rule. And so, Albertans had to be on their own. They couldn't rely on governments. They had to rely on themselves initially. They had to homestead the land and develop from their own sweat a future for themselves and their children. And so that makes Albertans really independent and self-reliant. They don't believe in institutions. They believe in hard work and independence." He believes that he would not have been able to lay the foundations of his architectural practice anywhere else because his work was very different from the status quo. "Alberta is a place of non-conformity in a world where lots of places are bent on conformity," he affirms.

"I'd describe it as a frontier province in some respects," opines Preston Manning. "This part of North America was one of last parts to be settled and it still has a lot of that frontier quality." He adds that another distinguishing characteristic of Alberta is that there is no better place to try to float a new idea. "Albertans' initial reaction tends to be one of enthusiasm—'By golly, that just might work'—and then have sober second thoughts, instead of as is often the case in Canada generally, where our initial reaction is one of reservation—'That probably won't work' or 'I don't know about that'—and then warm up to it later." Aritha van Herk agrees, adding, "Albertans are risk-takers. They're definitely the kinds of characters who don't want to be limited by anything and so they will test out the most difficult and the most unusual opportunities. And sometimes they will test out things that they shouldn't test out." Across the Bow River, Preston Manning continues this point with a reference to the province's controversial experiment with Social Credit in the Dirty Thirties: "If you put that argument to Aberhart, he would have said—in fact, he did say to my father—that in desperate times, the principal obligation of the politician is to give people hope. I think he felt that if he fouled up the banking system for a year to eighteen months and it prevented the foreclosure on one farm, it was worth doing." It's not unusual for one Albertan's method to be other people's madness.

What makes us this way? To Howard Palmer and Tamara Palmer, it's born of an "unstable juxtaposition of historical, economic, polit- ical and social forces…molded as much by the irrationality, doubt and anxiety by youth as by its innovation, energy and optimism."[7] Alberta's shingle as an optimist's paradise was hung resoundingly by her first premier, A.C. Rutherford, who is said to have exclaimed, "We have no pessimists in Alberta—a pessimist could not succeed. We are optimistic and always look on the brighter side of affairs."[8] This sunny view is echoed in place names like Eureka, Bonanza, Bluesky, Valhalla Centre and Paradise Valley though not so much in map-dots with monikers like Deadwood, Faust and Dead Man's Flats.

Jane Ash Poitras, whose fearlessness includes lambasting Anne of Green Gables as a cultural Uncle Tom at an awards dinner in Prince Edward Island, drops the m-word. Speaking not far from the site of her controversial outdoor sculpture of a bison skull—which she was compelled to dismantle in the absence of a permit—she observes, "There is a maverick sensibility in Alberta, yes, there is. You see all kinds of little mischievous things being done. But you have to have the mischief-makers, the heyokas and the contrarians to make the world a better place. If you don't have them and everyone is so comfort- able and fat and smoking their cigar at the pool and drinking a beer, nothing is going to get done." The award-winning, nouveau-Western singer-songwriter, Corb Lund, ties this quality back to the pioneering spirit in the province. Seated amidst musical and prairie parapher- nalia in his garage, he notes: "One of the things about Albertans that probably defines them is their ability to just go ahead and do things on their own. People out West are still sort of naïve enough and their spirit hasn't been drowned by bureaucracy enough that they're willing to have ideas and just follow through with them. There's enough freedom out here, still enough of an independent spirit, that people are willing to take chances and follow their dreams. It's very frontiers-y still." His comment was echoed in a rebranding exercise by the provincial government, which produced the motto, "Freedom to create, spirit to achieve" almost three years and $25 million later (ad budget included).

Tommy Banks sees that spirit leading to a disproportionate amount of cultural activity and a penchant to go for it despite being regarded as screwballs. His *In Concert* television series in the 1970s, featuring talent like Tony Bennett, Nana Mouskouri and Ray Charles and seen in seventy-eight countries, broke new ground. "The industry thought we were nuts because the convention in those days for variety shows was that the music was punctuated by comedy, variety, etcetera," he remembers. "We thought, 'Let's just do music and nothing else. That's unconventional—let's try it!' And it worked. And most people thought that *The Tommy Banks Show* came from Toronto. It didn't. It came from Edmonton."

On the subject of Hogtown behaviour, Ted Byfield adds, "I come from Toronto and this is not the way Toronto customarily behaves. It always has to have a centre of authority that it looks to. They just think, 'Well, this is what respectable opinion believes and so I believe it.' Here, you get, 'This is what respectable opinion believes in Toronto, so we doubt it.'" He observes that Canadians generally look around us for where authority is; initially this was to London, then Toronto in English Canada. While Ontarians ask, "Who can we depend on?" he suggests that Albertans are more likely to ask who has produced the best result and follow that. "What makes Alberta different is that it does not suffer from the Canadian disability," he says, "and the Canadian disability as defined by Bruce Hutchinson was that Canada is the affirmation of order and the United States is the affirmation of dissent. Well, Alberta is the affirmation of dissent. This makes it different than the rest of the country."

Albertans may be dissenters, but as Tamara Palmer Seiler suggests, we have a conflicted attitude toward authority. To her, the arrival of the North West Mounted Police in the West symbolizes the Canadian

approach to law and order with a notion that it starts from somewhere else and it's administered from a place of power rather than
being constructed on the spot, which is the American notion—or the
way that it's perceived. "In general, Albertans are very respectful of law
and order," she notes. "On the other hand, Albertans like to get things
done, and there's a sense that if you could get something done more
quickly, perhaps be a bit entrepreneurial, drive a little too fast, it might
happen in Alberta."

So Alberta's maverick-itude is rooted in essentially two camps.
The first covers what most would see as positive values: the energy
of youth, optimism, independence and adventurousness. The second
camp includes attitudes that can lead to positive results but tend to be
seen more negatively: mischief-making, contrariness and anti-authoritarianism. These last three run through Alberta like class-four rapids
on the Highwood River and explain some deeply held attitudes underlying the sunny side of Wild Rose Country. As we shall see, Albertans
come by our dissent honestly.

Autonomy

Alberta was born with a chip on her shoulder the size of Cascade
Mountain, which, happily, remains visible beyond the shops lining
Banff Avenue. Like that mountain, Alberta's independent streak
started well before she became a province.

Colonially speaking, Alberta joined the fur preserve chartered to
the Hudson's Bay Company in 1670 by Charles II of Britain under the
grand name of Rupert's Land. Named for His Majesty's cousin, the
territory covered the entire drainage basin for Hudson Bay, stretching
from Québec north of the Laurentians, across most of Ontario and
all of Manitoba, most of Saskatchewan, almost all of the southern half
of Alberta to the BC border and up into the present-day Northwest
Territories. (British monarchs could afford to be more generous in
the days before they paid taxes.) The original Canadian Constitution

of 1867 added Rupert's Land into the nascent nation. The national dreamer, Prime Minister Macdonald, noted the massive gap between the four settled provinces in central Canada and British Columbia, along with the creeping threat of the *American* national dream of "manifest destiny," which swallowed land with a zeal approaching Sir John A.'s appetite for liquid imports from his native Scotland. He knew that the American march of progress could easily turn from westward to northward and thereby smash his plan for souvenir plates bearing the legend, *A Mari usque ad Mare* ("from sea to sea," neglecting the coast in the true north). He needed the North-West Territories— as Alberta, Saskatchewan and most of Manitoba were then called— as his land bridge to BC for *his* march westward. So he passed legislation authorizing the sale of Rupert's Land from the Hudson's Bay Company to the new Dominion government in time for the fur-farming blanket-maker's bicentennial in 1870. Thus did the North-West Territories become a colony of a colony.

There were essential differences between the more settled provinces and the newly acquired territories. The original parties to Confederation— Nova Scotia, New Brunswick, Québec and Ontario—as well as later inductees like BC, PEI and Newfoundland—looked enough like separate entities to pass for provinces. In contrast, the North-West Territories did not, with its vast and imprecise area; sparse and fluid population; remoteness from centres of government, law and commerce; rough conditions for transportation, communication and public administration; and lack of economic base to exploit the land's vast resources and thus spur development and growth.[9]

After the North West Mounted Police and more homesteaders arrived, the feds divided the North-West Territories into the provisional districts of Assiniboia, Saskatchewan, Alberta and Athabasca in 1882, "for the convenience of settlers and for postal purposes."[10] But immigrants who had left provincehood behind were unsatisfied with convenience—or even a post office—that didn't come with political clout. An early Western demand for autonomy surfaced in the *Regina*

Journal in 1887, which declared, "The North-West is being settled by liberty-loving people, educated in self-government, who will be satisfied with nothing short of an administration responsible to the people in the fullest sense of the word. And if any makeshift is given, it will invite agitation and lead to an early struggle for the rights and privileges enjoyed by the Provinces."[11] Sure enough, in the first session of the Territorial Assembly in 1888, a committee demanded from Ottawa full responsible government except the power to borrow money.[12] Demands for autonomy were spurred by ex-Ontarians, who made up one-third of the immigrant population of the District of Alberta by 1891. (The 25,000 residents were split evenly between Natives and immigrants.) Although Ontarian expats' share would fall to a quarter of the immigrant population by 1901, their influence would be weighty as they made up nineteen of the first twenty-five Albertan legislators, five of the first seven premiers and three of the Famous Five women who fought the Persons Case in the late 1920s. But back in 1891, the *Calgary Herald* trumpeted the siren song of Alberta's dissent by declaring that "Albertans will not go to Winnipeg or Regina for advice" and "There are none in Canada better prepared to assume such responsibilities and better prepared to legislate for themselves; and those who assert the contrary either do not know Alberta or have sinister motives for wishing to see Alberta tied to the apron string of Regina or Ottawa."[13]

One James Reilly wrote of Alberta's difficulties in the midst of an economic depression, "Far removed from Ottawa, the only possible source of political or financial assistance, where the other Provinces derive their share of Dominion monies by constitutional right, but where the Territories have to appear as an annual mendicant for all we can get." Mr. Reilly asked, "Why keep boring for oil with a gimlet, when we might draw from the spring supplied from our own provincial credit and independence…"[14] Later, he spoke at a "mass meeting" in Calgary of local citizens and political leaders from across the North-West Territories. His supporters included the mayor of Calgary, a prominent Conservative senator and a future Liberal premier. But when Mr. Reilly approached the leader of the territorial council, Frederick Haultain, the latter resisted the idea as premature, as his focus was on winning responsible government within the territorial structure, keeping the Territories intact as one unit and avoiding a borrowing power that would put the new jurisdiction in debt. A pamphlet published in Calgary decried Alberta's status as "a minor" whose only "mouthpiece" in Ottawa was one of 215 MPs—the minister of the interior—"to whose department we belong along with the lunatics and Indians."[15] The pamphlet compared Albertans' clout in Ottawa to that of peasants in the imperial court at St. Petersburg.

But Mr. Reilly and his sycophants did not speak for all of Alberta. The territorial MLA turned MP from Edmonton, Frank Oliver, rebutted this in his other capacity as editor of the *Edmonton Bulletin*. Under the headline, "Hog Like Propensities," he accused "Jimmy Reilly and a few other political hacks" of serving Calgary's interests rather than those of all Albertans.[16] Rather than more autonomy, Mr. Oliver called for more representatives in Parliament and free transportation for farmers, their families and their livestock from south and central Alberta to the north. Calgary's motives were also distrusted by papers in towns like Macleod (Mr. Haultain's power base) and Lethbridge. In 1896 motions by the member for Banff in the territorial legislature demanding autonomy for Alberta and separating her from the rest of the Territories were defeated; Mr. Haultain argued persuasively that the time for provincehood was still not right. Meanwhile he continued his campaign to secure more autonomy and more revenue from Ottawa to meet the needs of the growing territorial population. He won full-fledged responsible government for the North-West Territories in 1897 and became premier, but when his demands to tie federal funding to actual local needs rather than the whims of Parliament went unheeded by Ottawa (for example, in the feds refusing requests for a larger grant from 1897–1899 even though the territorial population tripled in that time), he took up the fight for provincehood.[17] The assembly made a formal request to Parliament in 1900 without success. Eighteen months of head-banging later, Premier Haultain wrote to Prime Minister Laurier, "Then again, to require the people of the Territories to carry on the work of opening up and developing the country would not be to treat the early settlers in the North-West in the manner in which the people of the older Provinces have been treated."[18] When pressed to give up control over land and resources in the territories—which it had done for provinces entering Confederation—the Dominion (then Liberal) government refused "on the highest grounds of policy" so that it could continue to provide free homestead land as incentive for immigration. Clearly, the feds did not trust this task to authorities on the prairies. Mr. Haultain's case wasn't helped by the policy's opponents in the ranching industry, no bastion of federal Liberal support.

By the election campaign of 1902, the premier demanded equal rights with other provinces, including the same financial consideration; "control of the public domain in the West, by the West and for the West"; and compensation for the disposition of any part of public lands in the Territories for purely federal purposes.[19] By 1903 the premier's battle had captured national attention. The *Edmonton Journal* joined the fray, moaning, "The stigma of political inferiority has been attached to us too long."[20] (Recall that the *Journal*'s primary competitor was Frank Oliver, the owner of the *Edmonton Bulletin* and a Liberal MP to boot.) The feds waffled, citing disagreement among the districts themselves. But as the Conservative opposition pointed out, the real sticking point was disagreement over how to handle the rights of Catholics to their own schools, as the governing Liberals feared the ire of their supporters up Québec's religious ladder. Mr. Oliver claimed the Tory opposition was using the issue for political mileage (adopting the metric system being a good seven decades away). "The attitude of the Northwest," he editorialized, "is eminently practical; if autonomy means a betterment of our conditions it should be urged; otherwise it should be deferred. […] The people of the West care little for prestige."[21] Although the area's farmers, ranchers and business folks were divided on federal party grounds, they were more concerned with practical, financial issues than constitutional niceties.

A compelling case for provincehood was presented by the *Montreal Star* in 1904. That paper noted territorial residents' lack of control over their public land, minerals or timber, and their inability to raise money on their own credit, incorporate transportation companies, establish hospitals, administer criminal law or do various other things that provinces could do.[22] But by early 1905, the territories had grown sufficiently viable in the eyes of the feds—economically and politically—to turn the tide, and the Laurier government introduced bills to create autonomous government in the North-West Territories—but not quite as Mr. Haultain had envisioned. As noted earlier, he sought a super-province, perhaps called Buffalo, covering more than half a million square miles. Apparently, Team Laurier saw this as a political threat to British Columbia (359,279 square miles) and the recently augmented Québec (594,534 square miles) and Ontario (412,582 square miles), so they carved up what they called "the veritable commonwealth asked by the Haultain administration" into what we have come to know and love as Saskatchewan (251,700 square miles) and Alberta (255,285 square miles).[23]

The provincial autonomy bills attracted one of longest recorded debates in the House of Commons, consuming twenty-eight days over ten weeks and postponing the inauguration dates from July 1 to September 1. The feds picked Edmonton as the provisional capital because it was more centrally located than Calgary and Red Deer, which the PM noted had also presented good claims. Here began the singular skirmish between Calgary and Edmonton. Apart from the question of how many mini-Buffalos, the primary issues in granting provincehood were the ownership of public land, financial relations between the new provinces and the feds, and the right of Catholics in the provinces to their own schools within the public system. In defending the federal retention of public lands, the PM pointed out that (1) the other provinces were Crown colonies with control of their own natural resources before provincehood, except Manitoba; and (2) the federal government's power over immigration could be compromised by provincial public land ownership, though he admitted that Parliament needed to make "ample, even generous" compensation for this.

Premier Haultain disagreed with aspects of the autonomy bill and complained that Mr. Laurier did not consult him. Ultimately, he was frozen out for political reasons. As a Conservative, he campaigned against the federal Liberals in a pair of bellwether by-elections in Ontario in 1905. The *Calgary Herald* blasted the autonomy bill as an insult to the West, relieving the new provinces of the right to choose their own education systems and retaining control over coal royalties and irrigation "as a party privilege to be farmed out to Liberal supporters." To the Conservative *Herald*, "Sir Wilfrid audaciously extends the naked counterfeit to the west as the substance of provincial rights." The newssheet scoffed about Ontarians transplanted to Alberta and people 2,000 miles removed from Alberta debating over her education system, suggesting that easterners had little idea of Albertans' issues and concerns.[24]

Preston Manning reminds us that Alberta was born constitutionally unequal to the established provinces by having been denied control of her natural resources. "The federal government sold off or gave away six million acres of Alberta land to build railways when the federal government controlled Alberta's lands," he points out. "Alberta had a twenty-five-year struggle to overcome that and get constitutional equality. That's one of the reasons why equality and law arguments resonate with this province." After Alberta joined Confederation as a full-fledged partner, one might think she would have retired her protest placards and got down to business. As it turned out, nothing could be further from the reality.

Begging to Differ

The crucible out of which Western regional consciousness was forged was one of failure, depression and disappointed dreams. It became a defensive identity, seeking to locate blame in institutions and individuals outside the region, namely federal politicians, the Canadian Pacific Railway Company, and the people of Ontario.

—DOUGLAS FRANCIS, 1992 [25]

Becoming a province hardly handed Albertans a ticket to nirvana, particularly the new arrivals. From proposed settlement areas around Peace River that stretched too far north to sustain a homestead to the arid, drought-prone Palliser Triangle in the southeast, the province presented harsh realities behind the lush images of the golden prairie painted by the federal department of the interior. That office was now captained by Frank Oliver, the Edmontonian newspaperman who must have borrowed Bob Edwards's credo of never letting the truth stand in the way of a good story. At least Mr. Edwards was open about it.

The journey westward did not end happily for everyone. One woman who settled on the prairie with her family wrote, "I'll never forget the desolate feeling that came over me when we sat on a box and looked around, not a sign of any other human habitation or a road leading to one … Nothing but bluff and water and grass. Then I realized that this was to be our home, that if we wanted a house to cover us, a stable for our horses, a well for drinking water, it would all have to be the work of our own hands."[26] In a collection of life stories from Alberta's early days, the historian, David Jones, concluded, "What seems consistent in each life is some form of opposition, some constraint, some adversity. Without resistance, the sense of accomplishment is stillborn, the realization of self, stunted. A kite flies high against the wind—it is pushed aloft in its struggle to be what it is, and it must be confronted to reveal its nature."[27]

If Albertans' cherished can-do attitude is the yin of their success, then her culture of protest is undeniably the yang. Aritha van Herk referred to the province as "the country's canary for discontent."[28] The Ferguson brothers called Albertans the angriest people in Canada.[29] Douglas Cardinal observes, "There's a healthy disrespect for authority, so we question. We are probably the first to say that the emperor has no clothes and see through their rhetoric." And Jane Ash Poitras declares, "That's the way Alberta is. We don't like somebody, we deal with it right now. We're not afraid to be shakers and movers or to be mavericks." Ted Byfield sums up the yang part of the equation by noting, "Albertans have a profound conviction that there's a lot of BS in the world and that when told something, a Canadian affirms order and does it, while an Albertan says, 'Who says?' and is inclined to salute with a middle finger."

The image of Albertans' culture of dissent is hard to shake. Recall Premier Haultain's unanswered requests and demands to Ottawa before 1905. The unprecedented and tumultuous rise of Social Credit during the Depression. Premier Manning's resistance to official bilingualism and biculturalism, and his national appeal to Canadians to look before leaping into Medicare in the 1960s. Opposition to the federal government's White Paper on Indian Policy led by Alberta chiefs, who responded with a "Red Paper," and by the twenty-four-year-old president of the Indian Association of Alberta, Harold Cardinal, whose book, *The Unjust Society*, called Prime Minister Trudeau's proposals "extermination through assimilation." Opposition to the metric system by a mayor of Fort McMurray in the 1970s. Alberta's turning down the oil taps twice in response to the National Energy Program, and a small but loud minority's one-night stand with separatism in the early 1980s. The emergence of Preston Manning and the Reform Party, and their rallying cry of "The West wants in!" in the 1990s. The volley of proposals for proportional representation, the recall of MPs, a "triple-E" Senate (equal, elected and effective), a proposed firewall around the province. And all that is just the tip of the protest sign. Such is the culture of dissent in Alberta that a group called the Calgary Anti-Capitalist Convergence Group can rally about a thousand protesters at a summit of G8 countries in Kananaskis and get lost in the shuffle.

Of course, these are just the sound bites and the underlying issues are more complex. For example, Ernest Manning's opposition to bilingualism was based not on a wide-eyed loathing of French (he saved that for socialists, layabouts and eastern banks), but the like-lihood of Ukrainian, Scandinavian, German and American accents outnumbering English or French accents on the streets of Edmonton. He found bilingualism unrealistic and impractical. His caution against Medicare as proposed by Ottawa was not against its goal but the sweeping manner in which it was to be implemented. And the National Energy Program was and remains such a divine lightning rod for dissent in Alberta that its mere mention warrants an anger manage-ment regimen. It's a filthy job being the skeptic of Confederation but *someone* has to do it.

For Mark Lisac, "Western alienation is the only story that media organizations think Alberta has ever had."[30] Certainly the words "prairie" and "protest" have been steady companions over the last century in Canada. As a human land bridge and then as hewers of fur, grain and wood, and drawers of oil for central Canadian interests, Albertans and their prairie cousins have always served as grist for the nation-building mill in Ottawa and more recently, the money-making mill internationally. Even the province's descriptor as "Western" and her lineage from the "North-West Territories" are defined in relation to central Canada. Small wonder that Albertans' sense of unfairness and exploitation has fuelled an enduring culture of protest.

From a federal perspective, it was essential to keep the nation tightly controlled by Ottawa. Not only did the fledgling Dominion government face the spectre of Uncle Sam exporting his expan-sionist agenda to gobble up the Canadian prairies, there was also concern about holding together the new nation, as Confederation had occurred only two years after the end of the American Civil War. So the founding papas established a strong central government, empowering it to veto provincial legislation, choose provincial lieutenant-governors, appoint superior-court judges and so on. Prime Minister Macdonald clearly foresaw Parliament's taking precedence over provincial governments, and strong federal power was an essential driver of his National Policy.[31] The feds had to control public land to be able to manage settlement, to build a railroad to get the settlers to the prairies and to connect the rest of the country to British Columbia. Macdonald's railway minister, Charles Tupper, essentially admitted as much in Parliament in 1883, when he asked, "Are the interests of Manitoba and the North-West to be sacrificed to the policy of Canada? I say, if it is necessary—yes."[32] Like Eye Opener Bob, at least he was open about it.

But lest we get too caught up in the altruistic glory of nation-building, we should keep in mind that Sir John A.'s National Policy had an essential economic motive as well. Settling the West might have preempted American squatters, settlers and even soldiers but it also delivered a captive market for manufacturing interests based in central Canada. Primary producers and settlers in Alberta and in the West were forced to sell cheaply and buy expensively, paying up to 50 per cent more for goods made in central Canada than they would have buying from closer markets in the United States under free trade. Sir John A.'s tariffs on imported American goods made them unaffordable to most Westerners; on the other hand, Westerners had to sell their goods on an open market. Added to this was forcing Western farmers to sell their products through various middlemen, each of whom took a cut, lowering the producer's share of the ultimate selling price. Then came the cost of credit needed to buy the required land and machinery, plus raise buildings. All of this created and maintained Westerners' status as a colony of a colony.

For many, the financial burden was backbreaking. In the first quarter-century of Alberta's provincehood, 46 per cent of homesteads failed. (On a national basis, 40 per cent of the free homesteads failed from 1870–1927.) Small producers effectively worked for much larger interests like railway companies, grain traders, wholesalers, retailers, bankers and trust and insurance companies, all of which were unaccountable to, and beyond the control of, the actual producer.[33] In this light, given that Queen Victoria was portrayed as the "Great Mother" in the feds' dealings with Aboriginal people, it might not have been a stretch for Western farmers to call Ottawa the "Great Mother's Son" or, considering questions around paternity, the "Great Bastard." So they turned to protest, driven by a co-operative ethic, a belief in the righteousness of the farmer and a utopian desire to improve the world.

The unionist and social gospel influence of American immigrants, notably Henry Wise Wood, found a ready audience in Alberta. Recall that the UFA arose not as a political party but a principled protest movement fuelled by Christian values and driving for social reform. Two notable dualities about the province emerge here.[34] First, in a telling disconnect between the south and the north, the UFA's support was strongest south of Red Deer—where most folks came from Britain, the US, Germany and Scandinavia—and much weaker among the less WASP-ish crowd to the north. Second, although the social gospel movement sparked a famers' revolt, it was an urban creation of universities, civil servants and clerics, spread by city-based presses and preachers, and targeting exploitation by corporate overdogs rather than the capitalist system itself. One anonymous survivor of the Depression captured the sentiment fuelling Albertans' protests:

> *Aberhart, you know, he was smart. For all I know, he might have been the first Canadian politician to really use radio effectively. Maybe he took his lessons from Roosevelt. Remember Roosevelt's opening words, "Good evening, my fellow Americans?" Well, when Aberhart was talking, quoting chapter and verse in the Bible, he was*

*actually saying, "Good evening, you poor dumb Alberta farmers
who are getting a shit-kicking from those Eastern Canadian bankers
and that bastard R.B. Bennett sitting in his big expensive house in
Ottawa and eating T-bone steaks for breakfast, and those United
Farmers of Alberta in Edmonton are making a complete hash of
everything you and your fathers worked for since you busted the sod
with a hand plough and two horses." Yeah, that's a long sentence,
but that's what he was saying.*[35]

This ethos of protest was captured vividly by Harry Strom, a farmer who spent three years as Alberta's last Social Credit premier before giving way to Alberta's latest political juggernaut. He cited a cartoon of a cow standing on a map of Canada, chomping grass in Alberta and Saskatchewan while its milk poured into buckets located in Ontario. "To some, this problem is one of our own perceptions and insecurity," he said. "But there is also a basis for our resentment—we have felt the West was opened to settlement to line the pockets of eastern pot and pan salesmen."[36]

Over time, this protest shifted from its rural roots as agriculture became more mechanized, farms grew in size, the population grew increasingly urban and the economic base of the province shifted to energy.[37] Yet deep-rooted feelings around the land endure like a familial crest, both as a memorial badge of honour and as a call to arms against trespassers, whether actual or invented. So deep is Albertans' sense of protest that not even the province's rising economic clout can shake it off. In fact, the oil booms of the 1970s and the 2000s actually *reinforced* some people's frustrations by underlining the paradox between Alberta's economic clout and her perceived lack of political pull in Ottawa. Interviewed there, Geoff Poapst observes, "Albertans are very, very self-reliant, far more self-reliant than the rest of the country. But it's odd. For self-reliant people, they seem to always be complaining about being hard done by."

For some, the brouhaha from politicians and the media masks Alberta's strong influence on national affairs. In a landmark sociological study, Harry Hiller concluded from both statistics and personal interviews that the large inflow of interprovincial migrants during the last boom in particular has eroded Albertans' long-held hinterland mentality and sense of alienation, which has been replaced by "a new collective self-confidence that sometimes bordered on arrogance."[38] The political scientist, Allan Tupper, also found that Alberta's "portrayal as an oppressed, ignored and misunderstood hinterland is no longer convincing." Yet he added, "the national focus of elites, internationalism and interdependence, and advanced technology all weaken provincial distinctiveness and influence, but provincialism remains a potent force in Alberta and other parts of Canada."[39] In fact, time has whittled the edge of the powerful federalist vision behind Sir John A.'s National Policy. Decades of constitutional decisions by Canadian courts and the rising profile of areas within provincial jurisdiction such as health care, education and the environment have given the provinces more say than ever before.[40]

Preston Manning, no stranger to targeting Ottawa, wrote of Alberta's history as revealing six periods of bitter tension between the province and the federal government over issues of provincehood (up to 1905), natural resources (1905–1930), survival (1939–1945), national identity (1965 to date), oil pricing and revenue (1973–1988) and the structure of the federation (1987–2005).[41] Beyond the question of how much of it is deserved, the federal government has proven to be the best avenue for Albertans' frustration because, like all truly great bogeymen—from drought, frost and grasshoppers to commodity prices, foreign markets and freight rates—the feds can never be conquered. They can be voted out from time to time, but then the new bunch gets entrenched and starts behaving like the old. Any way you slice it, Albertans' dissent stems from forces well beyond our control.

For Mark Lisac, the notion of "Western alienation" is deliberately intangible because defining it would make it real, requiring action to

deal with it. "Better to leave it floating just out of reach—a combination of half-remembered history, a handful of genuine grievances and
shrewd current ambitions," he wrote. "That way it can exist forever.
A lot of people would no more want to get rid of it than a self-pitying
alcoholic would want to lose an excuse for drinking."[42] He makes a
superb point. Much as Canadians are bombarded with American
legends and images—from George Washington's tree-chopping to
Barack Obama's trend-setting—Albertans and other Westerners are
served up national dreams from a central-Canadian perspective.
When is the last time you heard about the Progressives, a national
political force in the 1920s? The Edmonton Grads, whom the inventor
of basketball called the finest team ever to play the game? Vern "Dry
Hole" Hunter, the legendarily unlucky tool push who gave it one last
try and hit black gold in Leduc? This is where actual history loses
out to fragments of memory, myths and folklore, which are far more
convenient, whether bandied about as water-cooler shorthand or
deployed as political weapons.

Alberta's politicians have used her culture of protest, cloaked in
the nebulous notion of Western alienation, shamelessly and repeatedly to rally homeys to circle the wagons against actual or perceived
threats, usually from Ontario. What better way to take the heat off
internal troubles or shortcomings than to batten down the hatches
and turn the cannons on the enemy out there? Albertans are played
like bull trout and don't seem to mind. In 2007 the provincial minister
of intergovernmental affairs called Albertans "kind of the bad boys of
Confederation" and let it be known that the province wouldn't be shy
about using her economic clout to demand favourable treatment like
Québec gets.[43] "Bad boys" dials up the province's deeply entrenched
and cherished traditions of protest and of daring to be different, to
challenge the status quo and not to take any guff from anyone—especially anyone from central Canada and especially, especially Ottawa.
In a gorgeous twist, this attitude has gone mainstream and caught on
in Ontario itself. The national columnist, Andrew Coyne, predicted

that Alberta-style populism would overpower Canada's political culture. "Ontario has taken up the 1980-Alberta mantle of protesting being the milk-cow of Canada, spawning a cottage industry calculating how much more it pays in than gets out, and shakes its fist at Ottawa," he wrote. "If Alberta is the new Ontario, Ontario is fast becoming the old Alberta."[44] But even if Albertans tone down their culture of protest, given Alberta's standing as both the energy powerhouse and the top polluter in Canada, it's unlikely that she will fade into the national wallpaper very soon.

An Early Dissident
Interview with Albertosaurus

Some Canadians see Alberta as a haven for certain prehistoric views. And they'd be right—about 70 million years ago, when Albertosaurus roamed the province. Albertosaurus was discovered in the Red Deer River valley by Joseph Tyrrell in 1884. As a new arts graduate from the University of Toronto, Dr. Tyrrell was hired by the federal government's geological survey agency to join an expedition for coal to fuel the coming railway. Descending a coulee, he found the exposed skull of a massive dinosaur staring up at him. The find was named for the new province in 1905. Albertosaurus is a close relative of Tyrannosaurus rex. Though smaller than his famous cousin—

Not again! T-rex, this! T-rex that! I'm twenty-seven feet tall, so cut me some slack, willya?

✳ *Is there a problem here, Al?*

That's *Big* Al to you, long-arms. So whaddya want?

✳ *I'm looking for the heart of Alberta. I'm hoping you can help us find it.*

Well, if it's a theropod like me, you've come to the right place. These badlands are crawling with us. Of course, we're only a shell of our

Big Al in his current role on a skeleton crew at the Royal Tyrrell Museum.
[Geo Takach]

former selves. (*Here he guffaws and stamps his huge, clawed feet,
causing the shale underfoot to shake.*)

✳ *A theropod meaning…*

"Beast-footed." You know, your basic fast-moving, lizard-hipped,
two-legged carnivore with small forelimbs and grasping arms. What
are you, mental? I'm the top carnivore here. The nasty one with the
killer teeth that ate all those sissy hadrosaurs. The original Big Hurt.
(*Here he lets loose a thundering roar and moves to thump his chest, but
with his disproportionately small arms, this comes off as more like a
playful slap.*)

✳ *If you're the king kahuna, how do you explain the teeth marks on your skull? You must have had predators. T-rex, perhaps?*

Will you shut up about T-rex already? Mr. T came two million years after me. I *made* T-rex, okay? I'm what you call a precursor. I was making with the cursor before T-rex was even a glint in anyone's antorbital fenestra. See, these tooth marks are so big, they could only have come from another large carnivore. So if I'm the only large carnivore in the epoch, I must have had a misunderstanding with one of the guys over one of two things: a meal or a dame. (*Here he shakes his head, causing a seismic tremor.*) Duh! If your people are so highly evolved, why do they send me such a doofus?

✳ *The eminent paleontologist, Philip Currie, tells me that you're "a very sophisticated, highly specialized animal, with a relatively big brain, long legs, incredibly powerful jaws that could munch through anything (and did), and teeth specialized enough to bite through bone. An incredible killer, not just an overgrown crocodile."*

At least you're not *all* doofuses. (*pause*) Excuse me. Doofii.

✳ *So, from that perspective, how do you approach the world?*

Lookit. Life is simple. There are just two rules. One: eat meat and lots of it. Two: kill or be killed. As my mom used to say, if you're not at the table, you're on the menu.

✳ *How Albertan can you get? Are you unique to this province?*

Your borders mean Bo Diddly to me, bub. But from what I've read, there's little trace of us found outside of this place. There's crud by way of terrestrial beds, mostly just marine sediments. So the full range of my territory is unknown. The only sure thing is that I was here, in your "Alberta." Can I go now? I've got a dental thing at three.

✳ *You seem to have issues with T-rex.*

Lookit. I'm just as ferocious. I've got longer limbs. I'm more nimble, probably a better hunter. Much better looking. But Cousin T gets all the respect, all the media buzz. Why? Just 'cause there's *more* of him! How fair is that?

✳ *Is this Mesozoic meanness envy?*

(There is no answer, though the recording picks up what sounds like basso profondo snarling.)

✳ *All right then, Big Al. So as a Westerner, how do you feel about the Torontosaurus?*

(Here the recording ends abruptly.)

The Great Divide

So entrenched is the culture of being different in Alberta that she seems to have borrowed from places like Italy and the US to create dissonance between north and south. Nowadays, that plays out in friendly and sometimes not-so-friendly competition between her two largest cities, Calgary and Edmonton, each of which claims about a third of the provincial population. But this bizarre bifurcation predates white settlement. There is a history of clashes between the Cree in the north and the Blackfoot Confederacy to the south. As legend has it, when Aboriginal peoples lost Alberta to the white man, they cursed that it would be divided eternally as it was divided between the Cree and the Blackfoot, along the Battle River. And the battle rolled on.

As white history goes, Fort Edmonton predated Fort Calgary by eight decades, but the inter-city rivalry didn't really pick up steam until the Canadian Pacific Railway entered the scene. In a fateful decision in 1881, the CPR diverted from the surveyed route for its main line across the West along the fertile valley of the North Saskatchewan River through Battleford, Edmonton and the Yellowhead Pass. Instead, the steel moved down to the dry belt three hundred kilometres to the south. When the iron horse chugged into Calgary in 1883, it brought businesses and a mercantile ethic, propelling the town on the banks of the Bow to dominance in the province into the new century.

When Edmonton claimed to be the geographical centre of the province, the *Calgary Herald* countered, "If the province was extended to the North Pole and if every member of the remote Indian tribes were added to those of white settlers, Edmonton would still not be the centre of Alberta's population."[45] Meanwhile, in the display of McDougall and Secord's store in the heart of downtown Edmonton, a mannequin, Mother Alberta, stood with her two daughters, Edmonton and Calgary, admiring a likeness of an imagined legislature building. With an outstretched hand and aided by a cartoon-style speech balloon, little Calgary cried, "I want it, Ma!" To which mom replied, "Now don't be naughty, Calgary. Let your sister have it. You're not old enough to handle it safely. Run and play with your C.P.R."[46] Rarely at a loss for comment, the great Bob Edwards captured the essence of the growing inter-city rhubarb when he wrote, "Edmonton now estimates that it has a population of over 4,000. Estimates are easy to make. Calgary, with her bona fide population of 11,000, is seriously thinking of estimating her population at 25,000 just to prove that its imagination is not inferior to Edmonton's."[47]

Imagine the locals' chagrin when the tide finally turned in the battle for provincehood, it came time to choose an interim capital city and the governing Laurier Liberals in Ottawa anointed Edmonton—coincidentally home of Frank Oliver, the minister of the interior. Imagine Calgarians' ire when the minister gerrymandered the new electoral map and the Liberals swept the first provincial election. Imagine their outraged howls when the public works minister, a good Calgarian, made a motion to move the capital to Calgary and it was defeated by a margin of more than two to one. The *Calgary Herald* railed against the "crowning infamy to a nefarious deal"[48] and raged that a "horde of Polacks and Galicians and innumerable imported pug uglies has inflicted the province with a form of government that is contrary to the traditions of law and fair play."[49] When Premier Rutherford floated the idea of a university for the new province, Calgarians assumed that it was their turn. Imagine their wrath when the University of Alberta wound up in the premier's riding of Strathcona, located across the river from Edmonton—and, to really twist the knife, absorbed by Edmonton in 1912. (Calgary did get a campus after World War II but only as a branch of the senior institution. In 1963 dissident students brandished the secessionist Confederate flag as they marched for independence, which was achieved in 1966.) When the first radio broadcast in the province came from Edmonton in 1922, the mayor signed it off by announcing, "Edmonton leads the way in all Alberta. Calgary and others follow. That is all. Goodnight."[50] By month-end, Calgary had *two* radio stations.

One hundred and one years to the day after the provincial inauguration, Preston Manning reminds me that Alberta is no more homogeneous than any other province. He views southern Alberta as the more radical part—harbouring the headquarters of the UFA, Social Credit and Reform parties (though Reform began in Edmonton)—while also giving birth to the CCF, and northern Alberta as the stabilizer, the ballast in the boat that says, "Wait a minute" and "This might be okay, but we're not sure about this." Time may have reversed that trend. Erin and Murray Chrusch, who have lived in both cities, report that the biggest apparent difference is the greater diversity of political viewpoints tolerated in Edmonton. They also point to a stronger inclination to maintain the status quo in Calgary, which finally adopted curbside recycling in 2009, twenty-one years after Edmonton and with far more controversy.

Politics creates long, if sometimes skewed, memories. To this day, many Albertans see "Redmonton" as leaning more to the left and Calgary and the rest of the province as leaning more in the other direction. These are generalizations, of course, but we can trace at least the north–south split back to the nineteenth century, when on the whole, the southern ranchers sided with the Conservatives (who had opened up leases for them under Sir John A. Macdonald), and the farmers and homesteaders leaned toward the Liberals, who favoured free trade at the time.[51] The Tories tended to be less keen on reforms such as women's suffrage, Prohibition and direct democracy that gained ground into the twentieth century, and their dislike of immigrants beyond the WASP persuasion stung many among the waves of newcomers that poured into the province. (As Liberal federal ministers of the interior, both Clifford Sifton, who openly welcomed "men in sheepskin coats," and Frank Oliver, who emphatically did not, respectively played to and against those generalizations, but each was only one guy.)

Both politics and patterns of settlement have reinforced the distinctions between Calgary and Edmonton. As David Ward, who has spent his life living and working in both cities, elucidates, "There was lots more eastern European settlement up north, which explains why a reference to the giant pyrohy in Glendon plays well in northern Alberta, but is lost on an audience in Bragg Creek. The American influence was heavier in the south, which is more managerial and businesslike. Edmonton is more relaxed and takes up less space, while Calgary is over the top now. About 50,000–55,000 people work in downtown Edmonton, while 125,000–130,000 work in downtown Calgary."

Fil Fraser comments, "Whoever put the provincial capital and the university in Edmonton may not have fully understood the consequences. This left Calgary as the frontier town and much more monocultural; the British and the Americans ruled the roost. In Edmonton, the British hegemony was never overwhelming; from day one, there was a much more even mix of cultures: Poles, Germans, Ukrainians and Czechs. This made Edmonton always a different place from Calgary, a more diverse and multicultural society."

The columnist, Richard Gwyn, observed that "Edmontonians look down on Calgary as uncultured; Calgarians look northwards at Edmonton and dismiss it as 'Siberia with government jobs.'"[52] Both claims are silly, as the two cities are hardly radically disproportionate in their cultural or climatic offerings. Yet Edmontonians still tell the one about the traffic cop stopping a speeding Calgarian and asking, "Do you have any ID?" whereupon the driver answers, "About what?" And Calgarians echo their former mayor, Ralph Klein, who once slyly remarked that "Edmonton isn't exactly the end of the world, but you can see it from there."[53]

There's a significant gap in self-perceptions, too. In a survey in 2008, 79 per cent of Calgarians described their city as world-class and 56 per cent thought others would agree, while only 61 per cent of Edmontonians called their city world-class and just 26 per cent felt that others would concur.[54] When asked to explain that gap, Edmonton's mayor, Stephen Mandel, cited Calgary's primary business: "I'm Big Oil. Got the big hat. From Texas." (Even in a province known for oddities, Calgary comes off as odd.)

And so it goes. Calgary was closer to the first oil boom at Turner Valley in 1914. Edmonton became the oilfield-servicing centre after Leduc in 1947. Calgary became the administrative and financial headquarters for the oil industry while Edmonton led in exploration and production. Calgary has proximity to the Rocky Mountains and hosts the Stampede. Edmonton has a really, really big shopping mall. Calgary held the Winter Olympics in 1988. Edmonton hosted sports dynasties with the Grads from 1915–1940, the Eskimos in the 1950s, 1970s and 1980s, and the Oilers in the 1980s. When provincial premiers, cabinet appointments or infrastructure dollars are at stake, politicians dance up a storm while Edmontonians and Calgarians break out their calculators to make sure their city doesn't get the short end of the shtick.

This inter-city, intra-provincial game of chicken is unusual in Canada. When asked whether such a rivalry exists in his home province—the one best known for its polarized politics—a Québecois, Howard Hassan, raises the distinction between smaller, governmental and administrative capitals like Québec City, Ottawa, Washington, DC, Sao Paolo and Tel Aviv, and neighbouring, correspondingly larger business capitals like Montréal, Toronto, NYC, Brasilia and Jerusalem, respectively. "Because the bases for their societies are different, there is a distinction in the way their inhabitants sense their own identity and some lack of sensitivity or resentment toward the other society," he states, then adds, "However, there is no intense rivalry between the inhabitants of Montreal and Quebec City today, and the one that did exist was limited to hockey fanatics."

Bruce McGillivray, the executive director of the Royal Alberta Museum (since retired), lived in Ottawa before moving to Edmonton and sees this tale of two cities as distinctive. "We joke about our football teams, the Stampeders versus the Eskimos, or our hockey teams, the Flames versus the Oilers. But in every facet of life, people ask, 'Are you a southern Albertan or you are a central-northern Albertan kind of person?' I'm sure our leaders struggle at times with what seems like almost an adolescent rivalry between our cities, and maybe we need to get over that, grow up and get on with making Alberta the best place it can be."

So although Alberta's politics have shifted over the decades, the attitudes established more than a century ago linger like garlic breath on the morning after trattoria night. Calgary is perceived as a centre for business while Edmonton claims the heartland of government and education in the province. Both of these identifiers were established early in the game. Of course, the cities share significant commonalities, notably the economic corridor expanding speedily between them. It's intriguing to speculate on the extent of the rivalry had Alberta and Saskatchewan been born as a single province in 1905 as envisioned by their territorial premier: would either Calgary or Edmonton ever have taken orders from Regina, the original capital of the North-West Territories? In any case, of Alberta's two largest cities, Calgary has been much more aggressive in sporting the maverick label, as the exhibit at the Glenbow Museum attests. It's significant that the exhibit focuses on southern Alberta, leaving the rest of the province's mavericks to go off and fend for themselves, as mavericks tend to do. Undeniably, elements of the maverick are part of Alberta's overall character, and wearing that badge like a sheriff's tin star goes with that character. But there's a lesser-known, darker side to the province's claim to maverick-icity.

The Sheep Factor

Albertans' claim to be the mavericks of Canada is anchored in more than a century of contrarianism, protest, restlessness and even mischief. But whether we are really, figuratively speaking, the bad boys of Confederation, a bunch of black sheep or merely a herd of sheep merits discussion. For openers, the provincial mammal is the bighorn sheep. Not that this noble ungulate isn't a primo poster mammal for the province, favouring wide-open spaces, mating into the winter and being the biggest sheep in its class. Perhaps there are reasons for this selection beyond the bighorn's obvious domicile preference.

To some, Albertans are really sheep in maverick's clothing. Mark Lisac agrees that Albertans are mavericks to some extent, but not much more so than many other Canadians. He believes that some Albertans tend to glory in the word, to establish a provincial identity and suggest that being Albertan somehow involves virtues that others lack. "The other thing about calling Albertans mavericks is it ignores a huge streak of conformism in the province, which is there often for very good reasons," he adds. "Usually it's a method of meeting all sorts of outside pressures. You can see it in the way that people approach community life and politics, where there's strong pressure to all belong to the same party and vote the same way, and even sometimes believing that Albertans are mavericks—that's a method of conformism, too."

The irony in this observation goes to the heart of one of the grand paradoxes called Alberta. It is *so* much cooler to wear the mantle of a maverick than the wool of a sheep. Hence the indelible legend of Albertans as rugged individualists, carving out a living and a future from dust. Like many great legends, this one is rooted in both truth and myth. While the province remains a bastion for individual initiative, her long-term growth probably owes more to local, cultural and religious communities, economic associations like wheat pools and other collective efforts. While this doesn't make Albertans sheep, it does cast a different light on our self-image as mavericks.

You could argue that Alberta is, in fact, a highly conformist society, in which the only tolerable targets of public dissent are central Canada and especially the federal government. (In Premier Manning's time, communists were fair game, too.) You could also suggest that the province's economic powerhouses, the primary resource industries, are just as beholden to government activity—favourable regulations, colossal subsidies, generous tax credits and so on—particularly during droughts, commodity price dives and other calamities.[55] "There are few other political universes where the prevailing myths are so completely at odds with reality," wrote the political scientist, David Taras. "As long as the popular myth remains strong and endures as part of the rhetoric of Alberta politicians, then the reality is somehow less observable, less important. Taken to an extreme, these conditions can generate what amounts to populism in reverse, a politics where ideas are rarely contested, where the public is increasingly apathetic and disconnected, and where politicians can hide from scrutiny and accountability."[56]

If our voting behaviour is any indication, then that extreme lives in Alberta, where one-party rule is the rule and disgruntled complaints about democratic dictatorship line the underbelly of public discourse. Implicit in allusions to dictatorship is the notion that voters have no choice at the ballot box and no say in their own governance. On one level, of course, there is unfettered freedom of choice in a democratic society. But an important wrinkle in Alberta, unprecedented in scope in Canada, is not only the *perception* that voters have no choice but also the pressure to conform to the political status quo. As Jackie Flanagan remarks, "It's almost like it's rude to disagree in Alberta. We all have to think the same way. We have to circle the wagons against Ottawa somehow and you're disloyal to your Alberta roots if you disagree."[57]

"Here in Alberta, we all vote for these clowns because that's what daddy did. We won't change the government!" fumes the filmmaker, Garth Pritchard. Jack Lewis, a senior who continues to work his family farm in Parkland County, explains that "Voting Conservative goes with the territory. You kind of get brought up that way and that's how you are." The editor of a biweekly, rural newspaper, Nancy Mereska, painted a harsh picture of life under a political juggernaut. She described rural Tory MLAs as bullies dispensing patronage favours to supporters, and accused local media of pro-government bias and election returning officers of disrespecting the rights of scrutineers. Noting that the local MLA had three campaign offices while his opponents worked out of their cars or supporters' homes, she lamented, "Standing up in rural Alberta and proclaiming that you do not support the Tories is akin to standing up in church and proclaiming you don't believe in God."[58]

Beyond the question of Alberta's conservatism, two notable phenomena emerge from Albertan's voting patterns over the last century.

The first is that on the numbers, Albertans actually do vote more monolithically than any other Canadians. Alberta stands alone as a truly one-party system, and this habit extends to the federal level, where her MPs have occupied the opposition benches in Parliament in greater proportions and for more time than the case of any other province.[59] In 27 provincial elections in Alberta, 15 governments earned more than 50 per cent of the popular vote. And just over half of Alberta's popular-vote majorities have occurred since the current ruling Conservative dynasty swept into office in 1971.[60] Small wonder that folks see Alberta as a one-party state.

To put this in context, in the federal sphere, only in 11 out of 40 elections between Confederation and 2008 did the government earn more than half of the popular vote. (Eight of those elections came before 1921, when the first "third" party, the Progressives—ironically, led by Albertans—broke the Liberal-Conservative duopoly on the ballot, if not the ballot box.[61]) In fact, the five safest seats in Canada in the 2006 federal election were all in Alberta, with the margins of victory between the winners and their runners-up falling between 65–75 per cent.[62]

Alberta's penchant for monopoly is reinforced in comparisons to other provincial votes at this writing, in which Saskatchewan recorded 8 popular-vote majorities out of 26 elections (the first 6 in a row), British Columbia had 6 of 37, Manitoba had 4 of 29 and Ontario had 8 of 30.[63] Québec rang up a higher total of 15 popular-vote majorities out of 29 elections, but at least *La Belle Province* has a true multi-party system, shown dramatically by three camps enjoying roughly comparable shares of the popular vote and seats in the 2007 election there.[64] Alberta's last two provincial governments rank among the longest-serving governments in the history of Confederation; the derby is led by the 42-year reign of the Conservatives in Ontario (1943–1985); the 41-year run by Alberta's Conservatives, presuming completion of their current mandate (1971–2012); the 39-year stretch by Québec's Liberals (1897–1936); and the 36-year turn by Social Credit in Alberta (1935–1971).[65] The staggering fact is that the Alberta government has changed ruling political parties just once since the Depression. This compares favourably to tenures in such bastions of electoral free will as the Soviet Union, North Korea and Cuba. Nor has Alberta ever harboured a minority government, joining only New Brunswick and Prince Edward Island in Canada since 1900.[66]

As always, these numbers don't tell the entire tale. In a study of the proportionality of the share of the popular vote to the number of seats won by parties in the provincial legislatures from 2002–2005, Alberta ranked next to last at 74 per cent, behind the national average of 83 per cent and ahead of only PEI.[67] Although the sample covers a brief time period, it suggests that Alberta's electoral results mask undercurrents of support for parties other than the ruling Conservatives, thereby contributing to the province's image as a monolithic voting bloc. Added to this is that Alberta has more MLAs than British Columbia, despite having a smaller population, and is slated to add even more. About half of our provincial seats are sprinkled across rural ridings, which boast a proportionately smaller share of the population. On the whole, this gives rural voters a bigger bang for their vote than their urban counterparts.

The second phenomenon to emerge from Albertans' voting record is not so much what they say as what they do not. Our apathy is outstanding, even astonishing. We rank dead last in Canada in voter turnout since at least the 1980s. In that decade, for example, Alberta's turnout in provincial elections was 57 per cent, a whopping 20 per cent below the provincial average across Canada.[68] Alberta's democratic deficit (or electile dysfunction) is evidenced by declining voter turn-outs in the last five provincial elections. For example, in the election of 2004, the Tories earned three-quarters of the seats based on 45 per cent of the popular vote. That only 21 per cent of eligible voters voted for Ralph's team belies the image of homogeneity in the province.[69] One would have figured that this marked the nadir of Albertans' indifference. And one would have been right—until the next provincial election in 2008. Despite iffy polls and rampant agitation for change in the media, the Conservatives corralled 53 per cent of the popular vote, more than double that of the Liberal opposition. In Wild Rose Country, that translates into 72 of 83 seats—almost 90 per cent of the spoils. A historically low voter turnout of 41 per cent meant that only about one in five eligible voters backed the government.[70] That turnout pales compared to elections in that same year in, say, PEI (84 per cent), Saskatchewan (76 per cent) and Québec (71 per cent), and even the lowest-ever turnout in a federal general election (61 per cent) in 2004.[71] With the Liberals scooping the remaining nine provincial seats in 2008, that left two-thirds of eligible voters with their wishes unrepresented under the dome of the Legislature. Letters to the editor expressed outrage and calls for another election, proportional representation (the allocation of seats based on parties' share of the popular vote) and a fat fine for not voting in the future; one missive noted Albertans' distaste for an opposition "of more than popgun proportions" and likened the political landscape to that of Russia.[72]

The system seems self-perpetuating, if calcifying. People in both rural and urban Alberta express dissatisfaction with the province's direction, but it never turns up at the ballot box. Young, engaged citizens like Erin Chrusch, a lawyer, and Murray Chrusch, a kinesiologist, can't find a vehicle to express their voices beyond the local level, where political party affiliation counts less. "It's almost like if you want to get involved in politics, unless you have a really strong familial tie to the Liberals or NDP, you'll become a Tory just because that's the only way you're going to have a political future," observes Ms. Chrusch. "There's no inspiring message and nothing to hang onto beyond, 'We're not the Tories.' That might be enough for some people, but not for us." Mr. Chrusch adds, "People just assume and resign themselves to the fact that the Conservatives are going to remain in power and that their vote is not going to matter."

For a province that values maverick-ery, Alberta seems to do a smashing job of rewarding conformity and keeping people in line. Some recent examples leap to mind.

When the medical health officer for the Palliser Health Authority, Dr. David Swann, indicated his approval of the Kyoto Protocol on reducing greenhouse gas emissions as a positive step for public health in the face of provincial government hostility to it, he was relieved of his duties. After the ensuing media outrage over his dismissal, in a genuinely maverick turn, he refused an offer to take his job back, ran as an opposition MLA and later became provincial opposition leader, surely the most thankless job in Alberta.

A significant number of members of provincial bodies were found to be staffed by card-carrying and often high-profile Conservatives in 2007, including all thirteen board members of the Peace Country Health Region and two-thirds of the board members of the ten former regional health authorities. Of about a thousand posts on Alberta's agencies, commissions, task forces, councils, college and university boards, health boards and health authorities, almost half were Tories even though only 3 per cent of Albertans held Tory membership cards. The party's president was offended by the suggestion of a conflict of interest, while one political scientist called it "a real slap in the face of democracy." Within a year, the face-slapping had fallen to just under a quarter of 281 appointments made over that subsequent period.[73]

The Alberta Energy and Utilities Board hired detectives to spy on local landowners who were opposed to an application before the board on a proposed transmission line in central Alberta in 2007. A report found that the agency violated rules of privacy. The year before, that same government-appointed board refused three separate submissions by elected representatives of the Regional Municipality of Wood Buffalo to decelerate the development of the oil sands to preserve a semblance of community in Fort McMurray.

Until 2010, provincial electoral returning officers were chosen not by the Chief Electoral Officer, who ventured to request that privilege, but by the ruling Progressive Conservative Party. This led to questions about the officers' objectivity and allegations of iffy practices at some polls in the 2008 election. After the chief electoral officer, Lorne Gibson, issued a post-mortem containing 182 suggestions for improvement, the government refused to reappoint him.

Also during that campaign, the Capital Health Authority departed from its policy of prohibiting political parties from using hospital property for political events. Defending the decision to allow the

Conservatives to announce an election promise on health care in the lobby of the University of Alberta Hospital, the health authority's chair (a Tory) agreed with the premier that the said public area was open to any activities that were appropriate to Capital Health's mission.

In 2007 the Alberta government appointed an independent panel to recommend the provincial royalty and tax regimes for oil and gas production, having regard to other provincial economies, the federal economy and energy sectors abroad. When the industry blasted the panel's recommendations to raise royalty rates, one of the six commissioners, Evan Chrapko, took the initiative to raise his concerns over: first, the panel's being disbanded immediately after the release of the report, precluding opportunities for Albertans to communicate their reaction to decision-makers; second, the apparently one-sided, closed-door access that industry had to government after the release of the report; and finally, the lack of an opportunity for the panel to defend its decision. Speaking only for himself, he offered his personal contact information and encouraged Albertans to make their views known to the politicians, the media and the community. Ultimately, the government adopted a lower increase in royalty rates than the panel recommended.[74] Still, the energy sector was displeased, and the government lowered the rates for conventional oil and natural gas in the less heady economic climate of 2010, returning to a regime similar to the one in place before the 2007 review.[75]

Noting that about 40 per cent of the Alberta government's revenues come from oil and gas royalties, the close ties between the energy industry and the ruling provincial Conservative party, and instances of government behaviour that he likened to official actions in Venezuela, Iran, Nigeria and Russia, the Albertan author and journalist, Andrew Nikiforuk, called his home province a poster child for the First Law of Petropolitics, which states that the quality of freedom is inversely proportional to the price of oil.[76]

Perhaps the most notorious example of the provincial government's flexing its muscle to squelch dissent occurred in 2004, when Premier Klein offended the local Chilean community with a reference to a coup in 1973 involving the dictator, Augusto Pinochet, during a debate in the Legislature on public automobile insurance. In response to the ensuing commotion, he tabled in the House an essay that he wrote for a communications class that he was taking by correspondence and invited the opposition and the Chileans to grade the thing. The premier's essay dealt with the Chilean coup and apparently contained passages pulled from the Internet but not cited as references, although he did include online sources in his bibliography—a practice that may technically constitute plagiarism. In that light, reporters questioned his grade of 77 per cent on the essay. Shortly after that, letters to the editor appeared from or on behalf of the presidents of the province's universities, praising the premier's commitment to lifelong learning. The minister of education confirmed that the letters came at his invitation, as he felt that reporters' questioning the academy's integrity was a serious issue. The letters didn't mention the financial pressure on the province's universities or the government's major impact on their purse-strings but the lesson was inescapable: toe the party line or have your next fiscal pedicure administered with a poleaxe.

So Alberta's popular diet of maverick-dom seems to come with a strong side order of sheep dip. On the one hand, as Premier Klein told the Canadian Club in Ottawa, "We're known as a province with a mind of its own. We're used to being branded as renegades, too willing to go our own way. We're used to controversy and we rarely shy away from problems just because they're tough or unpopular."[77] On the other hand, critics call this faux-populism, masking an agenda to protect the province's political and economic elites. Stifling dissent as "un-Albertan" or calling political opponents subversive feeds an apathy at the ballot box and in the public discourse that is already bloated to numbness by a ghoulish goulash of affluence, spiraling costs and user fees, aging and overburdened infrastructure, long waits for health care and other amenities, and the massive inertia that weighs against any kind of change. But Alberta's political leaders are shrewd; they know that Albertans need an outlet and a target for their maverick tendencies and their culture of political dissent. That's why the federal government is so important. Take away Ottawa, and Albertans actually might direct more of their culture of political dissent at the folks under the dome in Edmonton. Of course it's less convenient when an actual Albertan occupies the prime minister's office, but that hasn't happened very often or for very long over the last century. And even when it has, provincial politicians have found some clever reason to demonize the feds, like a depression (in the case of R.B. Bennett), oil pricing (Joe Clark) or emission targets for resource industries (Stephen Harper).

So the bottom line in Alberta, at least on the political front, is that protest is fine as long as it's directed at central Canada, primarily Ottawa, but if necessary, also Toronto, Québec City and, in extreme cases, maybe mid-sized centres like Kitchener-Waterloo. Rather than accept politics as the art of compromise, we draw a line in the tar sand. Mark Lisac suggests that there is pressure to absorb "the Albertan way of thinking," but questions whether it can last. "We are not native sons of the soil and more than half of Albertans now have to be taught," he posits. "The more we draw people here, the more tolerance there will be of their differences."

Bigger and Better

Alberta has been referred to lately as the Texas of Canada. It is a reference chiefly to its bountiful seas of oil. But it is more than that. An Albertan is as proud of his province as a Texan is of his state because, although he is more modest about it, he firmly believes his province has the biggest this and the biggest that and is the greatest in Canada.

—KEN LIDDELL, 1953

As a province that fancies itself as different from the rest, Alberta has done a decent job of convincing others of that. Boosterism ran rampant from the get-go. In the heady days of the settlers' boom before World War I, Premier Arthur Sifton exhorted Albertans to "boost and boost … so that this will be the banner province in the banner colony of the best empire which this world has ever witnessed"[78]—a triple-superlative updated by an Edmonton mayor almost a century later. A former Albertan in Ottawa, Andrew Varjas, comments, "What's quirky about Alberta is just how proud the people are of Alberta." Karman Kawchuk of the University of Saskatchewan notes, "Albertans un-ironically and proudly call themselves 'Albertans' while people in Saskatchewan rarely do the equivalent. Is this simply because of the lack of a euphonious adjective (Saskatchewanians? Saskatchewanites? Saskatchewanistas?) or is there something deeper here?" Let's check on that deeper part. Standing before a tractor that would dwarf Albertosaurus himself, Jack Lewis declares, "If it's Albertan, it's got to be the best, no matter who you are."

Is this credo applied in practice?

In the field of public health, Christine Meikle founded Canada's first government-funded school for the developmentally disabled in 1958; laid the groundwork for provincial and national associations for the neurologically disabled; and guided much of the planning for special education in Canada.

New antibiotics, improved treatments for leukemia and hemo-philia, and drugs to prevent the rejection of transplanted organs all stem from the work of the Albertan chemist, Raymond Lemieux. He was the first to chemically synthesize sucrose and to develop nuclear magnetic resonance spectroscopy, which examines the electromag-netic spectra generated when a substance interacts with energy. He held more than thirty patents, and his studies showing how carbo-hydrates bind to proteins are said to have changed chemistry and medicine forever.[79]

The Edmonton Protocol of islet-cell transplantation was the first medical treatment that enabled diabetics to stop taking insulin for years at a time. It's not a cure, but it could lead to one. Announced in 2000, it has been replicated in at least a dozen other facilities around the world, though the University of Alberta remains the only site in Canada to perform the transplants. A co-developer of the protocol, Dr. James Shapiro, tells me he came to the province from England "because it was a perfect environment for liver transplants and eyelet research. Without question, there is a climate for innovation, research and clinical practice in Alberta that's second to none."

The province was the first in the world to get drug-and-catheter therapy, also developed at the University of Alberta, which promises a dramatic recovery from a stroke by boosting the flow of blood to the brain by slowing the flow to the lower part of the body. Albertans pioneered electronic health records in Canada when they pulled together a province-wide network of existing channels. They also produced a plan to digitize diagnostic medical images and make them available in clinics across the province. The province boasts the first recognized centre of excellence in stereotactic radiosurgery for treating tumours and other problems of the brain. It also hosts what an American group calls one of the best pediatric cardiac surgery programs in North America, as well as the Alberta Heritage Foundation for Medical Research, which claims to provide the richest and longest health research grants in Canada. Health-related aids created in Alberta include an antimicrobial dressing for burns, a sand-filtered system that brings safe drinking water to developing nations, a laser digitizer system to produce prosthetics, and the Canadian Centre for Behavioural Neuroscience at the University of Lethbridge.

From its earliest days, Alberta has trumpeted the cause of education and has followed that up with enough landmarks in that field, along with arts and culture, to merit deferring to a separate chapter.

Alberta can claim some firsts for families and youth, even after notoriously being the last province to adopt the United Nations

Convention on the Rights of the Child. She is the nation's hotbed for the traditional family, with the lowest rate of single-parent homes in Canada. In the 2006 federal census, 73 per cent of Alberta's families were led by married couples, 4 per cent above the national average. One human ecologist suggested that the province's more socially conservative ways could support the greater strength of the nuclear family tradition in Alberta, though continued influxes from the rest of Canada could change that. Households led by unmarried couples make up 13 per cent of the total in Alberta, compared to 16 per cent nationally. And Alberta has the lowest share of young adults living at home, at 32 per cent of adults aged 20–29, compared to 44 per cent nationally—a statistic attributed partly to economic conditions that let young people afford to move out sooner here.[80] Alberta is the country's top producer of babies as well as home to the fastest-growing number of households populated by couples with children.[81] Although this isn't enough to bring the province's fertility rate up to the level at which the number of births equals the number of deaths, Alberta remains the most youthful province in an aging nation. Our median age of 36 is the lowest among the provinces in almost four decades, almost 4 per cent below the national average. Only 10 per cent of Alberta's population is over the age of 65, again, almost 4 per cent below the rest of Canada.[82] The crossover point at which more people are approaching retirement age than are working age is expected nationally before 2017, but not in Alberta until perhaps 2027.

In the area of protecting children, Edmonton's Zebra Child Protection Centre is Canada's only multidisciplinary team of child-protection experts, with police, social workers, Crown prosecutors, child advocates and volunteers working together under one roof. Apparently, Alberta has the only known adoption law in the Western world that lets adoptive families apply for an order preventing biological parents or adoptees from seeing the adoptee's file. This veto, only possible on adoptions before 2005, was so unique that a respected adoption researcher from Ontario called it bizarre.[83] And Alberta became the first authority in the world to protect children involved in prostitution with measures treating them as victims of sexual abuse (rather than as having made a lifestyle choice), including involuntary detention when their safety is at risk.[84] Yet Alberta has recorded the highest rate of domestic violence in Canada.

Although it's unlikely that any jurisdiction can claim a lily-white record in Aboriginal affairs, a few notable events on that front occurred in Alberta. Here are some.

After Alex Decoteau's family moved to Edmonton, he became the first Aboriginal cop in Canada in 1911, on the way to two European adventures, the 1912 Olympics in Stockholm as a sprinter and a more lethal run as a soldier at Passchendaele in 1917.

Besides being home for the most Métis in Canada—almost a quarter of the national total—Alberta claims an unrivalled landmark in the recognition of their rights. While the Métis' Aboriginal rights were affirmed under the *Constitution Act, 1982*—rights that traditionally require extensive visits to a courthouse to figure out—only the Alberta government saw fit to provide for Métis people, and that happened almost a half-century earlier. (A formative effort came in 1896 in the wake of the Riel Rebellion, when Père Albert Lacombe tried to start a farming colony. It ran aground.) In 1938, when many Métis were impoverished and starving, in response to grassroots work by the Métis Association of Alberta, the government moved to set aside twelve tracts of land in north-central Alberta as farming settlements. Unfortunately, much of that land was unfit for that. But in 1990, after years of extensive visits to the courthouse over whether that land grant included mineral rights, the Alberta Federation of Métis Settlements and the Government of Alberta signed an agreement that led to the constitutional entrenchment of the grant of 1.25 million acres (5,058 square kilometres) of settlement lands to the Métis Settlements General Council; the first and only Métis government in the country; and $310 million over 17 years. Only about 7 per cent of Alberta's 67,000 Métis live on that land. All of this remains unique.

"The fact that 'redneck' Alberta provided this kind of leadership often surprises the rest of Canada," wrote Fred Martin, a Métis lawyer. "How did it happen? The short answer is common sense and courage," he asserted. "Alberta has been different."[85]

Aboriginal Albertans are no strangers to the culture of dissent in the province. Although forming political organizations was strictly verboten under the federal *Indian Act*, Crees and Stoneys in Alberta started one in 1933. In the 1950s, the Indian Association of Alberta led the legal battle to keep 122 members of the Samson band on the Hobbema reserve in their homes after the federal government cancelled their Indian status on the basis of either illegitimacy or their ancestors' abandoning their Aboriginal rights by accepting scrip. This court ruling protected the rights of Aboriginals across Canada.

Two distinguished Albertans became pioneering members of the Canadian Senate: James Gladstone as its first Status Indian in 1958 (two years before Status Indians won the right to vote, which he supported) and Thelma Chalifoux as its first Aboriginal female in 1997. Another Albertan, Ralph Steinhauer, became the country's first Aboriginal lieutenant-governor in 1974. His brother, Eugene Steinhauer, was a pioneering broadcaster and an important advocate for Aboriginal rights. Victor Buffalo led the creation of Canada's first Aboriginal-owned financial institution in 1981, Peace Hills Trust, which in its first quarter-century, grew to eight branches and $400 million in assets while supporting scores of Aboriginal businesses across Canada.[86]

Albertans have certainly made their mark on the country's legal annals. They tried to get rid of party politics, both provincially and federally; pushed to create their own monetary system; challenged locally controversial federal legislation in court; and advocated for reforms to the Senate. Two legal experts, Richard Connors and John Law, wrote that Albertans "arguably have done as much or more to reconfigure the Canadian constitution in the last century than any other jurisdiction except Quebec."[87]

Famously, the so-called Persons Case, launched by five eminent Albertan women—Emily Murphy, Louise McKinney, Irene Parlby, Nellie McClung and Henrietta Muir Edwards—in 1929, set a powerful symbolic precedent in declaring women were actually "persons" in the eyes of the law and more specifically, capable of serving on the Canadian Senate. The case is also remembered fondly by lawyers for articulating a liberal interpretation of the Constitution as a "living tree" that must be read as changing with the times rather than frozen in time with the original intent of the legislators who produced it.[88] What is less celebrated is that Alberta's highest court said essentially the same thing about women being persons back in 1917, when some male lawyer challenged the right of the presiding magistrate (Emily Murphy, again), to hold judicial office, and he lost when the court declared women persons capable of holding judicial office.[89] (That was also the year that the province passed the first minimum-wage law for women.)

After quickly following Manitoba and Saskatchewan as the first to give women the vote provincially—well, some women, anyway, as some minorities and Aboriginals were excluded until years later—Alberta produced the first female cop in Canada (Annie May Jackson, 1912), the first female alderman in the British Empire (Annie Gale, 1917, who also acted as mayor, another imperial first), the first female judge (Alice Jamieson, 1914) and the first female magistrate (Emily Murphy, 1916). Albertans claim the first two females elected to a legislature (Louise McKinney and Roberta MacAdams Price, 1917) and the second female cabinet minister in the British Empire (Irene Parlby, in 1921, just five months after the first in neighbouring British Columbia). Alberta also has bragging rights to Canada's first black female lawyer (Violet King Henry, 1954), the first female big-city police chief in Canada (Christine Silverberg, 1995), the first female chief justice of Canada (Beverly McLachlin, 2000, though she was appointed from BC) and the first top-level court in which women made up the

The inventor of basketball called the Edmonton Grads (winning 526 and losing 22 against top international and even male competition from 1915–1940) the finest team ever to take the floor. [Provincial Archives of Alberta, A.11, 435]

majority (the Alberta Court of Appeal, eight of fourteen judges of which were women in 2006).

Why all these firsts for women, especially in the early twentieth century? Part of the answer might be that the chauvinism in more established areas did not travel well to the frontier, where women had to work just as hard as men and usually in concert with them simply to survive. Yet Alberta has recorded the country's highest reported incidents of domestic violence and stalking women.[90]

On the human rights front, the *Alberta Bill of Rights Act* of 1946 was at the crest of the country's wave of human rights legislation after

World War II. It set out the province's duty to protect property and civil rights, and it guaranteed fundamental freedoms such as speech, conscience and religion along with Albertans' right to either gainful employment or the necessities of life, educational benefits, medical benefits *and* a social security pension.[91] This went further than the landmark human rights legislation passed in Saskatchewan that year. Unfortunately, it was bundled together with Premier Manning's final attempt to implement the financial system of social credit as the way to fund his proposed social safety net. Because this got the entire legislation struck down by the British Privy Council (then Canada's highest court of appeal) on constitutional grounds, and because of an earlier but no less impressive glut of human rights abuses by the same Social Credit government, Alberta's bid for greatness in Canada's first wave of human rights has been consigned to the undertow of history.

The province led the pack in appointing North America's first ombudsman in 1967. A Swedish concept, an ombudsman independently investigates complaints by the public against the government or other outfit that appoints him or her.

Alberta was a strong advocate for provincial rights and equality of the provinces in the federal-provincial negotiations leading up to the repatriation of the Canadian Constitution in 1982. Alberta was the prime mover behind the constitutional amending formula and the constitutional amendment won by Premier Lougheed on resource development and taxation, the latter received in exchange for accepting Prime Minister Trudeau's Charter of Rights and Freedoms. These achievements were, as the historian, Michael Behiels, put it, "neither significantly understood nor appreciated by most Albertans or Canadians."[92]

On the administrative side, Alberta was the first to introduce mandatory business plans across government, outlaw deficits and eliminate its accumulated debt, all under Premier Klein. (As to debt, some believe that revenue from a finite asset like natural resources should not be considered as income any more than liquidated stocks or bonds; in this light, Roger Smith, a business professor emeritus, examined a total of $26.4 billion in actual and forecasted provincial net surpluses reported between 2000–2012 and saw *an accumulated debt of $87 billion*. Yet Alberta's debt-fighting legend lives on like the Marlboro Man. Any way you slice it, the government returned to deficits in 2009.[93]) Another notable precedent established by Ralph was becoming the first known political leader to attribute climate change to dinosaur flatulence—a startling, if tongue-in-cheek, comment from a man not known to put on airs.

In the civic bailiwick, Alberta was the first to give municipalities the powers of a natural person (in 1994), providing the freedom to do whatever you or I could do without requiring express statutory authority. The province performed a pioneering amalgamation of Fort McMurray and other municipalities to create Wood Buffalo, the country's largest municipality in terms of land area, not to mention mainland Newfoundlanders. In 1907 Edmonton became the first burg in Canada to adopt the idea of community-based organization, borrowing from the Social Centre movement for urban grass-roots democracy originating in the US in that era. The Edmonton Federation of Community Leagues, formed in 1921, is apparently the largest volunteer recreation organization in North America, representing 150 community leagues. The capital city was also the first in Canada to assess property tax based on the land's market value, a milestone less appreciated by homeowners during the boom part of the province's economic cycles. In place before World War I, this system aimed to prevent speculators who failed to improve their land from profiting at the expense of those who did.

Alberta's love affair with capital projects began in her early days, when more than half of the government's first budget was spent on public works.[94] The early demand for telephones was phenomenal, and citizens revolted against Bell Telephone, effectively a monopoly that the province's public works minister called "the most pernicious and iniquitous...ever perpetrated upon any people that have any claim to freedom."[95] So the Rutherford administration took it over in 1907, creating the first provincially owned telephone network in Canada and borrowing $2 million to expand it to rural areas. Two other early landmarks, both in the south of the province, are the High Level Bridge in Lethbridge, completed in 1909 over 11 months for $1.3 million, stretching 1.6 kilometres long and 96 metres high across the Oldman River valley and comprising the highest and longest steel railway bridge in the world;[96] and the Bassano Dam at Brooks, finished in 1914, "unique for its composite character, great length, and depth of water which would flow over the crest during flood periods," and now serving an irrigation district of 6 million hectares.[97] Even our prisoner-of-war camps were built on a grand scale: the facilities at Ozada, Lethbridge and Medicine Hat were the largest in Canada.[98]

This insatiable appetite for infrastructure continues to this day. For example, public spending on capital projects jumped by 22 per cent in 2008–2009 to a record $8.7 billion, or almost $2,500 for each Albertan, more than three times the average of the other provinces.[99]

In addition to the distinctive, radical and groundbreaking curvilinear work of Douglas Cardinal, another architectural wonder in Alberta is the Plus-15 pedway system in downtown Calgary. Designed by a native son, Harold Hanen, its 57 bridges, sprawling at about 5 metres (or 15 feet, hence the name) above ground over a walking distance of 16 kilometres, make the Plus-15 the most extensive elevated pedestrian system in the world. This marvy maze was the setting of a Canadian cult film, *waydowntown*, in which a clutch of yuppies bet a month's salary on who can remain in the system the longest. Linked to the Plus-15, the Husky (now Calgary) Tower was the tallest structure on the continent when it opened in 1968.[100]

Speaking of great connectors, the Alberta SuperNet is a fibre-optic broadband network linking 4,200 health facilities, schools and government offices in 429 communities. This can bring high-speed access to cyberspace to almost 90 per cent of Albertans, making Alberta pretty much the leader with this network, breaking new ground with the broad range of communities and geographic area served, especially in the social and economic development of remote places.[101] Albertans were the second-highest users of the Internet at 77 per cent (1 per cent behind BC) in 2007, though only 71 per cent reported broadband capability at home, which ranked second-last among the provinces.[102] And Albertans were the country's largest users of cellular telephones at 84 per cent in 2007 (12 per cent above the average), with a distantly nation-trailing 14 per cent using only a landline.[103]

In the broader field of science and technology, Alberta stands out for creating the first provincial research organization in Canada in 1921. From its original mandate to documenting the province's mineral and natural resources for the nascent local energy industry, the Alberta Research Council (ARC) has grown to an applied R&D corporation that serves almost 1,000 customers and partners around the world in the energy, life sciences, agriculture, environment, forestry and manufacturing sectors. Alberta has played a major role in developing new technologies for tapping the oil sands, turning aspen into value-added wood products, changing the paradigm in oil and gas production and even producing video games. While citing its successes, the ARC's CEO, John McDougall, feels that the system of innovation in Alberta has become fragmented, overlapping and competitive. But even if the system isn't perfect (and what is, really, besides the view of the Bow Valley from the terrace of the Banff Springs Hotel?), Alberta has given the world inventions like the flat-screen monitor, the JAVA language for computer programming, the SMART board for presentations, three-dimensional recording technology, computer games like *Baldur's Gate* and *Jade Empire*, and the peak limiter to modulate radio frequencies. (The latter was developed for the pioneering public broadcaster, CKUA Radio.) On a smaller note, the National Institute for Nanotechnology at the University of Alberta boasts one of the world's most technologically advanced research facilities.

As proof that being at the forefront does not always require novelty—and that everything old is new again—the province is a peerless place for dinosaur-seekers. Beyond the largest known dinosaur field, Alberta hosts the Royal Tyrrell Museum, Canada's only facility devoted exclusively to paleontology, one of the world's best of its kind and a Mecca for tweed-jacketed academics, adventurers, children and all combinations thereof. Nestled in the arid, eerie badlands, the facility offers not only first-hand adventures, but 120 virtual programs used by more than 3,500 students across Canada, the US and beyond. Dr. Don Brinkman, the museum's senior curator, highlights the province's pioneering paleontological work in trying to understand the animals' behaviour and communities, how they interacted and how they changed over time, and the effect of climate change on cretaceous vertebrates and on the ecology of animals and how they lived. "These kinds of questions were not seen as rigorous science, but thanks to Alberta's palaeo work in scenario-building, beginning in the early 1980s, this work is accepted," he says. Dr. Philip Currie adds, "It still irks me that the American Museum of Natural History in New York City has the best collection of Alberta dinosaurs for public display. But we have stronger backroom research."

Alberta is also a hotbed of work in a field that challenges the theory of evolution, which prevails at the Royal Tyrrell Museum and other venues. The village of Big Valley (population 351 in 2007), east of Red Deer, harbours a tidy bungalow with a dinosaur greeting visitors from an awning. Inside is Canada's first permanent museum devoted to creation science, premised on the belief that humans and dinosaurs coexisted when God created the world 10,000 years ago. As the museum's founder, Harry Nibourg, tells me, "Presenting the creation side of the origin debate can be a hot topic in coffee rooms." (Apparently, surveys indicated that the creation scientists' view is supported by more than half of the American population.) The displays at Big Valley cover geology, fossils, dinosaurs, DNA, dating methods, the genealogy of Queen Elizabeth II back to Adam and Eve, and an explanation of how fossilization can be faked. Mr. Nibourg's goal is to have creation science taught alongside what he calls "the lie of evolution" in schools. Visitors from around the world have signed his guestbook.

The world has benefitted greatly from inventions emanating from Wild Rose Country.

In the area of agriculture and food, Albertans have produced advancements such as an automated stoker; a frost-free nose-pump for water; a grain dryer; the Bradshaw Bale Booster to pick up, load and stack hay; a hoe-rake; the top-ranked Lacombe breed of swine; the mighty Noble Blade to knock out weeds without disturbing stubble; Radium Laying Mash, a healthy feed for chickens; and a system to convert manure to methane and bio-fertilizer. On the food side comes stuff like birch syrup, nut-free "peanut" butter, omega-3 bread, synthetic sugar, the Caesar cocktail and, for the canine crowd, frozen, biologically appropriate raw food, the acronym of which (BARF) reminds us that Albertans are not always as earnest as their longest-serving premier. On the gastronomic frontier, Culinary Team Alberta has won multiple world championships in its twenty-five-year career, and the team from the Northern Alberta Institute of Technology brought home five medals from the venerable Culinary Olympics in 2008.

Unsurprisingly, as a powerhouse of energy in every sense of the word, Alberta has been fertile ground for developments in the production, transportation and refining of coal, oil and gas. Examples are a system of transporting coal through pipelines, three-dimensional visualization for oil and gas extraction, the Smokey truck for fighting oil well fires, self-contained mobile drilling rigs, a device to direct and catch uncontrolled high-pressure drilling fluid, and steam-assisted gravity drainage to extract bitumen from oil sands.

Which brings us to the smokestack set and the world's largest industrial development, the tar sands in Fort McMurray. The annual production of oil from this resource has surpassed 1 million barrels per day and could well triple from 2006 levels by 2020 and even exceed 5 million barrels by 2030.[104] Further clever industrial contributions

The real Alberta for many of us: cities and shopping malls (especially the shopping malls), crowned by the mighty West Edmonton monolith. [Geo Takach]

include self-packaging portable housing structures (the ATCO trailer), ceramic brick, the detection of leaks in underground storage vessels and the recovery of silver from spent photographic solution.

On the leisure side come aids like the S-shaped compact-disc rack, a rubber curling hack and a system of analyzing motion for walkers, hikers and runners. As for consumer goods, Albertans have given the world forward steps like improvements to the water heater, furnace and thermostat, along with a hygienic mug and a bear-proof garbage bin.

In fact, consumerism in the province enjoys a status normally reserved for religion, harvest time and hockey. Albertans are the biggest shoppers per capita in Canada, consistently and by far. For example, Alberta's compounded annual growth in retail sales from

2000–2004 exceeded 8 per cent, more than 2 per cent above silver-medalist Manitoba and towering over the national average of fewer than 5 per cent.[105] In December 2006, we spent $1,113 per capita in retail stores, well above the national average of $874 for that month.[106] West Edmonton Mall gained fame as the world's largest shopping and entertainment complex, covering an area the size of forty-eight city blocks. Alas, the self-styled "eighth wonder of the world" has since lost the title to places like Beijing (the Great Mall of China?). Still, the province claims two of the country's top three so-called "power-shopping" Meccas (the second-largest is in Toronto)—as if spending cash is a talisman of strength, wisdom, respect, influence and heightened humanity.

Statistics like these are handily attributable to the province's wealth, primarily around the energy biz. Armchair social psychologists might speculate that this relatively nouveau-riche binge is compensating for the decades of hardship endured by homesteaders while living with alternating onslaughts of mosquitoes and minus-40, in frozen, leaky, sod huts and dirt.

Work has always been paramount in the province, and the lore of Albertans as roll-up-your-sleeves types is actually supported by statistics. For instance, in 2005, the province logged the lowest unemployment and the highest economic productivity, producing $40.34 in real gross domestic product (GDP) per hour worked, more than $3 above the national average.[107] Albertans also earned the highest after-tax incomes at $73,200, with the Canadian average at $64,800.[108] Of course, all of that entrepreneurship must play out on the bigger stage of the global economy, which includes not only free-market activity but its opposite, government intervention. As the commentator, Bill Longstaff, wrote, "Albertans should genuflect in gratitude to Muammar al-Qadhafi, catalyst of the shift in power from the cartel of oil companies to the cartel of oil countries, or perhaps to Sheik Yamani of Saudi Arabia, prime mover behind OPEC's 1973 machinations. These men, not Peter Lougheed or Ralph Klein, nor the CEOs of the oil companies, were the architects of Alberta's affluence."[109] Being the country's energy capital helps, of course, but there is an ethic that goes with it. You still need the wherewithal to put those resources to work. (More on the consequences of that later.)

Albertans work more than people in any other province (1,845 hours in 2007, half a dozen forty-hour weeks longer than the national average)[110] and record the most unused vacation days on average (2.81, just ahead of Saskatchewan and Manitoba).[111] Among full-time paid workers, Albertans lost less time due to illness or disability, at 6.2 days a year per worker from 1997–2007, a day below the national average; whether this means we're healthier or just too lazy to call in sick is unclear.[112] Albertans were the most mobile workers in Canada south of the territories according to the last census, with almost 9 per cent of the labour force having lived in another province or territory from 2001–2006, compared to a national figure of just 3.4 per cent.[113]

Perhaps part of all that energy comes from youth. Mark Breslin, who consolidated the administrative offices of his Yuk Yuk's comedy-club empire to Alberta—observes, "When I go to Alberta I'm very aware, it seems to me visiting the big cities like Edmonton and Calgary, how young everybody is. Very youthful. In fact, I understand that many of the people on both city councils are under twelve. And that's unheard of anywhere else in the country. But that's because Albertans are not afraid of new ideas. And I think that's great."

The territories boast Canada's youngest populations, but among the provinces, Albertans recorded the lowest median age, with almost 20 per cent of us under age 15 (0.2 per cent behind Manitoba) and the lowest share over 65 (just over 10 per cent).[114] On the other hand, Alberta has recorded notably high mortality rates for infants in the late 1990s and early 2000s, and consistently higher incidents of low birth weights and pre-term births from 1979–2004.[115] Still, Alberta maintained the highest birth rate among the provinces, averaging almost 13 per 1,000 people from 2002–2007, exceeding the national average of 10.6.[116] Albertans' life expectancy was higher than the national average for males (77.4 to 77.2), but lower for females (82.0 to 82.3) in 2004;[117] the Alberta government expressed concern about the disparity between people in lower and higher income groups, which is six years for men and two years for women. Albertans are more physically active than the national average (at almost 56 per cent, 4 per cent higher), though they have similar rates of obesity, with 42 per cent of men and 26 per cent of women overweight.[118] Finally, Albertans enjoyed the lowest death rate among the provinces from 2002–2007 at just below 6 per 1,000 population, with the national average at 7.2.[119]

Like many other numbers cited here, these may seem like minor statistical deviations to amateur number-crunchers, but they could support arguments for Alberta as a place that is at least a bit different from the rest.

One might be tempted to believe from her steady swirling of money and people that Alberta is the grand central station for vice in Canada. If you would have bet that swaggering Albertans smoke and drink more than any other Canadians, as one Albertan did in a street interview, then you might be out some money. The province's rate of smokers ranked third at 21 per cent, behind Saskatchewan (25 per cent) and Newfoundland (22 per cent) with BC trailing the pack (15 per cent).[120] Albertans came in seventh in per-capita alcohol-guzzling ($616 in 2004), a few ounces below the national average ($624) and only beating the latter in the realm of spirits.[121] But there is one area in which Albertans do lead the pack, and it's more likely to contain a jack of hearts than something unfiltered or triple-menthol. Albertans spent $890 per capita on gambling, or 70 per cent more than the $524 anted up by your average Canuck in 2007.[122] This doesn't mean that they are more addicted but they do have more money to spend, with the highest disposable income in Canada. Alberta's gaming profits were the highest in Canada by far in 2004.[123] This culture of risk-taking might explain why the provincial government spends more money on horse racing than on arts and culture in the province. Or it might not. In any case, Alberta's love for a good wager struck Mark Breslin in Toronto:

*Well I've noticed a couple of things about Alberta, cultural things
that are different. For instance, I've never seen so many video lottery
terminals in my life—everywhere, video lottery terminals. And
in places where you'd never think there would be these kinds of
machines. I went to the bathroom. I was about to urinate, and I saw
a video lottery terminal right in front of me so I could play it while I
urinated. That's unique. On a bus. In the maternity ward, a friend of
mine, the woman was giving birth and playing the lottery terminal at
the same time. And I thought, "That's so entrepreneurial.
That's so Alberta."*

As far as more grievous vices go, in 2007, Alberta finished fourth
among the provinces in per-capita crimes (the other Western provinces taking the top spots) with about 9,000 per 100,000 population
(the national average being about 7,000), and Edmonton and Calgary
ranking second and fourth among large cities, well ahead of Montréal
and Toronto.[124]

Whether by design or not, Alberta has taken the bigger-and-better
ethos to mammoth proportions by accumulating an astonishing array
of roadside attractions. Seated in his favourite chair in his office in the
Legislature, then Lieutenant-Governor Norman Kwong, notes, "The
only thing I find a little bit quirky are such things like the big monuments we have: the giant Easter egg in Vegreville, the dinosaurs in
Calgary and Drumheller, and the landing pad for UFOs, which I don't
think they've made use of yet, but it's there in case anybody wants to
use it." Indeed, the landscape is littered with not just big, but colossal
effigies of the oddest objects. A cowboy in Airdrie. A blue heron in
Barrhead. A milk bottle and a beer can in Edmonton. A baseball glove
in Heisler. A slingshot in Hughenden. A man made out of tires in
Grassland. A walleye in Lesser Slave Lake. A mosquito in Rainbow
Lake. A bicycle in Taber. A lapel pin in Willingdon.

Then come the world's largests. There's the trio mentioned by His
Honour: the pysanka (a decorative Ukrainian egg) in Vegreville, the

thirty-metre tall and forty-six-metre long dinosaur in the badlands and the world's first and only Martian welcome mat in St. Paul. But wait, there's more! A massive mallard duck in Andrew! A leviathan lamp in Donalda! A Promethean pyrohy—a doughy, filled dumpling of Ukrainian parentage—in Glendon! A sensational sausage-pair in Mundare! Monstrous mushrooms in Vilna! A Bunyan-esque badminton racquet in St. Albert! A gargantuan golf putter in Bow Island! A titanic tipi in Medicine Hat! A Brobdingnagian beaver in Beaverlodge! A horse-choking chuckwagon in Dewberry! An overgrown oil derrick in Redwater! A whopping wagon wheel in Fort Assiniboine! A behemoth of a bee in Falher! A soaring sundial in Lloydminster, Canada's only bi-provincial city! (Naturally, the world's-largest item is on the Alberta side.) A super-sized starship *Enterprise* from the *Star Trek* television series, which boldly sits where no five tons of solid concrete have sat before, in Vulcan, Alberta! One whale of a tractor weathervane in Westlock! A noticeably *non*-petite piggy bank in Coleman! And a quintessentially colossal cowboy boot in Edmonton!

If people don't get a large kick out of all this, they can at least ponder the burning question, *why?* Large attractions crop up all over the continent but perhaps not in such high density as in Alberta, where they seem a little more in context.

The Quintessential Albertan

As a place that's larger than life in many ways, Alberta has enjoyed her share of larger-than-life people, none more so than John Walter Grant MacEwan, who stood six-foot-four and is widely considered to be the greatest figure in the province's first century.

Like many Albertans, Grant MacEwan came from somewhere else. Born to pioneers on a farm north of Brandon, Manitoba, in 1902, he moved to Saskatchewan as a teenager and later graduated from Ontario Agricultural College and Iowa State University. While gracing

The quintessential Albertan, Grant MacEwan, on parade as lieutenant-governor in 1973. [Glenbow Archives, NA-2864-23347]

senior offices at the University of Saskatchewan and the University of Manitoba, he became renowned for teaching, judging livestock, writing and radio broadcasting. Coming to Calgary in 1951, he spent a dozen years on city council (three as mayor), then four years as a Liberal MLA and eight years as lieutenant-governor. He lightened the traditional stiffness of the latter office with folksy warmth and wit. He kept a punishing schedule that took him across the province continuously, averaging more than one official function per calendar day. Starting in his mid-forties, he became the author of more than fifty books focused mainly on popular Western Canadian history and on conservation, reflecting his crusades to link Canadians to their cultural and natural heritage. He was a tireless, beloved and profoundly influential figure until his passing at age ninety-seven in 2000, and his avalanche of contributions, achievements and honours is matched by the admiration and affection of the citizens that he served. In 2005 *Alberta Venture* magazine named him the outstanding Albertan of the century.[125]

Like thousands of Albertans, my first connection with this great man came through a tree. To the hordes dashing past it every day, this one is like any other, rising from suburban schoolyard grass even as a good chunk of its vicinity was paved over in the interests of more parking for teachers. This hardy elm, with three main branches sprouting from its slate, peeling trunk, now dwarfs the elementary school over which it watches.

As one witness recalls it, there was little hullabaloo on a sunny autumn day in 1967 when she was ushered out of her grade-two classroom along with everyone else to the front lawn to watch a tall, thin man brandishing a shovel and an elm shorter than he, one of thousands of centennial trees planted across Canada that year. But that seven-year-old girl had a strong sense of the moment because the man who was planting the tree was important. He had a fancy title—lieutenant-governor—and he was accompanied by bagpipes. But more than that, his name lined the spine of several volumes along the shelves in her family room. Except for a four-year hiatus, that girl saw that tree almost every day for the next four decades. I met the girl and the elm in 1977, heard the story of its planting, sensibly hung around and moved into the neighbourhood ten years later and saw that elm pretty much every day for almost two decades.

The tree took on further personal meaning in 1989 when I guest-taught the first of many classes at the college (now university) named for the man who planted it and caught the "MacEwan spirit," an energetic expression of lifelong learning and public service. In 2000, shortly before signing on to teach in the nascent professional writing program there, I was at a board meeting of the Writers Guild of Alberta when a colleague tabled a shortlist of potential recipients of the organization's highest honour, the Golden Pen Award for lifetime achievement. There had only been one award granted in the guild's first twenty years, to W.O. Mitchell. As we listened to the names of wonderful writers worthy of the prize, David Huggett took the floor in his direct way. Overriding the names on the list, he declared that we should recognize Dr. MacEwan, whose contributions through public service, education and conservation overshadowed his no less mighty literary output. I seconded the motion, adding that we should act quickly, while he was still with us.

A few months later, at the Alberta Literary Awards in Calgary, Dr. MacEwan arrived to accept his Golden Pen Award. He was in a motorized chair, due not to his ninety-seven years but to a nasty fall he had suffered. His eyes sparkled with the energy of two lifetimes. He wore a headset so he could hear Don Trembath introduce him, and he spoke at full volume to compensate for his own well-worn hearing. At his first words—"I'm going to stand"—a roomful of eyes welled as he hauled himself up by the handles of his chair. Shouting in a quavering voice, he spoke warmly and humbly of his life and his work, starting with his first publication (a short story that he pitched about his pet dog; the dog died, but he wrote and submitted the piece anyway), including an appeal to less-published writers that the best books remain to be written and read, and closing with a haunting "Thank you for remembering an old man." The applause was so thunderous that even he must have heard it. It was his last public appearance—though I expect that he would correct that by citing his state funeral.

Dr. MacEwan passed away just five weeks later. Of his abundant honours, only a handful appeared in the commemorative program at his memorial service; his Golden Pen Award was one of them. Regrettably, David Huggett, the poet who led the charge to bestow it, is also no longer with us. But that elm remains, along with many other legacies that Dr. MacEwan planted, literally, figuratively and formidably in almost a century on Earth, half of it in Alberta. His books still line our shelves, his causes are as vital as ever and his creed is as close to gospel truth as any carbon-based life form can prescribe.[126]

I still find the finest tribute to Grant MacEwan in that little elm, which I've watched grow for over three decades now. When I pedal past the old neighbourhood these days, I find his simple gift standing twelve metres tall and reaching for the sky.

MacEwan Creed

I believe instinctively in a God for whom I am prepared to search.

I believe it is an offence against the God of Nature for me to accept any hand-me-down, man-defined religion or creed without the test of reason. I believe no man dead or alive knows more about God than I can know by searching.

I believe that the God of Nature must be without prejudice, with exactly the same concern for all His children, and that the human invokes no more, no less of fatherly love than the beaver or sparrow.

I believe I am an integral part of the environment and, as a good subject, I must establish an enduring relationship with my surroundings. My dependence upon the land is fundamental.

I believe destructive waste and greedy exploitation are sins.

I believe the biggest challenge is in being a helper rather than a destroyer of the treasures in Nature's storehouse, a conserver, a husbandman and partner in caring for the Vineyard.

I accept, with apologies to Albert Schweitzer, "a Reverence for Life" and all that is of the Great Spirit's creation.

I believe morality is not complete until the individual holds all of the Great Spirit's creatures in brotherhood and has compassion for all. A fundamental concept of Good consists of working to preserve all creatures with feeling and the will to live.

I am prepared to stand before my Maker, the Ruler of the entire Universe, with no other plea than that I have tried to leave things in His Vineyard better than I found them.

—DR. J.W. GRANT MACEWAN, 1969
Reproduced with the kind permission of Heather MacEwan-Foran

Alberta Personified
Interview with Heather MacEwan-Foran and Max Foran

In seeking to understand more about Grant MacEwan as the quintessential Albertan, we are joined by his daughter, Heather MacEwan-Foran, and son-in-law, Max Foran, over dinner at a hearty Hungarian eatery in Calgary. The only child of Phyllis and Grant MacEwan, Heather shares her father's passion on environmental issues, while Max is a historian and professor at the University of Calgary, and a best-selling novelist to boot.

✳ *How did your dad feel about his adopted province?*

HEATHER: Oh, he absolutely loved Alberta. He wanted to come here as long as I can remember, even when I was a kid in

Winnipeg. He bought the land where Max and I now live before I was born. So he wanted a piece of Alberta, always. He was the personification of the Albertan.

* *How do you feel that he personified Alberta?*

HEATHER: Well, first of all, the look of him. He was tall and lanky and wore a Stetson or a big hat much of the time and just *looked* like the personification of the Westerner. He had a Western face. Also, his whole demeanour: he was very casual, very friendly. He spoke to everybody. No one was any more important than anyone else. At least before, Albertans prided themselves on being very friendly and welcoming. I don't know about now.

MAX: You've got to remember, he was foremost a livestock judge and he found probably the best opportunity to judge high-grade horses and cattle in Alberta. A lot of the horse-breeders and cattle-breeders, people who he got to know, and the agribusiness and livestock husbandry he was interested in as a university professor, were here in Alberta.

HEATHER: He absolutely loved the animals, the birds, the vegetation and everything in the foothills.

MAX: It's one of these classic Western stories about Westerners moving west until they come up to Rockies and realize they've found the best.

* *Do you have any favourite stories about your dad?*

HEATHER: When Father was mayor of Calgary, I used to walk down the street with him and every couple of feet somebody would accost Father, talk to him and act like he was a very best friend. And he would be the same; he would be nice to them all. I liked watching this because it didn't matter whether it was the street cleaner or the policeman or some big businessman or a bag lady. Whoever it was, he would stop and spend equal time with that person. He truly didn't believe that anybody was any more important than anybody else, and it was a real revelation to walk down the street with him and just see the people who treated him as a friend. A real buddy.

MAX: I remember in 1972, in January, I was going from Edmonton back to Calgary, and he saw me to the train station. I looked out the window as the train was leaving. It was about 25-below, cold and windy, and he's got his jacket wide open, his hands in his pockets and he's throwing his head back, roaring with laughter at some joke along with three CPR porters. You'd think he would be so fast off of that platform to get into the warm car but no, that was the man.

HEATHER: Yeah, that personified him.

MAX: My favourite story about Grant is when he was just appointed lieutenant-governor. It was just made public. He was dressed in his usual, very—

HEATHER: Casual. *Very* casual.

MAX: —very casual attire. He wandered into a secondhand bookstore in Edmonton. The proprietor looked at him inquisitively and finally said, "Damn it if you don't look like the new lieutenant-governor." And Grant said, "What would you say if I told you I *was*?" And the proprietor said, "I'd say you were a damn liar!"

HEATHER: I love that story, too.

MAX: I think he's also personified in his writing. A lot of it was set in Alberta. And of course, he wrote that column for the *Calgary Herald* every week for thirty years or some ridiculous amount of time without ever missing a column.

HEATHER: That's a wonderful repository of his writing, his thoughts and his philosophy. In some of these columns, years ahead of his time.

MAX: He told me the issue of the twenty-first century would be water. He told me this in the 1960s when no one else was talking about it.

HEATHER: People thought he was crazy. But he was quite prophetic on some of these things.

✳ *What do you think he would make of Alberta's direction today?*

MAX: He'd be very upset. He'd be absolutely appalled about the environment, at the accelerated resource rape of this land.

HEATHER: Yeah, he would. Not just Alberta, but Canada.

MAX: He would think that what happened last night with all the five hundred ducks killed up in Fort McMurray—[*on landing in an unguarded tar sands tailings pond; the number of ducks has since been revealed to be 1,606*]

HEATHER: He'd be just horrified, absolutely horrified.

MAX: He always believed that you can't spend the wealth of your heritage, the wealth of your children.

HEATHER: And what they're doing to the wolves in Alberta, he'd be just horrified at that sort of thing. He wouldn't like the sort of money that's being thrown around here, either.

✳ *What advice do you think he'd have for Albertans?*

MAX: He had simplistic solutions, probably the best ones. He would just say, "Cut back." He would be prepared to lower the standard of living if wealth could be spent more frugally and saved.

HEATHER: He was an enigma. He had these totally paradoxical viewpoints.

✳ *For example?*

MAX: He had a million acquaintances and no close personal friends.

HEATHER: His reverence for the past and yet thinking as a futurist.

MAX: The other one that is equally important: he was a great believer in the initiative, drive and responsibility of the individual. So he was very much an individualist. But on the other hand, he exalted and really liked institutions. He saw them as guardians of the way to do things.

HEATHER: People don't realize that about him. People who wrote about him missed the coin a lot of the time.

MAX: A very, very complex figure.

✳ *Much like Alberta, complex in so many ways and contrary to the image other Canadians have.*

MAX: That's a very good analogy. With Grant, in many ways what you see is what you get. But in many ways what you saw is not what you got.

HEATHER: That's right, absolutely.

✳ *What else stands out about your dad?*

MAX: His enormous ability to laugh. He had this roaring laugh. You couldn't help but laugh yourself. This booming, roaring laugh that would just go on and on.

HEATHER: It's funny because he was such a big guy and yet he loved small things. When he was young, he was six-foot-four. He loved small children and small animals. He was a real presence but he liked little things.

MAX: I helped him over the years to build things.

HEATHER: He liked little houses.

MAX: I'm very hopeless practically and in all my bumbling, I never once discerned in his face or his voice any level of censure, annoyance or impatience. And I used to make error after error.

HEATHER: I was the same. I worked with my dad a lot and I loved working with him. I'm quite good with my hands but I'd make terrible goofs sometimes, too, and he never lost his cool. I knew he was horrified at some of the things I did. Like the time we were building a barn and Father asked me to saw this piece of plywood in half. Of course you never, ever used a power tool; it had to be a hand tool. So I was sawing away with the saw and I thought, "Gee, this is hard. I don't know why this plywood is so hard to get through." All of a sudden I got through the plywood and the whole thing collapsed. He was up on the roof and I said, "Father, I think I sawed the sawhorse in two." He said, "Oh no, you wouldn't have done that. No one saws a sawhorse in two." And I said, "Well, I did. Here are the two pieces." He came by and shook his head. "By thunder," he said, "you did saw the sawhorse in two."

MAX: When he wrote about people, he was interested in what I call gentle knavery. He could appreciate Bob Edwards because of Edwards's humour and he could appreciate the funny little off-centre foibles of people even though he possessed none of those. He was always proper or it wasn't done. Human foibles just weren't part of him.

✳ *Which is why it's wonderful that he was Eye Opener Bob's biographer.*

HEATHER: Yes.

MAX: But you see, he'd write about Edwards, the gentle knave, but he wouldn't write about A.E. Cross because Cross owned a brewery. But Bob Edwards was fine.

HEATHER: And yet even though he was a teetotaller, he wrote this wonderful biography of Bob Edwards, who was definitely not a teetotaller.

MAX: He told me that he was always prepared to ignore the frailties in an individual in the interests of the big picture. And that made a big impression on me. I think he wanted not so much to inspire but to involve and engage people.

HEATHER: Yeah. One story personifies him to me. When he died and he was lying in state in the legislative building, our family was there the whole time, just to talk to people. I talked to a lot of people that I didn't know, and this one young person came up to me—she must've been thirty. (Of course, anyone's young to us now!) But she said she came to see my father lying in state because he came to judge a horse show in her small town in Saskatchewan. She said, "I had this horse that I absolutely adored. This was not a quality horse, a show horse or anything, and I probably came last in the class. But by the time your dad had talked to me about this horse, I felt as if I'd won. I came away thinking I had the best horse in the class." That was the way he was.

MAX: I never heard him praise himself in any way.

HEATHER: Oh, never. Never.

MAX: One day I really pushed him. I said, "What did you do at the university?" He did a lot at the university but he said, "Well, I didn't do anything." I kept on pushing him. I said, "If you really *had* to say what you accomplished there?" He said, "If I really *had* to, I'd say, well, maybe I was part of bringing the university to the farm." And I pushed and *pushed* him to get that.

HEATHER: That's why he was a really bad interview. But I have one other thing that I want to tell you about, and this again illustrates what you'd call a common touch or something. Father had a thing that when you made a date with anybody, you never broke that date, no matter what. So as lieutenant-governor, Father had dates a year in advance and one of the dates was with Boy Scouts somewhere in northern Alberta. Well, then the Queen came to Canada and he was issued an invitation to dine with the Queen on the Royal Yacht *Britannia* with all the other lieutenant-governors. Well, Father said, "No, I'm sorry, I can't come. I'm having dinner with the Boy Scouts." And to me that really illustrates the kind of guy he was. He truly didn't care whether it was the Queen or the Boy Scouts or the ditch digger or the gravel cart. My mother was a little disappointed because she wanted to go and have dinner on the *Britannia*. But your word was your bond and that was it.

✳ *Max, in an interview that you did with Dr. MacEwan in 1983, he mentioned that he turned from his earlier, church background to what we would now call environmentalism. He didn't say why, but could either of you hazard a guess?*

MAX: There was a fish and game group in High River that asked him to speak to them and he said, "You know, I'm a vegetarian and I don't eat my friends. Do you still want me to come?" And they said yes. I don't think it was sudden change of life but a gradual build-up. There comes a time when you say, "I don't like this anymore."

HEATHER: Yeah, it was gradual.

MAX: He was a conservationist, which is when you conserve things, but environmentalism is much wider than that. He crossed a bridge between conservationism and environmentalism in the mid-1950s or 1960s, when it was becoming vogue. With Rachel Carson's book [*Silent Spring*, 1962], the realization was, "We're not doing anything good here."

(Here we are joined by the Forans' longstanding friends, Judy Rogers Dundas and Joe Dundas.)

JOE: Are you allowed to put in some of the black side of the MacEwan family at all?

✳ *I'm all ears.*

JUDY: How long have you got?

HEATHER: It's a good story, actually.

JOE: They were caught fencing sheep back in Scotland. They'd be stolen and the MacEwans would buy them.

JUDY: Is that the truth or are you making that up?

HEATHER: He's making it up. Tell the whole story about when you were a kid.

JOE: Grant came to our hometown in Saskatchewan. He was going to speak to the community and stay at our place after. So I was bragging away to everybody that Grant MacEwan was coming to stay at our place. I didn't know him from Adam but I was a hero to my buddies.

JUDY: A little town in Saskatchewan.

JOE: We were sitting in the hall listening to his speech. And as he was closing he said he had to go out to the Dundases' for a reception and he said he didn't know whether he wanted to do that because the Dundases were kicked out of Scotland for stealing sheep. I was appalled.

JUDY: Joe turned from being the hero to the bum.

JOE: In an instant. And then on Grant's ninetieth birthday we were celebrating and I said that I had researched this and it was true that we were kicked out of Scotland for stealing sheep. But when you steal 'em, you have to give them to somebody to sell. And so the MacEwans were fencing our stolen sheep.

HEATHER: Payback time.

JOE: It took me forty years to do it but I got him.

HEATHER: And it felt good.

Rattus Non Gratus[127]

From Alberta's greatest hero, we move on to her greatest foe. When history's most formidable villains are tallied, we get usual suspects like Caligula, Genghis Khan or even Snidely Whiplash. But history, typically written by humans, neglects an insidious scourge of less humanity, but vastly greater consequence: *Rattus norvegicus*, also known as the Norway rat. According to the American Vertebrate Pests Council, the rat has caused more human deaths than every war ever unleashed. It is said to lay waste to $200 billion in damage around the world each year. And it destroys 20 per cent of the global food supply, or enough to consign world hunger to the dunghill of time, where it belongs along with the likes of Caligula, Khan and Snidely. So what has the Norway rat got to do with Alberta? In a word, nothing. And that's another aspect of this province that makes it so confounded special.

Alberta's claim as the world's only rat-free zone beyond the tundra (leaving other jurisdictions cold) has become the stuff of legend.

Alberta prides herself as the world's only rat-free zone outside of the tundra—excluding, as one interviewee kindly pointed out, our legislators.

[*Provincial Archives of Alberta, A.17, 2026b*]

And not merely urban legend, for its roots are singularly rural and as archetypically Albertan as oil-boom bumper stickers, Stetsons and Toronto-bashing. Outlets like *National Geographic*, Robert Sullivan's *New York Times*-bestselling meditation, *Rats*, and the 2007 Hollywood film, *Ratatouille*, have cited the province's singular crusade against a stealthy and cunning enemy that can climb a wall several stories high, burrow two metres deep, swim three kilometres, give birth at five weeks old and produce 15,000 heirs in just three years.

All this begs questions. What motivated Albertans to fight this? How in blazes can they beat an opponent that has, to quote Mr. Sullivan, "conquered every continent"? And what might this crusade reveal about Albertans beyond a discernibly dramatic distaste for rodents?

The motivation part is easy. The Norway rat spreads more than twenty often-fatal diseases and parasites, wipes out valuable crops, undermines water and sewer lines, and causes entire buildings to collapse or, by chewing up wiring, to burn down. And the $200 billion in damages that it causes each year is enough to run UN peacekeeping for almost a century. Money talks in Alberta, where the threat of rats *screams*.

But genius trades on both motivation and luck. As with other miracles of nature in the province (oil, gas, Gretzky), Alberta's place and time were perfect. The Norway rat, gifted to the New World by the Old around 1775, had soldiered inland from the east coast, hitting Saskatchewan in time for the Great Depression—and in extreme cases, Sunday dinner. A government field crew discovered the archvillain on our eastern border in 1950. Alberta Agriculture declared war, adding him to the list of *rattus non gratus* banned under pest control legislation, hosting conferences and town hall meetings, and unleashing posters and pamphlets in grain elevators, rail stations, post offices and schools. It was a good start, but it wasn't enough. Within two years, rats plied their trade along 270 kilometres of border, some as far as sixty clicks to the west. Less than a couple of dozen infestations in 1950 exploded to more than seven hundred by the late 1950s. Adapting one European legacy to fight another, the government borrowed from fifteenth-century Rome's notorious Borgia family and blew 63,600 kilograms of arsenic trioxide powder beneath 8,000 buildings between Provost and Medicine Hat. Though this enjoyed some success, the cost and danger of deploying arsenic prohibited its continued use. But it did buy Alberta Agriculture time to establish its rat control program, teaming up with seven local municipal entities to hire pest inspectors. This coincided with the advent of warfarin, the first anticoagulant rat poison, so safe that one official stunned a skeptical audience at a public meeting by chewing on it without keeling over.

Alberta's rat control program covers seven local jurisdictions within a 29-kilometre strip running 585 kilometres along the Saskatchewan border, from Cold Lake to Montana. It employs the equivalent of 5 full-time staff, who conduct field inspections each spring and fall covering 20 farms a day, respond to inquiries and potential sightings, and provide public education, all for $286,345 annually, plus another $50,000 for bait. That's less than 10 per cent of the cost of running the Calgary Stampede. (The program even emerged unscathed from the government's sweeping slashing of public spending in the 1990s.) Patrollers use poisoned bait, gas, buckshot and the odd shovel to dispatch their quarry, a nocturnal beast found under buildings, grain bins and bales. The patrol's esprit de corps crosses holy crusade and public service with a refreshing blend of gusto and humility.

"I have nothing but respect for this animal," declares John Bourne, who spent thirty-one years running the program. Glancing back at a large, stuffed, cartoony rat on his desk, he declares, "It poses the greatest threat to humanity. All bets are off with rats. Nothing surprises me anymore about them." Mr. Bourne praises the foresight of the program's founders. Its first employee, Joseph Gurba, was named the seventh-greatest Albertan in a provincial centennial poll by *Alberta Venture* magazine.

"Who'd think of starting a program to get rid of rats?'" marvels Orest Popil, a veteran patroller turned supervisor employed by the County of Vermilion River. "You never let the last rat go—that would be letting people down." Noting his positive dealings with landowners, he states, "It's the best job anybody could have, although being a rat-killer is not what your kids would brag about to their friends."

"Albertans take pride in being rat-free and hopefully, we'll hand that down to future generations," declares Cal McLean, a pest control officer with Vermilion River. He says his team is always looking for better ways to do the job, and when he and his colleagues phone the United States, they are told, "*You guys* are the experts!"

So is Alberta really rat-free? Emphatically yes, says Mr. Bourne. The logbook for Provost, for example, showed 147 infestations in 1983, falling to zero by 2003 and remaining there when I checked a few years later. Many centres have not reported an infestation in more than a decade, with the rest registering ongoing declines. Among the patrollers, stories abound of the rodents penetrating houses through toilets, scurrying up and down deserted barn walls by the hundreds, rushing right at you when they're cornered. When his team trains new inspectors, they have to travel to Saskatchewan to show them what rats look like. Mr. McLean recalls Mr. Popil reaching under a bale and pulling out a live rat by its neck. And after three decades of eradicating rats, Mr. Bourne, now retired in the US, admits to continuing, recurring nightmares of rats in his home—rats that he just cannot kill.

Nightmares aside, the program succeeds due to Alberta's fortunate circumstances. Our other boundaries—largely vacant rangeland in the south, mountains to the west and forests to the north—offer natural barriers to incoming rat hordes, which depend on people for food and shelter. The battle zone is relatively small. More isolated rural structures are easier to police than dense urban jungle. Legislation, low-toxic poison and the political will were in place *before* the threat spread out of control. (By comparison, Saskatchewan also launched a program, but it came too late because two-thirds of that province was already infested.) Landowners remain co-operative and vigilant, in part because the government's approach is more carrot than iron fist. When the first infestation in six years was reported in 2007—ground-zero being sundry hay bales in Sibbald, three kilometres west of the Saskatchewan border—it was front-page fodder for the *Edmonton Journal*, but nothing that a bale-shaking tractor and a volley of shotgun blasts couldn't cure. Alberta's *Agricultural Pests Act* bans rats and actually requires people to take measures to get rid of them. Except for hospitals, educational institutions and other authorized outlets, keeping any kind of *rattus* species in Alberta gets you up to six months in jail and a $5,000 fine.

The rat controllers warn against the dangers of complacency. Ever-increasing shipments of foreign goods and the pet-rat lobby threaten the province's cherished *rattus interruptus*. Indicating the gargantuan rubber rodent on Mr. Bourne's desk, his boss deadpans, "This is what's in store if we don't stay with the program."

What does all this say about Alberta?

"It bespeaks our frontier independence and our attitude to do what it takes," concludes Mr. Bourne. "It speaks of the farsightedness and willingness of people fifty years ago who knew the devastating consequences to people, wildlife and crops of not taking action. In Alberta, people aren't just more independent. More people tend to take action irrespective of mainstream thinking at the time, and we'll be damned if others don't agree!"

So Alberta owes its special, rat-free status to a singular soufflé of geography, circumstance, foresight, determination and pride. It's a potent mix. Apparently, even the scourge of humanity can't beat that.

4 Cultural Backwater or Fountain?

You go out to Alberta, you stand in the foothills, surrounded by the greatest livestock the world has ever seen and you ask, "What is Alberta giving Canada?" And the answer is blowing in the wind.

—DAVE BROADFOOT, 1978

The Rawhide Curtain

IS ALBERTA A BACKWATER OF CULTURE or a fountain of knowledge and the arts? My street interviews around the country reveal definite impressions on the subject from non-Albertans.

Decked out in khaki fatigues at a Canadian Armed Forces display on a sun-soaked Canada Day in Montréal, Sergeant Joao Barros offers this typical response: "Ah, Alberta. The first thing I think about is the Calgary Stampede and horses. They love their Stetsons and their cowboy boots. Even if they're from the city, they're all cowboys."

Up Highway 401 in Toronto, Mark Breslin recalls:

Another thing I noticed that's different is your restaurants, where you can actually eat live meat. I've never seen that. Out east in say, Halifax, they have those big tanks of lobsters. You point to one, they pick out the lobster and then they cook it for you. Well, I was in a number of restaurants in Alberta where they had these cows come by—I was wondering why the aisles were so wide in the restaurant—and when you say, "I'd like that one, I'll have Bessie," they

just narcotize the cow so it just stands there and you just bite into it.
Which is great if you're a beef lover. And I'm a beef lover.

In the shadow of the CN Tower, energetic Fielding Needleman pronounces, "Oh my god, they have people with pointy hats and pointy shoes! The people are friendly and an inordinate amount of them wear cowboy hats." Down the street at Queen's Park, Isabelle Babici muses with both bubblegum and tongue in cheek, "Alberta... it's the only place that I know that has vodka and pancakes in the same meal. I think I've had a hamburger from there, although it was probably made out of buffalo. I live in Toronto and we're multicultural, whereas you guys have buffalo." Uptown, against the semicircular twin towers of Toronto's City Hall, Rosina Banda Arteagu, a visiting Mexican student, mulls over her impressions of Alberta and declares, "It's part of Canada. It's cold. There are horses there... and no one else."

Aboard the Labrador ferry, three hardy, ballcapped fishermen don't hesitate to offer their first impressions of Alberta. Cornelius Smith mentions money, jobs and mad cow disease; Andy Langille flags oil, prairie and cattle; and Gary Martin declares, "The best steaks in Canada. We Newfs, we barbecue a lot of Alberta beef, I guess, 'cause our cows are no good." A genial tourist, Hoyeon Choi, puts beef at the top of his list, too.

Across the country, by the white fins of Canada Place at the port of Vancouver, Cora Noordman from Manitoba cites cowboys and horses. Anita Radmacher from Saskatchewan mentions cattle and oil rigs. Laura Sloot, a recent escapee from Calgary, observes that many Albertans wear Wranglers and cowboy boots.

And back home, whether it's locals on the streets of cities or international tourists in the Rocky Mountains, people's responses are usually peppered with references to beef. Among more than a hundred first impressions and comments about Wild Rose Country that I solicited from Canadians and international visitors, beef and cowboys stand out as our cultural hallmarks.

There must be a good reason for this. Of course, the beef industry revolves around Alberta. And yes, we do lead the land in horses, ponies and even bison.[1] But wait a minute. Québec is the country's top producer of breeding and market hogs, yet very few Canadians are likely to identify *La Belle Province* with swine (with pork-barrelling, perhaps, but not pigs per se).[2] Ditto Ontario with rams, ewes, lambs, goats, emus, rheas, ducks and goats;[3] Manitoba with geese;[4] and Saskatchewan with wild boars.[5] Alberta also happens to be the nation's heartland for llamas, alpacas and elk, not to mention boasting more than half of the ostriches.[6] But is she known for any of that? Heck, no.

The answer must lie with the Calgary Stampede—another response reiterated by interviewees from coast to coast—and the proud tradition, civic exuberance and marketing genius that have branded the entire province in its buckskin image. How did this happen? In a two-step, naturally.

The first step came back in 1912, when an entrepreneurial trick-roper from New York, Guy Weadick, got a well-heeled quartet of Calgary businessmen to pony up $100,000 to finance a weeklong rodeo. Originally intended as a one-time exercise in frontier nostalgia—a celebration of bygone days on the limitless range—the Calgary Stampede was reprised as a victory party after World War I and became an annual event when it linked to the city's agricultural exhibition in 1923. Its sizable purses immediately corralled the world's best cowboys and cowgirls. Two years later, an American silent film, deftly titled *The Calgary Stampede* and starring the legendary Hoot Gibson (an old barnstorming buddy of Mr. Weadick's), spread far and wide the alluring image of the Old Western rodeo, complete with Mounties and spiced with gamblin', rustlin' and good, old-fashioned killin'.

The second step, the one that really embedded the event into our national consciousness, dates from 1948. When the Calgary Stampeders qualified for the Grey Cup football game in Toronto, a local alderman and future mayor, Don Mackay, followed up his earlier invention of the city's white-hat ceremony by exporting the spirit of

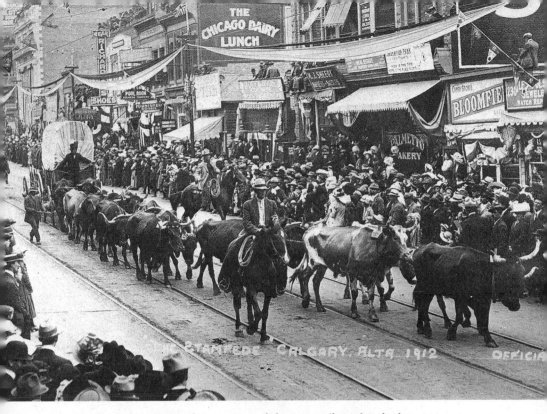

. *The first Calgary Stampede in 1912, intended as a one-off nostalgia-fest but now branded into the provincial hide—whether we like it or not.* [Glenbow Archives, NA-335-2]

Cowtown to Hogtown. The result was an invasion of 320 Calgarians in full cowboy dress, a parade with the visiting team to the game, a subsequent victory parade featuring two leaders of the Tsuu Tina Nation riding on horseback and leading a mounted posse of cowpersons, a Western band, sundry livestock, a chuckwagon and five hundred boisterous fans in motor vehicles. They stopped outside the tony Royal York Hotel to present a concert, a square dance and pancakes for the masses.[7] The spectacle is recalled almost six decades later by one of the Stampeders, the Honourable Norman Kwong. "That was Alberta's first venture into the sporting field Canadian-wide and it started the rebirth of the Canadian Football League," he says. "They created such a fuss in Toronto that the people really saw Albertans having fun and enjoying their team. And luckily Calgary won."

More than any other, this event crystallized Alberta's Western identity in the eyes of the Toronto media and by extension, the rest of the country. Of course, the cowboy culture lives on not only in Calgary for ten days every July but for even longer in the grasslands of southern Alberta, where it remains a working lifestyle, and in bustling rodeos held each year in places like Alder Flats, Bashaw, Carstairs, Debolt, Entwistle, Fort Assiniboine, Gimlet, High Prairie, Kinuso, Medicine Lodge, Ponoka, Sangudo, Tees, Valleyview and Wabasca, among other cowpunchers' hotspots. The Canadian Finals Rodeo leaves the chute each November in Edmonton. And in addition to that large deal in Calgary, said burg also features a rodeo presented by the Alberta Rockies Gay Rodeo Association.

But back to that mighty symbol of cowboy culture: the white hats worn in Calgary by good sports ranging from volunteer official greeters at the international airport to visiting dignitaries. If you're part of even an informal tour group that comes through Cowtown— along with five million other visitors each year—then you may be asked to repeat this version of the White Hatter's pledge: "I, *(your name here)*, havin' visited the only genuine western city in Canada, namely, Calgary, and havin' been duly treated to exceptional amounts of heart-warmin', hand-shakin', tongue-loosenin', back-slappin', neighbour-lovin' western spirit, do solemnly promise to spread this here brand of hospitality to all folks and critters who cross my trail hereafter. On the count of three, we will raise our hats and give a loud YAHOO!"[8] To the less cheerful, the cowboy costume becomes a faux social leveller in a city of extremes in both wealth and poverty. For Howard and Tamara Palmer, this ritualistic invocation of the province's ranching and agricultural histories was designed by the city's civic and business elites "to downplay social cleavages and to promote corporate interests."[9] For others, Alberta's Western guise has become a mockery. The filmmaker, Garth Pritchard, states, "We had a culture. The culture was rural. The culture was strong people who made decisions and shook each other's hands. Try to go into Calgary today with a cowboy hat on or as a farmer. God! Yeah, we're allowed to be a cowboy ten days a year; it's called the Stampede. The rest of the time, you'd better be an oilman."

In any case, Guy Weadick's nostalgia-fest lives on as your choice of "The Greatest Outdoor Show on Earth"—its official motto—or a less charitable rallying cry like "Ten Days of *Hee-Haw*." Anyway you barbecue it, Calgary deserves full credit for roping its annual summer party into the world's consciousness and giving the province an identity, for better or worse. And like it or not, from the great boreal forest in the north to the sweet grasslands of the south, a rawhide curtain has descended across the province. Behind that homogenous reflection lie people and values from diverse and ancient traditions, descended from First Nations, Europe, Asia and beyond. From places like Abbot Pass, Bawlf and Carrot Creek to Watkins Slough, Yule Meadow and Zama City, many people's views of all Albertans are filtered through a screen that is resolutely rugged, rural and rigorously repeated in the media.

One reason that the image, if not the culture, of cowboys and farmers continue to thrive while other forms of cultural expression fly lower under the radar might be the insularity that has held sway in Alberta. From her days as a territory, seeking ever-increasing autonomy from Ottawa under Premier Haultain through to the anti-establishment protests by political non-partisans, farmers and reformers, Alberta has cultivated a shoulder-chip that has led to her being labelled Canada's noisiest and angriest province.[10]

This reputation was cemented during the Social Credit era (1935–1971), the fourth-longest reign in Canadian electoral history. This was, after all, the regime that barred Eleanor Roosevelt from addressing the Legislature during her speaking tour to promote the formation of the United Nations even though she was welcomed in every other provincial legislature in the land. This was also the reign that, in its earlier stages, was hijacked by the Social Credit Board, an unelected gaggle of hardliners that feared any whiff of interference in Alberta's money supply, policing, tax regime or Christian, democratic society, which interference the board attributed to a conspiracy by mainly German and Jewish financial interests and socialists. Although these creative thinkers were cut loose by Premier Ernest Manning when they came out in favour of ending private land ownership and secret-ballot elections, he continued their penchant for isolationism. For some, the rural-centric insularity of the Social Credit era, in which film censors held sway and women and men could not drink together in bars, became unbearably oppressive. The writer, Myrna Kostash, fled Social Credit Alberta in 1965 and did not return for a decade. "I was very consciously Alberta-phobic, which I associated with Manning and censorship," she recalls. "The irony is that there was a stranglehold of rural, Christian values, but there were always pockets of resistance— university professors who were up in arms at what was going on in the Legislature, the Yardbird Suite [jazz club], where you would go to be Bohemian. There were ethnic enclaves and the communist hall. They were always producing against the grain."

Going against the grain is what prompted Jackie Flanagan to start *Alberta Views* magazine. While in Toronto and Montréal, she found that "Albertans are regarded with a certain amount of contempt, that we're hicks or we're rednecks. How narrow they thought I must be, how limited, and their impression of Alberta was very much shaped by *Alberta Report*." As a third-generation Albertan, she saw the need for a publication that reflected another Alberta, one with a tremendously rich, vibrant and interesting culture. "Our artists win the Vienna Biennial," she notes. "They're recognized all over the world. So Alberta is not that narrow stereotype, but when Klein speaks, he just reinforces that image of Alberta. I really wanted to redeem Alberta's reputation."[11]

Another reason for the propagation of cowboy culture in Alberta is that it fits with her official mythology of mavericks rolling up their plaid shirts, getting down to the business of making money, squinting defiantly at whatever the wind may be blowing their way from central Canada and expecting little or nothing from government. (That billions of public dollars have helped, if not bailed out, bucketfuls of businesses in down-to-earth industries like agriculture, energy and forestry doesn't fit the paradigm, so it's kept relatively quiet.) With the exception of Premier Lougheed's term—a fifteen-year interregnum fondly dubbed "Camelot" by the cultural Renaissance man, Fil Fraser—arts and culture have, ironically, had to live Alberta's maverick mythology to a greater extent than more favoured outlets for public funding like horse racing.

The ruling political juntas may tolerate, say, the odd cowboy poet—who in their right or left mind wouldn't like a champion sagebrush bard like Doris Daley?—but anyone who calls herself or himself an "artist" in Wild Rose Country risks being perceived as lazy, self-indulgent, irrelevant and possibly even homosexual. Arts and culture are seen largely as interesting hobbies and frills, something to do after the day's real work is done. (Case in point: the poet, Stephan Stephansson, who worked backbreaking days on his farm at Markerville near Red Deer, then spent "Wakeful Nights" penning verse in Icelandic that was hailed as among the finest poetry in human history.[12]) The more holistic, pantheistic and mystic view of arts and culture both underlying and expressing everything that a society does is reserved for well-meaning volunteers, idealistic arts administrators and deep thinkers who use phrases like "creative class," "smart cities" and "can your conference afford my speaking fee?"

Some folks in Alberta may see artists as a problem, and there are some perfectly good reasons for that.

First, creative types sometimes want money to make whatever it is they want to make: sculptures, films, books, beads, dance, songs, theatre, whatever. And that's annoying because in the world of people like Ernest Manning and Ralph Klein, people shouldn't ask what government can do for them but shut up, get a job and do something useful. If there's an official religion in Alberta, it's work, and although Premiers Manning and Klein came from different ends of the puritanical spectrum, their shared credo on this point seems deeply puritanical.

Second, even worse than wanting stuff, artists sometimes ask questions that make some people uncomfortable. And that can get darned inconvenient in a one-party state, where the entrenched political and economic interests view their opponents as anti-Albertan and vociferously encourage public emulation of our official mammal, which, as we have noted, is a sheep.

There's another reason for de-emphasizing an indigenous arts scene in the province over the years—Wilf Carter aside. "We can buy anything, and so we don't think about growing it ourselves," wrote Aritha van Herk. "Albertans have never been fond of seeds that must be coaxed to germinate. We prefer the inspiration-on-a-rocket, overnight-success, strike-it-rich, blast-to-the-top, blow-out model."[13]

Like Ms. van Herk, Myrna Kostash also led the province's provincial arts service organization for the literary arts, which gives her a good glimpse into official attitudes toward culture in Wild Rose Country. "Alberta is extraordinarily arts-friendly in terms of audiences," she says. "You have a population of readers and publishers. You go to a concert and feel the joy. There's a massive disconnect between the political class and audiences and producers." As a former president of the Writers Guild of Alberta as well, I can illustrate that disconnect with an experience from that group's annual general meeting in Red Deer back in 2000. The provincial government planned to use that occasion to announce a new award for writers in the name of Grant MacEwan. When the responsible cabinet minister (culture being lumped in the catch-all "community development" portfolio at the time) could not attend, a gracious local MLA stepped in. Seeking details for his introduction, I phoned his spouse and asked about his preferences in authors, hoping for a local reference that would inspire those of our then-eight hundred members who would be in the room that day. Alas, his pleasure reading was confined to bestselling American authors, and I feared that he had never heard of, let alone read, work by Albertan writers. This is not exactly getting sand kicked in artists' faces at the public beach; maybe it's more like going without the SPF 15 and getting burned by the UV rays of indifference.

Of course, none of this should stop indigenous art and culture. Isolation, official neglect and public indifference in these areas may chase some Albertan creators to places like Vancouver or Toronto. But they can't choke off inspirations like individual initiative, support from the private sector, the dazzling kaleidoscope of forms (both land and human), the brilliant sunlight or the rich, almost surrealistic colours found across the province. And much of the product of that inspiration is neatly obscured to outsiders and even some visitors, by that rawhide curtain. Not that there is anything wrong with the province's grand ranching heritage or taking pride in it. But as it represents only a sliver of Alberta's vast and diverse geography, her 10,000-year-old human history and her dining preferences, some of us feel compelled to remind anyone who will listen that it just ain't the whole story. For instance, there is also a rich history accompanying the fur trade and missionary life across the province, especially in the north, as recreated at a site like Historic Dunvegan in the Peace River valley and in a novel like Fred Stenson's *The Trade*.

Albertans realize that there is more to their province than cowboy culture, being, on the whole, more preoccupied or indifferent than stupid. And there are early signs that the creaky wheels of officialdom are moving forward on arts and culture as opposed to, say, grinding them into lint. After years of burying the file at the very back end of the last department in the cabinet pecking order, the Alberta government revived culture as a nearly stand-alone ministry in 2008, along with "community spirit," which presumably is not a veiled salute to Prohibition. In 2004 the province's funding for arts and culture ranked tenth among twelve provinces and territories.[14] That funding comes from gambling revenues, which critics claim is unstable and unpredictable—the same charge levelled at federal funding of the North-West Territories by Premier Haultain more than a century ago—not to mention tainted. As already noted (twice), the Alberta government funds horse racing more than the arts, even as its recently developed cultural policy proclaims that Albertans want culture and increased access to cultural activities to be a priority for their provincial government.[15]

One other thing about the cowboy culture in Alberta. Despite the fact that more than 80 per cent of Albertans live in urban centres, the political balance in the Legislature remains well over half a century out of whack demographically. In the 2008 provincial election, the one-third of Albertans who lived outside of Calgary and Edmonton elected more than half of the province's eighty-three MLAs. This may change some day, although as history has shown, governments that achieve fabulous electoral success don't exactly leap to fix the system. Economically, the recently faded energy boom took the public's attention away from rural Alberta's misfortune in the face of the BSE ("mad cow") crisis, unsteady commodity prices, the rising Loonie, soaring input costs like labour, fuel and machinery, and diminishing opportunities to serve the conventional oil drilling industry, which is also declining. If Henry Wise Wood and the United Farmers were alive today, they'd be weeping in their graves.

So whose job is it to try to make sense out of all this, express our values, confront our fears and show us the possibilities? If all else fails, we might as well send in the artists. Let's explore what Alberta has on offer.

More Culture than Bacteria?

On a spring day at the Legislature, Mark Lisac recollects his arrival to Alberta in 1978 and remembers the capital city as a larger, faster-paced version of Saskatoon. "But it's really changed," he says. "It's become much more of an urban metropolis. But people who've been here a long time sometimes get insecure. They think that the rest of the world sees Alberta as a backwater, and it's not, really. It hasn't been that for decades."

Across the North Saskatchewan River, downtown, at a festival screening of one of her films, Anne Wheeler describes the Alberta she knows as appreciating the arts, with a huge artistic community. "So it's really very different from what people outside of Alberta think," she tells me. "When I grew up, I had terrific music teachers, great drama teachers. In university, there were big productions. People came out to support their artists."

Seven blocks away, in a century-old building (fossilized by prairie standards), up in the control booth of the country's oldest continuing non-profit radio station, CKUA, Andy Donnelly, a popular, larger-than-life producer and announcer, has just wrapped his Friday-night *Celtic Show*, which has earned more than a kilt following. "Alberta's a leader in the world," he enthuses, citing international awareness of events like the Edmonton Fringe Festival, the Edmonton and Calgary Folk Festivals and the children's festivals. "Theatre, music, art, every-thing is there at all times. And you travel through this province and you'll always end up at something. It's phenomenal! And we've sent out to the world some of the greatest in all genres."

Following thousands of years of Aboriginal art, which encom-passed sacred, historic, symbolic, decorative and other representations on everything from rocks to bison hides, Alberta's artistic traditions have been influenced profoundly—like everything else—by the land, infused by and reflecting its magnificent and often overwhelming vast-ness, diversity, harshness and beauty. Early Eurocentric images of the area by painters like Paul Kane and the rash of sagebrush storytellers used romantic, even rococo lenses. Since white settlement, the torch of arts and culture has come from the grassroots, confined largely to the community level as the province came of age.

With urbanization, Vaudeville and other touring companies came through the province, giving local audiences a peek at everyone from Laurel and Hardy and the Marx Brothers on their way up to Sarah Bernhardt on her way out. An ambitious network of movie theatres dotted the landscape, some astonishing in their grandeur even by today's standards. Within three years of achieving provincehood, Edmonton claimed a population of 18,500 and six theatres, an opera house and the Thistle Arena, which had hosted the theatrics of the

Cultural life on the frontier: the Empire Theatre in Edmonton, 1913.
[*City of Edmonton Archives*, EB-11-15]

first provincial legislature. Three imports, Emily Murphy (as Janey
Canuck), Robert Stead and Nellie McClung, scored early successes
with prairie-flavoured novels, though in an eerie precursor to the
exodus of artists during the Klein era, Mr. Stead took a federal government job in Ottawa after World War I, apparently because his writing
did not pay enough for a living wage. Following the community
theatre movement, which sought to counterbalance mass-produced
professional entertainment in the early twentieth century, Elizabeth
Sterling Haynes, a pioneering drama specialist at the University
of Alberta, helped to produce the first provincial drama festival in
Canada in 1930. And thanks to the university's Faculty of Extension,
during the depths of the Depression, the province got radio drama

on CKUA and the Banff Theatre School, later the Banff School of Fine Arts and The Banff Centre. The school imported British painters whose landscapes set the tone for visual art in the province for decades; it has since become an international magnet for training in the performing, literary, new media and visual arts. After World War II, the government created the Alberta Music Board to promote the melodious arts across the province.

Arts and culture continued mostly at the amateur level in parlours, churches and community halls as Albertans coped with pursuits like infrastructure-building and economic survival. A major milestone for the province was the construction of the twin Jubilee Auditoria in Calgary and Edmonton for our golden anniversary in 1955. Under the leadership of Jeanne and Peter Lougheed, the premier from 1971–1985, and his tireless culture minister, Horst Schmid—Alberta's closest answer to the arts-loving Medicis—the province enjoyed a cultural awakening, exemplified by the government's matching private donations to arts organizations to a maximum of one-quarter of their budgets; relaxing the iron-fisted "blue laws" against drinking and importing smutty stateside magazines; axing film censorship; and contributing to Mel Hurtig's publication of the three-volume *Canadian Encyclopedia*, the first homegrown work of its kind in Canada. Mr. Hurtig asked for $2 million, but the provincial government kicked in double that (including 25,000 copies to distribute across Canada as Alberta's 75th anniversary gift to the country in 1980) on his promise *not* to involve the federal government.[16] This heady climate saw the birth of enduring and international extravaganzas like the Edmonton Heritage Festival, the Banff Television Festival and the Edmonton Fringe Festival, truly world leaders on their respective stages. These days of publicly supported pioneering are palpably passé.

As the veteran voice on arts and festivals for CKUA—an eclectic, province-wide radio service—Chris Allen has crisscrossed Alberta enough times to assess the cultural scene, beyond being a writer and actor himself. In a radio voice as rich and smooth as coffee, he intones, "Alberta is known as a volunteer province—people will volunteer for everything. That's why you have major projects like the Commonwealth Games, international sports events that took place here with a lot less money than in some other provinces. But this also supports local artistic ventures." He says culture in Alberta combines arts events produced from small areas brought to big cities and vice-versa, exemplified by a tiny community creating the Clive Cow Patti Theatre; a Francophone film festival in Waterton Park; and grassroots theatre in Edmonton's Walterdale Community Playhouse, growing into the Citadel, which became the largest regional theatre in Canada and one of the best facilities in the land. "We have an entrepreneurial, adventurous spirit which can embrace the history of theatre from Greek to the modern and more avant-garde productions," he adds. "Now this is theatre, but it's the same in music, the visual arts and Alberta arts in general."

Even if the hick label digs in like a golden retriever to a thrown stick, Alberta's artists may take some comfort in the irony of conforming to a different stereotype of the province: the independent entrepreneur. That spirit shows in several singular efforts. At the Rosebud Theatre, professional performances feature a company of resident players, student apprentices from the Rosebud School of the Arts and guest artists from around the world—in a hamlet of less than one hundred people. The Big Valley Jamboree in Camrose boasts Canada's biggest country music festival. The Yardbird Suite, an Edmonton mainstay for hepcats since 1957, is among the oldest jazz clubs in Canada, if not the oldest. *Beethoven in the Badlands* brings the Calgary Philharmonic Orchestra to the open air of Drumheller, dramatically linking heavenly music and otherworldly landscape.

For a province that some believe is a cultural backwater, Alberta offers seriously top-drawer museums. The aforementioned Royal Tyrrell Museum, a massive facility that seems embedded in the surrounding badlands, serves up a breathtaking blend of leading-edge science and natural history, with a healthy side of terror in the unforgettable hall of dinosaurs. The Remington Carriage Museum in Cardston showcases 250 carriages, wagons and sleighs in the largest collection of horse-drawn vehicles on the continent. The Reynolds-Alberta Museum in Wetaskiwin presents the province's mechanized history, focusing on transportation, agriculture, aviation and industry, with a particularly stunning array of vintage vehicles, like the rare, 1929 Duesenburg Phaeton Royale Model J. The Glenbow Museum, run by a private foundation in Calgary, grandly combines museum, art gallery, library and archives in Western Canada's largest museum, focusing on the cultural and military history, ethnology and geology of southern Alberta, with connections to art and artifacts from around the world. The Whyte Museum of the Canadian Rockies explores the special culture of the mountains, not only locally but also in terms of the relationship between mountains and culture throughout the world. Fort Edmonton—established by the Hudson's Bay Company in 1795 and prompting Robert Kroetsch to remark, "in Alberta, that ain't history, it's archaeology"[17]—was reconstructed upriver and reborn as the largest living historical museum in the country. And the flag-ship Royal Alberta Museum (known as the Provincial Museum until blessed by the Queen during her centennial visit in 2005) offers exceptional exhibits like an immense, multimedia exploration of Aboriginal history and culture (among the largest in North America), dioramas of the province's natural habitats and world-class homages to the fur trade, birds and bugs.

Moving outdoors, Alberta claims five of Canada's fifteen UNESCO-designated World Heritage Sites: Dinosaur Provincial Park, Head-Smashed-In Buffalo Jump, Writing-on-Stone Provincial Park, the Rocky Mountain Parks (Jasper and Banff) and Waterton Lakes National Park (joining Glacier National Park in Montana to form the world's first international peace park).[18]

Of course, all this is just a smattering of the province's ample cultural attractions. But culture in Alberta seems to be more than a happy accident. The province is believed to have brought in the first cultural development legislation in North America[19] and the first department of culture in Canada under Premier Lougheed in 1971.[20]

The province has its share of individual attention-grabbers, too.

Alex Janvier draws on Denésuliné (Chipewyan) and Saulteaux traditions to paint shapes of forests, lakes and animals woven together in a signature, bright, abstract style. A survivor of residential schools, he led the integration of Native motifs into Alberta's visual-arts landscape, achieving acclaim as a highly influential charter member of Professional National Indian Artists (the so-called "Indian Group of Seven") and the creator of work such as the glorious, 450-square-metre *Morning Star* at the Canadian Museum of Civilization.

Jane Ash Poitras is another internationally lauded and collected visual artist. Her work includes painting and mixed-media collages of historical and current imagery as well as painted elements. Her work has appeared in the National Gallery of Canada and many prestigious venues abroad. She lectures at universities and galleries across the continent and overseas, and is a creative activist (and a self-styled nuisance to authorities) supporting causes like Aboriginal rights and freedom of expression.

Pauline Gedge is an award-winning, bestselling author whose books have sold more than seven million copies and been translated into almost twenty languages. She sets most of her vividly researched work in ancient Egypt, lives in the hamlet of Edgerton (population: 373 in 2006) and in the finest Albertan tradition, told *Quill & Quire* magazine that she finds the Can-Lit mindset irritating and abhorrent.

The province's internationally lauded contributions to the literary vanguard include, for example, the work of the novelists, W.O. Mitchell (sample classic: *Who Has Seen the Wind?*) and Rudy Wiebe (*A Discovery of Strangers*), and the poet, Stephan Stephansson (*Andvökur* or *Wakeful Nights*).

And you've already met the great-granddaughter of one of the Mounties who marched westward in the 1870s, Doris Daley, who was named the best female cowboy poet in North America by the

Academy of Western Artists in 2004, the first Canadian of any gender to win that award for prime rhyme. Bucking the herd in what has been a traditionally male-dominated field, she rhapsodizes, "For me, Alberta is a grain field, a close-up of a wild rose in the dew of morning, a potluck to raise money for the curling rink, and all the scenery."

The work of the master puppeteer, Ronnie Burkett, has encompassed prairie gothic, bawdy burlesque, high drama, melodrama, social commentary and satire, mining topics like beauty, bereavement, aging, artists' freedoms and connections between elders and children. Lauded at home and abroad, his virtuoso performances have him dashing about the stage to play dozens of characters simultaneously.

Although Gordon Lightfoot famously sang about being "Alberta Bound," the province's unofficial anthem is "Four Strong Winds," written by her best-known adopted musician-rancher-cowboy-recluse, Ian Tyson, which also refers to going out to Alberta, in this case to find work. The government actually commissioned an official song for the provincial centennial, but it's unlikely that any officially prescribed art will approach the deep and popular resonance of Mr. Tyson's masterpiece. Stompin' Tom Connors penned a tune about the sensational songstress, k.d. lang, whose mildness he likened to an Irish wake; Ms. lang burst out of Consort (population: few) with what may be the most sublime set of pipes to come out of the West, bucking pretty much every testosterone-soaked sacred cow that the province had to offer on the way to lassoing four Grammies, eight Junos and no love from the beef business.

Corb Lund is a singer-songwriter who has won an arsenal of national and international awards in a hurry with a nouveau-Western style marrying respect for the frontier tradition with modern rhythms, rhymes and sensibilities: "Always keep an edge on your knife/ Cuz a good sharp edge is a man's best hedge/ Against the vague uncertainties of life." He calls his music "scruffy country," "ulterior country," "dissident country," "subversive country," "insubordinate country," "non-toxic country" or "Western music with some hair on it," and he rated his own comic book, *Corb Lund's Western Tales*, a collection of "rip-snortin', pistol-packin' dust-kickin' yarns" based on tunes from his oeuvre.[21] Descended from four generations of ranchers in the south of the province, he has no delusions about his influences. "Obviously, there's a lot of cultural and geographical reference in my lyric," he tells me. "The approach to my career has been influenced by being a rural Albertan, too, because up until recently, we'd done just about everything ourselves, and just rolled up our sleeves and printed our own T-shirts, fixed our own band and booked our own tour."

Keith Johnstone, a drama professor at the University of Calgary, invented improvisational "Theatresports" in 1976 as a way to knock down barriers between performers and audiences, in a revolt against what he called "the theatre of taxidermy." Theatresports involves putting improvisers in teams, squaring off in short games with limited rules, audiences calling out instructions and judges taking the heat off the performers as targets of the audience's wrath. Citing "the necessary joy in failure," its creator explained, "Like sports, it is the struggle for success that audiences want, even if they don't recognize it." His struggle spread across Canada and into twenty-one countries, and his other invented forms of improvisation (including Micetro Impro, Gorilla Theatre and The Life Game) also enjoy international adoption.[22]

The industrial designer, Tim Antoniuk, partnered in a modernist design, manufacturing and retail firm that served 750 clients internationally, placing furniture in Hollywood films and television programs like *Friends* and *Fresh Prince of Bel-Air*. His collaborations have won prizes and have been exhibited at the Smithsonian Museum and in marquee design shows in London and New York City. His latest work, teamed with sociology and chemical engineering professors, seeks to build high-end, sustainable products made from "memory plastics" that can morph into different shapes when consumers are ready to repurpose them. He describes the design aesthetic in Alberta as steeped in originality, openness and multicultural influences. "Being somewhat isolated from the major international centres of design, there's a sense of honesty to the work and an ethic that's deeply hard-working, committed and persistent—a farmer's work ethic, rather than something fleeting," he notes. "Alberta's successes have a lot to do with a long-term, pioneering spirit. When people are around constant development and progress—and these are loaded terms—they aspire to something greater than they are. Also, Alberta has always had its roots a little bit closer to nature, which keeps you grounded."

But for every smashing success out of Alberta, there are efforts that just don't get through to some people. When the Edmontonian comedy troupe, Three Dead Trolls in a Baggie, wrote "The Toronto Song" ("The rent's too high, the air's unclean/ The beaches are dirty and the people are mean"), the Toronto media took it as a musical assault on the inflated sense of self that most Canadians feel permeates the city on the lake. Sadly, the Hogtown hacks missed the *real* satirical target, which was Albertans' xenophobia, as the singers' spite escalates over the course of the tune from Toronto to the entire country, except Alberta, though it is careful to *include* Calgary. When a naval-gazing piece in the *Toronto Star* reprinted their lyrics and sniffed about an "obscure comedy troupe," the Trolls emerged from their lair to ask, "How can we be obscure when we are on the front page of the most important paper in Canada?" before concluding, "We may be obscure, but we've had over 1.7 million downloads of our stuff from mp3.com and pocketed a fistful of digital electronic loonies without ever 'making it' in Toronto."[23] Of course, there are a million more stories of artistic success in the naked province, both well known and not.

If the work of these artists has a common denominator, it seems to be a willingness to approach things differently. You might make the same observation for many people's artistic sensibilities, but in Alberta, the notion of going against the grain—as long as it's outside of politics—is acceptable practice, if not a religion. In fact, as we have seen, it's part of not only the popular image that Albertans like to project but indelibly part of our identity as well. Having to suffer the harrowing slings of indifference, particularly that of distant and more populous media centres, is common to all artists living outside of what "Taranna" administratively (and xenophobically) calls "the regions." But Alberta's longstanding culture of protest gives it an additional texture that just might make folks out here a touch hungrier and angrier for that elusive beast, acceptance, and its heftier, slipperier sibling, success.

A Constant Source of Amazement
Interview with the Honourable Tommy Banks

Tommy Banks is equally at home working in the Senate of Canada and performing at an intimate jazz club or leading a major orchestra. His television and musical work has won Gemini and Juno awards, and he has received a battery of other honours for a lifetime of cultural contributions to his province and country, from directing music at major events such as Expo 86 and the Calgary Winter Olympic Games to serving as founding chairman of the Alberta Foundation for the Performing Arts. This icon of Alberta's arts scene continues to perform and conduct music, while chairing the Senate Committee on Energy, the Environment and Natural Resources, serving on two other Senate bodies and performing other senatorial duties with little signs of slowing down. In a rehearsal room at the National Arts Centre, Senator Banks performs a composition in progress (his aptly titled Untitled) *and weighs in on the environment for arts and culture in his home province.*

✳ *Senator, please describe the culture in Alberta.*

The cultural life of Alberta in respect to the performing and creative arts and the arts and cultural industries is a constant source of amazement to everyone—even for some of us that live in Alberta but certainly to everybody who doesn't live in Alberta when they find out about it. Because it's disproportionate in every respect,

Tommy Banks stands out as nobody's fool on the Hill. [Daron Donahue]

both to the conventional perception of Alberta and to the size, the population and the age of the province. This is another of the things of which we should be really proud, because pound for pound, Alberta has always punched far above its weight.

✳ *Why is that?*

I once set out to try to find out why that was. I just concentrated in Edmonton because that's where I live, but the same thing would apply to Fort Macleod and lots of places. I went back in the archives to find why did this happen, how did this come about, why do we have more theatre, music, graphic art, sculptures and composers than you would think would be the case. I couldn't find an answer. But somewhere back there in every town or city, there must have been a Joe Shoctor [founder of the Citadel Theatre] who said, "Notwithstanding the difficulties and the impediments, we're going to do this"—someone who had the determination to galvanize the folks wherever they were and make it work. And that's true in every town and every city in Alberta. It's quite remarkable and that literally shocks many people.

A funny corollary of that is that Albertans are the lowest per-capita at applying for grants from Canada Council—a disparity that we've been trying to solve for a long time because it doesn't make any sense. We have this disproportionately huge activity in the arts and cultural industries, and yet one of the resources that can be used by creative people is not fully utilized by Albertans. We're continually trying to convince more Alberta creative people to apply more frequently for the kind of assistance that is available and to which people in other parts of the country all avail themselves. Albertans just don't.

✳ *Would you attribute that to Albertans' self-image of rugged individualism and independence?*

I don't think so. There are misimpressions that go both ways. Albertans have misimpressions, as I have, as I learn every day and have all my life, about what goes on in other parts of the country. In the same sense, most Canadians have a lot of misconceptions about Alberta and about how we do things in Alberta and why. So I don't think it's consciously saying we're not going to apply for grants because we're going to stand on our own two feet. That doesn't make any sense in some areas, particularly when you recognize that public assistance is required for all kinds of things, and we use it in Alberta for agricultural subsidies and tax forgiveness on certain business investments, all of which are very necessary.

But all kinds of wonderful things have happened in Alberta. The oil sands are the most recent, biggest and clearest example. That would not have happened were it not for a certain amount of favourable tax treatment for investments, which are highly risky. When they become less risky, when a thing becomes a proven fact, then those subsidies are no longer as necessary. But that kind of public assistance is given to all the resource industries and to the agricultural industry in Alberta. So I don't know why we don't take advantage of federal assistance to artists but I don't think it has to do with that thinking of independence. I hope it doesn't.

✳ *Is there any art or artist that, to your mind, sums up the spirit of Alberta?*

As in all things, Alberta's music, drama, theatre, graphic art, sculpture and literature are so diverse that it isn't possible to say what represents Alberta. But if I had to pick a source of music that represents Alberta, I would look among the compositions of Ian Tyson because he's an Albertan by choice. He's a real Albertan and he writes about things that Albertans understand intrinsically. He speaks for us in a lot of ways. So I would go there if I were looking for music to represent Alberta. But the music that is performed, created, composed and played well in Alberta is not limited to that by any means. The other end of the stick would be the opera, *Filumena*, which is grand opera in the truest sense of the word, by Albertans about an Albertan story that is redolent of a historical event in Alberta's history, which is pretty interesting and which most Albertans don't know about. [The opera tells the story, in English and Italian, of the last woman to be hanged in the province.] We're remarkably ignorant of ourselves sometimes, as others are.

※ *Is Alberta's arts scene a dark secret?*

Well, most Albertans aren't aware of the extent to which Alberta's performing artists and creators—poets, songwriters, composers and the like—are appreciated, played, read and performed elsewhere. I guess the most concentrated example would be the year before last, when "Alberta Scene" took place here at the National Arts Centre. Hundreds of artists from Alberta came here and performed and displayed in every conceivable genre of anything that could be thought of as arts. And that caused, as is the case when every other province comes here, eyebrows to rise because people, including Albertans, were continually running around saying, "We didn't know all this was going on in Alberta." *Filumena* was performed here during that time. I had the great pleasure of conducting the National Arts Centre Orchestra when Ian Tyson performed.

Whenever people see the depth and the breadth of art and other things, scientific undertakings and revolutionary agricultural things in Alberta, they're always surprised. And I don't know why they would be because Alberta has always provided a fertile field for innovation and creativity—"Let's try that, let's take that risk."

Nobody down here [Ottawa] cares that Alberta has the two best concert halls in Canada—the Winspear Centre in Edmonton and the EPCOR Centre for the Performing Arts in Calgary—and the largest theatre festival in North America, the Edmonton Fringe. The only places to have the complete Folkways Records collection are the Smithsonian and Edmonton, which doesn't come to mind as a place with any kind of critical mass.

It's not possible to stereotype Albertans any more than others based on historical trends. We used to be hicks, but not anymore.

Another item that people think grows like hayseed in Alberta is, of course, money. This also crops up among advocates for the arts across the land, notably when they make a business case for public

investment in a field that, at its heart, is driven by things less quanti-
fiable. A study commissioned by the Alberta Foundation for the Arts
(AFA) in 2005 revealed the economic impact of the arts in the province to include more than 3,500 full-time workers; spending of $120
million on operations and productions, and about $70 million to all
levels of government in tax revenue; a permanent annual increase of
$153 million in provincial gross domestic product (GDP) from creating
and producing artistic activities and events; and, based on a study by
Statistics Canada in 2001, a return-on-investment ratio of 12:1 for AFA's
grant of $13 million to arts organizations.[24] Statistics Canada reports
that Alberta's creative industries boosted her economy faster than the
cultural sectors in any other province, with growth of 74 per cent from
1996–2003, more than 25 per cent higher than the national average.
In 2003 television, radio, newspapers and other written media, adver
tising, film, visual and performing arts, architecture, festivals and so
on contributed $4.6 billion to Alberta's GDP (3.4 per cent of the total)
and 58,000 jobs (3 per cent of the lot).[25]

Okay, let's stop about the money for a second. As the playwright,
Tom Hendry, observed, "One can endlessly cite statistics to prove
employment, economic impact and tourist magnetism. What the
arts—given a chance—bring to a city is something in addition to all
these material rewards. They give a great city an image of its soul."[26]

Having gotten that out of the way, let's get back to the money.
Fans of the notion that Alberta does have more culture than bacteria
can take heart in the results of a face-to-face survey of 15,000 households by Statistics Canada revealing that Albertans ranked first in
consumers' cultural spending in 2001, 2003 and 2005, and—get this—
are almost *twice* as likely to spend money on concerts and theatre as
on hockey and football.

In 2005, 43 per cent of Albertans shelled out for arts events (to the
tune of $140 million), while only 23 per cent paid for sports events
($81 million). And to gild or even quilt the lily further, the average
Albertan spent more on the more narrowly defined category of

artwork and arts events—$114 per capita—than any other Canadians. The per-capita spending capitals in that category were Calgary ($139), Ottawa-Gatineau, St. John's and Edmonton ($116), with the national average at $88. Toting up all cultural items, defined by Stats Can as books, movie tickets, concerts, home entertainment, musical instruments and camera equipment, Albertans spent $971 per capita, beating the national average of $821. When broken down to cultural spending as a share of total consumer spending—in which Alberta led the land by a wide margin at $29,200 ($700 more than runner-up Ontario and $2,600 above the national average)—the province's 3.3 per cent was tied for third-highest in a close field, just 0.2 per cent behind both top-ranked Saskatchewan and the Canadian average.[27]

The study's researcher, Kelly Hill, noted, "In the rest of Canada, that's certainly not the perception of Alberta. That would surprise a lot of people."[28] The executive director of the Edmonton Arts Council, John Mahon, remarked, "It probably surprises some people who think that Albertans just get in their pickup truck, drive down Whyte Avenue and throw rocks. It challenges the stereotype. People who don't hang around theatre and concerts don't realize how many there are."[29]

"It surprises me a little that Albertans spend more on arts and culture than any other Canadians," admits Fil Fraser. "I would have expected Quebec to be at the top of that pile. But we live in an affluent society. We have a growing population, a very diverse population and people who appreciate the arts. Hockey and football are lovely, but they're not the whole thing. There's more theatre, dance and music going on."

Another notable item from that study is Alberta's sporting the largest gap between public and private spending on culture, at $3 billion for consumers and $540 million from the three levels of government. This raises questions. As the study's author pointed out, high spending in Alberta is at least partly attributable to her financial good fortune.[30] It would be interesting to know who is spending that money in terms of income levels. It can't be about wealth alone, or relatively poor old St. John's would not have finished third in per-capita spending on the arts.

In any case, Albertans certainly dig the arts. A battery of studies cited by the AFA indicate that 90 per cent of us attend or partici-pate in an arts event or activity each year and almost 12 million (well over thrice the provincial head count) attend the more than 40,000 arts events supported by the AFA each year. Albertans agree that it's important for every child to learn about the culture of the province (97 per cent agreed); that having a wide variety of cultural activi-ties and events makes Alberta a better place to live (94 per cent); and that taking part in cultural activities makes us feel good (86 per cent), helps relieve stress (81 per cent) and is enjoyable (about 75 per cent). Notably, 90 per cent of Albertans feel that it's important for the Government of Alberta to keep funding and supporting the arts. One might conclude from this that at least 88 per cent of Albertans favour motherhood statements, but again, the numbers trump the stereotype.[31]

Which brings us to another of those ironic disconnects between the *vox populi* and the still overwhelmingly white, male suits that represent us politically. That rank-and-file Albertans support the arts is apparent not only from attitudinal surveys but from hard numbers. Alberta ranked first in private-sector support of the performing arts in 2004 at $5.87 per capita.[32]

Yet we read stuff like Alberta ranking 11th out of 13 provinces and territories in per capita *public* funding for the arts, falling from $65 per capita in 1992–1993 to an inflation-adjusted $47 in 2002–2003, a decrease that led the nation at 18 per cent, 6 per cent above the national average; the Alberta government's funding for the arts, $63 per capita, was ahead of only Nova Scotia ($61) and Ontario ($51). In a poll of 600 Calgarians, 70 per cent believed that the province should partly fund the arts, notably music, theatre and visual arts, and to a lesser extent, dance, movies and publishing.[33] Even the *Calgary Herald* opined, "There are many reasons to support the arts, starting with the popular bohemian one: art for art's sake. It's the infrastructure of the soul. If you want a beautiful city, you have to build it with beauty."[34]

While fiscal hawks might argue that the private sector is picking up the slack, others clamour for a more generous expression of public support and disagree that the artist's way should include being "forced to plan for profitability, adequate market share and positive cash flow to qualify for funding."[35] As the journalist, Alan Kellogg, observed, "One of the major differences is that in Alberta, every organization must operate as a business and be guided by business principles."[36]

"I'm beyond outrage," stormed a senior arts administrator and admitted Tory voter. "I'm just embarrassed as an Albertan. It just goes to further fuel the perception that we're not really ready for primetime. This government is so behind the curve, so outdated. And the money for the AFA doesn't even come from general revenues, but from lotteries, which are also fat."[37]

From the artist's vantage point (here, from the roof of an office building in the downtown core of the capital city), the veteran, Juno Award-winning folksinger-songwriter, Bill Bourne, wonders why the oil industry—which he says has always been profitable—receives so much more support from the government than the arts. Down the hill, in the gold-flecked valley of the North Saskatchewan River on a crisp, autumn afternoon, Pat Darbasie observes that when her stage career began more than two decades ago, there were more theatres per capita in Edmonton than anywhere else in North America. She feels that "the art that happens here happens in spite of, not because of, why we are labelled 'that rich province.'"

Although lack of government support has driven much of the province's small but hardy book publishing and film industries out of the province or into the ground, an eclectic group of magazines survives to provide coverage of interest to audiences both within and beyond. In addition to the predictable paeans to cowboys, oil and commerce along with arts, lifestyle and other genres commonly available elsewhere, Alberta-based periodicals feature topics like purebred dogs,

African concerns, homeschooling and fly-fishing. There is leading national coverage of subjects from Aboriginal affairs (*Windspeaker*), emergency medical services (*The Emergency News*) and balancing mind, body and spirit (*Synchronicity*) to folk, roots and world music (*Penguin Eggs*), practical legal issues (*Law Now*) and the joys of the grape (*Wine Access*). *Legacy* magazine provided abundant evidence of the province's rich historical, cultural and artistic delights until it retired to its namesake in 2009.

Whether it's in theatre, music, the literary arts, drawing, painting, sculpture, ceramics, printmaking, quilting, weaving, photography, film or more, artists in Alberta have laboured not only behind a curtain of rawhide, but at least seven veils of distance from older, more crowded centres. Remarking on the "fierce individualists" and "confident otherness" that sustains the province's vigorous arts scene as it remains under the radar of others, the art historian, Patricia Ainslie, wrote, "In Alberta, as in many other jurisdictions situated on the periphery of the established art world, there was both the blessing of being an artist able to observe and absorb from afar and the curse of being in a distant place."[38] She observed that "colonial" attitudes that dismissed art created away from eastern centres failed to appreciate the incentive, provided by distance, to explore original perspectives rather than derivative work or attempts to pander to what is *au courant* in art.

In his landmark literary history of the province, George Melnyk traced the evolution of separate Aboriginal, ranching, agrarian, mountain and urban literary traditions into a postcolonial, postmodern, globalized synthesis, a process "full of intermingling, identities formed through differences and the clash of cultures." He found this process to have returned to its roots—the Aboriginal petroglyphs and pictographs at Writing-on-Stone—in requiring constantly new interpretation and understanding.[39] So culturally, Alberta remains a work in progress. Its dominant, white society is young relative to other provinces and places, and hardships associated with settlement, the Great Depression and even the last recession in the 1980s remain in the public's consciousness. As Chris Allen points out, "We understand how fleeting the economy can be and how important the more eternal things are, like the arts."

Diverse Roots

There is not one real Alberta. I have an image of clearly different people with different backgrounds—cowboys, East Indians, artists, scientists and more—getting together to create something beautiful. They stand up in all their diversity but collectively make music that every culture sings. The landscape brought different people, traditions and cultures, which created different ways of doing things.
    —DAVID WARD, 2007

For about 10,000 years, the area we call Alberta was home to first peoples like the Slavey, Beaver, Woodland Cree, Chipewyan, Plains Cree, Stoney, Blood, Peigan and Blackfoot. Then with the arrival of whitey, she transformed profoundly. Beginning in the 1870s, the North-West Territories became an immigrant society as the federal government surveyed and opened up the West for agricultural settlement, ushering in hordes of settlers, as the author, Ken Liddell, put it, "from all races but who now share a family tree that has stout-hearted roots in the courage of the explorers, police, traders and missionaries and its heritage in the great open-heartedness of the west."[40]

The first known pale face to see Alberta belonged to Anthony Henday, an ex-smuggler turned labourer tasked by the Hudson's Bay Company to drum up more Native trade in 1754. He was followed by French and British fur traders and missionaries, and by that uniquely Canadian creation, the Métis. Missionaries such as Robert Rundle, a Protestant from England, the Grey Nuns from Montréal and particularly Albert Lacombe, the influential Oblate who also served as teacher, Cree translator and treaty-maker, began establishing missions, hospitals and residential schools across the province. (The oldest building in the province is said to be Père Lacombe's mission from 1861, now resting in St. Albert.) The French settled from Lac La Biche to Red Deer in east-central Alberta, building communities like St. Paul and Bonnyville, as well as in the north of the province, which is dotted by centres with names like Grande Cache, Girouxville and Falher. The *Franco-Albertain* community has a hardy culture, as distinct from Québec as Jasper is from Rocky Harbour, Newfoundland.

In the 1870s the federal government unleashed a chain of events that changed the face of the West forever, from purchasing the North-West Territories from the Hudson's Bay Company, surveying the prairies and opening up the land for settlement (at prices so low, it was practically giving it away) to sending in the Mounties, making treaties with First Nations and ushering in the railway. The largest herd of immigrants would come from Ontario, a fact acknowledged by Albert Grey, 4th Earl Grey and Canada's governor general, at the provincial inauguration ceremony in 1905. Ex-Ontarians dominated the political, social and economic scenes to the point that Alberta was dubbed "Rural Ontario West" until the 1920s, and despite imports from a plethora of other origins, as the Heritage Community Foundation reminded us, "no other immigrant group did more to define the future of mainstream society in Alberta than the Ontarians."[41]

Two large groups targeted by Ottawa built on this white Anglo-Saxon Protestant base.

Perceived as at the cream of the empire's food chain, British citizens were warmly welcomed and they poured in from all social strata, from policemen, tradesman and professionals to remittance men, poverty cases and the obligatory butlers. They responded especially to opportunities for investment in land and ranching in southwestern Alberta and they helped to instill a respect for order as well as fuel a growing labour movement.

The other group that the feds pursued vigorously was Americans, many of whom had the equipment, money and experience needed to build the agricultural frontier. Most of the nearly 600,000 Yankees that poured in between 1898–1914 were Midwestern farmers. Some were originally Canadians who had left eastern Canada in the 1860s–1880s in search of land and returned to find homesteads for their children. Americans brought their sports, music, social gospel and optimism to Wild Rose Country. Twenty-eight religious sects moved into Alberta, notably the Mormons who settled around Cardston in the south, bringing their expertise in dryland farming, irrigation and sugar beets (which was welcomed) and their polygamy (which was not, and they met with less opposition once their church formally abandoned the practice in 1890). These religious groups had the advantage of living in strong communities rather than in isolated homesteads. American blacks were discouraged by Ottawa, which hired agents to frighten them off with horror stories of miserable weather and presumably even sadder soil. Undeterred, 149 settlers from Oklahoma established Amber Valley north of Athabasca in 1910.[42] By 1911 almost one quarter of Albertans were born in the United States, outnumbering British-born Albertans and leaving Canadian-born Albertans in the minority.[43] In his address to the Canadian Club of Ottawa in 1906, Premier A.C. Rutherford noted the "enormous influx" from the US and assured Prime Minister Laurier and the other premiers present that these settlers would make good British subjects rather than be disloyal to Canada.[44]

In addition to recruiting British and American settlers, Ottawa hired special agents to solicit other groups that it believed to be desirable: Norwegians, Danes, Dutch, Belgians, French Canadians, German Russians and religious minorities in the United States. The famous plea by the interior minister, Clifford Sifton, for hardy "men in sheepskin coats" cast a broader net and eventually, the cultural mosaic in Alberta grew to include, for example, Icelanders settling near Markerville; Swedes in Scandia; Norwegians in Claresholm, Edberg and Camrose; Germans in Stony Plain, Bashaw and Medicine Hat; Dutch in Granum, Nobleford and Strathmore; and in a departure from northern and western Europe, Ukrainians from the provinces of Galicia and Bukovina starting near Lamont and extending northeast to places like Mundare, Chipman and Vegreville; Poles in Wostok, Krakow and Kopernick; and Hungarians in Lethbridge, Ezterhazy and coal-mining towns of the south. Places in Alberta have been named by people from twenty-five nations, as diverse as Yemen (whose expats named Aden), Greece (Philomena, Orion), Italy (Vulcan, Bassano), Lebanon (New Sarepta), Lithuania (Vilna), South Africa (Krugerville, Vledt, Botha), Spain (Bonanza, Del Bonita, Granada), Syria (Abilene) and Ukraine (Ukrania).[45] Alberta's localities have been named after members of the military and police, geologists, royalty and aristocracy, missionaries and church leaders, ranchers, journalists, doctors and dentists, railroaders, developers, bankers and financiers, judges and lawyers, merchants and politicians.

In a period typical of the booms and busts that cycled through the last century in Alberta, her population grew fivefold from 1901 to almost 373,000 in 1911. As a sample of who was moving here, in 1910, for example, homesteaders from 27 nations made more than 18,000 homestead entries: 6,397 from the US, 3,248 from the rest of Canada, 2,348 from Britain, 1,032 from other parts of Alberta, 898 from Austria-Hungary, 665 from Russia, 421 from Sweden, 283 from Canadians returning from stateside, 12 from Iceland, 5 from New Zealand, a pair from Newfoundland and solos from each of China, Persia, Chile, Spain and Turkey. As an unnamed observer said at the time, "It may not generally be known how exceedingly cosmopolitan in character is the crowd of applicants for tracts of the free land of Alberta."[46]

A common denominator among most, if not all, of these immigrants was their aim to begin anew, whether it was fleeing hunger, poverty, social stratification, ethnic or religious persecution or creditors, or simply seeking adventure, new opportunity or some plot of land to call their own for awhile. An expression adopted by one Norwegian pioneer to title her memoir—"looking for country"[47]—refers to an animal bent on escaping, as in a stampeding herd or a spooked horse, but extends nicely to immigrants who sought freedom in a strange, new homeland.

The Ukrainian Cultural Heritage Village, a living history museum and park off the Yellowhead Highway in east-central Alberta, provides a vivid peek into immigrant life on the agricultural frontier in the early twentieth century. Interviewed there in front of an onion-domed church in her guise as the homesteader, Vaselina Hawreliak from Bukovina (circa 1928), the historical interpreter, Lessia Petriv, lyrically presents the immigrant ethic: "We came to new land. We brought seeds in our pockets. But we put our traditions, you know, our beliefs in our hearts. We came here, we threw seeds in a strange ground. We grow the good crop. We help others, contribute to the community. We want to share whatever we bring with us and plant it here, with our children." Today, there are nearly 300,000 Albertans of Ukrainian origin, just under 10 per cent of the provincial population. Edmonton is home to the world-famous Shumka Dancers (among other accomplished dance ensembles), as well as the Canadian Institute of Ukrainian Studies and the Ukrainian Canadian Archives & Museum of Alberta. The world's largest pysanka in Vegreville is a further monument to this heritage, while Mundare is home to the Basilian monastery and the Golgotha grotto, a popular site for Ukrainian Catholic pilgrims. Early Ukrainian organizations in Alberta often followed the "Prosvita" community groups from the old country, supporting education and culture through bodies like choirs and theatre companies.[48] Albertans elected the country's first MP of Ukrainian descent in 1926.

Anne Wheeler remains struck by how much Albertans have accomplished in so short a time, and "How all these different peoples came together to form communities and that the Ukrainians, the French, the Norwegians and everybody seemed to be levelled by the act of survival, getting through these winters, getting the communities together, delivering the babies, bringing the weddings together—all the things that they actually had to create out of nothing." The notion

of the province's cultural diversity as a great leveller is echoed by Fil
Fraser, who attributes it to a proximity to the frontier in her early
days. Speaking of that time, he says, "Because there was no overarch-
ingly dominant group, people learned to get along and developed a
much more relaxed approach to diversity, which serves us well today."
Ted Byfield suggests that there is no caste system here, though there's
still one in his native Toronto. Certainly, pedigree can't be discounted
entirely but personal observation suggests that it counts less in Alberta.
A prissy inquiry like "Takach? Where's *that* from?" is far more likely
to occur in Montréal, Ottawa or Toronto than in Calgary, Edmonton
or Grande Prairie. And it's not that today's Albertans don't care
about their heritage: on the whole, they just don't seem as interested
in ranking it in some patrician hierarchy any more than, say, tossing
their headwear into the political arena or even showing up to vote. A
generation ago, Robert Kroetsch wrote, "The process of losing ethnic
backgrounds is pretty much over in Alberta: the process of recovering
those backgrounds has begun. Unlike Ontario, there was in Alberta no
charter group that might absorb or alienate the newcomer." Blending
notions of a melting pot and starting afresh (if not mixing metaphors,
as he is too fine a writer for that), he continued, "But all were coming
into a vacuum created by the destruction of the buffalo and those
who depended upon them, and each newcomer, instead of feeling he
was being assimilated, felt instead that he was helping to create what
Alberta was to become."[49]

Today, Alberta's diversity endures in quiet ways. The 140 Christian,
communal Hutterite colonies in the province are the highest total
in Canada. In the town of Brooks, with about 11,000 people, more
than 100 languages or dialects are spoken, spurred by an influx from
Africa and the Middle East since the mid-1990s, drawn by jobs at a
local packing plant. Lac La Biche, a town of 2,700 located 200 kilometres northeast of Edmonton, claims the largest Lebanese population
per capita in Canada and the third mosque on the continent, built in
1958. This was no fluke. In the early 1930s, when there were less than

700 Muslims in Canada, a group of Muslim women in Edmonton set out to build the first mosque on these shores, but by the time the construction dust settled around the onion domes of the Al Rashid Mosque (attributable to the Ukrainian heritage of the project's contractor), a much smaller-scale project had opened in Cedar Rapids, Iowa. Still, Alberta can claim the first mosque in Canada and two of the first three in North America.[50] That tradition lives on in the capital city, where 500 filmgoers attended the Mosques Awards for young Muslim film and video artists in 2008.

Reflecting on the truth behind the image of white cowboys known to the rest of the country, Bruce McGillivray marvels, "There's a sense that here's farmers, ranchers, cowboys, oil-riggers and that's about it for this province. But there's well over a hundred different cultural communities here. This is a very different society than it's portrayed, a much more interesting society, one that's far more tolerant, engaging and culturally intriguing."

Contrary to popular images of Alberta as a bastion of intolerance— typified by a comment made in a street interview by a newcomer to the province from the Maritimes, who observes, "Albertans are not open to multiculturalism"[51]—Albertans tend to accept cultural diversity. In fact, a survey suggests that 31 per cent of Albertans think that increasing multiculturalism best describes the story of Canada, which ranks second to Saskatchewan and BC at 37 per cent and 4 per cent above the national average.[52] And Albertans scored third in the rankings of the most likely to socialize with people from other cultures, at 78 per cent, just 1 per cent behind leading Manitoba and 6 per cent above the national average.[53] Other Canadians often mistake Albertans' pluralism for anti-French sentiments. Preston Manning cited a story of his father telling Prime Minister Lester Pearson, "If you stood at the main downtown intersections of Alberta's largest cities and shouted, 'This is an equal partnership between two founding races, cultures and languages—the English and the French,' passersby would probably suggest that you seek psychiatric help. Such a definition in no way described the present-day reality of those particular parts of Canada."[54] Ernest Manning, like many Albertans, opposed singling out English and French and referring to other ethnic groups and their "cultural" contributions in an inferior sense.

Norman Kwong recalls that being the only Chinese-Canadian playing professional football in Canada caused fans to root *for* him. Having changed positions from fullback to lieutenant-governor of Alberta—a career that included a stint as national chairman of the Canadian Consultative Council on Multiculturalism—His Honour observes from his office, "I've been to very many high schools and different educational places across the province where I've seen the best diversity of students now. When I went to Western Canada High School in Calgary, there were over a thousand students and maybe two Chinese families. Now, there's a real cultural diversity and they all get along."

This sentiment seems to be shared widely though not unanimously across the province. "I'd argue that it's a tolerance for a spectrum of opinions that describes the West," wrote Jim Grey of Alberta's energy industry, noting that "There's not an *engrained* establishment that goes back generations and generations."[55] Miki Andrejevic, a former manager of the Belgrade Symphony Orchestra and now a prominent arts festival organizer and administrator in the province, enthuses, "Alberta is a land of opportunity, literally. What other province or country would accept as an executive director of a writer's organization [the Writers Guild of Alberta] a guy for whom English is a third language?"

And yet Alberta is far from the most popular destination for international immigrants. In 2006 Alberta's immigrant tally of just over 527,030 was 16 per cent of her total population, 4 per cent under the national average.[56] In 2001 Alberta enumerated her immigrants and found these origins, in order of frequency: the United Kingdom, southeast and eastern Asia, continental northern and western Europe, Eastern Europe (each between 10–14 per cent), southern

Asia, southern Europe, the United States, Africa, Central and South America, the Caribbean and Bermuda, and Oceana and other countries (2–7 per cent).[57] In 2006, Alberta's visible minority population of 14 per cent was 2 per cent less than the national average.[58] The province boasts the most Métis in Canada: more than 66,000 or 23 per cent of the total.[59]

In 2006 the Human Rights, Citizenship and Multiculturalism Education Fund held nine consultations across Alberta aimed at reducing discrimination at the community level. It found growing diversity in Alberta communities, which was generally welcomed; that more Albertans recognized that skills and knowledge acquired outside of Canada should be valued; that children and youth were more open to diversity and were discussing issues of inclusion and discrimination in schools and communities; and that Albertans were increasingly aware of inclusive communities and workplaces, and understood that our continued prosperity depends on that. However, lest anyone think that the province is a polyglot utopia, the fund also found that: many members of minority groups continue to experience discrimination, including homosexuals and since 9/11, Muslims; Aboriginal people face discrimination based on stereotypes, especially women and young people; there was a systemic discrimination in lack of diversity on boards of directors and among decision-makers in many government, public institution and high-level bodies; and that many Albertans are unaware of the ongoing prevalence of discrimination, particularly regarding employment amidst a growing population and economy.[60]

And yet the optics remain largely positive. The Edmonton Heritage Festival is the largest known multicultural party held in one location. It's a more than thirty-year-old celebration of diverse traditions, global harmony and overeating in which people from seventy-two nations gather in the usually sun-baked river valley to share culture, food and heartburn remedies. (It's like the United Nations, but without the paperwork or the peacekeeping.) When a killing tornado devastated the capital city in 1987, the show went on true Albertan style with a world-record conga line of 10,442 people.[61] Although no place is perfect, Alberta's tradition of attracting immigrants has created a diverse environment that largely tolerates cultural differences and even celebrates them now and then. With fewer years of white settlement than pretty much the rest of the country south of sixty, the province seems more concerned with what you have to sell than where your ancestors come from. Alberta has a longstanding openness to new people and ideas, enabling her to grow from the fringes of what passes for white civilization to a society as cosmopolitan and egalitarian as possible under the circumstances.

That openness, manifested through an overarching attitude toward learning and improving things, is where we will turn next.

Yearning for Learning

Audiences in Alberta are the most engaged, most informed, most serious audiences in Canada.
—NAOMI KLEIN, 2007

Often lost in the glut of energy and commerce in the province is another longstanding obsession. Confounding their image as simple cow-folk, Albertans have established an eye-catching penchant for forward motion and self-improvement. The exact causes of this— whether altruism, restlessness, greed or otherwise—remain to be seen.

Aritha van Herk tells me, "Some days I think Albertans are changing for the worse, and those are on days when all they're interested in is flaunting wealth and how much money they made yesterday. And on other days I think that they are changing for the better because they do have a sense of responsibility even if it isn't always visible to the outside world." She points to Albertans' relatively high levels of education and literacy, and believes that Albertans use libraries per capita more than people in any other province. "You've got to look for it in those small details that may be quite hidden," she advises, "especially when you're looking at edifices that are so huge that there's no detail visible." No less an authority than Margaret Atwood seems to agree: "Albertans have the highest per capita readership in the country," she told reporters. "It's not full of stupid people."[62]

Albertans' love of libraries was evident in the passage of a law during the first legislative assembly authorizing municipalities to create free public libraries. Visiting the province in 1913, the British neo-Romantic poet, Rupert Brooke, compared Calgary's public library highly favourably in both the quantity and quality of selections to "the dingy rooms and inadequate intellectual provision of Toronto and Winnipeg" and the inability of Montréal to support a library.[63] Today, Alberta has 310 public libraries from Zama City up north to Coutts down south, Bear Canyon in the west and Lloydminster in the east. Of 362 municipalities, 306 provide library service (many of those that don't are summer villages) and more than 98 per cent of Albertans have access to a library.[64] And by gum, do they use them. According to the Canadian Urban Libraries Council, in 2006, Alberta's libraries placed five of the top seven in circulation per registered borrower (including the top two, Medicine Hat and Lethbridge), two of the top three in questions per capita and two of the top five in circulation. Two notable dichotomies here are that the province's libraries placed only three of the top thirty-five in total spending (materials and operating costs) per capita, and the province failed to place a single library in the top thirty-three in registered borrowers as a percentage of the population.[65] It's anyone's guess whether this suggests a better overall bang for the taxpayer's buck in Alberta, a chasm between a cadre of rabid library-goers and other Albertans, or merely a lot of lapsed memberships due to overdue books and unpaid fines. In any bookcase, the library at the University of Alberta is Canada's second-largest research library and ranks first in volumes per student.[66] That institution also leads the country with thirty professors who have received national 3M Teaching Fellowships, Canada's highest award for undergraduate university teaching excellence; the runner-up, the University of Western Ontario, has twenty.[67]

The province made learning a *cause célèbre* early on when Premier Rutherford appointed himself minister of education and boosted the number of schools from 526 in 1905 to more than one thousand within three years.[68] Nor was he shy about his priorities. At a banquet in honour of Canada's premiers hosted by the Canadian Club of Ottawa in 1906, Prime Minister Laurier and seven premiers delivered speeches trumpeting the country's progress since Confederation. Speaking in order of provincial admission to Confederation—and thus last in that era—Mr. Rutherford opened by claiming the closest connection to Ottawa among the premiers by virtue of being born in Carleton County. Building on this broadside of charm, he expressed his hope that his "splendid" province, then barely a year old, would "lay the foundations of Empire" by adopting good features of "the older provinces" and "profit[ing] by the mistakes they have made." He focused on the importance of learning, booming, "I believe that in Alberta, the universal education of our people is the greatest glory of our province." He noted the organization of 140 new school districts in the preceding year and could not resist declaring that good measures adopted from other provinces included "taking out there the cream of the teaching staff of Ontario" and proudly paying the highest teacher's salaries in the Dominion, at least $500 per year. Having built up a head of steam to rival those belched by the railways that would later precipitate his political downfall, he closed by noting his compliance with the chairman's decree to keep the speeches brief.[69]

Earlier that year, in the first session of the new Legislature, the premier astounded some by passing a law creating a provincial university. When critics suggested this was premature, he argued that it was necessary to preempt dominance by religious institutions—an interesting statement coming from a deacon in the Baptist Church and an active Christian volunteer.[70] Classes started within two years. By 1916 the province had fourteen post-secondary institutions: a university, the first publicly funded technical institute in Canada, two "normal" schools for teaching teachers, three agricultural schools and seven privately supported colleges, six of the latter being church-related.[71] Meanwhile, at ground level, half of the children in Alberta were learning in one-room schoolhouses that combined up to eleven grades. At a time when the "three Rs" (reading, 'riting and 'rithmetic) were deemed sufficient, most students did not continue past grade eight. Teachers (mostly young women) were judged largely by their production of the annual rural school rite, the Christmas pageant, and on top of being poorly paid, they were the last in the British Empire to gain a pension in 1939. School budgets were slashed during the Depression. Education in Alberta only entered something like modernity along with the rest of the province after World War II, with the university's new faculty of education replacing the normal schools and breaking new ground in establishing: specialized departments in elementary education, educational psychology, secondary education and educational administration; new facilities to replace the one-room variety; high-school curricula expanded to include vocational and technical work; new post-secondary schools; and classrooms made more accessible to students with disabilities and special needs.[72]

Making up for lost time, the province took the lead on several fronts.

Alberta was the first province to establish quality-teaching standards to promote excellence in classroom instruction, setting out the knowledge, skills and attributes expected of teachers.

Alberta's charter schools were another first in Canada. These non-denominational hangouts operate autonomously like any other public school and increase students' choices within the public system. They cannot charge tuition fees, operate for profit or discriminate in admitting students. The difference lies in their charter, the contract between the ministry of education and the initiating parents and educators: the charter establishes the educational philosophy, mission, governance and organization of the school, giving parents autonomy and flexibility in governing their schools, while requiring accountability in meeting their mandate, earning parental satisfaction and improving students' learning in a measurable way. An early example was L'Académie Vimy Ridge Academy, combining a professional ballet program and a uniform-based cadet program and fondly known in district offices as "tanks and tutus."

The Edmonton Public School Board became what *Maclean's* magazine called "a darling of American educational reformers" and a model for "dramatic and controversial initiatives" in Oakland, California, and reforms in places like Seattle and Houston. Under innovations begun in the 1970s by Mike Strembitsky, a superintendent with relevant experience in both teaching and hog farming, schools ran on business principles and entrepreneurial vision, with principals having "unheard-of autonomy and budget control," plus the right to draw students from anywhere in the district. Beyond system-wide expenses like transportation and debt servicing charges, 92 per cent of the revenue spent by principals is based on priorities set by the staff at each school. As a result, almost half of the capital city's students attended schools outside of their neighbourhood catchment, more than double the national average of 20 per cent (leaving aside the thorny green issue). A professor of management in California called Edmonton the instigator and most successful proponent of running schools with entrepreneurial flair, declaring, "It is revolution."[73]

Apparently, the province is the best place to learn in Canada. The Composite Learning Index developed by the Canadian Council on Learning measures seventeen indicators of lifelong learning that cover both formal and other schooling, plus four kinds of learning: learning to know (youth literacy, high-school dropout rate, youth post-secondary education, university attainment, learning institutions), to do (workplace, job-related and vocational training), to live together (community institutions, volunteering, social clubs and organizations, learning from other cultures) and to be (access to media, culture, sports, broadband Internet and cultural resources).

Alberta earned top marks in Canada in each of the first five years of the index, scoring 83 in 2006 (national average: 73),[74] 86 in 2007 (nationally, 76),[75] 85 in 2008 (nationally, 77)[76] and 82 in both 2009 and 2010 (nationally, 75 in both years).[77] Calgary topped the list of large cities for the first four years. In 2008, Calgarians led a list of 37 cities in the share of the citizenry that spent on museums (54 per cent) and the live performing arts (52 per cent), which *Maclean's* magazine admitted made Calgarians Canada's most cultured citizens, even if it contradicted their "Wild West," "raucous" image.[78] Alberta's overall score sagged more than any other province's over those five years (minus-0.7 compared to a national average gain of plus-0.3 from 2006–2010). At this writing, she remains numero uno, followed precariously closely by Ontario (79) and BC (78).

When I asked him about Alberta's strong showing, Fil Fraser (speaking, appropriately, at Grant MacEwan University), professed not to be surprised. He cites two institutions as examples of the province's innovations on this front. Athabasca University is the first and most successful distance learning institution in Canada, modelled after the Open Learning University in Britain and serving about 34,000 students worldwide who never see a classroom. And he calls The Banff Centre the most unique educational institution in the country, the only place of its kind devoted completely to fine arts of all kinds and a place where artists go after they've completed their formal, academic education, to take their art to the next level: master classes with the greatest artists in the world in all disciplines. To provide a few other examples of leadership on the institutional side, the Northern Alberta Institute of Technology trains more skilled-trade apprentices than any other school in Canada, including 17 per cent of the country's tradespeople;[79] the University of Alberta has, at this writing, Canada's only Faculty of Native Studies; and the University of Calgary pioneered the larger-scale use of podcasting in Canadian universities.

Alberta also holds her own at the grassroots level. In a comparison of the reading and math skills of fifteen-year-olds among forty-one countries and Canadian provinces conducted by the Programme for International Students Association in 2003, Alberta ranked second behind Finland in reading skills, second behind Hong Kong-China in math and fifth in problem-solving skills.[80] In a similar survey among sixty-six countries and Canadian provinces in 2006, fifteen-year-old Albertans scored second in science, seventh in math and fifth in reading skills.[81] The Progress in International Reading Literacy Survey of 215,000 grade-four students in forty-five countries and Canadian provinces in 2006 ranked Albertan students third in reading, behind Russia and Hong Kong.[82] In a 2007 study of grade-four students across sixty systems internationally, Alberta rated a tie for fourth place in science, but only matched the international average in math.[83]

As home to twenty-nine universities and colleges, Alberta touts herself as having the most skilled and educated people in North America, with more than 40 per cent of her workforce holding post-secondary degrees or certificates[84]—and presumably the traditionally corresponding backpack-hernias, caffeine addictions and debt loads.

And yet all is not roses, even if they are wild. Alberta has ranked second-lowest in post-secondary funding per capita in Canada and harboured the lowest percentage of high-school graduates who flocked directly to post-secondary education.[85] Albertan seventeen- and eighteen-year-olds had the lowest high-school graduation rate among the provinces in 2006 (68 per cent, 7 per cent under the national average), though Alberta Education's figures are slightly higher and apparently improving.[86] Alberta also boasts the third-highest high-school dropout rate among twenty- to twenty-four-year-olds from 2004–2007 at about 11 per cent, almost 2 per cent above the national average, with especially alarming rates of 18 per cent in small towns and 20 per cent in rural areas, pretty much leading the country. Rural Albertan students racked up one of the highest rates of high-school dropouts in Canada (about 25 per cent in 2006), presumably beguiled by high pay for less skilled work and thus more vulnerable to the economic downturn that inevitably followed in late 2008.[87]

Yet Albertans' overall track record suggests that our headlong rush to get ahead in the world extends to the areas of research, arts, culture and learning. "Albertans are interested in learning more, interested in growing, achieving," declares Brian Dunsmore, a veteran of the radio world whom we'll meet shortly. "Alberta is a wonderful place and not by any stretch of the imagination the one-dimensional world that others would have us believe."

Ears a Little More Open[88]

Can you imagine an eighty-year-old product that people get delivered free, but happily pay almost $3 million a year for, just because they like it so much? A product demanded by everyone from surgeons in the operating room to long-distance truckers in their rigs? A product loved so much that some 1,500 unpaid volunteers line up to help deliver it?

Imagination meets reality at CKUA Radio, Canada's oldest continuing non-profit broadcaster. Over more than eight decades, the station has weathered the ravages of shifting tastes and technology, Byzantine broadcasting regulations, indifferent ownership, misman-agement and even a pulled plug. It has launched a litany of landmarks in Canadian broadcasting, become a favourite of artists and audiences alike, and belied an external stereotype of its native Alberta as boasting less culture than yogurt. The station's veteran program manager, Brian Dunsmore, observes, "People wonder why there's nothing like CKUA in Toronto, New York or London. It's a singular operation, and it says marvelous things about who we are and what we are, though we tend to hide it under a barrel."

Today, this unique outlet enjoys the cult-like devotion of some-where around 200,000 listeners and 17,000 donors who keep it afloat with astounding financial, logistical and emotional support. Why are they are so passionate about CKUA? And exactly what does CKUA's story say about Alberta?

"CKUA endures because it's willing and able to take risks," declares its station manager, Ken Regan. "It provides a real alternative to the CBC and the private broadcasters."

"The quality of the music and its informative presentation make CKUA unique," agrees Doug Penner, then the volunteer chair of the non-profit foundation that owns the station. "The announcers are constantly exploring and putting new music in context rather than repeating themselves. If you hear the same song twice in one week, you *know* it's a hot song!"

It wasn't always about the music, though the station did sign on with a live piano rendition of "God Save the King" on November 21, 1927. Broadcasting from a cramped shack at the University of Alberta (recognized in its last two call letters), CKUA fulfilled the vision of the campus's visual-aids specialist, H.P. Brown, to bring the institution to Albertans through the new medium. Most people lived on farms then, and Mr. Brown saw radio waves as a quantum leap from dispatching lecturers with magic-lantern shows to disparate communities isolated by distance, mud, snow or impassable combinations thereof.

Here began a string of broadcasting landmarks: the nation's first school broadcast in 1929; a special wartime newscast for American soldiers stationed in the Yukon in 1944; what we now call "multicultural" broadcasting after World War II; a pioneering stereo broadcast in 1959; the first broadcast of a proceeding of a legislative assembly in the British Commonwealth; and Canada's first online radio streaming in 1996.

Ownership moved from the cash-starved university to Alberta Government Telephones in 1945 and to the provincially owned ACCESS Corporation in 1974. When the Klein government privatized CKUA in 1994, it transferred ownership to a non-profit foundation, led by dubiously qualified appointees who drained its transition funding and, in what became the station's darkest hour, pulled the plug in

1997. As long-serving staffers were too crushed to do it, the junior-most announcer, Chris Martin, signed off—with the defiant (and prophetic) words, "We'll be back ... after this."

The ensuing dead air capped a history that reads like an epic struggle, a prairie picaresque brimming with heroic tales of clinging to bare survival. For most of a century, progressive, spirited do-gooders battled everything from threadbare technology, posturing politicians and convoluted broadcasting regulations to government neglect, money-sucking director-"consultants" and other natural and human-made disasters. A radio engineer interrupted his vacation in the 1940s to rebuild the station's sole, destroyed, remote amplifier from scratch on his own time and dime. A station manager fought the feds for enough wattage to keep the signal from being drowned out by competitors. A federal ruling in 1970 prohibited educational institutions from holding broadcasting licences.

But back to the nearly fatal shutdown in 1997. Within days, a groundswell of grassroots support from across Alberta saw donations of money pour into the silent station and letters of protest deluge Premier Klein's office. After weeks of occasionally rancorous negotiation, the former, government-appointed board was ousted by an impromptu, purely volunteer team led by the musician (and later, senator), Tommy Banks, and an Edmonton lawyer and occasional CFL referee, Bud Steen.

Two laid-off staffers, Lee Onisko and David Ward, embarked on a whistle-stop, cap-in-hand quest centred on the station's seventeen transmitters scattered around the province. An earnest, quiet pilgrimage soon became a media *cause célèbre*, with fans donating food, gas for the duo's vehicle and money. This "Touch the Transmitter Tour" raised about $25,000 in five days but it also became a metaphor for the station's unassailable grit and Albertans' refusal to allow anyone to take CKUA from them. ("This isn't a radio station," trumpeted Mr. Ward at the time, "it's a religion.") Meanwhile, an army of overnight crusaders raised $1 million in fourteen days, generating enough phone

CKUA's Steve Woodman, whose on-air exploits included duets with Doris Day records and eventual moves to the CBC (as Dr. Bundolo) and to NBC in NYC, spins the platter in 1952. [*Provincial Archives of Alberta, PA 1631/2*]

calls to pop CKUA's telephone circuits. CKUA returned triumphantly to the airwaves after five weeks and has stayed there since.

· "The irony is that when the station went off the air for the first time, people finally understood what a treasure it represented," explains Mr. Regan. This is echoed by the litany of volunteers who emerged to help save CKUA and by the social psychologist, Robert Sinclair, who tells me that people are more likely to have their passions raised when a freedom or something important to them is taken away.

Paradoxically, privatization has made CKUA more dependent on public largesse than ever. Donations accounted for 54 per cent of revenues in 2008–2009, with 23 per cent from advertising and sponsorships, 13 per cent from operating the province's emergency public warning system (which it created after Edmonton's killing tornado in 1987, and the contract for which the government awarded to some Ottawa-based firm in 2010) and 5 per cent from renting technical services. The station has staked its future on the novel notion of "subscription radio," a departure from its long history of institutional backing. Management sees this as an appropriate relationship between CKUA and its audience, inviting listeners to pay as they would for magazines or cable TV.

"We have no mechanism to withhold the service," explains Mr. Dunsmore, noting that it would be impossible to maintain CKUA on a conventional business model. "So we depend on people taking personal responsibility. The honour system works."

The numbers bear this out. There are 8,000 listeners with ongoing subscriptions. Donations totalled $2.9 million in 2008–2009, up from $1.3 million nine years earlier. Donations come from listeners in more then three dozen countries, as diverse as China, Norway and Sierre Leone.

But CKUA's support doesn't stop at cash donations. Volunteers contribute to every facet of its operations, be it serving on the foundation's board, running a music information line, cataloging and filing discs in the library, contacting donors, writing for the on-air *Arts and*

Culture Guide, or organizing and staffing fundraisers. Their contributions total 16,000 hours, which, even if calculated at Alberta's minimum-wage rate, saves the station more than $140,000 annually. That doesn't include the ten-day, biannual fundraisers, in which bluehairs, blue-rinses and in-betweens chip in another 3,000 hours each time. The station simply couldn't operate without them.

This brings us to the core of CKUA's popularity. It appeals to a segment of society united not by traditional geographic, social or economic strata but by an appreciation for expanding their horizons, an ethic consistent with the station's original mandate of providing academic outreach to the community.

"CKUA listeners are people with their minds awake and their ears a little more open, interested in music, art and culture, and striving to . improve their lives," says Mr. Dunsmore.

"I hate to criticize because the vast majority listen to 'Oops!...I Did It Again' or the Backstreet Boys," shrugs Tom Coxworth, who hosts the *Folk Routes* program. "The question is, are you going to find something that excites you and gives you a challenge, something you haven't heard before?"

CKUA's programming is ambitious, eclectic and highly personal to announcers and listeners alike. In any given week, you can hear music from classical, choral and jazz to new age, "wide cut" country and an aural collage of "minimal techno, Latin house, jazzy down-tempo, IDM and hybrids" called *Future Funk*. And the global diversity of daily programs like *Alberta Morning* defies categorization, not to mention the hoary stereotype of Albertans as homogenous rednecks.

Free from the dictates of hit parades or preformatted playlists, CKUA announcers can choose from one of Canada's leading musical collections, boasting 1.5 million pieces of music, including a basement full of 15,000 vintage 78-rpm records, which one volunteer spent eight months cataloguing. "We don't have everything," says Mr. Ward, "but we come pretty close."

"CKUA is a source of pride to me," declares Bernie Fritze, a listener. "It helps define me as an Albertan, as a member of a culturally rich community where differences are celebrated. If music is the food of the soul, CKUA is the maître d' of the finest restaurant in the world."

"Why do so many Albertans own music by African kora players, Tuvan throat singers, Cuban congeros or Brazilian singers?" muses Monica Miller, host of *How I Hear It.* "As we listen to music from places we've never been—Finland, Madagascar, Jamaica, Nashville or Cape Breton—we come to understand that cultures don't fit into boxes. Music travels independent of lines on a map, and 'cultural fabric' becomes so rich and wonderful. Our listeners understand that in a very profound way."

"CKUA is for thinking people who want to be really involved in the rest of the world—people who like James Brown, Celtic music and opera, and can smile at the difference," smiles Mr. Coxworth.

"The whole thing is a joy," enthuses Andy Donnelly, a popular producer and announcer. "It's all about the music and the people. They *get* it. We all feel the power, the spirit and the joy of it."

But CKUA announcers don't just play and talk about the music; they live it. Their ranks brim with accomplished vocalists and musicians in jazz, folk, bluegrass and blues, along with writers, actors and arts impresarios. A staple on the Celtic circuit, Mr. Donnelly is on a first-name basis with many of the acts he plays on-air. Lionel Rault (*Nine to Noon*) is an acclaimed folk-roots guitarist and songwriter with a career exceeding the forty-year mark. Holger Peterson (*Natch'l Blues*, Canada's longest-running blues program, dating from 1969) is a producer who runs Stony Plain Records, a Canadian roots music label of over three decades' standing. John Worthington, the station's beloved "Old-disc Jockey," has been there since 1949; these days, he devotes countless hours to restoring and remastering big-band and other venerable but damaged recordings for broadcast and CD release. Tom Coxworth has 12,000 LP discs in his collection and a recording studio in his basement. "We have a responsibility to the community and to the culture of the province in addition to the newsmakers," he says. "We're probably the most leading-edge in promoting local musicians who need to be heard. Many artists are respected and earning a living wage because CKUA gave them their start."

Reflecting the station's popularity with artists themselves, on-air tributes are spoken, sung and played by everyone from Africa's Black Umfolosi, the Bulgarian Women's Choir and the Cuban Institute of Friendship with the Peoples to the American jazz guitarist, Pat Methany, the Scottish folksinger, Dick Gaughan and the San Francisco-based activist and clown, Wavy Gravy. Pitching for CKUA here in Canada are the likes of the actor, Tom Jackson, the fiddler, Natalie MacMaster, the bluesman, Long John Baldry, the children's musical icon, Raffi, the talk-show host, Dini Petty and the then-existing folk duo of Kate and Anna McGarrigle. Internationally lauded performers like Corb Lund, Jann Arden, PJ Perry and k.d. lang credit the station with helping to launch their careers.

CKUA also has a long and strong record of contributing to arts, culture and education. "We tell people there's something good happening in Alberta," reports Chris Allen, host of *Arts Alive* and numerous arts-related programs over his three decades with the station. "I doubt there's a single arts or cultural group we haven't supported through our coverage. Other stations won't talk to the Cow Patti Theatre from Clive, Alberta, unless the theatre pays for it. We do."

Then came programs like *Innovation Anthology*, profiling science, research and technology; *Ecofile*, an award-winning environmental entry; and *Heritage Trails*, a series of five hundred historical vignettes. Though no longer on the air, the latter two are made freely available to Alberta schools and researchers. An ambitious trilogy of forty-eight-part documentary series chronicled popular music of the twentieth century. CKUA's monumental twenty-four-part series, *The Folkways Collection*, scooped the likes of PBS in documenting a vital slice of Americana, the amazing legacy of Moses Asch, the founder of Folkways Records. The series profiled the 30,000 musical performances, narratives, rituals, sounds and spoken word from around the world captured on that historic label. CKUA launched this unprecedented bi-national project by connecting personally with the late Mr. Asch's son, Michael (a fan of the station and then a University of Alberta professor) and the venerable Smithsonian Institution, which contributed funding and research assistance. A recent twenty-part series, *Inspiring Leadership*, explored best practices in, and the challenges of, leading in the twenty-first century. "Most people would look at that as a radio concept and laugh," laughs Mr. Regan. "But we feel that leadership in government, companies, communities and our own lives is fundamental to our society, especially today. It goes back to being willing to take chances. If we can present intelligent, credible content to our audience, even though it may be challenging, they'll listen and appreciate it."

Leadership is more than a buzzword at CKUA. The station is a strong advocate for community radio, fighting for a fund to support the operating activities of non-profit broadcasters. "CKUA might survive, but we fear that a lot of community and campus broadcasters won't," opines Mr. Regan. CKUA lobbied for the creation of a community radio support fund, financed initially with government seed money and contributions from private-sector broadcasters. Such a fund could become self-sustaining, based on a formula whereby community (non-profit) broadcasters would access monies on a matching-grant basis, drawing only an amount equal to what they earn through local community donations. The general manager believes that this would provide incentive for stations to be as relevant to their local audiences as possible. Community stations receiving funding could reinvest it to provide even better service, benefitting the stations, their communities and the broadcasting industry as a whole. "Remember, we don't own our broadcast licences, we're granted them," he states. "It's not a right, but a responsibility. At CKUA, we believe to the core that we have to work hard to earn our licence and to serve the public interest." CKUA's leadership has been recognized in awards at the provincial, regional and national levels, from disciplines as diverse as media, music, business, tourism, education, environmental communications and website design, not to mention coveted trophies from media slow-pitch league championships.

Yet the station remains an anomaly. Unlike the CBC, it no longer receives government funding. And unlike commercial radio stations, it is restricted by licence to four minutes of advertising per hour. This is why it seeks a support fund for community broadcasters. "On one hand," explains Mr. Regan, "we're prohibited from competing on an equal footing with the CBC and the private sector. On the other, we have no choice but to compete with them because we need an audience as much as they do". We face exactly the same challenges, but have none of the benefits they receive. I'm not complaining about the situation, but there is an inherent inequity in the way our current system is structured. A community radio support fund structured along the lines of what CKUA suggests would at least give our sector a fighting chance for survival. At least it would make our survival less dependent on external factors and more closely tied to our actual performance as broadcasters."

Beyond the competitive pressures of the marketplace, other daunting challenges lie ahead. Lacking a conventional capital budget, CKUA lives in a century-old building badly in need of upgrading, if not vacating. Its seventeen transmitters are also past their best-before dates, held together by what staffers affectionately call "glue, baling wire and duct tape." And the station must digitize its musical holdings, a half-million-dollar effort that will take years.

But Canada's oldest non-profit broadcaster remains optimistic even in a world of increasing fragmentation and competition. Donations continue to rise steadily, its website attracts over 100,000 people each month and it continues to meet its former board chair's promise to "engage and amaze" its growing body of listeners.

"CKUA will always be around if it stays true to its guiding principle," asserts Mr. Dunsmore, "which is to provide great music and useful information to its community."

"It's radio raised to a level that's really a public service," concludes Tommy Banks.

"That's Alberta, you know: the punter doing the right thing," enthuses Andy Donnelly, recalling the station's shutdown and revival back in 1997. "I'm not necessarily saying the politicians do it but the average man, woman and child in the street does. There's an integrity there that is totally Albertan, to do the right thing and sort things out, make it right. And that's what happened. CKUA has continued and it's continually supported."

Ultimately, CKUA's story reflects a larger political and cultural context, namely the rich and sometimes contradictory textures of the Wild Rose Province. From its pioneering days supporting outlying schools and bringing drama, music and new learning to remote audiences, the station has supported the public good in a society that glorifies private profit. Despite all of its challenges, CKUA continues courageously to serve a disparate and devoted patchwork of listeners, united only by their openness to eclectic sounds and fresh ideas, and to enriching themselves and their communities as a result.

So CKUA's story of pioneering, death and rebirth serves not only as a singularly Albertan story, but as a cautionary tale. In a world of increasingly uniform, preprogrammed playlists, where our choices as voters and consumers seem to be shrinking every day, one can only hope that CKUA's messages of exploration, originality and diversity remain a beacon, rather than a fading ray, of hope.

✳ Fil Fraser, Wild Rose Country's cultural Renaissance man, whose credits include serving as an announcer and producer at CKUA, takes us out of this foray into a deceptively vivid and complex cultural scene. "What would I say to people who would call Alberta a backwater of culture?" he asks. "They just haven't been here. Don't tell them, or they'll all want to come here. It's happening already. In many ways, Alberta is one of the best-kept secrets in Confederation. This is the most culturally advanced part of the country."

When it comes to advancement in Alberta, culture and every other sector enjoys a sibling relationship with the economy, with all of the attendant symbioses and blood feuds. Albertans' longstanding crusade for economic progress, played out nowadays through an increasingly wide environmental lens, is the focus of the next leg of our journey.

5   Boom, Bust and Eco?

[A] bumper crop, a gushing oil well, a boom in the stock market—

can vanish in a moment. The land has taught us that through cycles

of prosperity and poverty, through drought and deluge, through all

the vicissitudes of weather. It's our legacy.

—CATHERINE FORD, 2005

Overleaf: Looking up: an inside look at the legendary Leduc No. 1 (1947–1974), which gave Albertans plenty of reasons to gush. [Geo Takach]

Peaks and Valleys

SO MUCH OF ALBERTA is rooted and reflected in her landscape. The fortunes of the province rise and fall like the rolling foothills in Chinook Country. Since birth, Alberta has enjoyed the most dizzying heights and some of the dourest depths that the Canadian economy can dish out. Sharing the traditional prairie ethic of "next-year country"—typically tied to a plea for rain in the midst of drought—Alberta cultivated the reputation early on as a destination for builders, capitalists, hunters, scenery lovers and folks "who are seriously thinking of improving their condition by emigrating to a land where steady honest work meets with certain and speedy reward."[1] Photos accompanying that quotation from Alberta's volume in the American *Porter's Progress of Nations* series (published in 1912) depicted a wheat field and a train, an irrigation canal, the new Legislature building, grain elevators, a steam plough, a large cow and a simple tent in a field with a "Bank" sign and the invitation, "Ready for business." To this, the roving reporter, Leo Thwaite, added, "The most striking is the unfailing optimism which is infectious and which nothing seems to shake. This is no doubt partly attributable to the climate—to the clear dry, sunny atmosphere in which the people work—and partly to the realization of the fact that there are within reach potent forces, natural conditions and opportunities upon which a great future can be built."[2] Almost half a century later, another writer replied, "In Mr. Thwaite's time, all Albertans looked forward, if only because there was little to look back upon."[3]

Although the province was a massive money-magnet during the extended, recently faded boom in particular, busy Albertans, largely addled by wealth and living in the moment, overlook by hope, ignorance or attention-deficit the relentless sine wave that not only washes in wealth but sucks it right back out, leaving wreckage in its wake.

A five-star poster boy for this syndrome is the truck driver, amateur geologist and early oilman, Bill Herron. Stopping for lunch on the road one day in 1911, he noticed gas percolating from some rocks and did what any rugged, individualistic, maverick entrepreneur would do: come back later, take samples, send them to a couple of American labs (which confirmed his suspicion that it had something to do with oil), buy the land and the mineral rights from an illiterate farmer, painstakingly flog his find to people with money and equipment, and then get rich off what became the province's first oil boom at Turner Valley in 1914. When capital dried up and drilling stopped during the Great War, he went back into the hauling business and earned enough to buy a nice mansion in Calgary. After the next big strike at Turner Valley, including a find on his original property in 1928, he rode high until the Depression, when he lost his house because he couldn't pay the property tax. So he did what any sensible Albertan would do: go prospecting for gold up in British Columbia. Although that didn't pan out, another rugged, individualistic, maverick entrepreneur struck oil on land to which Mr. Herron happened to have an interest. So he came home, got his house back and had the good sense to expire before the next bust.[4]

This is Alberta in a nutshell: luck, smarts, hustle, lucre, a good kick in the pants and then more hard work and luck. In the hockey game of life, Alberta is the forward who jumps off the bench in time to grab the puck on the opposing team's blue line while everyone else is caught up-ice. Sure, we get a big breakaway but we still have to charge the net and bedevil the goalie to score. Yet the province continues to trade on a longstanding reputation as a Mecca for money—a guise questioned by the historian, Tamara Palmer Seiler, who believes that the notion of Alberta as a land of unlimited opportunity was a myth for many. "There were a lot of stories of failure that we don't hear so much about as the success stories," she says, citing the scores of homesteading farmers whose efforts were doomed by dryness in the 1920s, "but certainly there is enough evidence of great success in Alberta that the myth continues."

By 1900 settlers were sweeping into Western Canada like tumble-weeds, encouraged by federal immigration campaigns, free land and a wheat boom that lasted until almost World War I. A promotional booklet produced by Ottawa in 1911 captured the "optimistic feeling everywhere" on the prairies, "the world's largest wheat farm." The high-colour cover depicted a cowboy on a horse with two others on tether and extolled the unlimited potential of "ranching, dairying, grain raising, fruit raising, mixed farming." Photos featured cattle, hogs, fields of wheat and oats, and homesteads with massive stacks of harvested grain. "During the past 10 years hundreds of thousands have taken advantage of it," boomed the booklet. "All are satisfied, doing well, and becoming prosperous, and there is no longer any worry as to future prospects."[5] Declaring that all the prerequisites for prosperity were present, the feds called for settlers to simply show up and apply some elbow grease. It worked. Born midway through that wheat boom, Alberta saw her population double between 1906 and 1911, which jacked up the demand for infrastructure and led the government to invest overzealously in schemes like a $20-million telephone network and various railway expansions, irrigation projects and agricultural incentives. An early challenge was to diversify the economy, which was so heavily dependent on one commodity, agriculture. (Does any of this sound familiar today?) Before the imposition of income tax in 1917, governments seeking to finance these kinds of adventures had to borrow the money, and Albertans have always borrowed with the best of them. By 1922 the provincial debt was 50 per cent higher than Manitoba's and double Saskatchewan's (even though her sister province had a population one-third larger), and Alberta's net debt would grow by one-third to $98 million in 1929.

When the United Farmers of Alberta succeeded the province's first and only four Liberal administrations in 1921, it inherited bushels of red ink along with labour unrest in the coal mines and the disastrous drought and famine in the southeastern drylands that led to perhaps the largest abandonment of farms in Canadian history.[6] Even in good years, at least 38 per cent of the province's net spending went to interest on its accumulated debt.[7] Still, the UFA refused to feed the debt monster by raising taxes—which were lower than in other provinces—even with rising operating costs and growing demands for schools, roads, public works and public welfare. Within a year, almost 2.2 million bushels of relief went from northern Alberta to the south in 2,700 cars of hay and 1,000 cars of feed oats, and by 1923, provincial government aid to the south had reached $8 million and the province was near bankruptcy.[8] The government did raise taxes and sell its railway assets to cut its debt in 1929–1930, but by then the Depression made the effort laughable. In 1929 nearly 40 per cent of Albertans' income came from the work of independent commodity producers— primarily farmers—and wage labour hired by farmers, so the province was pummelled when the price of wheat plummeted from $1.14 per bushel to 32¢ in 1932.[9] From 1929–1933, per capita income in the province fell by 61 per cent and the provincial gross domestic product was almost halved, while provincial revenue dropped by almost one-third between 1930–1932 alone. In a hallmark of the horror, the government unleashed a provincial income tax and hiked all other taxes in 1933. (Not that it collected much, as income was only at one-quarter of 1928 levels that year.) At one point, half of farmers' earnings went to cover threshing and transportation.[10] Meanwhile, payments of relief more than doubled from 1929–1936.[11]

Far beyond the numbers, this era and a decade of drought left scars on Alberta's psyche, brought home by haunting images of menacing clouds of dust, grasshopper-stripped crops, buildings turned gooey brown from dead insects, abandoned farmsteads, shoeless children and gaunt horses pulling "Bennett buggies." As one survivor of the Depression from the dry belt south of Medicine Hat recalled, "That dirt which blew off my hand, that wasn't dirt, mister. That was my land, and it was going south into Montana or north up towards Regina or east or west and it was never coming back. The land just blew away."[12] Rudy Wiebe recalls, "Alberta was incredibly and especially poor and the furthest west, the driest and the worst agricultural land on the prairie. We're still terrified of poverty."

This was the stage set for Bible Bill Aberhart, who campaigned for office in 1935 on a promise to pay Albertans $25 a month when a family on relief might get half that. Decades later, an unnamed observer recalled, "[S]ure, he was a phoney, but he was the phoney people were looking for. They'd have voted for a guy selling snake oil if he could show them a way out. [...] Aberhart offered them hope, and spell that in capital letters, when nobody else offered them sweet bugger all but the old promises."[13] Preston Manning explains the challenge facing the new Social Credit government when it swept into office: "In the Depression when my father was first elected to the Legislature, the budget of the Alberta government was $15 million and $8 or $9 million of that was debt service charges on $160 million dollars of debt, and so you ran the province on $6–$7 million. Now it's a $30-billion-a-year enterprise. That's come a long, long way, and it's wise for Albertans to remember there was a time this province was flat on its back." As Mr. Manning tells it, Alberta's was the only government allowed to go bankrupt because the province rejected the Liberals under W.L. Mackenzie King in 1935: "He [King] said, 'I'll help you out if you vote for me,' and good old Albertans, they were flat on their back, but they said, 'Don't try that' and they gave him the back of the hand, so he let 'em go bankrupt, and Alberta couldn't borrow from 1938 to 1951."

Seared into Alberta's psyche, the Great Depression offered exciting opportunities to travel. [Glenbow Archives, NC-6-12955b]

On taking office, Premier Aberhart stormed Ottawa, cap in hand, to borrow $2.2 million to help pay Alberta's provincial employees, who received a 10 per cent cut along with teachers.[14] (In Saskatchewan, they tried to cover teachers' salaries with a special sales tax—a telling contrast.) Back in the Legislature, the government passed a battery of legislation to try to stop the hemorrhaging of red ink among the citizenry. These laws rewrote the rules between private debtors and their creditors to ease the burden of debt and limited the rights of the courts to enforce debts and foreclosures. This did not sit well with the banks, which, of course, were based in central Canada and worked closely with the Bank of Canada to resist Alberta's disruptions. Nor did the constitutionality of the Social Credit government's efforts sit well with the feds or the Supreme Court of Canada, which disallowed them en masse.

By 1936, $2 of every $5 earned by the Alberta government went to interest on the provincial debt. In a hallmark of Alberta's desperate straits, the province resorted to the ultimate atrocity: a sales tax of 3 per cent. Although it was yanked in 1937 after howls of protest, the hurt simmers to this day in an apparently genetically encoded revulsion to any perceived interference in our sacred right to shop. The government cut interest rates on its bonds and savings by half and failed to redeem bonds except in emergencies. The province—which had already earned the lowest credit rating in Canada in 1930—could not accept the strings attached to the allegedly string-less loan of $2 million offered by the federal government (supervision over Alberta's budgeting and borrowing), and the Bank of Canada refused to help. So in 1936, Alberta became the first and only province to default on a maturing principal debt payment.[15] Federal officials strove to isolate Alberta and to calm the financial markets with assurances that the province's case was exceptional and that she was a poor cousin whose antics were emphatically unappreciated by Ottawa. Thus, extreme economic misfortune, compounded by a radical, desperate agenda for reform and a historically testy relationship with the feds, tossed Alberta in a class by herself, somewhat like the proverbial child sporting conically shaped headwear on a stool in the corner of the country schoolroom. Though few recall it first-hand, the humiliation remains etched into Alberta's soul.

Yet the province may have a last laugh on Ottawa. Faced with plummeting incomes and foreclosing banks during the Depression, the Social Credit government created the Alberta Treasury Branches to serve Albertans in outlying communities and to provide credit when the central-based banks were scaling back their service in the province. As basically a socialistic enterprise operating on a capitalist model, this institution lives on as ATB Financial, competing against national and foreign banks many times its size. Although it seems to conduct the business of banking—a matter exclusively within federal jurisdiction under the Canadian Constitution—it has escaped the fate of the

Leduc No. 1, February 13, 1947. Enough said. [*Provincial Archives of Alberta, No. 86.393/65*]

rest of Premier Aberhart's misadventures in implementing social credit and a homegrown solution to the Dirty Thirties. In another of those magnificent ironies that abound here, the province with apparently the most deep-seated distrust of banks has the only state-owned financial institution in the land.

The province's economy improved from 1937–1945, seeded by the recovery of grain prices during World War II and the mechanization of agriculture. Yet Albertans were leaving for British Columbia, Ontario and the Untied States, and those who stayed gravitated toward the cities, tipping the balance of rural dominance that had held sway since white settlement.

And then came the gusher at Leduc No. 1, celebrated on the frosty morning of February 13, 1947, changing everything for province and country. Typically, it came with its own epic, a dramatist's dream that almost never happened. After spending almost 35 years and $23 million exploring for oil in Western Canada, Imperial Oil looked at the dismal outlook for Canada's oil industry, the dwindling fields in southern Alberta and a possible-record 133 consecutive dry holes drilled into the prairie soil, and was ready to throw in the oilcloth. The company's chief geologist, the irrepressible Ted Link, narrowly sold the directors on one last try, rather than moving ahead on their plan to produce synthetic oil from natural gas. When their legendary lead driller, Vern "Dry Hole" Hunter, struck pay dirt, 1,532 metres deep in the dolomite limestone in a wildcat well (so called where there are no productive wells known in the area), the riches of the Devonian reef were unlocked. Within a decade, the number of drilled wells in the province flared from 523 to 7,400, Alberta's annual bounty of oil erupted from 6.7 million barrels to 144 million,[16] and, as Preston Manning notes, "Of course, the second oil was discovered, the banks called up and said, 'Your credit is now fine.'"

The next and biggest-ever oil boom was on, reversing the net outflow of people from the province, boosting investment in Alberta from $122 million to $909 million in a decade, propelling the province into modernity, eventually taking over half of Alberta's economy[17] and consigning the Depression to the mists of memory. Jack Lewis, a senior citizen and second-generation farmer, remembers, "I went to the Toronto Royal Fair in 1952, and they were still talking about having to help the Alberta farmers to survive. I guess they did ship feed out here [during the Depression]." As the wells fruitfully multiplied at Leduc in 1947 and beyond, the province was still paying off its debts from its darkest days. Resentment at this national embarrassment continued to simmer beneath sunny statistics like government revenues rising from $45 million in 1947 to $250 million in 1957 (about half of the latter from energy royalties, leases and rentals) and the asset ledger tilting from $118 million in the red to $253 million in the black.[18] But the demands of economic growth were equally fierce and expenses caught up to revenues by 1957, due mainly to transfers to municipal governments for local infrastructure. Premier Manning deftly managed the melee while keeping taxes relatively low and budgets more or less balanced. Meanwhile, the power in the province shifted from agrarian populism to an urban, business class. Bucking the widespread political turbulence of the 1960s, Albertans enjoyed relative economic stability during that decade, with increased production compensating for falling investment and (in real terms) energy prices. Albertans' standard of living and per capita income did not catch up to the national average until the early 1970s.

The new Conservative government under Peter Lougheed continued to sing the praises of free enterprise while actively intervening in the economy in an effort to smooth out the province's historical cycles of boom and bust before the next dive in energy prices. After the oil cartel, OPEC, jacked up its rates in 1973 and the Alberta government tied its royalties to energy prices, the province's take more than doubled to $560 million in 1974. Provincial budgets from 1971–1982 cut all kinds of taxes, while a 62 per cent hike in real, per-capita program spending from 1979–1982 was, as the economist, Paul Boothe, observed, "probably unmatched elsewhere in Canada in peacetime."[19]

In 1980, when oil created 25 per cent of Alberta's GDP and 80 per cent of the government's revenues, the province's economy fell victim to the notorious National Energy Program, which siphoned billions of tax dollars to Ottawa and scared piles of people and investment away from Alberta. The high interest rates hurt, too. From 1980–1983, unemployment increased from under 4 per cent to about 11 per cent while net migration plummeted from almost plus-70,000 to about minus-30,000.[20] To add further tumult to injury, the world price of oil tumbled by about half from 1985–1986, grain prices fell and exports dropped by 25 per cent.[21] The next premier, Don Getty, took over a budget based on $40 per barrel of oil when the actual price was $13. Economic growth fell below the national average from 1982–1988. Recovery was slow in coming into the 1990s. In the capital city, for example, downtown buildings remained boarded up for years, West Edmonton Mall sunk into receivership and there was even talk of the hallowed Oilers skipping town.

Then came the good times, the longest period of prosperity in memory.

Alberta's population grew at about 10 per cent from 1996–2001 and 10 per cent again from 2001–2006, almost double the national average, and in 2006 it topped 10 per cent of Canada's total for the first time.[22] As the only province in which the population did not decline naturally from 2001–2006, Alberta gained people through interprovincial migration, although the international inflow had been rising, too. At that pace, Alberta's population would double by the mid-2030s. Alberta claimed the fastest-growing large city (Edmonton), seven of the top eight fastest-growing mid-sized urban centres and two of the top ten fastest-growing small towns and rural communities in Canada from 2001–2006, though she also claimed the fastest-declining small town and rural community (the historically ill-fated Crowsnest Pass).[23] But these figures may be deceptive, as many of the growing numbers of non-permanent residents and even interprovincial migrants may not stay, and a survey in 2008 suggested that more than 11 per cent of Albertans claimed that it was somewhat or very unlikely that they will be here in five years.[24] All of this reminds us that Alberta's population is highly fluid. Following a history of dramatic rises and falls mirroring the province's economic fortunes, the number of Albertans almost tripled from 1.1 million in 1956 to about 3.3 million in the past fifty years. In the 2006 census, more than 11 per cent of Albertans over age five were living outside of the province five years previously; the comparable national figure is under 7 per cent.[25]

On the economic front, Alberta brims with superlatives. She led the nation in economic growth during the 2000s, though that torch has been forecast to be passed to Saskatchewan and Manitoba. Albertans' incomes climbed at twice the rate as the rest of Canada, and our after-tax median household income from all sources of $64,700 in 2005 was

$8,700 higher than the national figure.[26] Wood Buffalo, the munici-
pality that includes the tar sands titan, Fort McMurray, led the nation
with a median *individual* income of $48,900 in 2005.[27] One report
gushed that Calgary had "the lowest downtown office vacancy rate on
the planet," rivalling all major centres at 0.6 per cent in 2006.[28] Retail
sales jumped by almost 16 per cent from 2005–2006 and followed
nation-leading retail growth exceeding 8 per cent from 2001–2004,
with the national average at under 5 per cent and no other province
reaching 6 per cent.[29] A national bank called the corridor between
Calgary and Edmonton the "only Canadian urban centre to amass
U.S.-level wealth while preserving Canadian-style quality of life,"
citing GDP per capita of 10 per cent above the average of American
metropolitan areas and 40 per cent above Alberta's Canuck counterparts, with the potential to widen her economic lead in Canada and
be considered one of best places to live in North America.[30] Economic
output in the corridor between Edmonton and Calgary topped that of
every country in the world except Luxembourg.[31] Alberta's last boom
echoed across the country, with Albertans paying $9 billion more to
the federal government than they received in benefits, and 60 per cent
of the output and employment benefits from the oil sands flowing to
other provinces. Statistics Canada went as far as declaring Alberta's
last boom the strongest period of economic growth of any province in
Canadian history.[32]

But Albertans see the dark side of the boom. Take the last one, for
example. Please.

Health care felt the strain. In a national survey of physicians,
doctors in Alberta expressed the most concern about the state of
emergency care in their province.[33] Alberta's inflation rate of 6.3 per
cent in 2007 was almost thrice the national average of 2.2 per cent
over the previous year, led by ridiculous increases in housing costs in
the face of surging growth in the economy and the population.[34] And
although the rich get richer, the only ones believing in the trickle-
down effect in Alberta are drips. For instance, in 2005 dollars, most

Edmonton households were only $300 ahead of the $32,000 that they earned in 1981; median earnings were lower in all intervening years and as much as $7,500 lower in 1995. That the local economy was twice as large per capita than 25 years earlier suggests that most of the gains in earnings went to business rather than individuals.[35] That year, 198,000 Albertans between the ages of 18 and 64—almost 9 per cent of the working-age crowd—lived below the poverty line and almost one-third of them worked at least half time for the entire year and posted family incomes below the low-income cut-off. In constant, 2005 dollars, households in the capital city earning less than $40,000 grew from 18 per cent of the population in 1981 to 27 per cent in 2005 (peaking at 38 per cent in 1995), while stabilizing middle-income households earning $40,000–$100,000 fell from 55 per cent to 43 per cent of the total and households earning $100,000 sashayed up slightly from 27 per cent to 30 per cent.[36] Meanwhile, the Conference Board of Canada warned that the province could face a shortage of 332,000 workers by 2025, and the Auditor General of Alberta estimated that the province was short on required infrastructure to the tune of $6.1 billion in 2007.[37]

"Alberta is a victim of its own success," says Tom, a musician, in a music store in Jasper. "It's a boom and bust province and right now [2007] it's a boom. Everything has gone up in price. Young families can't afford to buy a home. A huge influx and a huge demand for property have put a lot of people out of the market. It's a very difficult place to live and afford." His plan to handle the boom: move to Saskatchewan.

Booms can be hard on businesses, too. The computer manufacturer, Dell, and the TD Bank pulled their call centres out of the province. The software maker, Intuit, moved its national head office from Edmonton to Toronto, citing the difficulty of keeping staff and the rising cost of living.[38] For farmers like Ken Lewis, an economic boom "is fantastic if you're sitting on land outside of expanding cities," but daily operations are difficult because they have to compete with Fort McMurray for labour and for services. "I can see why everyone envies it," he says, "but being in the middle of it, it's got its hang-ups, for sure. Expansion is difficult with higher operating costs, and our labour costs are killing us."

From his perch on a picket fence around an acreage in the foothills, the documentary filmmaker, Garth Pritchard, assesses the ethic of Alberta today relative to when he arrived here from Montréal a generation ago. "When I first came here, I never, ever sat down with a group of people who sat around the kitchen table and talked about what they had just bought on the stock market yesterday," he recalls. "The culture of Alberta has been destroyed by people who have come here and are raping it for greed and money and arrogance. What makes me mad about Alberta is that these people who came here for three days and then left, they all went back with these wild-ass stories about Alberta and how much money was being made." Mr. Pritchard observes a slow, silent exodus of young Albertans, even during the last boom. He tells the tale of a young farmer who tried the oil patch and proudly drove the biggest trucks in the world in Fort McMurray, but his $98,000 salary wasn't enough to cover the cost of a house up there (even if he could find one). So the young man had to buy a house in his native Calgary and commute every five days; in the end, he had to quit his job. "It destroyed him," says Mr. Pritchard. At least he wasn't one of the litany of commuters who die in high-speed collisions on Highway 63 leading up there. "Alberta's in trouble, true trouble," he states, "and the greed and money are dragging us down a deep hole I don't know if we can get out of. I don't know how you take a $1.5-million piece of hay land and ever be able to allow a cow or a horse back on it if you don't build a $2-million house. Think of Bre-x. How do you take nothing and turn it into $900 per share and there's nothing there? That's what seems to be happening to us. Very sad."

"The values defining Alberta are money," declares Nyambura Belcourt, the executive director of the Edmonton Multicultural Society and a recent immigrant from Kenya. "Misdirected materialism bankrupts your mind and your sense of analysis."

Given Alberta's economic extremes, it figures that the gap between rich and poor is greater than anywhere else in Canada and widening. "Supposedly we make a lot of money," says a twenty-something in dark glasses on the streets of Edmonton, "but you don't really see it." Down the hill, in the North Saskatchewan River valley, Alison Turner observes that as a member of the arts community, the boom hadn't benefitted her at all, and when she walks around downtown Edmonton, she sees a lot more homeless people than before. "So there seems to be this false illusion of prosperity," she says. "Everything seems very frenetic right now, like the whole province has been shook up in a snow globe. It doesn't feel very real." A ballcapped man on a downtown street opines, "The boom is 50–50. It puts us on the world map, but a lot of people come here looking for the dream. When they don't find the dream, a lot of them turn to other avenues for income and whatnot."

Across the country, in Vieux-Montréal, Robert O'Callaghan sees Alberta's economic good fortune as a cautionary tale. "Throughout history, most people at some point have done well and then the tide has gone the other way," he notes. "So it's not so good to be smug when everything is going very, very well, because the tar sands eventually will be used up and the oil will be used up. And we'll be back to clovering cows."

Another danger is that the greater the boom, the greater tendency to rely on the increasingly specialized sector that both depends on and supports that boom. This is the "staple trap" of pouring resources into the dominant activity that pays so well. As leader of the provincial opposition in the 1960s, Peter Lougheed warned of the need to diversify the province's economy rather than coast on oil money—a concern that remains pressing even after his later efforts to bankroll private industry, which cost taxpayers billions of the dollars that they were supposed to save. Compounding this challenge is the recurring threat of volatility. Because Alberta's private sector depends largely on commodity prices and her public sector relies on revenue from royalties on resources extracted from the province, the Alberta government's revenue and spending are vastly more variable than any other authority in Canada.[39] Also, Alberta garners more of her income from investments (more than 40 per cent in 2003–2004) and less of it from consumption taxes (13 per cent, including sales taxes) than any other province or territory,[40] and her royalty rate on provincially owned energy resources is the lowest among comparable jurisdictions in the United States, including Texas, Alaska, New Mexico and Colorado.[41]

These uncertainties, reinforced by nightmares of the Dirty Thirties, motivated Premier Lougheed to establish the Alberta Heritage Savings Trust Fund in 1976 as primarily a rainy-day repository for citizens' share of energy royalties. A few billion dollars were tossed in during that boom but withdrawals for program spending began in 1982 and contributions dried up after the price of oil went south for the winter (and spring, summer and fall), and the slow recovery that followed. The fund declined by more than $2 billion from 1996–2002, while an analogous adventure, the Alaska Permanent Fund, also born in 1976, grew by almost $13 billion and another, the Norway Petroleum Fund, launched in 1990, ballooned by almost $90 billion over the same period. The government has drawn fire for mismanaging the fund and for collecting only 69 per cent of the available revenue due to Albertans from oil and gas royalties from 1995–2002 compared to 99 per cent in Alaska, 88 per cent in Norway and 93 per cent in British Columbia. That the Yukon and Northwest Territories also scored 69 per cent and Saskatchewan scored 63 per cent doesn't seem to make anyone feel better.[42]

The sociologist, Tami Bereska, posits a snapshot of Alberta from the lens of other Canadians. "The wealth of our province stands out," she says, noting our image as wealthy fat cats, though that's not to say we're actually wealthier. She cites the astronomical wealth and deep poverty here. "We have the stereotypical masculine, testosterone rig pigs versus big businessmen in three-piece suits, the same kind of wealth in two completely different groups and cultures in Alberta,"

A view of Calgary on an upside of the Ferris wheel of construction cranes and foreclosure notices that characterize Alberta's economic joyride. [*Geo Takach*]

she says. "Somehow they meet and interact here. It's almost a surreal experience with roughnecks and oil executives in the same run in Fort McMurray, 'north of the middle of nowhere.' It's such a macho environment—even the women!" The national media frequently paint Albertans as nouveau-riche rubes, especially during boom times, singling out Calgary as a world of "bonanza glam" where "five-figure art routinely sells out, often sight-unseen," and folks buy $5,000 of wine in fifteen minutes, while driving up the prices of vacation properties in BC.[43] Even some longtime locals and other Albertans see the city they used to call Cowtown as the new Toronto—arrogant, self-absorbed, cocky and out of control.[44]

In keeping with what many Albertans see as the national media's propensity to portray the province as a boorish backwater, the CBC commissioned a documentary film called *Tar Sands: The Selling of*

Alberta, which aired in 2008. Credited to Albertan filmmakers, the piece painted a calamitous portrait of "'Fort McMoney,' a modern-day Eldorado, where rents are skyrocketing and cocaine abuse is four times the provincial average" and "a Florida-sized 'environmental sacrifice zone' has become Canada's contribution to U.S. energy security in the post-9/11 world."[45] Unsurprisingly, some Albertans—perhaps the same ones who loathe the CBC for its ostensible leftward bias and focus on central Canada—criticized the film as a political hatchet job, with a venom that they normally reserve for notions like global warming being caused by pollution. But even political hatchet jobs can be accurate.

Alberta's wealth puts her on the firing line. As Max Foran observes through the lens of our national pastime, "Who gets booed when he goes on the ice in another city? Ovechkin today and Gretzky earlier. You always go after the best because the best are easy targets to hammer. And Alberta's right up there, so 'Cut 'em down!' We're victims of our own success."

Although few outside the industry dispute the harshness of the oil sands on the environment, the resulting emissions account for less than 0.1 per cent of the world's carbon dioxide emissions.[46] Yet Alberta has a reputation to uphold: for one thing, we continue to build much more emission-heavy coal-fired plants while every other province moves away from them.

In our own, ceaseless quest for truth, we turn to the artist's perspective. The veteran folksinger and songwriter, Bill Bourne, sees a schism between the wealth of natural resources in his home province and the quality of their stewardship. "Alberta has this enormous potential," he sighs. "We have this huge gift, all this oil and all this money. But it seems that it's being squandered away at this point, which makes me feel pretty sad because my grandparents emigrated here from Europe a long time ago and they worked hard. Now there's all this kind of buffoonery going on around here. So it's a bit of a paradox." Doris Daley has further concerns about our ethics and our manners. "Our

Bronco Buddy, billed as Canada's first non-rodeo cowboy clown and almost famous since 1983, says "Albertans don't always count their blessings like they should."
[Geo Takach]

affluence makes us different and it's something to be on guard against," she says. "The huge houses and skyscrapers…I don't get it. I worry a bit about our affluence and how the rest of the country, and even the rest of the world, perceives our affluence. It's almost embarrassing and almost something to overcome. We all grew up with parents who cautioned us to not eat all the Christmas candy before you sat down to dinner. Having so much, is that so good?"

Pat McGaffigan, a retired nurse whose work took her to Nepal, quotes the late leader of her mission there, Oliver Howard, a BC native who called Alberta "the only province to go from abject poverty to affluence without a period of civilization in between." She observes,

"Sometimes we're too caught up around our wealth, maybe because we haven't always had it."

At a children's festival in High River, we meet Bronco Buddy (Bud Edgar), billed as Canada's first non-rodeo cowboy clown and "almost famous since 1983." Clad in Western gear and a red fright-wig, the irrepressible Buddy rides a unicycle horse called Blister, performs eye-popping rope tricks, plays a plunger-fiddle with a rubber chicken (his "Dixie chick") and declares, "People in Alberta are like spoiled teenagers in the sense that they have it all and take it all for granted. They expect it all to be there, the ones who haven't had an opportunity to see other people, be in other cultures and see how other people have to live—and that those people don't have the advantages that we have. They would miss it if it weren't all there. It's the old, 'You don't miss your water until your well goes dry,' right?" Max Foran, who does not wear size-16 footwear, agrees, stating, "Generally, we've got it so darn good that we don't really know how bad the rest of the First World is, let alone the bloody Second or Third."

When the inevitable bust followed in late 2008, Alberta was, characteristically, hit hard. One bank predicted that the province's economic decline would be Canada's steepest in 2009, and building permits fell by 22 per cent in a month in which the national drop was under 5 per cent.[47] Even our retail sales tumbled by a nation-leading 6.2 per cent in one month.[48] However, the Conference Board of Canada forecasts solid growth of 2.6 per cent per year (that's compounded annual average growth) from 2008–2030, led by the oil sands.[49]

The pursuit of affluence—whether born of the challenge of scraping to survive on a harsh, isolated frontier or a more contemporary craving to commute around town in a hulking, air-conditioned, auto-starting, DVD-playing, US Army vehicle—has always taken centre stage here. Alberta's history of booms and busts reads like a polygraph needle on steroids, a symphony of soaring peaks and steep chasms that recalls her geography, from the precipitous peak of Mt. Columbia in Jasper National Park to the Slave River lowlands in the northeast. "The province has come a long, long way, and anyone that studies its history should be encouraged by that," advises Preston Manning. "You can be flat on your back and down and out, but if you have that pioneering spirit and the desire to succeed, it's possible to do so."

Reflecting on Alberta's journeys through boom and bust over the last hundred-plus years, Mark Lisac sees Alberta as forward-looking, growth-oriented and restless. "We never feel that what's here is good enough and never reach our ultimate goal, always looking for ways to make things bigger and better," he muses. "Our economy is built on constant growth and the construction of physical assets, both public and private. The oil dollars don't always flow steadily. Maybe these characteristics are inherited from earlier days of the province: immense expansion and great dreams of a trade route to Asia. We had the same dreams in 1905 that we have today." He points to tremendous pressure in the province to achieve material, intellectual and all manner of success—and a parallel, underlying fear that we aren't going to achieve things, and that even if we do, something or someone is going to come along and take it away. Repeated cycles of boom and bust have conditioned us to accept that everything we have could disappear. As Mr. Lisac observes, that feeds into the sense of insecurity found in relatively small communities surrounded by larger metropolitan areas and even larger international forces. So there is a constant tension in Alberta between riches gained and the prospect of losing them.

Today, that tension is playing out epically in the emerging clash between the economy and the environment. The shift from conventional to synthetic crude oil is a prime culprit. With every announcement of zillions of dollars of new investment in the oil sands—which generate three times more carbon dioxide than conventional oil production—come increasingly dire and pervasive warnings of environmental Armageddon and rumblings from other provinces, nations and international bodies about Alberta's "dirty" oil. It's a spectacular collision course that the World Wrestling Foundation would envy.

Eco Ground Zero

Alberta has lots of natural attributes and a lot worth protecting. Unfortunately, we're not doing a very good job. It seems we're trying to catch up with other areas while destroying the environment. The quest for development and money places far ahead of our desire to protect our environment.

—MARTHA KOSTUCH, 2005

The issue of Albertans' environmental stewardship is heating up both in and out of the province with an intensity ordinarily reserved for the Stanley Cup playoffs—but without the beer comercials. Different messages emanate from different quarters.

The provincial government called its standards as rigorous as any in Canada and in the United States for air quality and "among the world's toughest" for water quality.[50] Of course, no standards can measure a government's keenness or capacity to enforce them, so perhaps it's the results that should count—say, the actual volume of pollutants produced rather than standards, public spending or dedicated personnel. Alberta's success had better not be measured by public spending, as Alberta Environment was gutted by a staff cut of 40 per cent over a decade, with a budget of $143 million in 2007 dwarfed by that of Saskatchewan, which spent $180 million with one-third of Alberta's population and none of her tar sands development.[51]

The province has an abominable record in the court of public opinion. This reached an apogee in a recent book, *Stupid To the Last Drop: How Alberta is Bringing Environmental Armageddon to Canada (And Doesn't Seem to Care)*, which painted a devastating picture of ravaged land, toxic air, poisoned water and rampant political nepotism and corruption. *Canadian Geographic* magazine used calmer phrases, like "carbon time bomb" and "disaster zone"[52] while *Maclean's* opted for "doomsday."[53] Even the venerable *National Geographic* took a break from pygmies and astral extravaganzas to drop the eco-anvil on Alberta's economic roadrunner, complete with glossy centrefold of the boreal forest (before and after mining operations) and references to dirty oil, "dark satanic mills," a "tarry stench," contaminated water, unusual cancer cases in downstream Fort Chipewyan and the conclusion that Alberta has sacrificed environmental concerns to the free market.[54] The Alberta government takes pride in its *Special Places* program—billed as an effort to set aside and protect large tracts of wilderness for conservation, recreation and tourism—and calls it a success for adding two million hectares of protected land.[55] But others see it less charitably as having lost all credibility in what Andrew Nikiforuk called "an Orwellian conservation ruse for 'rape and pillage,'" abandoned by participating environmental groups and neutered and doomed by disinformation and scare tactics from the industry-friendly provincial departments of energy and forestry. In measured prose, supported by ample facts and figures,[56] Mr. Nikiforuk's book, *Tar Sands: Dirty Oil and the Future of a Continent*, presents the environmental equivalent of a slasher film, painting a blood-freezing portrait of systemic and monumental shortsightedness, greed, regulatory indifference and destruction; the book opens by declaring a political emergency and gets increasingly frightening from there. The province's auditor general attacked the government's failure to proceed with promises on integrated resource management.[57] The Sierra Club has consistently ranked Alberta last in Canada with failing grades on biodiversity and climate change, awarding two of the five F-grades assigned to the thirteen provinces and territories in 2006, following fourteen years of awarding almost uninterrupted Fs to Wild Rose Country.[58]

The list goes on. Is it all warranted? To find out, let's touch on Albertans' record on each of the four elements of antiquity: earth, air, fire and water.

Regarding earth, Albertans' ecological footprint—the land and resources needed to satisfy our lifestyles—is 10.7 hectares (26.4 acres) per person. That trumps the Canadian average of 7.7 hectares and finishes just out of the international medals after the land hogs in the United Arab Emirates, Singapore and the United States.[59] Tree-huggers have a rough row to hoe in Alberta, where in relative terms, the deforestation of the southern boreal forest outpaces that of the Amazon, and the province's litany of well sites, seismic lines, clear-cut logging, roads and tar sands have left only 21 per cent of its boreal forest standing, the second-lowest proportion in Canada after Prince Edward Island but on 117 times the land area.[60] An international forest protection group called Forest Ethics ran ads in downtown Toronto bus shelters, subway stations and billboards using Alberta as a poster child for environmental destruction, depicting a massive pulp mill and denuded land with the words, "Klein's Alberta? Nope. McGuinty's Ontario."[61] The eastern edge of Jasper National Park has been devastated by coal mining at Mountain Park, where powerful corporate interests and regulatory indifference have run roughshod over a ragtag, volunteer band of local and environmental groups trying to stop it. Assessing the regulatory approval process for projects like Mountain Park, the coalition's lawyer, Jennifer Klimek, noted, "In Alberta, the test of public interest is so skewed toward economics that I wonder what we would have to prove to show that any industrial project, no matter how bad it is, shouldn't go ahead."[62] The province's fragile southern ecosystem, which has the highest biodiversity in the province, is also in peril, says Roxy Hastings, a bio-geographer and the curator of botany at the Royal Alberta Museum. The biggest loss of biodiversity due to ploughing and farming is near Writing-on-Stone Provincial Park in Alberta and Grasslands National Park in southwestern Saskatchewan.

Rapid urbanization is not unique to Alberta, but in no other province has the city steamrollered over the countryside so suddenly. After growing slowly from 29 per cent of the provincial head count in 1911 to 32 per cent in 1941, the urban population leaped to 73 per cent in 1971, doubling from 800,000 in 1946 to 1.6 million.[63] In the last two decades of that span, Calgary and Edmonton grew by 158 per cent and 135 per cent, respectively; they account for about two-thirds of the population today. Recently dubbed "Calgreedy" and "the new Toronto" by those who feel the city has lost its way, Calgary has doubled its area since 1980, if not the infrastructure to go with it. At that rate, by 2050, it should swallow Langdon, Airdrie and Cochrane, each about 20 kilometres away today.[64] The city takes up roughly the same space as New York City with a tenth of the population. Among Canada's ten largest census metropolitan areas in 2006, Calgary ranked sixth in area and fifth in both population and population density; Edmonton came first in area, sixth in population and third in population density.[65] The capital city has 60 per cent more land than Toronto but only 20 per cent of the residents, a ratio aided by its network of river valley parks, ballyhooed as the continent's largest.[66] Mill Woods, an über-neighbourhood in the city's southeast end, was the largest publicly sponsored compilation of land ever undertaken in North America, starting in 1970 with 6,500 hectares of woods and farmland. Today, it hosts almost 100,000 people, which would make it the third-largest city in the province.[67]

Edmonton continues to elevate retail to a religion. Adding to a tradition that includes perhaps the country's oldest big mall (Westmount, 1955), a new, 128-hectare "power-shopping" nirvana mushroomed in the city's south end to join the sainted West Edmonton Mall and Toronto's Yorkdale Shopping Centre as the largest orgasms of retail in the land. This addition, which consumes the area of 213 football fields—that's *Canadian* football fields—ensnarled enough traffic to hinder access to the airport and our main highway, inspiring the accelerated construction of a new interchange at an approved cost of $107 million in 2005, which morphed into $260 million within two years in the boom-time economy.[68] Highway 2 (upgraded to the Queen Elizabeth II during the 2005 royal visit) is one of four routes cited by Statistics Canada as supporting urban sprawl.[69] Down the road, Okotoks, just south of Calgary, grew by almost 47 per cent and Airdrie, just north of Calgary, grew by almost

42 per cent from 2001–2006, making them the second- and third-fastest growing communities in Canada over that period. Small wonder that Calgarians are the likeliest among seven major urban centres in Canada to call urban sprawl a problem for their city (almost three-quarters of them said so in a survey in 2007) and are the most frequent users of urban green space along with Vancouverites.[70] Urban sprawl, the darling of chambers of commerce and urban development institutes—blessed by, as the Parkland Institute put it, "large campaign donations from developers sitting on large swatches of farmland and natural areas on urban edges"—fuels Albertans' addiction to motor vehicles and causes about 350 illnesses and deaths from breathing polluted air in each of Edmonton and Calgary each year.[71]

But it's not just urban creep that's chewing up land in Alberta. The world's insatiable addiction to oil and some 1.7 trillion barrels of it said to lie under the tar sands have dropped the largest industrial project on Earth onto the boreal forest in northeastern Alberta. (You can tell the attitude from the terminology: pro-development forces in industry and the provincial government prefer "oil sands" to "tar sands," which sounds more foul and is deployed by folks who worry more about pesky environmental issues. This book uses them interchangeably, to annoy both groups equally.) Just how big a project is it? The industry's daily natural gas consumption in 2005 could heat 3.2 million homes for a day and that could well triple by 2015.[72]

The oil sands are a messy business. The natural mixture of sand, clay and rock contains bitumen, a thick, sticky tar made of oil. It's accessed by knocking down the trees, clearing off the topsoil, sand, clay and gravel, and then digging up the tar sand with an immense vehicle called a shovel, which scoops a hundred tonnes at a time, stands as tall as fifty-eight elephants, and feeds the largest trucks in the world, with tires three metres tall. The booty—5,000 tonnes of surface material and sand every minute of every day—is hauled to a crusher, which breaks up lumps and removes rocks. The oil sand gets mixed with hot water to separate the bitumen, which is cleaned in several

stages to be made into gasoline, heating oil, motor oil and so on.[73]
The land is supposed to be restored with clean sand, fresh topsoil and
newly planted shrubs and trees but reclamation has been substantially
slower than extraction. The inventor in the 1920s of the hot-water flota-
tion process to separate the bitumen, Karl Clark, once called the tar
sands "a taunt to North America for generations" that "wear[s] a smirk
which seems to say, 'When are you going to do something?'"[74] Nearing
his death in 1966, after he saw the sod turned on the opening of the
first oil sands plant, he expressed grief at the scarring of his beloved
landscape.[75]

As for the second element, air, the tar sands are part of why
Albertans have been known to give the ozone layer a good workout.
Alberta is the leading greenhouse-gas polluter in Canada, contributing
39 per cent of the country's industrial emissions and six of the top ten
sources of greenhouse gases. Alberta's oil sands are the single largest
perpetrator and are expected to boost contributions of 20 megatonnes
to between 70–90 megatonnes in the next four years, threatening to
dry out prairie rivers, ignite the boreal forest and reduce already arid
southern Alberta to John Palliser's mid-Victorian vision of a desert.[76]
The tar sands led all industries with a 104 per cent increase in greenhouse gas emissions from 1990–2003, with oil and gas following at a
rise of 41 per cent while pulp and paper and construction emissions
each dropped by about one-third.[77]

For its part, the provincial government claimed to be the first in
North America to require large industrial polluters to reduce their
greenhouse gas emissions, and the first to fund technology to capture
and store carbon underground.[78] This earned full marks on paper but
shrieks of protest from critics for targeting not the crucial, absolute
reductions but the intensity of the emissions (the equivalent of a 12 per
cent reduction in intensity per year), because intensity becomes irrelevant if actual production at least quadruples from 1 to 4 or 5 million
barrels a day by 2020. So Alberta's plan actually calls for *more* toxins
and greenhouse gases for a dozen years before improved technology

(mainly the capture and storage of carbon) is hoped to level off emissions by 2020 and reduce them from 2005 levels by a whopping 14 per cent by 2050. This leads to media descriptors like "shockingly irresponsible," "fraudulence" and "a study in political deception" that, "if unchanged, will make it the pariah of jurisdictions internationally."[79] Signs of this occurred in 2008, when Premier Stelmach addressed a gathering of the Western Governors' Association in Wyoming. The state's largest local daily carried an ad by a coalition of Canuck and Yankee eco-groups inviting the governors to meet in Canada's oil sands, where they can "watch as pristine boreal forests and wetlands are destroyed to make some of the dirtiest oil" and admire spectacular sunsets over giant lagoons of toxic waste.[80] (In an earlier trip to Washington, DC, the premier was dogged by protesters both in and out of polar-bear costume.) The governors didn't seem too bothered, no doubt preferring Alberta's cheap product to the vagaries of less friendly oil-rich regimes. Measures introduced under President Barack Obama purport to eschew "dirty" oil in a symptom of mounting international pressure against Alberta's oil sands, though America's own coal-fired record is far from clean.

On the subject of gasoline—which can get more expensive in Alberta than in central Canada—rank-and-file Albertans are also making their mark on the environment. A national study showed that Edmontonians and Calgarians rely more on their cars than those living in any other large census metropolitan areas. More than three-quarters of respondents from those burgs used their vehicles for all of their trips on the survey's reference day, compared to less than two-thirds in Toronto and Montréal.[81] A dealership in Edmonton claimed to be the first in Canada to sell a thousand vehicles in one month,[82] and an outfit in Fort McMurray sold the most trucks in Canada, unhindered by an official local population of just over 60,000.[83]

On the fire side of the elemental quartet, the rise in Alberta's greenhouse gas emissions stands to spark massive blazes in the boreal forest, aided by the famous dry climate and by the notorious pine beetle, the menace of which has been attributed to global warming in that our winters are no longer cold enough to kill it off. In their peak years, forest fires are said to spew emissions amounting to 90 per cent of those of industry.[84]

As for the last of the four elements, Albertans have a vigorous appreciation for water. We consume more than twice the national average, although almost two-thirds of Canada's irrigated farmland is found in Wild Rose Country. The big bifurcation here is between the south where most Albertans live, and the north where more than 86 per cent of the river flow is, notably the Peace and the Athabasca, which feed the Arctic Ocean.[85] The droughts of the 1920s and 1930s may be a distant nightmare, but a dry climate and growing global warming have raised the alarm—only this time, we won't be able to turn to the famed American professional rainmaker of that bygone era, Charles Hatfield, with his tall towers and fakir gear.

Added to this is that our demands on this most precious of resources are skyrocketing. In 2004 half of the oil production in the province required water, led by the oil sands companies, which were expected to hike their use in situ by about 300 per cent from 2002–2020—and that's *without* expansion.[86] Already, the oil sands suck almost 200 million cubic metres of surface water and groundwater runoff per year (about 40 per cent of Toronto's consumption),[87] and one report suggested that companies are licensed to draw 349 million cubic metres per year.[88] Each barrel of oil produced from the tar sands requires between two and six barrels of water,[89] and once that water is used, only 8 per cent of it can be returned to the Athabasca River. The rest of the resulting poisonous, clay-ridden, gruel-ish slurry is dumped into tailings ponds, which have reached the size of Vancouver and were expected to reach a volume of a billion cubic metres by 2010. It will take decades for the clay to settle.[90] Already, the ponds are instant suicide for waterfowl, as a malfunctioning warning system proved one spring day in 2008, when 1,606 unlucky ducks perished pretty much on contact with the toxic sludge.

One scientist, William Donohue, pointed out that Alberta's management of oil sands development in the Lower Athabasca River suffered from seriously understaffed and underfunded environmental staff; a failure to consider vital information on the effects of climate change; and an appalling lack of science and political will that have made critical science and monitoring programs practically non-existent over the past decade. He warned that the industry's goal of quadrupling output from the oil sands by 2030 on the back of the Athabasca or its tributaries during a period of declining water supply raises extreme environmental and economic risks.[91] The Athabasca, one of Canada's largest groundwater systems, is believed to be the largest aquifer in the North American Plains region, with "Perrier-quality" water that environmental and Métis groups claim could be contaminated by leakage from the steam-assisted gravity drainage used to extract oil between Lac La Biche and Fort McMurray.[92] Many tar sands plants operate directly above the aquifer.

It's not just Fort McMurray. More than 90 per cent of Alberta's streams have phosphorous content exceeding national guidelines, and nine of twenty-one areas in Canada with the highest levels of fecal coliform bacteria are here.[93] Dr. David Schindler, an internationally lauded water scientist armed with decades of hard data and leading-edge science, is among many who have warned of imminent and catastrophic danger to Alberta's air, land and water. He has likened the province's situation to that of Newfoundland, where a rising population eliminated the forests and fish stocks and destroyed people's livelihoods, requiring them to move, ironically, to Alberta, which he predicts will suffer a similar fate unless development is curbed.[94] In Alberta, Dr. Schindler is dismissed by some political interests as an academic with a political agenda. If you're not with the prevailing program—which, of course, is run by politicians—then you are a "special interest" out to derail what's good for all Albertans, and economic development is as close to sacred here as anything that any religion has on offer. Although the province has been widely and roundly trashed for grossly mismanaging its essential resources, it seems fitting to save the worst for the stewardship of our surface water and groundwater, the essence of life as we know it.

As befits her egalitarian ethic, the province is as tough on her fauna as she is on her elements. Over the millennia, Alberta's geographic cornucopia attracted diverse wildlife, and the relatively low numbers of Aboriginal people and their nomadic lifestyles had only a local effect on animals' numbers and habitats. After white folks moved in, their firearms and unregulated hunting drove species like the elk and the pronghorn antelope to the brink of decimation. The province launched a bounty system for offing predators (wolves, coyotes, birds of prey and cougars) in 1907, but it didn't increase the number of game animals and was dumped in 1954. Trained wildlife biologists hired after the Leduc discovery focused mostly on game animals before diversifying mainly into endangered wildlife.[95]

Although land in Alberta has been set aside for parks and such, only 1.4 per cent of Alberta's provincially managed land is protected for wildlife conservation, effective water management or sustainable use. One study ranked Alberta 112th among 141 nations.[96] An advocate for animals and wildlife, Heather MacEwan-Foran, tells me, "I am embarrassed to be an Albertan because of the way we've treated our wildlife and our environment. We've raped the environment." She cites a development in Canmore in the Rockies that is supposed to be a wildlife corridor but is about as wide as a restaurant table, with bears and other wildlife expected to share it with cyclists, joggers and more. "Alberta's record on the environment is disgusting," she declares. "Development takes precedence over everything. People—the developers and the government—see the dollar signs and they don't care about the environment or the animals."

A signature case is the mighty grizzly, which saw its habitat overrun by settlers, the railway, hunters and the forestry industry to the point where it could be gone from outside our national parks within thirty years.[97] Alberta's Endangered Species Conservation Committee recommended in 2002 that the government treat the grizzly as an endangered species, suspend the grizzly hunt and devise an effective recovery plan. In response, the government set up a recovery team and spent $250,000 on a study to estimate the grizzly population, which was found to be down to five hundred and which may be extinct in a century.[98] The woodland caribou is also endangered owing to the rapid disappearance of its natural habitat, a victim of expanded coal-mining north of Grand Cache (which stops their migration), oil and gas exploration, tourism, poaching and accidental hunting—a curse of resembling deer, moose and elk.[99] The Alberta Wilderness Association cites a lack of political will and potentially costly changes as barriers to saving the caribou, and even the government admits that the unfortunate ungulate is slipping from endangered to doomed.[100] Other endangered life in the province includes the western spiderwort and western blue flag plants, the northern long-eared bat, the whooping crane, livestock at the Calgary Stampede and pretty much any opposition political party.

It's not easy being an Albertan, with growing numbers of people against you even as they continue to guzzle your resources. Stopping in Calgary during his "If You Were Prime Minister" tour in 2007, the eco-crusader, David Suzuki, called on the Alberta government to ease up on the oil and gas expansion. "You think you need the tar sands to go gung-ho," he implored. "Albertans have always had the highest standard of living of any province in the country. Why the hell do you need all this unlimited expansion? For God's sake, that's crazy."[101] The problem, of course, is that there is money to be made and in the world of the nouveau riche in particular, the present always trumps the future. In a Statistics Canada study in 2006 of household environmental behaviour covering recycling, composting, temperature-lowering, switching to more efficient lighting and reducing water consumption, Albertans ranked below the national average.[102] And we are the nation's top producers of trash, at 1,136 kilograms per person and rising from 2004–2006 at thrice the national average rate.[103]

The epicentre of the ultimate, winner-take-all showdown between the economy and the environment is, of course, Fort McMurray, which is part of the fastest growing population centre in Canada. It's also Canada's largest municipality in area, at one-tenth the size of the province and larger than Nova Scotia. The place ballooned from 36,000 people in 1996 to 65,000 in just over a decade, paying the highest average income in the country while renting two-bedroom units for $1,717 on average and selling your average single-family home for $486,962 in 2007.[104] Even Costco cannot build there. "We would love to be a green leader but we are financially challenged," Mayor Melissa Blake advises me before addressing an environmental conference in Edmonton. "The environment is something that's important to Albertans. When I think about my region in particular, we do struggle to try and make the right decisions all the time but the opportunities that come economically are something that drives our reason for being there. But we wouldn't have that reason if we can't protect the environment. So when it comes down to the attitudes that I hear from people, there's an expectation that we are going to do our best in integrating that protection while not circumventing their ability to make a living."

It's a razor-sharp balance and one so laden with foreign and powerful interests beyond Her Worship's control that one wonders whether any municipality would have the jurisdiction or capacity to resolve it. Wood Buffalo's elected municipal council asked the Alberta Energy and Utility Board—an administrative, unelected body—to slow down development but was refused, and the provincial government remains adamantly against curbing development.[105] Noting that Alberta's economic boom brought more crime, labour shortages, inadequate school space, unsustainable population growth, traffic congestion and disastrous land-use planning, Andrew Nikiforuk observed, "All of Alberta seems to be coming down with a Fort McMurray fever because the government doesn't have the courage or good sense to pace growth." Decrying that we are "using water and natural gas to produce synthetic oil, or gold to produce lead," he wrote that Alberta has "constructed a toxic house without proper ventilation and with no plan for alternative energy resources," and "no game plan other than the rapid liquidation of its hydrocarbons" at an indecently low royalty rate for citizens.[106]

The alarm echoes from the grassroots. In a letter to the editor, Peter Lee wondered why his province needs groups like Greenpeace to raise critical issues and why Albertans are unquestioningly becoming the Americans' supplier of "the dirtiest and [most] energy-consumptive petroleum the world has ever seen" while earning a rep for boasting the developed world's highest rate of loss of our natural environment and wildlife, and "becoming ground zero for provincial, regional, national, hemispheric and global environmental degradation."[107]

The international angle is significant. As the refusnik folk hero, Naomi Klein, observed during a visit to Alberta, "The connection between disaster capitalism and big oil is so direct, so obvious. This boom, which is a part of everyone's life in this province, is intricately linked to the spiralling chaos around the world—which assures oil prices remain high."[108] Beyond economic chaos, there is another, more insidious disaster afoot. According to the "First Law of Petropolitics" coined by the American columnist, Thomas Freidman, the price of oil and the quality of freedom inevitably move in opposite directions, so "petro-tyrannies" like Iran, Nigeria and Venezuela can make money from energy and thus don't need to listen to their people. Critics find this law applied in Alberta, which Andrew Nikiforuk suggested makes no distinctions between government and business, and where "the democratic gap between rulers and ruled grows wider every day." Citing polls showing that although Albertans overwhelmingly favour absolute reductions of carbon emissions, their government deliberately does nothing, Mr. Nikiforuk adds that rural Albertans' demands for rigorous protection of groundwater are met with further oil and gas drilling in their backyards.[109]

Addressing this apparent democratic deficit, the journalist, Gordon Laird, commented, "Alberta is a province locked in political adolescence, with ongoing issues of delayed democracy, under-investment in public welfare, environmental absenteeism and cheap resource rents not uncommon to other oil-rich jurisdictions. Yet, unlike other places like Nigeria, Saudi Arabia and Venezuela, Alberta is a self-determining democracy, one that should be more able to steward its own resources and provide for the long-term well-being of its citizens."[110]

But as much as some environmentalists might feel that the future is lost, the voice of Premier Rutherford from over a century ago reminds us that Alberta is a place for optimism. The province's *official* record on the economy versus the environment seems clearer than, say, the air over refinery row on a windless, winter day. Now let's turn to the question of just how green the grassroots in Alberta really are.

Green Streak

I would rather that my grandchildren found themselves short of money because a process closed down than short of breath because it didn't.

—BRYAN TAYLOR, letter to the editor, 2007 [111]

As you would imagine, it's not easy being green in a province that was built for economic growth, with exploitation of every opportunity encoded so deeply into the local DNA that not even radiation could fry it out. But contrary to tankers full of evidence, it's not flat-out impossible. Many might be astonished to find an undercurrent in Alberta that is less than fully committed to development at all costs.

The accomplished actor, Tantoo Cardinal, has seen everything from the northern lights of her birthplace near Fort McMurray to more southerly and earthly luminaries in Hollywood. She expresses a lesser-known perspective from Alberta amidst the greenery inside a hotel in downtown Edmonton: "We get to be the front lines of this disaster. Not everybody is after the oil money. There are a lot of people that are very upset and distressed and enraged over what's going on with our environment. We could be in alternate energy already. We could be in the future. But no, we're not. Because of that power and greed." She fantasizes about Albertans turning to alternate energy and letting the fossil fuels sit but she also understands the sense of powerlessness and the need to earn a living that stand in the way. "That fear of survival can block so much," she says. "There has to be clarity of faith, clarity of spiritual vision. I can see a struggle towards it. But people need to understand that the earth is alive. My father's people didn't understand that until some scientific instrument went like this," she continues, indicating a dancing seismic needle with her hand, "whereas my mother's people have known that since *forever*. There has to be some respect for us Neanderthals over here on this side of the track!" She calls on people to reassess and remember where life really comes from, have some faith that life still comes from the land; "and know that what the oil industry is doing to the planet overall is destructive and anti-life. People have to remember that the planet is a living, breathing thing and we're a part of it."

Her concerns are echoed by Corb Lund, speaking from his writing studio in his garage as a fourth-generation Albertan from a ranching background. "There's a bit of a groundswell of conservationism going on in Alberta now," he says. "You're starting to see some of the traditional ranchers speaking out about urban sprawl, development and stuff like that. Which is interesting because for years, you've associated the twenty-one-year-old dreadlock hippie with environmental concerns, and people tend to dismiss that, which isn't right, but it's true. But it seems to have an impact when a sixty-year-old generational rancher who's wearing a cowboy hat and looks very conservative actually speaks out about these things." He speaks of the importance of protecting the slopes of the Rockies and ranchland containing huge swaths of untouched native grass. And he attributes Albertans' increasingly apparent streak of environmentalism to the accelerated volume and pace of development in the province during the last boom.

This attitude also surfaces among many people in my street interviews in Alberta and in a battery of surveys. One poll in 2006 showed that 54 per cent of Albertans actually supported a carbon tax "to increase the cost of burning fossil fuels like oil, gas and coal for consumers and industry [to] ... promote energy efficiency and help the environment." But as Premier Klein added, the poll was incomplete for not asking Albertans whether and how much they'd be willing to pay by way of a carbon tax.[112] Before the federal government unveiled its regulatory framework in 2007, a poll suggested that 70 per cent of Albertans believe that we should pursue absolute emission cuts rather than the proposed intensity emission targets even if it costs industry more.[113] (Again, though, we don't know what Albertans would say if those costs were passed on to us.) About six months before the 2008 provincial election, Albertans told pollsters that environmental concerns should outweigh economic considerations. They ranked wildlife habitat, greenhouse gas emissions and water usage ahead of royalties, land use and economic impacts as their top concerns related to developing the oil sands. True to Albertans' form, the poll indicated that we don't trust the leaders of the major political parties to manage the province's growth, with 43 per cent trusting "none of the above" and only 33 per cent trusting the Tory premier. Yet approval and disapproval of the provincial government's management of growth and the tar sands were split at about 40 per cent each.[114] In another poll, just days before the election, nearly two-thirds of Albertans said that the government should limit the overall amount of greenhouse gas emissions produced by oil sands projects even if it means delaying or cancelling some projects and 57 per cent felt that the government wasn't doing enough to help reduce Canada's greenhouse gas emissions.[115] But in the poll that matters the most, the provincial government was returned with just over half of the popular vote, although the turnout was a record-low 41 per cent. The emerging lightning rod for environmental priorities, the Green Party, ran in 79 of 83 races, capturing 5 per cent of the vote and not even a back pocket, let alone a seat, though optimists would note a slow rise from 11 nominees and 0.2 per cent of the vote in 1993 through to 49 nominees and almost 3 per cent of vote in 2004 (when it was having trouble finding candidates) to 79 nominees and 4.6 per cent of the vote in 2008, when it claimed the distinction of being the only opposition party to boost its vote total from 2004.[116] Internal feuding over the Alberta Green Party's finances led to its deregistering itself in 2009, leaving us at least temporarily without the political equivalent of Dr. Suess's immortal Lorax to speak for the trees.

Curiously, though, in the 2006 *federal* election, the Greens did better in Alberta than anywhere else in Canada: of their 4.5 per cent of the popular vote nationally, 14 per cent came from here. The Greens drew 6.6 per cent in Alberta, another top ranking. Three Green candidates in Calgary, home of the prime minister's riding, got more than 10 per cent of the vote—only eight Green candidates did that nationally— and a Green took second place in Wild Rose, in southwest Alberta. The Green Party captured 8.5 per cent of the vote in Calgary, one point up from 2004 and a quantum leap from 1997 and 2000, when it barely registered.[117] That put the Greens in behind the Liberals (16 per cent) and the NDP (10 per cent), prompting the *Herald* to snipe, "As far as Calgary is concerned, if the Green Party is a fringe party, so are the NDP and the Grits."[118] In the 2008 federal vote, Albertans' support for the Greens sprouted to 8.8 per cent of the popular vote, behind only the Yukon and BC , with the national total at 6.8 per cent. Alberta's share of the Green vote nationally was almost 12 per cent.[119]

Fittingly, the battle to save Alberta's land and water, at least from the tar sands, may be led by those with the oldest connections to the earth. After a conference on water in 2008, a coalition of Aboriginal chiefs from three provinces and the Northwest Territories announced that local First Nations would seek to negotiate a moratorium on development, failing which they would sue to enforce their Aboriginal rights. Local Cree and Chipewyan bands pulled out of various oil sands stakeholders' groups, which they felt were driven by industry and not responsive to their concerns. The chief of the Athabasca Chipewyan, Allan Adam, vowed that First Nations would no longer sit by while corporations failed to consult with Native people on the colossal oil sands projects or properly assess their impact.[120]

As on other fronts, it would be so easy to dismiss Alberta as a black hole when it comes to green concerns. Defying such simplicity, the province has achieved several distinctions of a more positive nature on this front.

During the early oil boom at Turner Valley, naphtha gas had to be burned off to get the oil, a process that not only unleashed noxious hydrogen sulfide gas but squandered $10 in gas to produce $1 of oil. This led the Social Credit government to establish the Oil and Gas (later Energy) Resources Conservation Board in 1938. Alberta was also the first in Canada to create a body dedicated to environmental matters—the Environment Conservation Authority in 1970, since dismantled and replaced by Alberta Environment in 1971.[121] Alberta created Canada's first electronic recycling program in 2004, starting with computer hardware and televisions.[122] She was also the first province to require producers of consumer electronics to take back their products at the end of their usefulness, the goal being to reduce 360,000 kilograms of lead from the province's landfills each year.[123]

The capital city in particular is a leader in green-ness. Beyond harbouring North America's largest continuous stretch of urban parkland in a 7,400-hectare stretch of the North Saskatchewan River valley, Edmonton launched Canada's largest curbside recycling program in 1988 and diverts up to 60 per cent of residential waste from landfills (one of the few cities to reach the national goal of 50 per cent), targeting 90 per cent by 2012. It's the continent's first and perhaps only city to recycle road sand. It has North America's largest collection of advanced, sustainable waste processing and research facilities. The city is a world leader in recycling wastewater and was the first centre on the continent with a population of under one million to sport a light rail transit system.[124] Continuing its push to the edge of the lid of waste management, Edmonton proposes to be the first municipality to turn garbage into ethanol, a clean biofuel, by creating a gasification plant to produce synthetic gas from an annual total of 100,000 tonnes of plastic, textiles, contaminated stuff and other trash that can't be recycled or composted; municipal and provincial officials know of no other facility of its kind.[125]

In the south of the province, the legendary chinook winds blowing in from over the Rockies are borrowed by formidable, 660-kw turbines standing on towers fifty metres tall with a rotor diameter of forty-seven metres. In two hours, one turbine can produce enough power to supply a home for a month.[126] A Hutterite community south of Viking produces electricity by enclosing swine manure in a concrete container and harnessing the methane gas.[127] And building on their principals' innovations in using cow manure—up to a hundred tonnes of it each day—to produce power, natural gas and ethanol, a company is developing what it calls the first integrated "BioRefinery" in Canada, to produce green power, bio-fertilizer and ethanol.[128]

In the remote northwest, oil and gas producers agreed to pull out of the 486-square-kilometre Hay-Zama Lakes Wildland Park, a wetland of internationally designated significance that members of Dene Tha' First Nation plan to transform from industrial use to eco-tourism. With its focus on depleting reserves as soon as possible, the agreement is hailed as a model for discontinuing nonconforming pursuits in Alberta's protected areas.[129]

In 2008 the political scientist, David Kahane, took on the province's juggernaut of apathy to convene twenty people drawn from industry, government, environmental interests and international experts on deliberative democracy, a growing popular movement designed to include citizens in making important decisions on public policy. His task: to find ways for Albertans to become leaders in addressing the effects of climate change.[130]

These are incremental but refreshing variations on the mighty wind, hot air and organic matter being spread on the environmental front, often by those whose position, privilege and pocketbook require stoking the furnace of economic progress at a record-shattering rate. Now let's hear from one leader traditionally associated with conservative, business-friendly interests and another on the environmental side.

Going Green Meets Making Green
Interview with Preston Manning

Some Albertans see the potential for harmony between going green and making green. Preston Manning, now a management consultant and the leader of an institute called the Manning Centre for Building Democracy, joins us at the meeting table in his office in a downtown Calgary high-rise to assesses the context in the province that could make such an alliance possible.

✴ *You've spoken about a possible blending of eco green and Tory blue in this province. How so?*

One of the issues that keeps rising in the polls if you ask Albertans about their top-of-mind concern is environmental conservation. There are impending water shortages, concern about the management of the boreal forest, concerns about the environmental demands that intensive energy development, particularly the oil sands, puts on the environment. The question that raises for Albertans is, can you marry this rising interest or commitment to genuine conservation—not just token statements about sustainability—but can you marry a genuine commitment to conversation with Alberta's market-based approach to economic development, particularly in the energy industry?

✴ *Some might see that as an oxymoron.*

Conservation and conservatism come from the same root: the basic principle is that conservatives believe in living within their

Preston Manning watched over by another one-time national leader who did time in Ottawa. [Peter Takach]

means. Fiscally, that means balancing your budget. But on a broader scale, it means balancing the ecological budget, which is what a lot of Albertans would like to see. So if someone can come along and show how those two concepts can be effectively married and apply them in practical circumstance to our water situation, our land use, our energy development, then that idea would have a lot of momentum behind it, a lot of public support.

✳ *What indications of that support do you see?*

That the Green Party, with no MP behind it, finished second in Myron Thompson's rock-ribbed conservative riding [in the 2006 federal election] shows a commonality between conservatism and conservation. If this support could be combined, you'd capture a big chunk of the province, combining conservancy and a market-driven approach to economic development.

✳ *Would Canadians be surprised by this?*

I think so, because they've been told by some of the media and political elites in central Canada that Alberta is indifferent to the environment. Alberta was never keen about the Kyoto Agreement, but that wasn't because Albertans weren't concerned about the results of the combustion of hydrocarbons. It was because most Albertans, myself included, did not believe that the Liberal adminis-tration that signed Kyoto had any intention of ever implementing it. Because that agreement cannot be implemented without the concurrence of the provinces and the private sector, who have to do many of the mitigated measures that Kyoto calls for. And I don't think there was ever any serious attempt made by the Chrétien administration to get the support of the biggest hydrocarbon-producing province, Alberta, or the biggest hydrocarbon-consuming province, Ontario. So I think the impression may be given by Alberta's cool reaction to Kyoto that it doesn't care about these things. It does care about them. But Albertans would be much more open to a different approach: how can you harness the marketplace, the pricing signals, to conserve the environment rather than trying to do it through orders and agreements by government?

✳ *How would that work in practice?*

When you talk about marrying conservation and conservatism, or market-based approaches to environmental conservation, we have to start with what's called full-cost accounting: that if you're under-taking an economic development project, you have to identify the environmental consequences. You have to propose measures for mitigating or avoiding those and build the cost of those measures into the price of the good or service that you're producing, so that the price includes not just the price of the developmental side, but the price of the environmental conservation. That concept cuts the other way, too. If someone's going to propose a big environmental protection measure, there's an obligation on them to spell out what are the economic impacts of that and how that can be integrated into the economy.

So Many Challenges
Interview with Martha Kostuch

Martha Kostuch (1949–2008) was the leading face of environmentalism in Alberta for a generation. After arriving from her native Minnesota to start a veterinary clinic in Rocky Mountain House in 1975, she linked a high rate of reproductive disorders in cattle to sour-gas emissions from oil and gas drilling nearby. The reduction of those emissions capped the first of many battles that she waged to protect Alberta's air, water, forests, wilderness and wildlife. Preferring consensus to shrillness, she won the respect of adversaries in industry and government, and called many of her enemies her friends. Dr. Kostuch passed away eleven months after this interview, which took place in the earlier stages of her illness, along a sunlit, wooded trail in the North Saskatchewan River valley.

✳ *What brought you to Alberta?*

The mountains were the main thing that led me here. Being close to the mountains, beautiful rivers, wonderful forests, the wilderness, the wildlife. And that, to me, is what makes Alberta very special.

✳ *What does living here mean to you?*

Alberta's both a very wonderful place and a very challenging place to be. Albertans care about the environment very much, but at the

Martha Kostuch, whose vision, commitment and compassion embraced the forest as well as the trees. [Daron Donahue]

same time Alberta is being very much damaged by some activities within the province. There's a big fight going on between protecting the environment and destroying the environment.

✳ *Tell us about it.*

Alberta is one of the best places to live, but it also has the dubious honour of being one of the worst places to live as far as environmental protection. Albertans are number one in destroying the environment in very many areas. We're the number-one producers of carbon dioxide, climate change and greenhouse gases. Our industries rate up among the top polluters in Canada. We consume huge amounts of water in Alberta—agriculture in particular— our irrigation districts, but also cooling ponds. And our own consumption of water is one of the highest in Canada per capita. The oil sands development is the largest development happening anywhere in the world—*massive* development. We're also using up agricultural land at a very high rate. So we have the dubious honour of being in first place in many areas of environmental destruction.

✳ *Is environmentalism dead in Alberta?*

Albertans care for the environment. In fact, in many ways, the polls show we lead in many areas for concern for the environment. We had the highest percentage of votes for the Green Party anywhere in Canada. The polls show we have one of the highest rates of support for the Kyoto Accord. So certainly, Albertans care about the environment. That's not necessarily being translated into government policy, unfortunately.

✳ *Why might that be?*

I think governments often follow public opinion and in this case they certainly are behind. Industry has a lot of political sway in Alberta. Also, governments tend to think in very short time periods—four years at the most—and the environment is a long-term concern. It's not something that you can solve overnight. So I think Albertans are ahead of the game and certainly ahead of the government when it comes to caring about the environment.

✳ *What makes you most proud to be an Albertan?*

Just being here. It's such a wonderful environment. That makes me most proud, but also the people. They are very committed, very concerned, and we do make a difference. I've seen Albertans make a difference and make changes in the way we do things. A lot of significant improvements have occurred as a result of Albertans speaking up.

* *What, if anything, makes you most embarrassed to be an Albertan?*

Our poor record as far as our government not taking a leadership role in environmental protection. In fact, we've been the drag on Canada. The reason Canada can't meet, and isn't going to meet, the Kyoto commitment is because of Alberta—the Alberta government and Alberta industry. Certainly the fact that the government is a bad actor, and industry, for example, said we can't afford a raise in the royalty rate. Right, you know, we should feel sorry for industry when they're turning in billions of dollars in profits and yet they say they can't afford to pay any more royalties! That makes me ashamed to have those industries operating in Alberta.

* *How would you describe being an environmentalist in Alberta?*

Alberta's the best place to be an environmentalist because there are so many challenges. It wouldn't do to be an environmentalist where there were no challenges; it wouldn't be very interesting. To be in Alberta is to have no end of activities to be involved in: everything from local issues and saving small areas all the way up to climate change at an international level. And the oil sands! So certainly there's no end of activities and challenges for environmental activists in Alberta.

We as Albertans have a responsibility, not just to other Albertans—and here I include other species—but to the whole world to do a better job. Our activities are not just affecting Alberta; they're affecting the entire world. So it's a great place to live, but it's also very important that we in Alberta do our share and make it a better place to live.

* *What is your greatest hope for the future in this province?*

I do see a different future for Alberta. Through the oil sands process, we're trying to figure out what that future should look like.

What do we want Alberta to be like in fifty or one hundred years from now? Do we want it to be one huge urban development? Do we want it to be huge oil sands mines and oil sands developments everywhere? Do we want beautiful forests and wildlife? Do we want energy that's sustainable, renewable and solar-based instead of living off fossil fuels, which are non-sustainable?

So we're working on what that vision should be. It's important for Albertans to say what they want the future to be for Alberta, for our children, for our grandchildren, for other species. And my hope is that in fifty and one hundred years, we'll have a healthy Alberta with a diversity of wildlife. A place where people can enjoy and appreciate the outdoors, with renewable sources of energy—solar and wind. A place where we will no longer be dependent upon fossil fuels as our main source of energy or as the staple of Alberta's economy.

Perhaps the perspectives of the business community, as suggested by Preston Manning, and those of environmentalists, as expressed by Martha Kostuch, are not as mutually repelling as, say, oil and water. As Mr. Manning told us earlier, Alberta has been fertile ground for new, homegrown political movements that come out of left field— and right field—to capture the public's fancy and push for change. Some Albertans believe that true grassroots conservatives have disconnected from their governing party because it has become too cozy with big business. As the kinesiologist, Murray Chrusch, notes, "Sometimes big oil's needs get met before those of average Joe Albertans, especially those who run farms and worry about how their farmland is potentially being destroyed by the government's allowing big oil to do what they like to it." At some point, Albertans might be ready for an artful palette-mixing of Tory blue and environmental green. It has already been done in nature, as any visitor to Peyto Lake or any number of stunning, aqueous gatherings in the Rockies can testify. One dictionary defines teal as "a moderate or dark bluish green to greenish blue."[131] Perhaps someday, that hue and spirit of moderation will colour and harmonize Alberta's ecological and economic landscapes as well. And while we're at it, perhaps the gaseous inferno of a basement that Rudyard Kipling observed underlying the region of Medicine Hat will ice up, too.

The brilliant backstop philosopher, Yogi Berra—who, by his own admission, really didn't say everything he said—actually did say, "The future ain't what it used to be."[132] With that inspiration after flitting through Alberta's century of boom and bust and some of the ecological effects, let's hear from people on what the province's future might be—or used to be.

The Future (Ain't What It Used to Be)

From an economic perspective, in more than a century of provincehood, Alberta has experienced more altitudinal variations than the sky tram to the Whistlers. Change is as much a way of life as something that folks ask you for on downtown streets. As Tamara Palmer Seiler tells me:

> Summing up Alberta is certainly no easy job, probably not possible to do. It's a place that has changed a great deal in a short period. There were many events that happened rather quickly: the end of the fur trade, the end of the dominance of Aboriginal peoples of the area, the coming of the farmers and ranchers, and then the railroad coming to southern Alberta in particular. So you have the fur-trade wilderness becoming a farming economy and then a ranching economy—in certain parts of the province anyway—and then the growth of other industries. So Alberta's economic base has changed dramatically and rapidly.

In my four years of interviews in the streets, parks, offices and rooftops of the land, I asked eminent Albertans and other accommodating

Canadians whether they felt that Alberta's character was changing; if so, how; and where they thought and hoped that the province was headed. Here are some of their replies.

I think Alberta's trying to refine its identity because we've had so many people move here over the last ten, fifteen years. And it'll come.
　—DON BURNSTICK, comedian

If there is any change, it will come from more of a rural, grassroots area than from people who immigrate to our cities.
　—ERIN CHRUSCH, lawyer

No doubt about it, the economic focus is shifting to the West in this country. Alberta's a growing force, the West is a growing force and if Alberta really wants to move into the mainstream, it's got to find another Peter Lougheed. I think Peter Lougheed is the greatest statesman we've produced in this country in generations.
　—GEOFF POAPST, writer-consultant in Ottawa

The past is past, but as we look forward, we're in an interesting position. Alberta could use this century's Lougheed at the helm to deal with education, the royalty review, etcetera. Do we have vision? Can we impact and lead the country? We have the opportunity now to lead—possibly not just commercially, as in the word, "opportunity." What can we do? How can we learn to sing together to make that choir? The basic elements are there. Do we have the will, the energy and the vision to make something happen that's lasting?
　—DAVID WARD, producer and announcer, CKUA Radio

We need to look a little more into the future as far as our energy policies go. At the moment, the world is on a petroleum economy and we should take advantage of that. At the same time, we should look to the future and take a lot of our extra money and invest it. It'd be

interesting to see what Albertans could do with researching alterna-
tive energy sources and stuff like that, so that when the world does
move away from petroleum, whether it's ten or fifty years from now,
we can be viewed as world leaders in that kind of thing, too. Because
otherwise we may end up like the Maritimes and the fish, right? I
think that we should support the oil industry for the moment. That's
what's made the province fantastically wealthy in the last while. Part
of my family works in the oil industry. At the same time, I think we
should look to the future and plan for what's around the corner, too.

—CORB LUND, singer-songwriter

I have some hopes for the future. One of the things that I hope the
new leader will address is an integrated energy policy, because we
need to take advantage of the tremendous brainpower that we have
amassed over the years relative to conventional and oil-sands oil and
gas, and funnel those energies into alternate forms of energy for the
future. By that I mean coal, coal gasification, coalbed methane, solar
power, wind power, nuclear power, hydro power, all forms of energy
other than conventional and oil-sands gas and oil.

—RALPH KLEIN, premier, 1992–2006

I don't know if there's any hope for Alberta's future. I can only hope
there is. We're in trouble, get it? The money is gone. We're making
deals for oil that have nothing to do with Albertans. It's our natural
resource. All of us. But so few have control over it. So if there is one
word for all of this, it's hope. We can only hope that somebody gets
a hold of it and gets some control back. We just cannot allow so few
to get so much of our natural resources without thinking about the
future of Alberta, our children and their children. Quebec doesn't do
that, Quebec's thinking about their children. Quebec knows what it
is. Quebec has a history and a future. We've become two words.
Oil. Greed.

—GARTH PRITCHARD, documentary filmmaker

One aspect of Alberta's image that is absolutely true is Fort McMurray. We are this global polluter and we don't give a damn. It's horrendous. I don't even know if Alberta is going to be recognizable in another thirty years, given what's going on up there. And I have my fears about Edmonton as an urbanized zone: that when the bitumen runs out, it's going to be a ghost town. All those new suburbs are going to be deserted. People will have to sell their houses, and there's just going to be abandonment. There will be this last hard-core group of Edmontonians living in the centre, trying to hang on. It's a terrible image.

There's probably no hope. I look at my friend's new baby boy, this tiny, perfect human being, and I think, "Oh, baby. Are you going to have water to drink? Will you have trees to shade you or birdsong to gladden your heart?" At that level, it's apocalyptic and global but we are going to be a major contributor to that.

You can read the business section of the newspaper on how soft the Alberta economy really is. Yes, we've got all these labourers coming into the province, but a lot of them are on short-term certificates. They're coming in without families. They are not citizens, not unionized, not part of our communities. They're exploited and they're going to be flown out or they'll leave. This is the first time in an economic zone in Canada that people aren't coming to actually live here. They're not being encouraged to stay. It bodes very ill for Alberta if we have a labour force that's temporary.

All this points to the soft underbelly of all this wealth. If you can't encourage the next generation to settle here, their kids to school here, pay their taxes here, send and go to concerts here, then what the hell? We may be blowing off our critical mass.

—MYRNA KOSTASH, writer

When you're a cowboy poet, not only are you not part of the boom, you're not even at the edge of the slick! But, I'm proud to be an Albertan when I hear voices speaking up to say, "Let's do it right and let's do it maybe slowly and let's preserve what we have." To me, it doesn't take a whole lot of wisdom to go rushing pell-mell to get up to the banqueting table. But it takes a whole lot of smarts to be selective when you do get up to the banqueting table and try to make sure there's something left for the next generations to come. I hope there's an Alberta for the next generation. I hope the bigger part of Alberta is the legacy we leave, saying we weren't so eager to have millionaires but we were eager to have enough.

—DORIS DALEY, cowboy poet

In many ways, Alberta's a bit of a baby, but I think that's all going to change. The people are going to change it. More and more, people are going to demand from their leaders that this place becomes progressive. I believe this place has the potential to be a world leader in so many areas: environmentalism and sustainable development, agriculture and all kinds of things. It's just a matter of getting that agenda in place.

—BILL BOURNE, singer-songwriter

Some days, I think Albertans are changing for the worse, and those are on days when all they're interested in is flaunting wealth and how much money they made yesterday. And on other days, I think that they are changing for the better because they do have a sense of responsibility even if it isn't always visible to the outside world. One of the problems of a really exciting, booming moment is that you have to think about the future and sometimes you worry that Alberta's going to hell in the future, partly because we are people of the moment and we don't look as far down the road as we should.

I would like to see us not just learning from all of the past booms and busts, and of course the bust always follows the boom. I'd like to see us learning from the present. In this moment, what we can do with all this promise and all this wealth and all this energy is imagine a future that takes advantage of the gifts that we have—

the resources, the beauty and the personal, the people energy—
and moves us toward a future that actually encompasses all of those
aspects and that really does something different—culturally, politic-
ally, and, I would hope, socially.

—ARITHA VAN HERK, writer

6 Will the Real Alberta Please Stand Up?

Thus the root of fear, the reason many people feel trapped, even despairing, about the direction of our world, is not what we've assumed it was. It's not just a shaky economy or suicide bombers or ecological meltdown. It's that we've been forced to deny who we are.

—FRANCES MOORE LAPPÉ AND JEFFREY PERKINS, 2004

Overleaf: It's hard to toe the line on a subject as complex, contradictory and (digitally) composited as Alberta. [Photo montage by Bonnie Sadler Takach.]

What's in a Name?
Interview with H.R.H. Princess Louise Caroline Alberta[1]

On May 8, 1882, the federal government, in an early and literal version of going postal, partitioned a portion of the North-West Territories into the districts of Saskatchewan, Athabasca, Assiniboia and Alberta. The latter was named in honour of Princess Louise Caroline Alberta, the fourth daughter of Queen Victoria and Prince Albert. Princess Louise joins us for a quintessentially colonial compromise, medium tea.

✳ *Welcome, Your Highness. How did your name come to grace one of the farthest-flung provinces of Canada?*

It was the handiwork of my husband, the Marquis of Lorne. He was your governor general at the time and apparently influential on Sir John A. Macdonald, the day's prime minister and minister of the interior. They considered my first name, but the Americans had already taken Louisiana. My second name had gone to the Carolinas. This did not displease me, as I favoured my third name,

Self-portrait sculpted by Princess Louise Caroline Alberta, whom Albertans might take for granite. [*National Portrait Gallery, London, No. 4455*]

which honoured my dear father. My husband was fond of it as well, for he called me Alba for short. You may count yourselves fortunate that the Canadian government did not follow *that* lead!

✳ *Hmm. Imagine a province called "Alba for short."*

Let us not be *too* frivolous, sir.

✳ *Sorry about that. How do you feel about this distinction?*

At first, I felt intensely proud to have this most wonderful province called after me. Today, with the blessing of hindsight, I am more humbled by it. One might only hope that whatever qualities I possessed bear the glimmer of an approximation to your beautiful, sunlit and prosperous Alberta.

✳ *You're being modest. Historians call you intelligent, unaffected and possessing a "radiant," "uncommon," and "uncontested" natural beauty. Surely these are qualities for which Albertans would love to be known.*

Perhaps. But not everyone harboured that opinion, least of all the editor of the *Edmonton Bulletin*, who would have preferred the honour on a buffalo. I still recall the stinging screed in his Dominion Day edition in 1882: "Alberta may be a nice name for a baby girl, although that is a matter of opinion, but there can scarcely be two opinions as to its being inappropriate as the name of a great province of a great country. To name this province after any man who has yet appeared in Canada is too much honor for the amount of good any one of them has done this country. Many names could be found, some appropriate, but none less so than Alberta."[2]

✳ *Harsh!*

I might think myself fortunate that *he* was not minister of the interior at the time. *(courtly pause)* How lovely it must have been for him to be holding that office twenty-three years later, when my namesake district was promoted to provincehood. I understand that your Prime Minister Laurier preferred the name Assiniboia. Pity.

✳ *My money is still on your being a fitting namesake for the Wild Rose Province.*

I would not leap so quickly. The inexorable sword dance of time can change one's perspective. Rigor mortis is a wonderful equalizer, you know.

✳ *Perish the thought, Your Highness!*

(*Here she casts a sidelong glance through narrowed eyes.*)
Let us examine the facts. I was known for a gentle manner. Your province is avowedly not.

✳ *A good point, but—*

Mind your interruptions, man! Note also that my being born during a time of social unrest in the mid-nineteenth century caused my beloved mama, Her Majesty the Queen, to fret about the possibility that I might become...peculiar.

✳ *Ah, but Albertans have always liked the notion of standing out in a crowd. Surely you fit this bill.*

As the sixth of nine children, I never received as much attention as some of my dear siblings. I compensated for this by exhibiting a curiosity that evidently overwhelmed my family. They bestowed upon me the title of "Little Miss Why." I was always fond of new ideas. My husband and I would host gatherings of eminent educators in our home.

✳ *Albertans are naturally curious, too. There is a fierce love of the new here. You know, learning new things, trying out new ideas, buying new SUVS...*

Here, in all fairness to your argument—if not auguring my own—I note that I could execute the sword dance with greater ginger than any of my sisters. And I dare say that I had three older ones, too.

✳ *There you go! You were known among royal-watchers for your exuberance, wit and flair. Albertans like to think we're known for our energy and our sunny disposition. Again, I see a fine match here.*

Do you? I spent a good many years in a state of melancholy after I lost my father at age thirteen. If that is sunny, then your colonial definition differs from the one back home.

✳ *But Your Highness, your provincial namesake spent her formative years grieving the loss of a loved one as well. It took a quarter-century for Alberta to win the right to her own natural resources from Ottawa— a right that was granted to all but the Prairie provinces on joining Confederation.*

Ah, yes, Ottawa. My husband and I had a catastrophic accident there. On the way to a function at the Senate, our sleigh overturned. Our steeds, apparently alarmed, dragged us along the street for a substantial distance. I suffered a phalanx of injuries and was shipped back home to recover.

✳ *Ouch.*

To be truthful, my time in your country was wrought with ill fortune. We arrived in Halifax bereft of the small matter of our mainsail, an unscheduled offering to the great Atlantic. Our train almost had a calamitous altercation with the Montreal-Ottawa Express. Once, the royal yacht broadsided a schooner on the St. Lawrence River.

✳ *With the greatest of respect, Your Highness, it couldn't have been all* bad.

(laughs) There were swirling rumours of a Fenian plot to kidnap me as ransom for the return of Irish militants awaiting trial back in Britain. So in 1883 I was packed off to Bermuda, where I was hailed as its first official tourist and memorialized with the name of a hotel. Several Canadian newssheets took issue with my departure. I could understand the anti-monarchists in Britain and the American rags. But frankly, I expected more politeness from your country.

✳ *Then you might have a problem with your namesake province, which some say has become the least politically correct, or polite, part of the country.*

As that less than polite newspaper editor noted, I never did visit Alberta. My husband reached Fort Calgary, Fort Macleod and High River while I was convalescing back in England. Not seeing your Alberta remains among my greatest regrets. I could have strapped myself to the cowcatcher of a Canadian Pacific Railway train in your spectacular Rocky Mountains, like that insufferable Lady Macdonald. *(grand pause)* Or at least brought home a porcelain souvenir plate.

✳ *You are remembered as a magnificent non-conformist, even a rebel. These attributes are prized highly in Alberta. Would you describe yourself that way?*

Well, Mama did call my behaviour as a teenager "very odd, dreadfully contradictory, very indiscreet and from that, making mischief frequently." Dear Mama. It took me seven years after my father's death to convince her to sing again. Family whimsy holds that my brother, the Prince of Wales, spent forty more years trying to get her to stop. *(stately pause)* Now where was I?

✳ *We were discussing your independent spirit.*

So we were. How I loathed invitations dictating my place at
the table and my choice of wardrobe. As if I were nothing but a
dummy! And then came the biggest blow of all. Mama wanted
to marry me off to a German prince, as was the custom since the
Hanoverians. But I would have none of it. I dissuaded suitors by
donning dresses that were light in colour and wearing my hair down
to my shoulders or piled upon my pate. In an age in which women
wore dark, heavy apparel and their hair crimped up with tongs,
this offended some of our subjects. I detested the thought of being
saddled with a European royal like my sisters. I was independent, as
you say. I knew what I wanted.

✳ *Which was?*

What I wanted was to marry a Briton. Did you know that I
announced my own intention to wed? This caused quite a little
cacophony back home. The least objectionable candidate was Sir
John Campbell, the Marquis of Lorne. He was no royal, though he
was from the Scottish nobility and a Member of Parliament. Imagine
the audacity of my marrying one of our subjects, a practice disused
since the Plantagenets, who ruled Britannia in the late Middle Ages.
However, Mama, being accustomed to my face, I suppose, was good
enough to grant my wish. I designed my own veil.

✳ *With the greatest of respect, Your Highness, how Albertan can you get?*

If you find that anecdote resonant, then you may favour these
others. I prepared my own oyster pâté for guests. When Rideau
Hall entertained scarlet fever and our servants would not attend to
the sick, I played the nurse myself. And while in Bermuda, walking
to a function rather than using a carriage, I stopped at a house for
water. The presiding matron demurred, exhorting me to wait until

she finished ironing a shirt. I instructed her to fetch the water while I finished the shirt.

✳ *You actually ironed the shirt?*

I most certainly did. I would have starched the collar if she possessed the necessary equipment.

✳ *Starch?*

No, a collar.

✳ *Splendid! Did you flaunt convention to the very end?*

I suppose so. I was the only one of nine children in my family not to have children. (As it turns out, dear Lorne was not so, ah, oriented.) And I arranged to be cremated, an uncommon practice among royalty at the time. *The Times* was good enough to remind its readers that I was "the least bound by convention and etiquette of any of the Royal Family."

✳ *On that point, you were also noted for your wit. Is there any truth to that story of you and the bird at the royal mausoleum?*

Good heavens, yes. My family and I were at Frogmore on an anniversary of Mama's death, during the 1920s, I believe. As we knelt in prayer, a dove flew inside. "Dear Mama's spirit," whispered my loved ones. I knew it was no such thing and told them why: Mama's spirit would never have ruined Beatrice's hat.

✳ *Can you drop a hint about some of your accomplishments?*

Marrying Lorne allowed me to stay home and pursue my art. I painted both oils and watercolours. My drawings were published. I studied sculpture at the National Art Training School. I was the first female sculptor to have work displayed in London, a likeness of Her Majesty the Queen near Kensington Palace. There is another one at Victoria College in Montreal; I believe they call it the Strathcona Music Building now. *(regal pause)* That's 555 Sherbrooke Street West if any readers are in that vicinity.

✳ *Duly noted. Artistic flair is another characteristic of Albertans. Although it's not the first thing to leap to mind when folks think of our province.*

If they think about it all!

✳ *Right.*

I understand anonymity. In fact, I embraced it. I stole away, alone, to church in Halifax, to give thanks for surviving our first journey to your shores. My disdain for stuffy receptions and idle chatter moved me to withdraw from many public appearances, which certainly did not sit gladly with the public. I enjoyed travelling under assumed names. I attended public lectures without any escort. Just imagine my position on trumpet fanfares! Tell me now, just how "Albertan" is that?

✳ *Touché. Albertans do seem to like hoopla. On the other hand, many of us would probably appreciate your disdain for formality.*

Would your well-known haven for cowboys also appreciate my advocating for the rights and the interests of women? I wrote letters to newspapers and made speeches. I served as the first president of the National Union for the Higher Education of Women.

✳ *Don't let the lariats mislead you, Your Highness. Alberta rocked the cradle of the feminist movement in Canada. Following your*

distinguished example, Albertans are proud to call themselves
"mavericks"—

(*laughs imperially*) Forgive me. I have been called many things, but never an unbranded calf. If my ancestors were here, they would relieve you of your head quicker than Lucifer could scorch a feather!

✳ *A century of sorries, Your Highness. No disrespect intended. May the force of ten thousand hair-crimping tongs meld my two lips into one.*

Satisfactory. Now if you will be good enough to partition your remaining lip into halves, we can conclude this little audience.

✳ *How would you like Albertans to remember you?*

I would hope that they remember me at least as well as my own countrymen! Today, my name lives on mostly through a pub in London dating from the late Victorian era. Apparently the establishment is noted for its epicurean delights, not to mention the superb plumbing fixtures in the gentlemen's lavatory.

More seriously, perhaps, blessed Bermuda boasted of hosting the first exhibition of my watercolours in 1989. Alas, I do not anticipate many more. I had some technical facility, but I preferred the classical tradition to the modernist work of Monsieur Rodin and his Impressionist confreres. So I shan't be remembered as an artist.

If I could choose my testament, then I suppose it would be my efforts for charity. My husband and I founded affordable schools for girls. We supported several schools, a shelter for girls, the welfare of veterans, literacy for the impoverished, books for the blind, temperance, the preservation of historical sites and natural areas. His tenure in your Dominion ushered in the National Gallery of Canada, the Royal Canadian Academy of Arts and the Royal Society of Canada. There were others.

✳ *Well, Albertans are generous privately, although in the eyes of some, less so publicly. Still, on the whole, there seems to be a decent case for linking your attributes and interests to the character of our province.*

The contradictions are of interest but one might be content with the course of events. It could have been worse. You could have been christened for my youngest sister, Princess Beatrice.

✳ *Beatrice? That's not so bad.*

I was contemplating one of *her* middle names: Feodore.

✳ *Indeed. Thank you for joining us, Your Highness, contradictions and all.*

(Her Royal Highness sashays out, accompanied by a simply heavenly trumpet fanfare.)

The Princess's third name, Alberta, also graces a 3,619-metre mountain found about one hundred kilometres south of Jasper. Her second name, Caroline, embellishes a town near the foothills of the Rockies. And her first name, Louise, adorns four distinguished Canadian army regiments, a world-famous lake and a klatch of tourist cabins, gas pumps and other delights comprising the hamlet near that lake.

Myths and Contradictions (Or Not)

It's a paradox but it's amazing, man!
—BILL BOURNE, 2007

Trying to define anything, let alone a place like Alberta, is complicated by the panoply of perspectives involved. Like the blind man approaching the elephant, each of us grasps a piece of the thing—as big or small as we choose to muster—and draws conclusions about the whole. Given Alberta's elephantine size and her variety of textures, appendages and orifices, getting to the soul of the beast is certainly no small tusk. And it's a moving target to boot. As Tamara Palmer Seiler tells us, forming an identity is always an evolving process. "Alberta has changed a lot and its identity has changed and evolved," she says, observing that our province seems to have a distinct identity in other parts of Canada, while adding, "Whether or not that is an identity that most Albertans would say is accurate is another matter."

With the rapid social, demographic and economic change in Alberta, spurred by commodities like fur, wheat, beef, gas and oil, and steeped in the uncertainties of cycles of boom and bust, it's arguable that the province hasn't had much time to develop an identity.[3] The writer, Ray Djuff, warned against searching for the real Alberta. "Try to define an Albertan and any number of stereotypes jump to mind," he wrote. "Don't waste your time—they don't stand up to critical examination." He believes that finding an iconic Albertan is as difficult as getting a Calgarian and an Edmontonian to agree on whose city is superior and concludes that "a great deal of the myth and reality of what is an Albertan is wrapped up in contrariness and contradiction."[4]

"There has been contradiction throughout Alberta's history, such as Emily Murphy being both a women's rights advocate and a racist," notes the sociologist, Tami Bereska. She looks at different parts of the province and sees contrasts.

As we have seen in these pages, the contrasts are stunning.

Albertans' history, outlook and economic survival are rooted in the land even as we lay waste to it with recklessness and indifference.

We are fiercely traditional in our ties to previous ways but boldly progressive when it comes to changing them.

We celebrate departing from the herd in many fields—especially down south, where they have more herd to depart from—while twirling a lariat of political conformity that would freeze Dumbo's biggest brother in his tracks.

Alberta is full of cow culture—and plenty of the other kind.

We are fearful for the present and hopeful for the future, sometimes in the same breath.

And we adopt the larger-than-life persona that befits the big skies, big trucks and free enterprise for which the province is known—even if it doesn't always fit. As Aritha van Herk comments, "One of the strangest traps for Albertans is that they believe their own mythology. After awhile, they start to step into the story that has been invented about them and they love it so much that they can't resist dressing up in that costume."

So what are Alberta's myths? Or more precisely, what perceptions do others commonly declare about Wild Rose Country, the accuracy of which may have been ploughed over by the harrow of time and eventually combined and baled into convenient, rhetorical sound bites?

That the province is all bald prairie, punctuated westwardly by some mountains.

That we are predominantly rural in our outlook and lifestyle, collectively fixated on cows, horses and Stetsons.

That we are archly, unflinchingly and uniformly conservative in our social, political and economic orientation.

That our necks are redder than the guests of honour at church basement suppers in Cavendish, the home jerseys of *Les Glorieux*, maple leaves during hunting season in Muskoka, flags brandished by marching disciples of Tommy Douglas or double-decker buses cruising Victoria at teatime.

That we thump Bibles like a pumpjack stuck in overdrive.

That we don't give a darn about the rest of Canada.

That we are more Texan than Canadian.

That we are mavericks who do what we want, when we want, with whomever we want.

That bacteria have more culture than we do.

That we are mainly a bunch of good ol' white boys.

That we're a stagnant place, not big on the whole education and innovation thing.

That we're always booming and we're all filthy rich.

And that we are all out to get even richer at the expense of our land, air, water and wildlife.

So if these are all myths, or at least exaggerated truths or former truths, why are they persistently thrown in our face in the media? And why do we perpetuate them ourselves? Maybe the better questions to ask are who is being served by these myths and why.

After Mother Nature's work over the eons and then a few millennia as Aboriginal country, the land was recast as the Canadian North-West, of which Alberta became a part. This move profoundly shaped her identity, defining her in relation to something else, something perceived as greater than she. For people like the Cree and the Blackfoot, for instance, the term "North-West" had all the significance of bison dung, except the dung was actually useful for heating and for building driving lanes for (ironically) bison hunts. As a colony of a colony, Alberta was seen as grist for the mill of empire, be it beaver-felt hats for the haberdasheries of jolly olde England, grain for the national breadbasket, a captive market to prop up manufacturers in central Canada, the missing link in a sea-to-sea umbilical chord of steel, or black-gold products for foreign interests enmeshed in global political struggles. In short, by virtue of her geography and since colonial times, Alberta has existed to serve the political and economic interests of people who do not live here.

For two centuries, this was largely terra incognita for non-inhabitants beyond accounts from fur traders, the work of pictorial artists and the odd tourist like the Marquis of Lorne, the upscale remittance man married to the royal who lent the eventual province her name. It was a vast, remote, frigid wilderness, contentedly left by imperial powers to fur-plunderers and profiteers. The myth-making began in earnest in late Victorian times when the bosses of the new Dominion government, bent on agricultural settlement to thwart the threat of American incursion, decided that Wild Rose Country was the second coming of Eden—despite expert advice to the contrary. But the promise of cheap land, freedom from social, ethnic or political repression and the siren song of economic opportunity attracted millions to the Last Best West. The feds' gambit worked: they got the settlers, farmers, customers, citizens and taxpayers that they sought. And many of those who endured the hardships of homesteading got the freedom that *they* wanted.

The result was an indelible popular image: the self-reliant, rugged individualist on the frontier who carved a life from the prairie stubble on sheer strength, wits and grit. While this portrayal contains truth, other realities often get lost in the folklore. For example, people did band together to survive and communities, churches and wheat pools played huge roles in their stories. "We value community spirit and cooperation," observes Michael Phair, a community relations director and a longtime community volunteer and activist. "This is under-played many times by the sense that you should take care of yourself and do it on your own, but I think that our community and coopera-tive spirit are stronger." Myth-making persists on other fronts, too. The oft-mentioned harshness of the climate and the insects were matched by the less-mentioned sting of centrally based bankers, railways and grain monopolies. Popular media glorify Alberta's postwar industrial-ization while mostly bypassing the well-developed coal industry in the Crowsnest Pass, the clay works in Medicine Hat and many other local economies. And the persistent spotlight on cowboys, rumrunners, gunslingers and other aspects of the American Wild West ignores, first, the enormous power and influence of the ranching barons and the British-Ontarian culture that they brought to the province; and second, the vastly longer history of the northern fur trade, along with other aspects and areas of the province, which is certainly not all bald-ass prairie. Those aspects include at least 10,000 years of Aboriginal history and culture.

Ironically, this emphasis on Alberta's physical landscape is evident even in what our historic sites project to the world. A former director of the government's cultural facilities and historical resources services,

Frits Pannekoek, observed during his tenure that the province's spectacular scenery and wildlife were easier to interpret than the "subtle
meandering of Alberta's coal-mining, industrial, settlement or intellectual history." Noting the aforementioned transfer of central Canadian
and American settlement mythologies to the province and that
Alberta was the last in the land to establish a provincial museum or
archives, Dr. Pannekoek observed the common belief that Wild Rose
Country is a blank slate despite centuries of occupation. "Where there
is no past, any newcomers create a future and, more significantly, a
new past," he wrote, tracing the first rewriting of Alberta's history to
the arrival of the North West Mounted Police in the mid-1870s and the
next one to Ontarian and British ranchers, who, within twenty years of
their arrival, were "consciously endeavouring to preserve the past they
had created for themselves." Then came the "wheat miners" and subsequent waves of immigrants after World War II, all of whom the good
doctor suggests were convinced that they, too, were writing history.[5]

In certain parts of the province, the dominant historical moving
force has been the fight to preserve group culture against Alberta's
dominant Ontario-American political and social culture.[6] Yet the
province remains coloured by an increasingly small and remote
caricature of that culture: the backwater, nouveau-riche, cowboy-
maverick-redneck. One might attribute the cowboy part of this to
the marketing geniuses at the Calgary Stampede, glorifying a tradition that reached its zenith in one part of Alberta more than a century
ago and echoing aspects of the mythical American Wild West that
never travelled north. According to the historian, Sarah Carter: "The
two Wests shared administration from a distant and often insensitive
federal government, powerful railroad interests, the confinement of
aboriginal people to reserves, the survey of the land into the same grid
pattern, despoilment of the environment, technologies, politics and
religion. They shared blizzards, dust, weeds and baseball."[7] But Alberta
did not share other aspects of the American West, notably in her
retaining British traditions and institutions, and in her perhaps mildly

less genocidal approach to Aboriginal affairs. In any case, the enduring image of the cowboy only touches some of the myths and stereotypes of Alberta, ignoring forces beyond tourism as motivation for perpetuating a specific image.

Myths have proven to be powerful ways to influence individual and group behaviour and thus not only reinvent our past but affect our present and future. Seen as such, a myth is not only a story but a message aimed at achieving a purpose—an appropriation and distortion of history for a political end.[8] Creating and perpetuating myths is a way to mobilize public opinion and support. Myths, whether based on actual or manufactured events, have been used by political, economic, cultural and other interests for a battery of reasons: to create symbolic reality and provide meaning, emotion and motive for human action; to bestow values through stories to justify actions; to create or maintain order, structure and control; to protect one's image, identity and autonomy; to foster conformity with group decision-making; and to conceal, distort or manipulate, among other ends.

We saw this kind of myth-making a century ago when the federal government encouraged settlement in the Last Best West by portraying the arid Palliser Triangle as a lush, agricultural paradise. We saw it after the rise of the Progressives, who tend to be portrayed by revisionists as self-sufficient, pioneer farmers rather than organized, sophisticated grain specialists who sought to replace unfavourable tariffs with wheat boards and other government services.[9] We saw this throughout the Lougheed era and beyond, when the provincial government sang the praises of free enterprise while subsidizing business and industrial interests to the point that critics claim is shameless and indecent. We see it today when media snobs from Ontario ignore or slag Wild Rose Country as culturally inferior and, by implication, less worthy of national attention. And we certainly see it when political and economic interests in Alberta invoke the spectre of the National Energy Program each time anyone broaches introducing a tax on carbon emissions, as if Ottawa was singlehandedly responsible for falling oil prices and every one of a complex series of factors that precipitated the 1980s' bust in the province. Dead for years, the NEP has become a powerful symbolic weapon to be deployed by Alberta's government against any real or perceived incursion by the feds, just as central Canada continues to serve as bogeyman-on-demand to distract Albertans from provincial problems or shortcomings, and particularly from the need for an opposition in the Legislature. Individuality is trumpeted to the moon, while on the ground, conformity is orchestrated carefully, quietly and ruthlessly.

Although this sort of historical revisionism and manipulation is a standard tool of the political trade, it has been used with dazzling success in Alberta, the race-paced, come-for-the-money, attention-deficit capital of a country of citizens whom surveys repeatedly show couldn't pass an elementary-school history test. As Michael Phair points out, Canada's relatively small population and few media channels, compounded by American media domination, gives provincial governments a higher profile than they might have otherwise. Hence, the portrait of Alberta that emerges from our Legislature is predominantly rural, white, male, older and laughably obsolete.

The diversity of the province belies its monocultural profiling in the popular media. As the dramaturge and filmmaker, Gerry Potter, tells me, "It's a wide-open place, with people with wide-open minds. It's exciting, full of life, full of contrasts." He says that everything in the world is here in microcosm: "There's cultural diversity. There's every kind of climate zone you want. There's every kind of geography. We have inner-city problems and we have wide-open spaces. We have cowboys. We have Indians. We have everything. We're not the stereotype that people think we are."

So here lies the grand paradox that is Alberta.

Not just prairie and mountains but a vast landscape, dizzying in its geographic diversity, with more biomes than almost any other part of Canada and more biodiversity than just about anywhere else on the planet.

No longer predominantly rural people-wise—despite harbouring nation-leading numbers of cows, horses and Smithbilts, not to mention llamas, alpacas and ostriches—but pretty much the most urbanized and certainly the most rapidly urbanized, population in the country.

Home to not only chuckwagons but world-leading treatment for diabetes, the proto-feminist Persons Case and the grandmaster puppeteer Ronnie Burkett—and according to the Canadian Council on Learning, the best learning opportunities in Canada.

Not entirely conservative within the true meaning of the term, with a formative history of politically non-partisan and even radical behaviour, a latter-day bent for economic neo-liberalism under Ralph Klein and Preston Manning, and a lifelong pull to lead the charge for reform.

No more redneck than other parts of the nation and not colossally divergent from other Canucks at the grassroots level on major social issues.

Further from the buckle of Canada's Bible belt than any other province in the loop except British Columbia and by far the most ardent worshippers at the altar of retail.

Proudest of our province and our communities but still fiercely committed to our country and a mostly uncomplaining, highest net-contributor to Confederation.

Admittedly comparable to Texas in terms of oil, bravado and living large, but probably nowhere nearly as anti-American.

Prone to calling ourselves mavericks, taking big risks and thumbing our noses at authority, but mostly true to our provincial mammal, a sheep, when it comes to political and business elites enforcing the status quo and to citizens voting (or not voting) in elections.

Boasting even more culture than bacteria as Canada's largest per-capita consumers of cultural products, which we seem to value twice as much as sainted hockey and football.

Not all old, white and male—nor the visible minority capital of Canada—but the youngest population among the provinces; more homogenous in terms of class structure and more racially tolerant than many; and generally more interested in your progress than your pedigree.

Not a stagnant backwater but a cauldron of rapid change with a penchant for education, innovation and self-improvement as ideals, practices and lifestyle choices.

Still filthy rich as a province but also home to the nation's widest (and ever-widening) gap between wealthy and impoverished; brutal on folks with low and fixed incomes; and deeply insecure after continually riding the volatile waves of boom and bust in an economy tethered overwhelmingly to resource commodities and their market prices.

Holding a catastrophic record on our land, air, water and wildlife— while growing grassroots resistance to rampant, massive industrial development.

To many, Albertans are united by a fierce need to face challenges head-on and improve their lot in life. On the other hand, there is record-setting apathy at the ballot box and on matters of collective social, economic and environmental concern in a province where people are too affluent, disinterested or distracted to care.

Perhaps Alberta is too well off or complacent to reconcile her astonishing paradoxes. Maybe that's simply asking too much of any place or people. It's easier to stay mired in the rhetorical muck and spin a slurry back at others than to confront oneself, challenge longstanding assumptions and possibly even change them. Yet we Albertans pride ourselves on defying the status quo, with ample justification. When you get a handle like the Last Best West, you can do that. And as the American philosopher, George Santayana, warned, "Those who cannot remember the past are condemned to repeat it."[10]

Albertans have proven highly adept at remembering our past but what's even more remarkable is how selective that memory has been and how it has been channelled. We have been much less vigorous in framing our bigger historical picture and in questioning apparently traditional beliefs and attitudes. Whether this is due to political manipulation by the people we elect, our own laziness or some cruel combination of both makes interesting argument but ultimately is not the point. As we traipse through our second century of provincehood, the unprecedented onslaught—dare we say stampede—of incoming economic migrants could help change our cherished Albertan stereotypes or simply adopt and entrench them further. As Aritha van Herk tells us, new Albertans step into the myths that have been created for them.

Undeniably, Alberta is a grand place, blessed immensely by geography, both physical and human, costume and all. But her true greatness, measured by our contributions to our society, our country and our planet, remains to be seen. Perhaps ditching some of the rhetorical baggage and its labels—especially our semi-mythical, evil-twin image as eco-killing, selfish-redneck, backwater-dwelling, political sheep—would be a dandy place to start. Nobody is perfect, but Alberta's titanic natural and value-added advantages, channelled through a perplexing maze of contradictions to reach a heightened sense of self-awareness and purpose, just might give us a better shot at it than most.

So, in a nutshell, what is the real Alberta?

In One Word

During streetside interviews from the left coast to the right, I asked people to sum up their thoughts, feelings and impressions of Alberta in a single word. Beyond the merry parade of references to beef, cowboys, oil, conservatism, rednecks, money, jobs, Ralph Klein, the Calgary Stampede and West Edmonton Mall from other Canadians and foreign visitors, here are some replies from Wild Rose Country itself (except as otherwise noted), loosely grouped and classified:

Temporal:
Ancient, intriguing (*Jack Brink, archaeologist*)
Fresh (*Jackie Flanagan, publisher; Chris Allen, radio producer/announcer*)

Natural:

Open *(Don Brinkman, paleontologist)*

Grandeur *(Andy Donnelly, radio producer/announcer)*

Beautiful *(Martha Kostuch, environmentalist)*

Bright *(Anne Wheeler, filmmaker)*

Grass (rough fescue) *(Doris Daley, cowboy poet)*

The Alberta rose *(Jane Ash Poitras, visual artist; a grade-two student in Leduc)*

Freedom *(Pat McGaffigan, retired nurse)*

Hardy:

Individualistic *(Douglas Cardinal, architect)*

Independent *(Don Burnstick, comedian)*

Pragmatic *(Karen Lynch, administrator)*

Resilient *(Scott Pfeifer, curler)*

Strong *(Marcel Rocque, curler)*

Community *(Pat Darbasie, actor)*

Forward-looking:

Possibility *(David Ward, radio producer/announcer)*

Potential *(Fil Fraser, film producer/broadcaster/etc.)*

Imagination *(Ted Byfield, journalist)*

Determined, adventurous *(Tommy Banks, senator/jazzman)*

Initiative *(Link Byfield, journalist)*

Passionate *(David Nedohin, curler)*

Optimistic *(Douglas Cardinal, architect)*

Opportunity *(James Shapiro, surgeon; Melissa Blake, mayor; John McDougall, CEO)*

Frontier *(Corb Lund, singer-songwriter; Preston Manning, éminence grise)*

Superlative:

Joy *(Anne Chandler, farmer; a tween immigrant in Edmonton)*

Amazing *(Bill Bourne, singer-songwriter)*

Outstanding *(Randy Ferbey, curler)*

Great *(Hon. Ralph Klein, premier)*

Best *(Philip Currie, paleontologist)*

Confident, cocky *(Geoff Poapst, writer-consultant in Ottawa)*

Lucky *(Bronco Buddy, non-rodeo cowboy clown)*

Evolving:

Changing *(Mark Lisac, journalist)*

Massive flux *(Tim Antoniuk, industrial designer)*

Dynamic *(Max Foran, historian/author)*

Diverse *(Hon. Norman Kwong, lieutenant-governor/*CFL *Hall of Famer; Bruce McGillivray, museum director)*

Urban(e) *(Michael Phair, community relations director/community advocate)*

Elusive:

Complex, contradiction, indefinable *(Tamara Palmer Seiler, historian)*

Like the large monuments singled out by Lieutenant-Governor Kwong, Alberta is an overstatement, a larger-than-life embodiment of the breadth and depth of human energy, invention and absurdity. As Aritha van Herk says, "One of the very strange parts of Alberta is that it is such a hyperbolic place, right out of a tall tale. We start to take it for granted, and we think that all this excess, all this energy, all these crazy passions that we have are ordinary. You couldn't invent a place as crazy as this in any story, and yet here it is and we're living in it and we're a part of that craziness in everything we do."

From everything I have heard, learned and experienced, I would distill the essence of the province to six qualities:

1. The desire, courage and capacity to start anew, encompassing the values of pioneering, optimism and opportunity

2. A passion for freedom, with a desire to escape social, cultural, political or economic strictures of the past and *any* bureaucratic restrictions of the present

3. A profound connection to the land—physical, economic and psychological—playing out in open spaces and open people

4. A propensity to do it oneself, whether individually or as a community, reflecting the values of invention, learning, self-reliance and industry

5. A penchant for taking risks, born of the volatility of a singularly commodity-based economy (ranching, agriculture, fossil fuels)

6. Alienation, anti-authoritarianism and a sense of exploitation from being situated far from the centres of political and economic power.

The common denominator, the well from which these qualities spring, seems to be the notion of Alberta as the Last Best West—the frontier plus the mythology that has arisen around it. Of all the people that I interviewed, a few mentioned or alluded to it in passing, but only two named "frontier" as the one word that best sums up Alberta for them. One is Preston Manning, the founder of the Reform Party, retired national opposition leader, now the head of the Manning Centre for Building Democracy and incidentally, the son of the longest-serving premier in Alberta's history. The other is someone quite different: the nouveau-country singer, songwriter and musician, Corb Lund, the winner of several national music awards and a fourth-generation Albertan. Different as different can be in terms of generations, haircuts and fingerpicking styles, but united on this overarching summary of their province. As Mr. Lund puts it, "I still think it's frontiers-y enough here that people are able to follow their goals and get their work done and just go ahead and do things on their own. I think that's partly because there's a real wilderness-y, out-on-the-open-plains, frontier kind of spirit here."

So let's look closer at that deep-rooted frontier spirit, our penultimate stop en route to the soul of Wild Rose Country.

The Last Best West

The lure of distant places, the promise of greener fields, the desire to own land—all of these, combined and collectively expressed in the movement of people to a new frontier, constitute one of the most forceful drives in society.
—JOHN ARCHER, 1970

In its provincial incarnation, Alberta has always embodied what Robert Kroetsch called "that old North American impulse to be off to the simpler, freer, more elemental frontier."[11] Her formative event as a province can be traced not to, for example, the leadership of Louis Riel (Manitoba) or the coming of the transcontinental railway (British Columbia), but to a foreign consequence, the evaporation of the American frontier by 1896.[12] When that happened, Alberta truly became the Last Best West advertised by federal authorities: the final frontier of free land for folks who yearned to start anew, escape the oppression and poverty of their homeland or open fire on livestock-threatening coyotes.

Back in 1912, an American report by Leo Thwaite urged those who sought to improve their fortunes and their children's prospects to look seriously at Alberta and act immediately.[13] A century later, the mythological West continues to beckon Canadians and others with its siren song of limitless possibility, untapped prosperity and freedom, a fresh start in an open, unfettered space.[14] Alberta's continuing frontier ethos explains some fundamental underlying incidents of her character.

An iconic siren song from the turn of the twentieth century that apparently still resonates today. [Provincial Archives of Alberta, A5738]

The frontier was a great leveller, often eroding differences of ethnicity and class.[15] As Grant MacEwan put it, "The new West with its fresh ideals about human behaviour was no place for social differences determined by wealth."[16] The province's egalitarian, anti-elitist tradition may be another legacy of the frontier. Preston Manning traces the roots of democracy at least partly to ancient Greek frontier settlements that the city-state established to meet its agricultural needs. "In that frontier environment, people could invent their own governing structures," he explains. "People had to be relatively independent and resourceful in those communities, and there was a natural equality on the frontier. It wasn't imposed but you were as good as what you could do, and it didn't matter much what your family was or what your background was." Mr. Manning suggests that those conditions precipitated the democratic ideal and resurfaced more recently on the Western frontier, sparking Albertans' interest in democratic reforms. He believes that every democratic reform idea that's ever been floated in North America has found some kind of an audience in Alberta, and he calls her democratic heritage a distinguishing provincial characteristic.

Almost a century and a half after the first wave of white settlement hit the prairies, the spirit of the Western frontier lingers. In the United States, the frontier enjoys an almost spiritual significance. Rejecting the prevailing theory that new societies are formed simply from fragments of the old, the historian, Frederick Jackson Turner, born in Wisconsin in the mid-nineteenth century, turned the tables with a Western perspective on the development of American society. He felt that the US was reborn with each westward expansion of its frontier, which represented a steady, incremental movement away from dependence on Europe and toward American independence. He saw this expansion as a constant remarriage of "civilization" and wilderness, promoting democracy, individualism and hostility to authority, with coarseness, strength and an attendant prejudice to the civic spirit. While recognizing the subsistence of old ways, Professor Turner argued that each frontier provided a gate of escape from the shackles of the past, accompanied by disdain for the more established society left behind, impatience with its restraints and old ideas, and indifference to its lessons. He viewed the West as a form of society rather than

NO. 20

Photo J. H. GANO, WAINWRIGHT ALT.

(Top) A homesteaders' caravan bound for Milk River, Alberta, as re-enacted in a National Film Board documentary in 1939 [Glenbow Archives, NA-5633-4]*; (Bottom) Apparently the real deal—at least as it appears from this image from around Wainwright in 1906—also featured firearms.* [Glenbow Archives, NA-424-26]

an area—a new order born of older institutions and ideas transformed by free land; a place of new opportunities, broken customs and new growth, institutions and ideals. At that point, he wrote, a new society emerges and gradually loses its primitive conditions as it assimilates into the older social conditions back east (while retaining vestiges of its frontier experience), and the "West" passes to a new frontier.[17]

This explanation of the growth of democracy in the lower forty-eight has been debated by scholars and applied to the wide-open spaces of Canada, Australia, New Zealand, the Soviet Union, Brazil, Argentina and South Africa.[18] Regardless of the merits of Professor Turner's argument, for our purposes, there is a distinctly Albertan sensibility to his populist assertions that frontier regions bring democratic influences and sweep away the privileges of officialdom.[19] Written in the 1890s, his sentiments resonate in comments offered for this inquiry by Albertans as diverse as Senator Tommy Banks, Ted Byfield, Douglas Cardinal, Premier Ralph Klein, Preston Manning, Anne Wheeler, Max Foran, Aritha van Herk, Doris Daley, Jackie Flanagan, Mark Lisac, Don Burnstick, Corb Lund and Mayor Melissa Blake—to name just two—and a century earlier by Alberta's first premier, A.C. Rutherford, and the travelling scribe, Leo Thwaite. When a broad spectrum of eminent achievers—everyone from poets and politicians to reporters and rat patrollers—expresses similar sentiments about the same place, they must be onto something. In this spirit, one could easily substitute "Albertan" for "American" (along with more gender-inclusive language) in this transcendent thought from Frederick Jackson Turner: "Best of all, the West gave, not only to the American, but to the unhappy and oppressed of all lands, a vision of hope, and assurance that the world held a place where were to be found high faith in man and the will and the power to furnish him the opportunity to grow to the full measure of his own capacity."[20]

The notion of starting anew with possibilities as limitless as the prairie sky was equally apparent north of the 49th parallel. Idealists saw homesteading of the Canadian West as the last chance to improve on more established white societies in Europe and easterly North America, and thus create a new society.[21] In an elaborate booklet extolling the virtues of "Canada West: The Last Best West" to potential immigrants in 1911, the federal government boomed, "Here is the field for the world's next farming race. Nature knows no political parties, no race exclusiveness; she recognizes no dividing parallels of latitude." Channelling Professor Turner, the feds continued, "The frontier is advancing daily. New railways are blazing new trails for settlement. Improved social conditions keep pace with industrial progress. And thus, gradually, healthily, and with sure momentum, the inflowing tide of robust citizenship is opening up the Last Best West."[22] Invoking images of a virgin Eden and the rampant optimism found there, the booklet guaranteed success and prosperity to those who applied their own resources.

The feds' rhapsodic reference to resources reminds us that the Last Best West was settled not to spread democracy but to further political and economic interests entrenched in central Canada. Although the West was a formative composer of American mythology, the Canadian soundtrack offers not so much bugle-calling and gunplay as the shuffling of paper and the *ka-ching* of the cash register. As the great historian, Harold Innis, wrote, the major economic, political and cultural developments in Canadian history occurred not on the Western frontier, but in the metropolitan centres of central Canada, notably Ottawa politically and Montréal and Toronto economically. These centres assumed and maintained control of the economy of staples produced in the hinterland, which in Alberta's case meant mostly fur, wheat, wood and fossil fuels.[23] As Professor Innis put it, "Western Canada has paid for the development of Canadian nationality, and it would appear that it must continue to pay."[24]

This cross-country habit of living off the avails of hewing wood and drawing water for others without a sustainable, long-term vision has been criticized by nationalists, environmentalists and people not making a buck off resource industries. In that regard, Albertans are largely in the same canoe as other Canadians. The province paddles near the middle of the pack in evolving from primary to secondary and tertiary economic sectors over most of a century, shifting from a split of 54–11–35 per cent among those respective sectors in 1911 to 36–14–50 per cent in 1951 and 10–17–72 per cent in 2001.[25]

Yet Albertans seem to resent their subservience more (or at least more loudly) than others, cultivating a reputation as the most dissatisfied, angriest people in Canada, outdone only when the economy heads south and the Péquistes need an extra-provincial bogeyman, too. Alberta's resentment is rooted immutably in the myth and the spirit of the frontier, which remains deeply engrained in her psyche. Through a Freudian lens, we might see the pull of the frontier as a repressed desire to escape from the shackles of the old, be it tyranny and poverty across the pond or the dominant, central Canadian political and economic powers by and for the benefit of which the province was birthed.[26] Over the last dozen decades, we tried to escape it all— their control over our finances and development, their political parties, their federal elections (sometimes decided before our polls even close), their stranglehold on our natural resources, their railways, their grain pricing, their tariffs, their banking system, their social liberalism, their Medicare, their bilingualism and biculturalism, their energy policies, their federal spending proclivities and priorities, their GST, their gun registry, their Kyoto Accord and their failure to consult us on the renos at 24 Sussex Drive. The province's tradition of protest reminds us that as the back end of the Last Best West, Alberta was created by a distant and more established metropolitan centre with far greater power in areas like capital, communications, transportation and product marketing; as such, frontier places tend to be dependent more than self-reliant, requiring help from the metropolitan centre even as frontier residents resist and resent the perceived intervention.[27]

Where many Albertans might divert from this view is in perceiving a continuing need for "help" through regulation by political and

economic forces in central Canada. Au contraire, it is others—
be it Canadians, Americans, Chinese, Norwegians, etcetera—who
need Alberta's friendly oil more than ever, even if that friendliness is economic rather than environmental. Having come of age (at
least economically), Alberta is still coming to terms with her place
in Confederation. As Max Foran observes, people move west from
Manitoba and Saskatchewan until they hit the end of the line and the
Rockies—the Last *Best* West—and because we believe firmly that
we've found it, we behave like we belong in the Last Best West. Citing
the federal National Policy and its tariffs that prejudiced Western
Canada, Professor Foran tells me, "The only province that could ever
say 'Shove it!' is Alberta. The only way the feds can get what they want
done is to coerce the provinces, but you can't coerce Alberta."

Today, after ploughing ahead full-bore in the longest and strongest stretch of economic growth ever recorded in the nation, with the
attendant ratcheting up of everything from house prices to road rage,
Alberta needs to take a breath and come to terms with herself. The
steady, long-term influx of people is altering the landscape. Our sense
of who we are as Albertans has become as fluid as the wave pool at
West Edmonton Mall but without the swim diapers.

After the First Nations, this is a province of relatively recent immigrants, motivated mostly by economics. The population has more than
doubled since the provincial government last changed in 1971; that
has a huge impact on the identity of a place. In the nation's hotbed of
economic volatility and labour mobility, where do new Albertans turn
to make sense of what they find here in a provincial, let alone national
or global, context? Where do we find traditions and cultural meaning
that can help define us? With such rampant rootlessness, especially in
the wake of the last, protracted boom, the more humanistic, community-
focused strains of Alberta's history seem lost in the cloud of dust raised
by the pursuit of cold, hard lucre that lures people here. This disen-
gagement is manifested in the widening gap between rich and poor,
record-low electoral turnouts and rampant environmental rape.

In the young twenty-first century, Alberta is at a turning point—socially, culturally, economically and environmentally. And there is an eerie parallel between the economic plunderers mentioned by Garth Pritchard and the environmental indifference of Alberta's political and economic decision-makers and the resource profiteers. It should not have to end badly; Alberta does not have to be the final frontier of human greed. For example, the national director of the Sierra Youth Coalition, Youri Cormier, suggested that in the duel between the economy and the environment, Albertans are not the culprits, but the solution: rather than rely on oil for our continued prosperity, we could lead the green revolution with our natural strengths in solar and wind power; the nation's best expertise in generating energy; and our financial strength, which can afford measures like carbon-neutral transit, building retrofits and the detoxification of land.[28]

Back in 1912, our friend, Leo Thwaite, wrote that although pioneering days were almost over in Alberta, "the real West is still the land of the toiler and the tiller" and "a country of beginnings."[29] This holds as true as ever today. For although Alberta is far from tabula rasa, her greatest story—how her citizens respond to the massive social, cultural and economic challenges of the nascent millennium without destroying our exquisite, essential and endangered natural environment—remains to be written. As Woody Allen wailed, "More than any other time in history, mankind faces a crossroads. One path leads to despair and utter hopelessness. The other, to total extinction. Let us pray we have the wisdom to choose correctly."[30]

Standing Up

So ends this glimpse into the elusive essence of Alberta. To answer the five questions floated in our introduction:

1. Are Albertans down to earth or are we destroying it?

Despite urbanizing with record dispatch, Albertans retain deep historical, cultural, economic and emotional connections to our rich and diverse landscape. This doesn't seem to have stopped us from significantly desecrating and devastating what's left of the earth, air and water as whitey found it, though there are gopher-pockets of resistance. If Grant MacEwan were alive today, even he might have a fatal coronary.

✳ Alberta has a rural soul with a developer's appetite.

2. Are we rednecks or radicals?

While alternately revelling in and bridling at our latter-day redneck reputation, Albertans, being creatures of the moment, overlook the earlier, non-politically conservative half of the province's political odyssey. Lost in the distant mists of primordial Alberta (that is, before Ernest Manning and his postwar tilt to the right) are an initial, fierce opposition to conventional party politics, followed by stretches of co-operativism and even unionism. If there is a provincial political stripe here, it's apathy. We'd make that official, but nobody cares enough.

✳ Time and prosperity have muted Alberta's early non-partisan streak and radicalism, while the media and some obliging local politicos have fashioned a retro redneck cartoon.

3. Are we truly mavericks or are we more like sheep?

Individualism may be the unofficial state mantra, but things like wheat pools, quilting bees and the odd protest rally reveal that often we practise our individualism together. Only relatively recently removed from sodbusting days, Albertans seem torn between a deep-seated urge to buck the herd and a powerful, wagon-circling mob mentality. Remarkably, both extremes surface when the feds do the driving. Protesting against injustices—actual or imagined, in good times or bad, especially from Ottawa—is the best smokescreen Alberta's politicians have ever had.

✳ As adopters of the frontier, Albertans love a big, open sky and an even bigger challenge, but have a complicated relationship with authority.

4. Is Alberta a cultural backwater or a flowing fountain of knowledge and the arts?

Perhaps overcompensating for the Last Best West mantle, Wild Rose Country has tended to punch above her weight in areas of human advancement such as education, the arts and the small but growing field of nanotechnology. Where else will you find world-class concert halls, a province-wide broadband network *and* gay rodeo?

✳ Albertans are hungry for learning, self-improvement, creative expression and innovation; the hick label is backwater under the bridge.

5. Just what does Alberta bring to Confederation?

Shaped by decades of dealings with Ottawa in which we perceive the feds' attitude as "If we want your opinion, we'll give it to you," Albertans are willing, if occasionally wary, participants in Canada's ongoing, tri-sea party. Though there are some nuanced variances, Albertans are not, on the whole, extraordinarily out of whack with other Canadians on major issues of the day. Of course, we have never been shy about expressing our opinion, whether it's welcome or not.

✳ Albertans bring to Canada energy, individuality and a
healthy skepticism.

Barrelling boldly into her second century of provincehood, Alberta
seems ready to challenge her sagging stereotypes. At her core, like
the large monuments singled out by Lieutenant-Governor Norman
Kwong, Alberta is an overstatement, a larger-than-life embodiment of
the breadth and depth of human energy, invention and frailty. And this
is self-fulfilling, for Albertans can't help embracing and perpetuating
our own myths and stereotypes.

Wild Rose Country remains the frontier of human potential, excess
and peril. As Bill Bourne points out, we have the capability to lead the
world in so many areas. But as Tantoo Cardinal reminds us, the environmental stakes are massive and the province has become a poster
child for eco-catastrophe.

In struggling to balance it all, we might consider a possible parallel
from the mists of time in southern Alberta. Beyond claiming the title
of Canada's sunniest city, Medicine Hat had an earlier brush with
greatness. Back in 1910, Calgarians mocked the Hat for exporting
its erratic weather, which offered fluctuations between record high
and low temperatures from November to April of up to 137°F (58°C),
unmatched in Canada.[31] Sensitive to further ridicule, some city coun-
cillors made noises about changing the Hat's name—derived from
Cree lore—fearing that it would look bush-league to potential investors. Facing a plebiscite on the issue, outraged local fans of the name
turned to no less than Rudyard Kipling. The great British author had
visited three years earlier and was impressed enough to dispatch a
reply, "both as a citizen of the Empire and as a lover of Medicine Hat:"

Accept the charge [of brewing bad weather] joyously and proudly go
forth as Medicine Hat, the only city officially recognized as capable
of freezing out the United States and giving the continent cold feet.
[...]

[The name] echoes the old Cree and Blackfoot tradition of red mystery and romance that once filled the prairies. Also, it hints at the magic that underlies the city in the shape of your natural gas. Believe me, the very name is an asset, and as years go on it will become more and more of an asset. It has no duplicate in the world: it makes men ask questions, and as I know, more than twenty years ago, draws the feet of the young towards it; it has the qualities of uniqueness, individuality, assertion and power.

Above all, it is the lawful, original, sweat-and-dust-won name of the city, and to change it would be to risk the luck of the city, to disgust and dishearten old-timers, not in the city alone, but the world over, and to advertise abroad the city's lack of faith in itself.[32]

Reprinted in the local paper and in newssheets around the world, Mr. Kipling's letter turned the public tide against the suggested rebranding, which was defeated by a ratio of ten to one. An excerpt appears on a Western-flavoured, outdoor mural in town, reminding Medicine Hatters and all Albertans to remember our roots and not only to protect but celebrate our distinctiveness in our headlong charge into tomorrow.

If there's a lesson offered by Alberta, Canada's ongoing experiment in frontierism, it is this triad...

- Honour the work of those who came before by remembering them, learning from them and never repeating their mistakes.
- Endure the jokes: at least they're talking about you.
- And for heaven's sake, to invoke Grant MacEwan's creed, try to leave the vineyard in better shape than you found it.

Alberta's first hundred-odd years of provincehood have shown immense human energy and a less conspicuous but comparably fierce defiance of the caricature that she has sometimes become. Wild Rose Country has a genuinely pioneering ethos and a legacy that I'd like to believe was built on something less fleeting than self-interest. If Albertans can face the global and domestic challenges of the twenty-first century by resisting the insular lethargy of affluence and by leading with long-term stewardship rather than instant gratification, maybe then we will finally break free of our largely unflattering stereotypes.

Maybe then we will be worthy of the province's grand gifts and the titanic responsibilities that come with them.

Maybe then we will see the real Alberta stand up.

Notes

Opening Questions

1. A shorter version of this introduction appeared as "Eclectic Alberta" in *Alberta Views* 8:8 (December 2005–January 2006).
2. Studin, 267.
3. *Alberta Online Encyclopedia*, "Local, Regional, National," Web.

1 | Down to Earth?

1. Berry and Brink, 11.
2. The Natural Tourist, "Alberta Native Culture," Web.
3. King, Foreword.
4. Berry and Brink, 159.
5. *Canadian Encyclopedia*, "Columbia Icefield."
6. Takach, "How about a Hand for Our Arms?"; Alberta Legislative Assembly, Web; Massey, 83.
7. Kyi, 5.
8. Keewatin Publications, *Biodiversity Perspectives, Alberta Edition*.
9. MacEwan and Macdonald, 20.
10. Statistics Canada, "Alberta Weather Winners," Web.

11. Anonymous, "Alberta. A Province," 1.

12. Gould, 7.

13. Sandburg, Web.

14. Martin, 374.

15. Thwaite, 218, 227, 229.

16. Bibby, A19.

17. Statistics Canada, "Where We Live? Prairie Provinces," Web.

18. Ibid., "Population and Dwelling Counts, for Canada, Provinces and Territories, 2006 and 2001 Censuses," Web.

19. Thwaite, 244.

20. Tyson and Escott, 48.

21. Jedwab, Web.

22. Wirth, 1–24.

23. Lisac, *Alberta Politics Uncovered*, 3.

24. Kroetsch, 147–48.

25. Statistics Canada, "Population Urban and Rural, by Province and Territory (Canada)" and "Population Urban and Rural, by Province and Territory (Alberta)," Web.

26. Richards and Pratt, 233–34.

27. D'Aliesio, E6.

28. Alberta Agriculture and Rural Development, "Alberta's Rural Demography," Web; Statistics Canada, "Portrait of the Canadian Population in 2006: Subprovincial Population Dynamics," Web.

29. Statistics Canada, "Number of Municipalities (Census Subdivisions) and Percentage Distribution by Province, Territory, and Type of Region, Canada, 2001," Web.

30. Ibid., "Portrait of the Canadian Population," Web.

31. Ibid., "Small Towns and Rural Communities with the Fastest Population Decline since 2001," Web.

32. Finalyson, F4.

33. Taras, "Alberta in 2004," 758.

34. MacEwan and Macdonald, 18.

35. Wetherell, "Making New Identities," 193.

36. Epp, 736–46.

37. The Applied History Group, "Calgary and Southern Alberta: Palliser's Triangle," Web.

38. Marty, Foreword.

39. Breen, 16–18.

40. Jameson, 8; The Applied History Research Group, "Calgary and Southern Alberta: Ranching," Web; Government of Canada, *Canada West*, 1.

41. Tyerman, BonBernard and Cardinal, 49; Alberta Agriculture and Rural Development, "Agriculture and Food Value Chain Facts 2008," Web; Growing Alberta, Web; Statistics Canada, *Cattle Statistics 2007*, 7; Statistics Canada, "Study: Canada's Bison Industry," Web.

42. Thwaite, 95.

43. Alberta Agriculture and Rural Development, "Agriculture and Food Value Chain Facts 2008," Web.

44. Alberta Forest Products Association, Web.

45. *Canadian Encyclopedia, s.v.* "Alberta: Land and Resources," Web.

46. Gould, iii.

47. Alberta Energy, "Our Business," Web; *Canadian Encyclopedia, s.v.* "Alberta," Web.

48. Oil Sands Discovery Centre, Web.

49. Palmer and Palmer, *Alberta: A New History*, 154–59.

50. Gulless, Web.

51. Wcpipeline.com, Web.

52. Parks Canada, "National Parks of Canada: National Parks List," Web.

53. Quoted in Lisac, "Birth of a Province," 28–52, 34.

54. Grey and Laurier speeches quoted in Owram, *The Formation of Alberta*, 372, 373.

55. Chester Martin, 207.

56. Macdonald, *Canada. House of Commons Debates*. May 2, 1870.

57. Hopkins, *1906*, 472, 476–78.

58. Quoted in Babcock, 153.

59. Jaques, 43–58.

60. Collins, 307; *Canadian Encyclopedia, s.v.* "Energy Policy," Web.

61. Friesen, 93.

62. Quoted in Thomson, A10.

2 | Rednecks or Radicals?

1. O'Leary, "Conservatism," 159–61.

2. Ibid., "Liberalism," 422–24.

3. Stewart and Carty, 99, 101, 110.

4. Quoted in Robert F. Nixon, Web.

5. Haultain, 249.

6. Babcock, 73; quoted in Babcock, 42, 73.

7. *Calgary Daily Herald*, "The Provincial Elections," March 23, 1909.

8. Quoted in Babcock, 73.

9. Cormack, 95.

10. Morton, 158.

11. Allen, 145–46.

12. Nelson Wiseman, 50.

13. Schultz, 185, 191.

14. Quoted in Pal, 5–6.

15. Rennie, xii, xi.

16. Cormack, 65.

17. Elections Alberta, "Voter Turnout in Recent Canadian Elections," Web.

18. Laird, 11.

19. Government of Canada, *Canada West: The Last Best West*, 2.

20. Nelson Wiseman, 32–33.

21. Paulsen, 322.

22. Hiller, 48on6.

23. Statistics Canada, "Population, Urban and Rural, by Province and Territory (Alberta)," Web.

24. MacEwan, *Poking into Politics*, 117–19; Byrne, 64.

25. Elliott, 23.

26. Quoted in Conway, 121–22.

27. Mansell, 21–22.

28. Allexperts.com, "Alberta General Election, 1944: Encyclopedia," Web.

29. Quoted in Flanagan and Lee, 192.

30. E.C. Manning, "Alberta Government Policy," 21.

31. Laird, 48.

32. E.C. Manning, *A White Paper on Human Resources Development*, 97.

33. Barr, 134.

34. Basavarajappa and Ram, Web.

35. Harrison, 13.

36. Friesen, 90.

37. Taft, 112, 117.

38. Henton, A2.

39. Government of Alberta, "Budget 2008: The Right Plan for Today and Tomorrow," 5.

40. Palmer and Palmer, *Alberta: A New History*, 300, 306.

41. Rennie.

42. Elections Alberta, "Candidate Summary of Results (General Elections 1905–2004)," Web.

43. Harrison and Laxer, 3.

44. Ford, 246.

45. Palmer and Palmer, "The Alberta Experience," 33.

46. Berdahl, Web.

47. Solomon, FP13.

48. McKeen, D2.

49. *Miriam Webster's Online Dictionary.*

50. Howard Palmer, *Patterns of Prejudice.*

51. Wetherell, "Upholding Social Decency," 54–59.

52. Howard Palmer, *Patterns of Prejudice*, 178, 181.

53. Auger, 130.

54. *R. v. Mahé.*

55. Statistics Canada, "Official Languages in Canada," Web.

56. Jedwab, Web, 8.

57. Alberta Education, "About the International Languages Programs," Web.

58. Nelson Wiseman, 31–33.

59. Proudfoot, "Majority Accepts Mixed Marriages," A7.

60. Richelle Wiseman, Web; Geddes, "What Canadians Think of Sikhs, Jews, Christians, Muslims…," 20–24.

61. *Alberta Online Encyclopedia, s.v.* "Alberta Settlement: Amber Valley," Web.

62. Brennan, 180.

63. Coalition for Gun Control, Web.

64. Statistics Canada, "Study: Firearms and Violent Crime: 2006," Web.

65. Hartnagal, 403–23.

66. Thwaite, 214.

67. Aberhart and Manning, 21.

68. Reichwein, Web.

69. Greg Flanagan, 115–35.

70. Government of Alberta, "What's in Budget 2008 for Albertans?," 14.

71. *Reference re Goods and Services Tax Act.*

72. *R. v. Big M Drug Mart Ltd.*

73. Howlett, 364; Government of Alberta, "What's in Budget 2008 for Albertans?," Web.

74. Don Martin, A3.

75. Lafrance, 269–84.

76. Bencz, A15.

77. Statistics Canada, "Charitable Donors," Web.

78. Ibid., "Cornerstones of Community," Web.

79. Ibid.

80. Volunteer Canada, Web; Volunteer Alberta, "Who are Alberta's Volunteers?," Web.

81. Volunteer Alberta, "Who are Alberta's Volunteers?," Web.

82. Fuller and Hughes-Fuller, 327.

83. Swimmer and Bartkiw, 530.

84. Ray Martin, 670.

85. Bibby, A19.

86. Retson, B3.

87. Applied History Group, "Calgary and Southern Alberta: The Jewish Community," Web.

88. Marsh, Web.

89. Radford and Park, 73–84.

90. Vivequin, Web.

91. Cairney, 789–92.

92. Kahane, Sharp and Tweedale, Web.

93. Clift, 64–65.

94. Statistics Canada, "Population by Religion, Province and Territory," Web; O'Neill, 481.

95. Horne, Web.

96. Harrison, Johnston and Krahn, 83–84.

97. Bibby, A15.

98. Nelson Wiseman, 34.

99. Harrison, *Of Passionate Intensity*, 29, 252.

100. Archer, xiii, x.

101. Kawchuk, interview; Elections Saskatchewan, Web; Siaroff, 175–211.

102. Clift, 68.

103. Fraser, 24.

104. Sinclair, 199–201.

105. Taft, 117.

106. Emery and Kneebone, Web.

107. McClinton, 58–66.

108. *Alberta Online Encyclopedia*, "Famous Five," Web.

109. Ferguson, "Bull's Eye," 40.

110. Howlett, 373.

111. Jedwab, Web.

112. Boswell, A5.

113. Government of Canada, "Shared Values."

114. Government of Alberta, "Budget 2008," Web.

115. Dyck, 94.

116. Howlett, 353.

117. Bibby, A15.

118. Barrie, *The Other Alberta*, 40.

119. CBC News, "Klein Threatens to Abandon Equalization," Web.

120. Lisac, *Alberta Politics Uncovered*, 27.

121. PRA Inc., Web; CBC News, "Nearly One in Five Ballots Spoiled in Alberta Senate Elections," Web.

122. Lisac, "Ignoring Alberta's Antiwar Protesters," 13.

123. Hiller, 426.

124. Clift, 69.

3 | Mavericks or Sheep?

1. Howlett, 361.

2. Quoted in Geddes, Demont, Beltrame et al., Web.

3. van Herk, *The Story of Maverick Alberta*, 11; van Herk, *Mavericks*.

4. Thwaite, 65, 66.

5. Quoted in Colombo, 2.

6. Quoted in Mander, 14.

7. Palmer and Palmer, "The Alberta Experience," 33.

8. Quoted in Colombo, 8.

9. Tardi, 341.

10. Canada, Minister of the Interior, Web.

11. Quoted in Lewis Robert Thomas, 151.

12. *Journals of the Legislative Assembly of the North-West Territories 1888*, 105–06.

13. Quoted in Owram, *The Formation of Alberta*, 81–82.

14. Ibid., 84–85.

15. Ibid., 91.

16. Ibid., 95.

17. Lingard, 257.

18. Ibid., 245.

19. Owram, *The Formation of Alberta*, xxvii, xxx.

20. Ibid., 248.

21. Quoted in Cormack, 83.

22. Quoted in Hopkins, *1904*, 243.

23. Lingard, 247.

24. Quoted in Owram, *The Formation of Alberta*, 274–75, 299–300, 333.

25. Francis, "In Search of Prairie Myth," 27.

26. Anonymous, quoted in Bercuson and Palmer, 51.

27. Jones, *Feasting on Misfortune*, 1.

28. van Herk, *Mavericks*, 11.

29. Ferguson and Ferguson, 52.

30. Lisac, *Alberta Politics Uncovered*, 105.

31. Public Archives of Canada.

32. Tupper, 971.

33. Conway, 31, 32.

34. Allen, 138–47.

35. Anonymous, quoted in Broadfoot, 312.

36. Strom, 32.

37. Gibbins, 215–16.

38. Hiller, 420.

39. Allan Tupper, 479, 494–95.

40. Owram, "The Perfect Storm," 393.

41. Preston Manning, "Federal-Provincial Tensions," 338–39.

42. Lisac, *Alberta Politics Uncovered*, 2.

43. Fekete, A14.

44. Coyne, 33.

45. Taras and Rasporich, 410.

46. Clark.

47. Edwards, 232.

48. Taras and Rasporich, 410.

49. Lisac, "Birth of a Province," 30.

50. Don Hill, 216–17.

51. Palmer and Palmer, *Alberta: A New History*, 136–37.

52. Gwyn.

53. Cernetig, A8.

54. Staples, E4.

55. Lisac, *Alberta Politics Uncovered*, 3.

56. Taras, "Alberta in 2004," 763–64.

57. Quoted in Takach, *Will the Real Alberta Please Stand Up?* [Film]

58. Mereska, A17.

59. Stewart and Carty, 105.

60. Siaroff, 186–87; Elections Alberta, "Unofficial Poll Results: Provincial," Web.

61. David A. MacDonald, Web.

62. Anonymous, "Inside the Numbers," A9.

63. Siaroff, 181, 185, 187–88, 183–84; Elections Alberta, "Voter Turnout in Recent Canadian Elections," Web; Elections BC, "2009 Preliminary Voting Results," Web.

64. Le directeur générale des élections du Québec, 2008, Web.

65. Siaroff, 207–09.

66. White, 263.

67. Blake, 138.

68. Stewart and Carty, 111; Gidengil et al., 117; *Edmonton Journal*, "National Turnout," A2.

69. Elections Alberta, "Voter Turnout in Recent Canadian Elections."

70. CBC News, "Alberta Votes 2008," Web.

71. Ibid., "Voter Turnout at Federal Elections and Referendums, 1867–2006," Web.

72. Beard, A14.

73. Henton and Markusoff, A1; Anonymous, "Government Agencies and Conservative Appointees," Web; Anonymous, "Less Patronage," A14.

74. Chrapko, A19.

75. CBC News, "Alberta Retreats on Energy Royalties," Web.

76. Nikiforuk, "Is Canada the Latest Emerging Petro-Tyranny?" A15.

77. Ralph Klein, A19.

78. Quoted in Hall, 27.

79. University of Alberta, "University of Alberta Facts 2007–08," Web.

80. Zabjek and Audette, A1.

81. Audette, A2.

82. Zabjek, A1.

83. Anonymous, "Alberta Law Gives Power to Adoptive Parents," A3.

84. Human Resources and Skills Development Canada, Web.

85. Fred V. Martin, 346.

86. New Federation House, Web.

87. Connors and Law, xxix.

88. *Henrietta Muir Edwards et al. v. A.G. Canada* (1930).

89. *R. v. Cyr* (1917).

90. Statistics Canada, "Family Violence in Canada," 15; Alberta Justice, 26.

91. *Alberta Bill of Rights Act*, chapter 11.

92. Behiels, 450.

93. Roger Smith, A19.

94. Hopkins, *1906*, 477.

95. L.G. Thomas, 52.

96. City of Lethbridge, Web.

97. City of Brooks, Web.

98. *Alberta Online Encyclopedia, s.v.* "POW Camps in Alberta and Internment Camp 13," Web.

99. Alberta Finance and Enterprise, "Budget 2008 Highlights," Web.

100. Calgary Public Library, Web.

101. Government of Alberta, "Alberta SuperNet Now Operational," Web.

102. Statistics Canada, "Canadian Internet Use Survey," Web; Canadian Council on Learning, *Canada's Progress in Lifelong Learning*, Web.

103. Statistics Canada, "Residential Telephone Service Survey," Web.

104. Alberta Energy, "Alberta's Oil Sands," Web.

105. Statistics Canada, "Study: The Alberta Economic Juggernaut," Web.

106. Ibid., "Study: Christmas Shopping, 2006 in Review," Web.

107. Alberta Employment, Immigration and Industry, "Facts on Alberta: Living and Doing Business in Alberta, "15.

108. Statistics Canada, "Average After-tax Income of Families, Canada and Provinces," Web.

109. Longstaff, Web.

110. Statistics Canada, "Hours worked and labour productivity in the provinces and territories," Web.

111. Expedia.ca, G7.

112. Statistics Canada, "Absence Rates for Full-Time Employees by Sex and Geography," 100–12.

113. Anonymous, "Census Snapshot, Canada's Changing Labour Force, 2006 Census," Web.

114. Statistics Canada, "Age Characteristics," Web; Foot, 444.

115. Statistics Canada, "Deaths 2002," Web.

116. Ibid., "Births and Birth Rate, by Province and Territory," Web.

117. Pembina Institute, "Life Expectancy in Alberta: How Much?," Web.

118. Alberta Health and Wellness, "Comparable Health Indicators: Keeping Albertans Healthy," Web.

119. Statistics Canada, "Deaths and Death Rate, by Province and Territory (Death Rate)," Web.

120. Zdeb, D1.

121. Statistics Canada, "Control and Sale of Alcoholic Beverages: Sales of Alcoholic Beverages Per Capita 15 Years or Older," Web.

122. Proudfoot, "Albertans Biggest Gamblers Last Year," A6.

123. Greg Flanagan, 133.

124. Statistics Canada, "Crime Statistics, 2007," Web.

125. Grant MacEwan University, "About Our Namesake"; Anonymous, "The 50 Greatest Albertans."

126. MacEwan, "MacEwan Creed," Web.

127. This section is adapted from the author's article originally published in *Alberta Views*, "Rattus Non Gratus," 40–43.

4 | Cultural Backwater or Fountain?

1. Statistics Canada, "Table 1. Horses and Ponies," Web, Ibid., "Table 2: Bison," Web.

2. Ibid., "Hog Inventories," Web.

3. Ibid., "Agricultural Overview, Canada and the Provinces," Web; Ibid., "Table 3: Goats," Web; Ibid., "Table 10: Emus and Rheas," Web; Ibid., "Table 11: Ducks," Web.

4. Ibid., "Table 12: Geese," Web.

5. Ibid., "Table 4: Wild Boards," Web.

6. Ibid., "Table 7: Llamas and Alpacas," Web; Ibid., "Table 6: Elks/Wapiti," Web; Ibid., "Table 9: Ostriches," Web.

7. Seiler and Seiler, 32.

8. Ibid., 43.

9. Ibid., 30.

10. Friesen, 84; Ferguson and Ferguson, 52.

11. Quoted in Takach, *Will the Real Alberta Please Stand Up?* [Film]

12. Jonasson, 1.

13. van Herk, "Who You Callin' Cultured?" 30–32.

14. Statistics Canada, "Government Expenditures on Culture," Web.

15. Government of Alberta, "The Spirit of Alberta: Alberta's Cultural Policy," 1.

16. Fraser, 118.

17. Kroetsch, 144.

18. Canadian Commission for UNESCO. "World Heritage Sites: Canada's World Heritage Sites." Web.

19. Graff, *Dreamers and Doers*; Mandryk, Web; *Cultural Development Act, 1946*.

20. Stenson, "The Writer's Life," 34.

21. Volmers, D1.

22. Chris Wiebe, 42–47.

23. Borg, Grahn and Bird, Web.

24. Econometrics Research Ltd., Web.

25. Withey, C1.

26. Hendry, "History," Web.

27. Hill Strategies Research, Web.

28. Kelly Hill, quoted in Stolte, D1.

29. Mahon, quoted in Stolte, D1.

30. Kelly Hill, D1.

31. Alberta Foundation for the Arts, "Fast Facts," Web.

32. Government of Alberta, "Highlights of the Alberta Economy 2007," 44.

33. Withey, B1; McCoy, B4.

34. *Calgary Herald*, "Arts Funding a Shared Duty," A16.

35. Edwards, Cosgrove and Lawes, 48–49, 49–50.

36. Kellogg, A2.

37. Ibid.

38. Ainslie and Laviolette, xi.

39. Melnyk, *The Literary History of Alberta, Volume 1*, xvi, 174; Ibid., *Volume 2*, 225.

40. Liddell, 1.

41. *Alberta Online Encyclopedia, s.v.* "Ontarians as a Charter Group," Web.

42. Bercuson and Palmer.

43. Nelson Wiseman, 33, 49.

44. Rutherford, Address to the Canadian Club of Ottawa.

45. Colin A. Thomson, 11–12, 14–15.

46. Byrne, 63–64.

47. Merriken, *Looking for Country*.

48. *Encyclopedia of Ukraine, s.v.* "Alberta," Web.

49. Kroetsch, 14–16.

50. British Broadcasting Corporation, Web.

51. Anonymous, quoted in Takach, *Will the Real Alberta Please Stand Up?* [Film]

52. Jedwab, Web.

53. Canadian Council on Learning, *The 2008 Composite Learning Index*, 28.

54. Preston Manning, "Federal-Provincial Tensions and the Evolution of a Province," 328.

55. Collins, 197, 199.

56. Statistics Canada, "Population by Immigration Status and Period of Immigration, 2006 Counts, for Canada, Provinces and Territories," Web.

57. Ibid.

58. Ibid., "Visible Minority Population, by Province and Territory (2006 Census)," Web.

59. Ibid., "Aboriginal Peoples in Canada in 2006," Web.

60. Cooper and Bartlett, Web.

61. Heritage Festival Edmonton, Web.

62. Atwood, D1.

63. Kroetsch, 119.

64. Anonymous, "Libraries: The Story So Far," B1.

65. Canadian Urban Libraries Council, Web.

66. University of Alberta, "University of Alberta Facts 2007–08," Web.

67. Ibid., "Teaching Excellence," Web.

68. Hopkins, 1908, 511.

69. Rutherford, Address to the Canadian Club of Ottawa, 56–57.

70. Babcock, 36, 48.

71. Byrne, 206.

72. Ell, Web.

73. MacQueen and Wells, 36–39.

74. Canadian Council on Learning, The 2006 Composite Learning Index, Web.

75. Ibid., The 2007 Composite Learning Index, Web.

76. Ibid., The 2008 Composite Learning Index, Web.

77. Ibid., The 2009 Composite Learning Index, Web; Ibid.; The 2010 Composite Learning Index, Web.

78. Gulli, 49.

79. Lamphier, E1; Maurier, personal correspondence.

80. Canadian Council on Learning, State of Learning in Canada, 93–94; Ibid., The 2007 Composite Learning Index, 9–11.

81. Ibid., The 2008 Composite Learning Index, 13–15.

82. Tibbetts, A1.

83. Alberta Education, "Alberta Students Place 4th in the World in Science," Web.

84. Canadian Bureau for International Education, Web.

85. Marshall, 759.

86. Zabjek, "Alberta's High School Graduation Rate Lowest among Provinces," B6.

87. Canadian Council on Learning, *The 2008 Composite Learning Index*, 17.

88. Earlier versions of "Ears a Little More Open" were published in *Alberta Views*, 36–40; and *Broadcast Dialogue*, 30–36.

5 | Boom, Bust and Eco?

1. Thwaite, 8.

2. Ibid., 116–17, 180, 196–97, 227.

3. Liddell, vii.

4. Brennan, 35–38.

5. Government of Canada, *Canada West: The Last Best West*, 3, 36, 38.

6. David C. Jones, "Herbert W. Greenfield," 62.

7. Richards and Pratt, 19.

8. David C. Jones, *Empire of Dust*, 122; Ibid., "Herbert W. Greenfield," 63.

9. Mansell, 18–19, 55; Ascah, 55–56.

10. Gibbins, "Why Alberta is Different," A21.

11. Ascah, 54–56.

12. Anonymous, quoted in Barry Broadfoot, 38.

13. Anonymous, quoted in ibid., 312, 313.

14. Ascah, 61.

15. Ibid., 54–56.

16. Anonymous, *The Discovery that Made History*, Web.

17. Mansell, 19.

18. Ibid, 20; Boothe and Edwards.

19. Boothe, 14

20. Statistics Canada, Cat. No. 91–002 and 71–201.

21. Mansell, 17–31.

22. Statistics Canada, "Portrait of the Canadian Population in 2006: Population of the Provinces and Territories: Alberta: The Engine of Population Growth in the Prairie Provinces," Web.

23. Ibid.; Ibid., "Population of Canada, Provinces and Territories in the Last 50 Years," Web; Ibid., "Growth Rate for Canada, Provinces and Territories in the Last 50 Years," Web; Ibid., "Mid-size Urban Centres," Web; Ibid., "Small towns and rural communities," Web; *Edmonton Journal* Staff, "Edmonton's Net Gain Highest in Canada," A3.

24. Hirsch, A19.

25. Statistics Canada, "All Data" under "Mobility Status—Place of Residence 1 Year Ago" and "Mobility Status—Place of Residence 5 Years Ago," Web.

26. Jaremko, E1.

27. *Edmonton Journal* Staff, E1.

28. Canadian Press, A16.

29. Statistics Canada, "Retail Sales, Canada and Provinces, and Selected Socio-Economic," Web.

30. Anonymous, "Calgary-Edmonton Corridor," Web.

31. Chalmers, E7.

32. Statistics Canada, "Study: The Alberta Economic Juggernaut," Web.

33. *Calgary Herald* Staff, B5.

34. Jaremko, E1.

35. Thorne, B3.

36. Kolkman, Web.

37. Hodgson, Web; Henton, A2.

38. Finlayson, "Intuit See Need to Jump to Toronto," F1.

39. Mansell, "Fiscal Restructuring," 20, 39.

40. Hale, 377.

41. Barrie, "Will Alberta's Tory Government Be Able to Protect the Public Interest?" A18.

42. Taylor, Severson-Baker, Winfield, Woynillowicz and Griffiths, Web.

43. Kingston, 16–22; Millar, 51.

44. Remington, A19.

45. Tom Radford, *Tar Sands: The Selling of Alberta*.

46. Kunzig, 44.

47. Canwest News Service, "Alberta Hurting Most," E1; *Financial Post*, E1.

48. Isfeld and Abma, E1.

49. Crawford, Web.

50. Alberta Environmental Protection, ii.

51. Nikiforuk, "The Tar Age," 37–38.

52. Gillespie, cover, 65.

53. Köhler, 20.

54. Kunzig, 34–59.

55. Alberta Tourism, Parks and Recreation, Web.

56. Nikiforuk, "Oh, Wilderness," 24, 26.

57. Urquhart, 142, 144.

58. Sierra Club of Canada, *Rio+14*, Web.

59. Collins, 12.

60. Urquhart, 140.

61. Archie McLean, A6.

62. Gadd, 26.

63. Richards and Pratt, 233–34.

64. Chandler, 37, 41.

65. Statistics Canada, "Population and Dwelling Counts, for Canada, Provinces and Territories, 2006 and 2001 Censuses—100% Data," Web.

66. Guerin, 11.

67. Edmonton Economic Development Corporation, Web.

68. Chandler, 39–40; City of Edmonton, "Major South Edmonton Roadway Project Moves Forward," Web.

69. Bonnell, Web.

70. Berdahl, Web, 5, 7.

71. Chamberlain, Web.

72. Köhler, 21–22.

73. Gillespie, 72.

74. McMaster, Web.

75. Brennan, 70.

76. Sierra Club of Canada, *Kyoto Report Card 2007*, Web.

77. Mittelstaedt, A5.

78. Alberta Environment, *Climate Change: Alberta's Strategy for Reduced Emissions*, Web; Alberta Environment, *Alberta's 2008 Climate Change Strategy*, Web.

79. Pembina Institute, quoted in Brooymans and Makaroff, A1; Gillespie, 70; Simpson, A21.

80. McLean, A1.

81. Turcotte, Web.

82. Derrick Dodge Chrysler Jeep, Web.

83. Green, 120.

84. Köhler, 22.

85. James Byrne, 175.

86. Urquhart, 148.

87. Gillespie, 72.

88. Marsden, 114.

89. Köhler, 21.

90. Gillespie, 70–72.

91. Donahue, A19.

92. Yang, B1.

93. Urquhart, 144–45.

94. Marsden, 105, 116.

95. Alberta Environment, "Focus on Wildlife Management," 7–8.

96. Galius, 44.

97. Ibid.

98. Douglas, A18; Nixon, A3.

99. Alward, Web.

100. Alberta Wilderness Association, Web.

101. Anonymous, "Suzuki Slams Stelmach," B5.

102. Statistics Canada, "Household Participation Rates for Environmental Behaviours, by Province, 2006," Web; Statistics Canada, "Prince Edward Island Has the Highest Proportion of Very Active Households, 2006," Web.

103. Statistics Canada, "Disposal and Diversion of Waste, by Province and Territory, 2004 and 2006," Web.

104. Melissa Blake.

105. Nikiforuk, "Is Canada the Latest Emerging Petro-Tyranny?" A13.

106. Ibid., "The Tar Age," 38, 40.

107. Peter Lee, A19.

108. Naomi Klein, D1.

109. Nikiforuk, "Is Canada the Latest Emerging Petro-Tyranny?" A13.

110. Laird, "Spent Energy: Refueling the Alberta Advantage," 170.

111. Brian Taylor, A19.

112. Woods, A1; Anonymous, "Klein Questions Poll," Web.

113. de Souza, A3.

114. Henton, "Oilsands Must Go Green: Poll," A3.

115. Henton, "Environment Trumps Oilsands: Poll," A1.

116. CBC News, "Alberta Votes 2008." Web; Green Party of Canada, "Alberta Greens: Best Ever Result with 23% Second Place Finish," Web.

117. Elections Canada, "Official Voting Results of the 39th General Election," Web; Brooymans, "Breakthrough Eludes Party, Even in Canada's Greenest Province," A4.

118. *Calgary Herald* Editorial, "Greens Need Ripening," A24.

119. Elections Canada, "Official Voting Results of the 40th General Election—Poll-by-Poll Results—Raw Data," Web.

120. Henton, "Natives United to Fight Oilsands," A1.

121. Alberta Environment, "Waste Not," Web.

122. Veno, Web.

123. Ostroff, Web.

124. City of Edmonton, "Leading in Environmental Excellence," Web.

125. Kent, A1.

126. Tyerman, BonBernard and Cardinal, 67.

127. McClinton, "Hog Farm Converts Manure to Electricity," Web.

128. Highmark Renewables, Web.

129. Henton, "Goodbye Oil and Gas, Hello Ecotourism," A1.

130. Pratt, A19.

131. *The American Heritage Dictionary of the English Language.*

132. Berra, 9, 118–19.

6 | Will the Real Alberta Please Stand Up?

1. This scripted interview draws on the following sources: Benson; Forbes; McDougall; Owram, *The Formation of Alberta*, 55–56; Stemp.

2. Oliver, quoted in Owram, *The Formation of Alberta*, 55–56.

3. Palmer and Palmer, "The Alberta Experience," 23.

4. Djuff, 362.

5. Pannekoek, 18, 19.

6. Ibid., 20.

7. Carter, 109.

8. Barthes, 109–59.

9. Careless, 13.

10. Santayana, 82.

11. Kroetsch, 190.

12. Nelson Wiseman, 28.

13. Thwaite, 12.

14. Laird, *Slumming It at the Rodeo*, xv.

15. Palmer and Palmer, "The Alberta Experience," 22.

16. MacEwan, *Eye Opener Bob*, 141.

17. Turner, 38, 205.

18. Winks, 19.

19. Turner, 247, 268.

20. Ibid., 268.

21. *Alberta Online Encyclopedia, s.v.* "The New West," Web.

22. Government of Canada, *Canada West: The Last Best West*, 1, 2, 36, 38.

23. Innis, *The Fur Trade in Canada*, 383, 385, 400–01; Francis, "Turner versus Innis," 17–22.

24. Innis, *A History of the Canadian Pacific Railway*, 294.

25. Howlett, 355.

26. Mitchell, 150.

27. Careless, 18–19.

28. Cormier, A15.

29. Thwaite, 64.

30. Allen, 57.

31. David C. Jones, *Empire of Dust*, 43.

32. Kipling, 11.

Interviews Cited

Scheduled Interviews

Allen, Chris. Edmonton, November 14, 2007.

Andrejevic, Miki. Telephone, November 2, 2005.

Antoniuk, Tim. Telephone, June 17, 2008.

Babici, Isabelle. Toronto, June 27, 2005.

Banks, Hon. Tommy. Telephone, November 29, 2005. Ottawa, June 14, 2007.

Beauregard, Paula. Edmonton, October 18, 2008.

Belcourt, Nyambura. Edmonton, October 23, 2006.

Bencz, Marjorie. Edmonton, August 5, 2006.

Bereska, Tami. Edmonton, December 12, 2005.

Blake, Melissa. Fort McMurray, October 14, 2006. Edmonton, May 10, 2007.

Bourne, Bill. Edmonton, May 11, 2007.

Bourne, John. Vermilion, November 23, 2005.

Breslin, Mark. Toronto, June 27, 2005.

Brink, Jack. Edmonton, May 14, 2007.

Brinkman, Don. Telephone, May 28, 2007. Drumheller, June 9, 2007.

Burnstick, Don. St. Albert, October 9, 2005.

Byfield, Link. Telephone, December 2, 2005.

Byfield, Ted. Telephone, November 25, 2005. Edmonton, May 10, 2007.

Cardinal, Douglas. Telephone, October 31, 2005. Gatineau, Québec, June 14, 2007.

Cardinal, Tantoo. Edmonton, May 5, 2007.

Chandler, Anne. Hay Lakes, October 5, 2007.

Chrusch, Erin. Videoconference, May 11, 2009.

Chrusch, Murray. Videoconference, May 11, 2009.

Currie, Philip. Edmonton, June 26, 2007.

Daley, Doris. Edmonton, October 27, 2005. Turner Valley, September 10, 2006.

Darbasie, Pat. Edmonton. October 18, 2007.

Donnelly, Andy. Edmonton, May 11, 2007.

Dundas, Joe. Calgary, April 30, 2008.

Edgar, Bud (Bronco Buddy). High River, June 9, 2007.

Fassbender, Norm. Edmonton, October 18, 2007.

Ferbey, Randy. Edmonton, May 11, 2006.

Flanagan, Jackie. Calgary, April 29, 2008.

Foran, Max. Calgary, April 30, 2008.

Hastings, Roxanne. Telephone, October 29, 2005.

Kawchuk, Karman. Telephone, May 12, 2008.

Klein, Hon. Ralph. Calgary, September 1, 2006.

Kostash, Myrna. Edmonton, December 18, 2007.

Kostuch, Martha. Telephone, November 25, 2005. Edmonton, May 11, 2007.

Kwong, Hon. Norman. Edmonton, May 24, 2007.

Lewis, Jack. County of Parkland, October 18, 2007.

Lewis, Ken. County of Parkland, October 18, 2007.

Lisac, Mark. Telephone, November 21, 2005. Edmonton, May 24, 2007.

Lund, Corb. Edmonton, August 21, 2006.

Lynch, Karen. Telephone, November 28, 2005.

MacEwan-Foran, Heather. Calgary, April 30, 2008.

Manning, Preston. Telephone, March 27, 2006. Calgary, September 1, 2006.

McGaffigan, Brian. Strome, May 3, 2009.

McGaffigan, Pat. Strome, May 3, 2009.

McGillivray, Bruce. Edmonton, May 10, 2007.

Nedohin, David. Edmonton, May 11, 2006.

Needleman, Fielding. Toronto, June 27, 2005.

Nibourg, Harry. Big Valley, June 9, 2007.

Petriv, Lessia (as Vaselina Hawreliak). Ukrainian Cultural Heritage Village, June 5,
2007.

Pfiefer, Scott. Edmonton, May 11, 2006.

Phair, Michael. Edmonton, May 13, 2009.

Poapst, Geoff. Ottawa, June 14, 2007.

Poitras, Jane Ash. Edmonton, September 27, 2005 and October 18, 2007.

Potter, Gerry. Edmonton, October 18, 2007.

Pritchard, Garth. Priddis, September 1, 2006.

Rocque, Marcel. Edmonton, May 11, 2006.

Rogers Dundas, Judy. Calgary, April 30, 2008.

Seiler, Tamara Palmer. Calgary, December 8, 2005.

Shapiro, James. Telephone, January 27, 2006.

Shapiro, Lorne. Dorval, Québec, June 28, 2005.

Takach, Leslie. Edmonton, October 15, 2007 and January 10, 2008.

Thomas, Lorna. Edmonton, October 18, 2007.

Turner, Alison. Edmonton, October 18, 2007.

van Herk, Aritha. Telephone, April 20, 2005. Calgary, April 25, 2006.

Varjas, Andrew. Ottawa, June 14, 2007.

Veldkamp, Coba. Edmonton, October 18, 2007.

Ward, David. Calgary, May 20, 2007.

Wheeler, Anne. Edmonton, May 5, 2007.

Wiebe, Rudy. Edmonton, July 19, 2006.

Street Interviews

Anonymous. Calgary, April 25, 2005. Edmonton, May 4, 2006 and October 18, 2007.

Bakken, Judd. Vancouver, October 11, 2006.

Banda Arteaga, Rosina. Toronto, June 28, 2005.

Barros, Sgt. Joao. Montréal, July 1, 2005.

Carey, Carol. Sally's Cove, Newfoundland, July 5, 2005.

Choi, Hoyeon. Labrador Straits, July 6, 2005.

Dufoy, Lise. Montréal. June 28, 2005.

Langille, Andy. Labrador Straits, July 6, 2005.

Martin, Gary. Labrador Straits, July 6, 2005.

Miller, Uta. Labrador Straits, July 6, 2005.

Noordman, Cora. Vancouver, October 11, 2006.

O'Callaghan, Robert. Montréal, June 30, 2005.

Plenkiewicz, Adam. Montréal, July 1, 2005.

Radmacher, Anita. Vancouver, October 11, 2006.

Santos, Roger. Montréal, June 28, 2005.

Simm, Rick. Cow Head, Newfoundland, July 8, 2005.

Sloot, Laura. Vancouver, October 11, 2006.

Smith, Henry Cornelius. Labrador Straits, July 6, 2005.

Trahan, Marie-Christine. Montréal, July 1, 2005.

Williams, Shirley. Toronto, June 28, 2005.

Young, Mariah. Gunner's Cove, Newfoundland, July 7, 2005.

Bibliography

Ainslie, Patricia and Mary-Beth Laviolette. *Alberta Art and Artists*. Calgary: Fifth
House, 2007.

Alberta Agriculture and Rural Development. "Agriculture and Food Value Chain Facts
2008." June 2008. Web.

———. "Alberta's Rural Demography." March 27, 2009. Web.

Alberta Bill of Rights Act. Statues of Alberta 1946, ch. 11.

Alberta Community Foundation. "Elders' Voices." 2005. Web.

Alberta Education. "About the International Languages Programs." Web.

———. "Alberta Students Place 4th in the World in Science." December 2008. Web.

———. "Implementation Activities." Web.

Alberta Employment, Immigration and Industry. "Facts on Alberta: Living and Doing
Business in Alberta." 2007. Web.

Alberta Energy. "Alberta's Oil Sands." June 5, 2008. Web.

———. "Our Business." June 10, 2008. Web.

Alberta Environment. "Focus on Wildlife Management." Pub. No. 1/761. November
1999. Web.

———. "Waste Not." Web.

————. *Alberta's 2008 Climate Change Strategy: Responsibility/Leadership/Action*. February 20, 2008. Web.

————. *Climate Change: Alberta's Strategy for Reduced Emissions*. September 12, 2007. Web.

Alberta Environmental Protection. *A Comparison of Alberta's Environmental Standards to those of Other North American Jurisdictions*. Edmonton: Government of Alberta, 1999. Web.

Alberta Finance and Enterprise. "Budget 2008 Highlights." Web.

Alberta Forest Products Association. "Facts and Figures." Web.

Alberta Foundation for the Arts. "Fast Facts." Web.

Alberta Health and Wellness. "Comparable Health Indicators: Keeping Albertans Healthy." April 17, 2006. Web.

Alberta Justice. "What We Do Know of Domestic Violence." 2008. Web.

Alberta Legislative Assembly. "The Citizen's Guide to the Alberta Legislature." Web.

Alberta Online Encyclopedia. s.v. "Alberta Settlement: Amber Valley." Web.

————. *s.v.* "Local, Regional, National." Web.

————. *s.v.* "Ontarians as a Charter Group." Web.

————. *s.v.* "POW Camps in Alberta and Internment Camp 13." Web.

————. *s.v.* "The New West." Web.

Alberta Tourism, Parks and Recreation. "Managing Parks and Protected Areas: Establishing Protected Areas." Web.

Alberta Wilderness Association. "Will the Woodland Caribou be Alberta's Dodo?" May 13, 2004. Web.

Allen, Richard. "The Social Gospel as the Religion of the Agrarian Revolt." In Melnyk, *Riel to Reform*, 138–47.

Allen, Woody. *Side Effects*. New York: Random House, 1980.

Allexperts.com. "Alberta General Election, 1944: Encyclopedia." Web.

Alward, Mary M. "Alberta's Woodland Caribou." April 6, 2002. Web.

American Heritage Dictionary of the English Language. "Redneck." Boston, MA: Houghton Mifflin, 2000. Web.

Anonymous. *Aberhart–Manning*. Liverpool, UK: K.R.P. Publications, 1943. [Glenbow acc. no. 6762, call no. 332.56 E24a Pam.]

————. "Alberta Law Gives Power to Adoptive Parents." *Edmonton Journal*. January 27, 2008: A3.

————. "Alberta. A Province." *Evening Journal*. September 2, 1905: 1.

————. "Autonomy that Insults the West." *Calgary Herald*. April 26, 1905. Quoted in Owram, *The Formation of Alberta*, 333–34.

————. "Calgary-Edmonton Corridor Only Canadian Urban Centre to Amass U.S.-Level Wealth While Preserving Canadian-Style Quality of Life, Say TD Economists." April 23, 2003. Web.

————. "Census Snapshot, Canada's Changing Labour Force, 2006 Census." *Canadian Social Trends* 85 (Summer 2008). Web.

————. "Government Agencies and Conservative Appointees." *Edmonton Journal*. September 16, 2007. Web.

————. "Hog Like Propensities." *Edmonton Bulletin*. April 15, 1895. Quoted in Owram, *The Formation of Alberta*, 95–96.

————. "Inside the Numbers." *Edmonton Journal*. January 24, 2006: A9.

————. "Klein Questions Poll Showing Albertans Would Support Carbon Tax." *Whitehorse Star*. November 8, 2006: 20. Web.

————. "Less Patronage." *Edmonton Journal*. August 6, 2008: A14.

————. "Libraries: The Story So Far." *Edmonton Journal*. March 14, 2007: B1.

————. "National Turnout." *Edmonton Journal*. March 3, 2008: A2.

————. "Provincial Government for Alberta. Its Meaning and Necessity." [Pamphlet] Calgary. 1895. Quoted in Owram, *The Formation of Alberta*, 89–95.

————. Quoted in Takach, *Will the Real Alberta Please Stand Up?* [Film]

————. "Suzuki Slams Stelmach over Gung-ho Oilsands Plan." *Edmonton Journal*. February 24, 2007: B5.

————. "The 50 Greatest Albertans." *Alberta Venture* 9:10 (December 2005): insert.

————. *The Discovery that Made History: The Legacy of Leduc*. n.p.: Imperial Oil Limited, 1997. Quoted in Canadian Petroleum Discovery Centre. "Leduc History." Web.

Applied History Group (University of Calgary). "Calgary and Southern Alberta: Palliser's Triangle." Web.

————. "Calgary and Southern Alberta: Ranching." 1997. Web.

————. "Calgary and Southern Alberta: The Jewish Community." Web.

Archer, John. "Introduction: Alberta 1911." In *Land of Plenty*, edited by John H. Blackburn. Toronto: Macmillan of Canada, 1970. ix–xiii.

Ascah, Robert L. *Politics and the Public Debt: The Dominion, the Banks and Alberta's Social Credit*. Edmonton: University of Alberta Press, 1999.

Atwood, Margaret. Quoted in Richard Helm, "Atwood Sounds the Alarm." *Edmonton Journal*. January 23, 2007: D1.

Audette, Trish. "Mini-Baby Boom on Base Mirrors Rest of Alberta." *Edmonton Journal*. September 13, 2007: A2.

Auger, Edmund A. "One Language and One Nationality: The Forcible Constitution of a Unilingual Province in a Bilingual Country, 1870–2005." In Connors and Law, 193–35.

Babcock, D.R. *A Gentleman of Strathcona: Alexander Cameron Rutherford.* Calgary: University of Calgary Press, 1989. [Quoting three sources: A.C. Rutherford, *Strathcona Plaindealer* and *Edmonton Journal.*]

Barr, John J. *The Dynasty: The Rise and Fall of Social Credit in Alberta.* Toronto: McClelland & Stewart, 1974.

Barrie, Doreen. *The Other Alberta: Decoding a Political Enigma.* Regina, Saskatchewan: Canadian Plains Research Center, 2006. [Quoting Centre for Information and Research on Canada. November 2004.]

———. "Will Alberta's Tory Government Be Able to Protect the Public Interest?" *Edmonton Journal.* October 1, 2007: A18.

Barthes, Roland. *Mythologies,* translated by Annette Lavers. London: Trinity Press, 1972.

Basavarajappa, K.G. and Bali Ram (Statistics Canada). "Historical Statistics of Canada: Section A; Population and Migration." Web.

Beard, Bill. Letter to the editor. *Edmonton Journal.* March 5, 2008: A14.

Behiels, Michael D. "Premier Peter Lougheed, Alberta and the Transformation of Constitutionalism in Canada, 1971–1985." In Connors and Law, 411–58.

Bencz, Marjorie. "Hunger Doesn't Take a Summer Vacation." Letter to the editor. *Edmonton Journal.* July 24, 2007: A15.

Benson, E.F. *Queen Victoria's Daughters.* New York: D. Appleton-Century, 1938.

Bercuson, David and Howard Palmer. *Settling the Canadian West.* Toronto: Grolier, 1984.

Berdahl, Loleen (Canada West Foundation). "Looking West 2007, Segment 1: Urban Environment." Web.

———. "Under 35: An Analysis of the Looking West 2006 Survey." Web.

Berra, Yogi. *The Yogi Book: "I Really Didn't Say Everything I Said!"* New York: Workman Publishing, 1998.

Berry, Susan and Jack Brink. *Aboriginal Cultures in Alberta: Five Hundred Generations.* Edmonton: Provincial Museum of Alberta, 2004.

Bibby, Reginald. "Albertans: Are We Really All That Different?" *Edmonton Journal.* December 18, 2004: A19.

Blaché, Herbert [director], Raymond L. Schrock, Donald W. Lee and Richard Schayer [writers]. *The Calgary Stampede.* Produced by Carl Laemmle. Los Angeles: Universal, 1925.

Blake, Donald E. "Electoral Democracy in the Provinces and Territories." In Dunn, 115–44.

Blake, Melissa. "Mega Projects, Mega Growth, Mega Impacts." Presentation to the Parkland Institute. University of Alberta. Edmonton, May 10, 2007.

Bonnell, Gregory. "Green Issues? Canadians Choose Urban Sprawl in Staggering Numbers: Census." March 13, 2007. Web.

Boothe, Paul. "Public Sector Saving and Long-Term Fiscal Balance in a Resource-Based Economy: Alberta 1969–89." Research Paper No. 90–13, Department of Economics. Edmonton: University of Alberta, 1990.

Boothe, Paul and Heather Edwards, eds. *Eric J. Hanson's Financial History of Alberta, 1905–1950.* Calgary: University of Calgary Press, 2003.

Borg, Wes, Neil Grahn and Joe Bird (Three Dead Trolls in a Baggie). Letter to the editor. *Toronto Star.* Web.

Boswell, Randy. "Albertans Well Aware of 'Have' Status." *Edmonton Journal.* February 17, 2009: A5.

Bourne, Bill. "Ole Buffalo." In Bill Bourne and Alan Macleod, *Dance and Celebrate.* Rynde Records Ltd./Peer Music [CD, track no. 5], 1990.

Bramley-Moore, Alwyn. *Canada and her Colonies, Or Home Rule for Alberta.* London: Stewart, 1911.

Brennan, Brian. *Alberta Originals.* Calgary: Fifth House, 2001.

British Broadcasting Corporation. "The Al Rashid Mosque, Edmonton, Canada." July 30, 2003. Web.

Broadfoot, Barry. *Ten Lost Years 1929–1939: Memories of Canadians Who Survived the Depression.* Toronto: Doubleday, 1973.

Broadfoot, Dave. "Dave Broadfoot's Canada." Address to the Empire Club of Canada. March 9, 1978. Web.

Brooymans, Hanneke. "Breakthrough Eludes Party, Even in Canada's Greenest Province." *Edmonton Journal.* January 25, 2006: A4.

Bruce, Christopher J., Ronald D. Kneebone and Kenneth J. McKenzie, eds. *A Government Reinvented: A Study of Alberta's Deficit Elimination Program.* Toronto: Oxford University Press, 1997.

Burns, Gary [writer-director]. *waydowntown.* Produced by Gary Burns and Shirley Vercruysse. Calgary: Burns Film, 2000.

Byrne, James M. "Silent Lies and Alberta's Looming Water Crisis." In Harrison, *Return of the Trojan Horse,* 173–89.

Byrne, T.C. *Alberta's Revolutionary Leaders.* Calgary: Detselig, 1991.

Cairney, Richard. "Democracy Was Never Intended for Degenerates." *Canadian Medical Association Journal* 155:6 (September 15, 1996): 789–92. Web.

Calgary Daily Herald. Editorial. March 23, 1909.

Calgary Herald. July 6, 1891. Quoted in Owram, *The Formation of Alberta*, 81–82.

———. "Meddling with the West." February 9, 1905. Quoted in Owram, *The Formation of Alberta*, 274–75.

———. "Without Alberta's Consent." March 2, 1905. Quoted in Owram, *The Formation of Alberta*, 299–300.

Calgary Herald. Editorial. "Arts Funding a Shared Duty: Albertans' Support Suggests Growing Role for Government." March 19, 2007: A16.

———. "Greens Need Ripening." January 28, 2006: A24.

Calgary Herald Staff. "Alberta MDs Most Concerned about Delays." *Edmonton Journal*. March 18, 2008: B5.

Calgary Public Library. "Calgary Tower." 2005. Web.

Canada, Minister of the Interior, O.C. 1882–0982, "Provisional Districts, North West Territories." May 8, 1882. Web.

Canadian Broadcasting Corporation. "Tar Sands: The Selling of Alberta." Web.

Canadian Bureau for International Education. "Alberta." Web.

Canadian Commission for UNESCO. "World Heritage Sites: Canada's World Heritage Sites." Web.

Canadian Council on Learning. *The 2006 Composite Learning Index: Putting Lifelong Learning on the Map*. 2006. Web.

———. *The 2007 Composite Learning Index: Helping Communities Improve their Quality of Life*. 2007. Web.

———. *The 2008 Composite Learning Index: Measuring Canada's Progress in Lifelong Learning*. 2008. Web.

———. *The 2009 Composite Learning Index: Measuring Canada's Progress in Lifelong Learning*. 2009. Web.

———. *The 2010 Composite Learning Index: Five Years of Measuring Canada's Progress in Lifelong Learning*. 2010. Web.

Canadian Encyclopedia. s.v. "Alberta." Web.

———. s.v. "Alberta: Land and Resources." Web.

———. s.v. "Columbia Icefield." Web.

———. s.v. "Energy Policy." Web.

———. s.v. "Prince Albert: Cultural Life." Web.

———. s.v. "Writing-on-Stone, Archaeological Site." Web.

Canadian Press. "Office Space in Calgary's Core Virtually Nil." *Edmonton Journal.*
August 27, 2006: A16.

Canadian Urban Libraries Council. "Canadian Public Library Statistics." July 5, 2007.
Web.

Canwest News Service. "Alberta Hurting Most: RBC." *Edmonton Journal.* March 13,
2009: E1.

———. "Edmonton No. 3 in Nation for Learning." *Edmonton Journal.* May 30, 2007:
A7.

Careless, J.M.S. "Frontierism, Metropolitanism, and Canadian History." *Canadian
Historical Review* 35:1 (March 1954): 1–21.

Carter, Sarah. "Transnational Perspectives on the History of Great Plains Women." In
Higham and Thacker, 84–114.

CBC News. "Alberta Retreats on Energy Royalties." Web.

———. "Alberta Votes 2008." Web. "

———."Klein Threatens to Abandon Equalization." May 24, 2006. Web.

———. "Nearly One in Five Ballots Spoiled in Alberta Senate Elections." December
2, 2004. Web.

Cernetig, Miro. "Edmonton: Will Klein Commit a Capital Offence?" *Globe and Mail.*
December 10, 1992: A8.

Chalmers, Ron. "Alberta Boom Echoes Throughout Canada." *Edmonton Journal.*
September 29, 2007: E7.

Chamberlain, Chuck (Parkland Institute). "City Councils Approve Deaths from
Sprawl." *The Post.* Fall 2000. Web.

Chandler, Margaret. "Sprawl Pox." *Alberta Views* 7:4 (July–August 2004): 37–41.

Chrapko, Evan. "Time to Demand Action on Royalties." *Edmonton Journal.* October
13, 2007: A19.

City of Brooks. "Bassano Dam." Web.

City of Edmonton. "Leading in Environmental Excellence." Web.

———. "Major South Edmonton Roadway Project Moves Forward." August 29, 2008.
Web.

City of Lethbridge. "High Level Bridge." Web.

Clark, George. "McDougall and Secord Window Display." 1904. Provincial Archives
of Alberta, Edmonton, No. B6736. City of Edmonton Archives, EA-10-812.
[photograph]

Clift, Dominique. *The Secret Kingdom: Interpretations of the Canadian Character.*
Toronto: McClelland & Stewart, 1989.

Coalition for Gun Control. "The Case For Gun Control." Web.

Collins, Robert. *Prairie People: A Celebration of My Homeland*. Toronto: McClelland & Stewart, 2003.

Collum Peter, ed. *Alberta: 100 Years a Home*. Edmonton and Calgary: Edmonton Journal Group and Calgary Herald Group, 2005.

Colombo, John Robert. *New Canadian Quotations*. Edmonton: Hurtig Publishers, 1987.

Connors, Richard and John M. Law, eds. *Forging Alberta's Constitutional Framework*. Edmonton: University of Alberta Press, 2005.

———. "Legal and Constitutional History of Alberta." In Connors and Law, xxix–xxxvi.

Connors, Stompin' Tom. "Lady, K.D. Lang." In *Stompin' Tom—Fiddle and Song*. A-C-T Records, 1994 [CD, track no. 1].

Conway, John F. *The West: The History of a Region in Confederation*. 3rd ed. Toronto: James Lorimer, 2006.

Cooper, Merrill and Deborah Bartlett. "Creating Inclusive Communities Stakeholder Consultation: What We Heard." July 24, 2006. Web.

Cormack, Barbara Villy. *Perennials and Politics: The Life Story of Hon. Irene Parlby, LL.D.* Sherwood Park, AB: Professional Printing, 1968.

Cormier, Youri. Letter to the editor. *Edmonton Journal*. July 17, 2008: A15.

Coyne, Andrew. "From Protest to Power." *Saturday Night*. Summer 2005: 33.

Cragan, John F. and Donald C. Shields, *Understanding Communication Theory*. Needham Heights, MA: Allyn & Bacon, 1998.

Crawford, Todd (Conference Board of Canada). "Alberta." In *Provincial Outlook 2009*. Web.

Cultural Development Act, Statutes of Alberta, 1946, ch. 9.

D'Aliesio, Renata. "Bitter Urban-Rural Split amid Land Rush Chaos." *Edmonton Journal*. March 4, 2007: E6.

de Souza, Mike. "Albertans Back Tougher Oilsands Stance: Poll." *Edmonton Journal*. May 7, 2007: A3.

Derrick Dodge Chrysler Jeep. Web. Confirmed in a telephone conversation with the author, January 26, 2008.

Directeur générale des élections du Québec. "Résultats officiels par parti politique." 2008. Web.

Djuff, Ray. "Contradictions and Contrariness." In Collum, 362–73.

Donahue, William F. "Even Regulators Don't Know Impact of Oilsands Projects." *Edmonton Journal*. November 15, 2007: A19.

Douglas, Nigel. "Grizzly Bears Roadkill under Stelmach's Tires." *Edmonton Journal*.
June 18, 2007: A18.

Dunn, Christopher J., ed. *Provinces: Canadian Provincial Politics*. 2nd ed.
Peterborough, ON: Broadview Press, 2006.

Dyck, Rand. "Provincial Politics in the Modern Era." In Dunn, 57–94.

Econometrics Research Ltd. "The Economic Impact of the Arts in Alberta: Measuring
the Value of the Arts." 2005. Web.

Edmonton Economic Development Corporation. "Community: Mill Woods." April
10, 2007. Web.

Edmonton Journal. Editorial. "The Stigma of Inferiority." December 2, 1903. Quoted in
Owram, *The Formation of Alberta*, 248.

Edmonton Journal Staff. "Edmonton's Net Gain Highest in Canada." *Edmonton Journal*.
December 5, 2007: A3.

———. "Highest Wages in Canada May Lure New Workers to Alberta." *Edmonton
Journal*. May 31, 2008: E1.

Edwards, Bob. *Eye Opener*. February 4, 1905. Quoted in *The Best of Bob Edwards*,
edited by Hugh A. Dempsey. Edmonton: Hurtig, 1975.

Edwards, Loria Ann, Blair Cosgrove and Mark Lawes. "Three Views on Funding the
Arts." *Alberta Views* 7:1 (January–February 2004): 48–50.

Elections Alberta. "Candidate Summary of Results. General Elections 1905–2004."
Web.

———. "Unofficial Poll Results: Provincial." March 4, 2008. Web.

———. "Voter Turnout in Recent Canadian Elections." 2008. Web.

Elections BC. "2009 Preliminary Voting Results." May 15, 2009. Web.

Elections Canada. "History of Federal Ridings since 1867." Web.

———. "Prime Ministers of Canada: Electoral Information: Candidate in Federal
Elections while Serving as Prime Minister." Web.

———. "Official Voting Results of the 39th General Election." Web.

———. "Official Voting Results of the 40th General Election." Tables 3, 8, 9. Web.

———. "Voter Turnout at Federal Elections and Referendums, 1867–2006." Web.

Elections Saskatchewan. "Historical Provincial Vote Summaries." Web.

Ell, Jerome F. *A Brief History of Public Education in Alberta*. 2002. Web.

Elliott, David. "William Aberhart: Right or Left?" In *The Dirty Thirties in Prairie
Canada: 11th Western Canada Studies Conference*, edited by R.D. Francis and H.
Ganzevoort. Vancouver: Tantalus Research, 1980.

Emery, J.C. Herbert and Ronald D. Kneebone. "Mostly Harmless: Socialists, Populists,
Policies and the Economic Development of Alberta and Saskatchewan." Web.

Encyclopedia of Ukraine. s.v. "Alberta." 2001, Web.

Epp, Roger. "Two Albertas: Rural and Urban Trajectories." In *Alberta Formed–Alberta Transformed,* edited by Payne, Wetherell and Cavanaugh, vol. 2, 736–46.

Expedia.ca. "By the Numbers." *Edmonton Journal.* May 14, 2009: G7.

Fekete, Jason. "Alberta Won't Shy Away from a Scrap." *Edmonton Journal.* January 6, 2007: A14.

Ferguson, Will. "Bull's Eye: Remembering Bob Edwards, the Crusader behind *The Eye Opener.*" *Alberta Views* 7:4 (May–June 2004): 38–40.

Ferguson, Will and Ian Ferguson. *How to Be a Canadian.* Vancouver: Douglas & McIntyre, 2001.

Financial Post. "Grim Forecast for Alberta." *Edmonton Journal.* March 6, 2009: E1.

Finlayson, David. "Alberta Farm Numbers Shrink—But Less than Sask. and Man." *Edmonton Journal.* May 17, 2007: F4.

———. "Intuit Sees Need to Jump to Toronto." *Edmonton Journal.* March 6, 2008: F1.

Flanagan, Greg. "Not Just About Money: Provincial Budgets and Political Ideology." In Harrison, *Return of the Trojan Horse,* 115–35.

Flanagan, Jackie. In Takach, *Will the Real Alberta Please Stand Up?* [Film]

Foot, David K. "The Policy Implications of Provincial Demographics." In Dunn. 435–66.

Forbes, Keith Archibald (Bermuda Online). "Bermuda's Connections with and Ties to Canada." August 18, 2005. Web.

Ford, Catherine. *Against the Grain.* Toronto: McClelland & Stewart, 2005.

Francis, Douglas. "In Search of Prairie Myth: A Survey of the Intellectual and Cultural Historiography of Prairie Canada." In Melnyk, *Riel to Reform,* 20–42.

———. "Turner versus Innis: Two Mythic Wests." In Higham and Thacker, 15–30.

Fraser, Fil. *Alberta's Camelot: Culture and the Arts in the Lougheed Years.* Edmonton: Lone Pine Publishing, 2003.

Friesen, Gerald. *The West: Regional Ambitions, National Debates, Global Age.* Toronto: Penguin Books, 1999.

Fuller, Tom and Patricia Hughes-Fuller. "Exceptional Measures: Public Sector Labour Relations in Alberta." In Harrison, *Return of the Trojan Horse,* 313–27.

Gadd, Ben. "Fighting Frankenmine." *Alberta Views* 8:5 (July–August 2005): 23–27.

Galius, Jeff. "Alberta's Grizzly Century." *Alberta Views* 8:8 (December 2005–January 2006): 40–44.

Geddes, John. "What Canadians Think of Sikhs, Jews, Christians, Muslims..." *Maclean's.* May 4, 2009: 20–24.

Geddes, John, John Demont, Julian Beltrame et al. "Liberals Win Election." *Maclean's*. December 4, 2000. Web.

Gibbins, Roger. "Regionalism in Decline: 1940 to the Present." In Melnyk, *Riel to Reform*, 215–23.

———. "Why Alberta is Different." *National Post*. July 13, 2005: A21.

Gidengil, Elisabeth, Andre Blais, Neil Nevitte and Richard Nadeau. *Citizens*. Vancouver: University of British Columbia Press, 2004.

Gillespie, Curtis. "Scar Sands." *Canadian Geographic* 128:3 (June 2008): 64–78.

Gould, Ed. *All Hell for a Basement: Medicine Hat 1883–1983*. Medicine Hat, AB: City of Medicine Hat, 1981.

Government of Alberta, "Alberta SuperNet Now Operational throughout the Province." September 30, 2005. Web.

———. "Budget 2008 Fiscal Plan." Web.

———. "Budget 2008: The Right Plan for Today and Tomorrow." April 22, 2008. Web.

———. "Highlights of the Alberta Economy 2007." Web.

———. "The Spirit of Alberta: Alberta's Cultural Policy." 2008. Web.

———. "What's in Budget 2008 for Albertans?" Web.

Government of Canada. *Canada West: The Last Best West*. Ottawa, Government of Canada, 1911.

———. "Shared Values: The Canadian Identity." Cat. No. CP22–29/1991E, 1991.

Graff, Les. Quoted in *Dreamers and Doers: 100 Years of Arts and Culture in Alberta*, directed by Marriane Garrah, produced by DTM Inc. ACCESS Television, 2005. "Second Segment." Web.

Graham, David. "Not Your Dad's Alberta." *Toronto Star*. June 17, 2006: F1.

Grant MacEwan University. "About our Namesake." Web.

Green, Kim. "F-150 City." *Alberta Venture* 11:4 (April 2007): 120. Web.

Green Party of Canada, "Alberta Greens: Best Ever Result with 23% Second Place Finish," Web.

Grey, Albert Henry George, 4th Earl Grey. Speech at the Ceremonies Inaugurating the Province of Alberta. September 1, 1905. In Owram, *The Formation of Alberta*, 373–74.

Growing Alberta. "Beef." 2007. Web.

Guerin, David (David Suzuki Foundation). *Understanding Sprawl: A Citizen's Guide*. Vancouver: David Suzuki Foundation, 2003. Web.

Gulless, Mickey (Petroleum History Society). "Alberta's First Natural Gas Discovery." Web.

Gulli, Cathy. "Canada's Smartest Cities." *Maclean's*. September 8, 2008: 49.

Gwyn, Richard. *Toronto Star*. April 4, 1978. Quoted in Colombo, 111.

Hall, David. "Arthur L. Sifton, 1910–1917." In Rennie, 19–42.

Harrison, Trevor W. Introduction. In Harrison, *Return of the Trojan Horse*, 1–22.

———. *Of Passionate Intensity: Right-Wing Populism and the Reform Party of Canada*. Toronto: University of Toronto Press, 1995.

———. *Return of the Trojan Horse: Alberta and the New World (Dis)Order*. Montréal: Black Rose, 2005.

Harrison, Trevor and Gordon Laxer. Introduction. In Laxer and Harrison, 1–21.

Harrison, Trevor W., William Johnston and Harvey Krahn, "Language and Power: 'Special Interests' in Alberta's Political Discourse." In Harrison, *Return of the Trojan Horse*, 82–94.

Hartnagel, Timothy F. "Gun Control in Alberta: Explaining Public Attitudes concerning Legislative Change." *Canadian Journal of Criminology* 44:4 (October 2002): 403–23.

Haultain, Frederick. "Policy and Speeches of Mr. Haultain: Speech to Territorial Legislature, April 22, 1903." In *Canadian Annual of Public Affairs 1905*, edited by J. Castell Hopkins.

Hendry, Tom. Quoted in Manitoba Theatre Centre. "History." Web.

Henrietta Muir Edwards et al. v. A.G. Canada [1930] Appeal Cases 124. (J.C.P.C.)

Henton, Darcy. "Environment Trumps Oilsands: Poll." *Edmonton Journal*. February 28, 2008: A1.

———. "Goodbye Oil and Gas, Hello Ecotourism." *Edmonton Journal*. May 31, 2008: A1.

———. "Natives United to Fight Oilsands." *Edmonton Journal*. August 18, 2008: A1.

———. "Oilsands Must Go Green: Poll." *Edmonton Journal*. January 28, 2008: A3.

———. "Province Losing Race with Infrastructure Debt." *Edmonton Journal*. October 2, 2007: A2.

Henton, Darcy and Jason Markusoff. "Tories Stack Alberta Boards." *Edmonton Journal*. September 16, 2007: A1.

Heritage Festival Edmonton. "Fun Festival Facts." Web.

Higham, C.L. and Robert Thacker, eds. *One West, Two Myths II*. Calgary: University of Calgary Press, 2006.

Highmark Renewables. "Growing Power Hairy Hill." Web; Trevor Nickel [Growing Power Group]. E-mail to the author. August 31, 2008.

Hill Strategies Research Inc. "Consumer Spending on Culture in Canada, the Provinces and 15 Metropolitan Areas in 2005." Web.

Hill, Don. "With Wire, Quips and Bye-Bye Blues Radio Mania Sweeps into Alberta." In *Alberta in the Twentieth Century*. Vol. v: *Brownlee and the Triumph of Populism 1920–1930*, edited by Ted Byfield. Edmonton: United Western Communications, 1996. 216–17.

Hiller, Harry H. *Second Promised Land: Migration to Alberta and the Transformation of Canadian Society*. Montréal and Kingston: McGill-Queen's University Press, 2009.

Hirsch, Todd. "Alberta's Artificially Robust Population Surge." *Edmonton Journal*. June 28, 2008: A19.

Hodgson, Glen (Conference Board of Canada). "Taking Sides: Is Alberta's Labour Shortage a Doomsday Scenario?" July 17, 2006. Web.

Hopkins, J. Castell, ed. *The Canada Annual Review of Public Affairs 1904*. Toronto: The Annual Review Publishing Company, 1905.

——. *The Canada Annual Review of Public Affairs 1906*. Toronto: The Annual Review Publishing Company, 1907.

——. *The Canada Annual Review of Public Affairs 1908*. Toronto: The Annual Review Publishing Company, 1909.

Horne, Tammy. "Privatizing Responsibility: Public Health in Alberta." *The Post* (Parkland Institute). Fall 2004. Web.

Howlett, Michael. "De-Mythologizing Provincial Political Economies." In Dunn, 353–72.

Hubbard, G. D. Rev. of. *Alberta: An Account of its Wealth and Progress*, *Bulletin of the American Geographical Society* 44:9 (1912): 693–94. Web.

Human Resources and Skills Development Canada, "Child Welfare in Canada 2000"/"Child Abuse and Neglect." Web.

Innis, Harold. *A History of the Canadian Pacific Railway*. Rev. ed. Toronto: University of Toronto Press, 1971.

——. *The Fur Trade in Canada: An Introduction to Canadian Economic History*. Rev. ed. 1956. Repr. Toronto: University of Toronto Press, 1999.

Innovation Alberta. "#153—Woodland Caribou Numbers in Drastic Decline." February 22, 2005. Web.

Isfeld, Gordon and Derek Abma. "No Wind in Retailers' Sales." *Edmonton Journal*. February 24, 2009: E1.

Jameson, Sheilagh. *Ranches, Cowboys and Characters*. Calgary: Glenbow Alberta Institute, 1987.

Jaques, Carrol. "Charles Stewart." In Rennie, 43–58.

Jaremko, Gordon. "Alta. Costs Soar Three Times as Fast." *Edmonton Journal*. July 19, 2007: E1.

Jedwab, Jack. "Alberta, Canada's History and Canadian Identity: Knowledge, Interest and Access." May 18, 2005. Web.

Jonasson, Stefan M. "Out in the Open Air: The Liberating Legacy of Stephan G. Stephansson." Web.

Jones, David C. *Empire of Dust*. Edmonton: University of Alberta Press, 1987.

——. *Feasting on Misfortune: Journeys of the Human Spirit in Alberta's Past*. Edmonton: University of Alberta Press, 1998.

——. "Herbert W. Greenfield, 1921–25." In Rennie, 59–76.

Journals of the Legislative Assembly of the North-West Territories 1888. Regina, SK: Government of the NWT, 1889.

Kahane, D., W.D. Sharp and M. Tweedale. *Report of the MacEachran Subcommittee*. Edmonton: University of Alberta, Department of Philosophy, 1998. Web.

Kawchuk, Karman. E-mail to the author. May 27, 2008.

Keewatin Publications. *Biodiversity Perspectives, Alberta Edition*. Regina, SK: Keewatin Publications, 2005.

Kellogg, Alan. "Alberta Arts Sector is Infrastructure, and Should Be Funded as Such." *Edmonton Journal*. March 26, 2006: A2.

Kent, Gordon. "City Eyes Gas from Trash." *Edmonton Journal*. March 14, 2008: A1.

King, D.R. *Alberta Archaeology: A Handbook for Amateurs*. High River, AB: The High River Times, 1968.

Kingston, Anne. "Bonanza Glam." *Maclean's*. March 27, 2006: 16–22.

Kipling, Rudyard. Letter to Francis F. Fatt, December 9, 1910. Quoted in Gould, 11.

Klein, Naomi. Quoted in Babiak, Todd. "The Other Klein Has a Vision—and It's Not Pretty." *Edmonton Journal*. October 4, 2007: D1.

Klein, Ralph. Speech to the Canadian Club, Ottawa, November 21, 2005. Quoted in "Sharing the Wealth." *Edmonton Journal*. November 22, 2005: A19.

Köhler, Nicholas. "Doomsday: Alberta Stands Accused." *Maclean's*. October 8, 2007: 20–24.

Kohit.net. "Three Dead Trolls in a Baggie—The Toronto Song." 2001. Web.

Kolkman, John. "Standing Still in a Booming Economy." October 2007. Web.

Kostash, Myrna. *All of Baba's Children*. Edmonton: Hurtig, 1977.

Kostash, Myrna and Duane Burton. *Reading the River: A Traveller's Companion to the North Saskatchewan River*. Regina, SK: Coteau, 2005.

Kroetsch, Robert. *Alberta*. Toronto: Macmillan, 1968.

Kunzig, Robert. "The Canadian Oil Boom: Scraping Bottom." *National Geographic* 215:3 (March 2009): 34–59.

Kyi, Tanya Lloyd. *Alberta*. 2nd ed. Vancouver: Whitecap Books, 2005.

Lafrance, Jean. "Does Our Path Have a Heart? Children's Services in Alberta." In Harrison, *Return of the Trojan Horse*, 269–84. [Quoting National Council of Welfare. "Fact Sheet 2004"]

Laird, Gordon. *Slumming It at the Rodeo: The Cultural Roots of Canada's Right-Wing Revolution*. Vancouver: Douglas & McIntyre, 1998.

———. "Spent Energy: Refueling the Alberta Advantage." In Harrison, *Return of the Trojan Horse*, 156–72.

Lamphier, Guy. "Oberg Balks at National Watchdog." *Edmonton Journal*. March 29, 2007: E1.

Lappé, Frances Moore and Jeffrey Perkins. *You Have the Power: Choosing Courage in a Culture of Fear*. New York: Jeremy P. Tarcher/Penguin, 2004.

Laurier, Sir Wilfrid. Speech at the Ceremonies Inaugurating the Province of Alberta. September 1, 1905. In Owram, *The Formation of Alberta*, 374–77.

Laxer, Gordon and Trevor Harrison. *The Trojan Horse: Alberta and the Future of Canada*. Montréal: Black Rose, 1995.

Lee, Peter. Letter to the editor. *Edmonton Journal*. November 13, 2007: A19.

Liddell, Ken E. *This is Alberta*. Toronto: Ryerson Press, 1953.

Lightfoot, Gordon. "Alberta Bound." In *Don Quixote*. Reprise Records, 1972 [CD, track no. 3].

Lingard, C. Cecil. *Territorial Government in Canada: The Autonomy Question in the Old North-West Territories*. Toronto: University of Toronto Press, 1946.

Lisac, Mark. *Alberta Politics Uncovered*. Edmonton: NeWest Press, 2004.

———. "Birth of a Province." In Collum, 28–51. "

———. "Ignoring Alberta's Antiwar Protesters." *Media* (Canadian Association of Journalists) 10:1 (Spring 2003): 13–14.

Longstaff, Bill. "OPEC and the Alberta Advantage." February 1, 2005. Web.

Lund, Corb. "Always Keep an Edge On Your Knife." In *Hair in My Eyes Like a Highland Steer*. Stony Plain Records, 2005 [CD, track no. 3].

MacDonald, David A. (nodice.ca). "Popular Vote Results." Web.

Macdonald, Sir John A., PM. *Canada. House of Commons Debates*. May 2, 1870.

———. Quoted in Nixon, Robert F. (Empire Club Foundation). "Democracy in Ontario." Speech to the Empire Club of Canada. April 20, 1967. Web.

MacEwan, Grant. *Eye Opener Bob: The Story of Bob Edwards*. Edmonton: The Institute of Applied Art, 1957.

————, (Grant MacEwen University). "MacEwan Creed." 1969. Web.

————. *Poking into Politics*. Edmonton: The Institute of Applied Art, Ltd., 1966.

MacEwan, Grant and Rusty Macdonald. *Alberta Landscapes*. Saskatoon, SK: Western Producer Prairie Books, 1982.

MacQueen, Ken and Paul Wells. "Class Revolution." *Maclean's*. January 16, 2006: 36–39.

Mander, Christine. *Emily Murphy, Rebel: First Female Magistrate in the British Empire*. Toronto: Simon & Pierre, 1985.

Mandryk, Rosalette. "Symbols in Civilization." Alberta Society of Artists. Web.

Manning, E.C. "Alberta Government Policy." Speech. June 11, 1943. Quoted in Anonymous, *Aberhart–Manning*.

————. *A White Paper on Human Resources Development*. Edmonton: Queen's Printer, 1967.

————. Quoted in Flanagan, Thomas and Martha Lee. "From Social Credit to Social Conservatism: The Evolution of an Ideology." In Melnyk, *Riel to Reform*, 1992. 182–95.

Manning, Preston. "Federal-Provincial Tensions and the Evolution of a Province." In Connors and Law, 315–44.

Mansell, Robert. "Fiscal Restructuring in Alberta: An Overview." In Bruce et al., 17–31.

Marsden, William. *Stupid To the Last Drop: How Alberta is Bringing Environmental Armageddon to Canada (And Doesn't Seem to Care)*. Toronto: Knopf, 2007.

Marsh, James H. (*The Canadian Encyclopedia*). "Eugenics: Keeping Canada Sane." Web.

Marshall, David. *Alberta: Leading and Learning in Post-Secondary Education*. January 2005. Quoted in Taras, "Alberta in 2004," 759.

Martin, Chester. *"Dominion Lands" Policy*. Toronto: MacMillan, 1938.

Martin, Claire. "If You Don't Like the Weather…Wait Five Minutes." In Collum, 374–87.

Martin, Don. "Revitalized B.C. Eager to Expand Alberta Ties." *Calgary Herald*. September 10, 2005: A3.

Martin, Fred V. "Alberta's Métis Settlements: A Brief History." In Connors and Law, 345–89.

Martin, Ray, MLA. *Alberta Hansard*. April 19, 2007.

Marty, Syd. Foreword. In Sherman Hines, *Alberta*. Toronto: McClelland & Stewart, 1981.

Massey, Don, MLA. *Alberta Hansard*. August 28, 2003. 83.

Maurier, Raquel (Northern Alberta Institute of Technology). E-mail to the author. March 19, 2008.

McClinton, Lorne. "Hog Farm Converts Manure to Electricity." *National Hog Farmer*. September 15, 2003. Web.

———. "Twenty-Five Things You Didn't Know About Saskatchewan. But Ought To." *Alberta Venture* 12:5 (May 2008): 58–66.

McClung, Nellie. Quoted in Colombo, 2.

McCoy, Heath. "Alberta Lags in Culture Funding." *Edmonton Journal*. April 15, 2007: B4.

McDougall, D. Blake. *Princess Louise Caroline Alberta*. Edmonton: Legislature Library, 1988.

McKeen, Scott. "Obama Isn't Good for Maher." *Edmonton Journal*. March 14, 2009: D2.

McLean, Archie. "Ontario Ads Use Alberta as Example of Desolation." *Edmonton Journal*. October 23, 2006: A6.

———. "Premier Braces for Oilsands Showdown." *Edmonton Journal*. June 28, 2008: A1.

McLeish, Kenneth, ed. *Key Ideas in Human Thought*. New York: Facts on File, 1993.

McMaster, Geoff. "U of A Influence Felt in Alberta Oilsands." *Express News*. June 27, 2008. Web.

Melnyk, George. *The Literary History of Alberta, Volume One: From Writing-on-Stone to World War Two*. Edmonton: University of Alberta Press, 1998.

———. *The Literary History of Alberta, Volume Two: From the End of the War to the End of the Century*. Edmonton: University of Alberta Press, 1999.

———. *Riel to Reform: A History of Protest in Western Canada*. Saskatoon, SK: Fifth House Publishers, 1992.

Mereska, Nancy. Letter to the editor. *Edmonton Journal*. February 22, 2008: A17.

Merriken, Ellenor Ranghild. *Looking for Country: A Norwegian Immigrant's Alberta Memoir*. Calgary: University of Calgary Press, 1999.

Millar, Erin. "Whose Town Is It?" *Maclean's*. August 4, 2008: 51.

Miriam Webster's Online Dictionary. "Redneck." Web.

Mitchell, Lee Clark. "Whose West is it Anyway? Or, What's Myth Got to Do with It? The Role of 'America' in the Creation of the West." In Higham and Thacker, 139–51.

Mittelstaedt, Martin. "Slowpokes Win the Race to Cut Emissions." *Globe and Mail*. June 11, 2007: A5.

Montreal Star. April 8, 1904. Quoted in Hopkins. *The Canadian Annual Review of Public Affairs 1904*, 343.

Morton, W.L. "The Western Progressive Movement." In Melnyk, *Riel to Reform*, 149–61.

Natural Tourist, The. "Alberta Native Culture." Web.

New Federation House. "Native Leaders of Canada." Web.

Nicholson, Dennis (Government of Alberta). Telephone interview with the author. February 7, 2006.

Nikiforuk, Andrew. "Is Canada the Latest Emerging Petro-Tyranny?" *Globe and Mail*. June 11, 2007: A15.

———. "Oh, Wilderness." *Alberta Views* 1:4 (Fall 1998): 20–28.

———. *Tar Sands: Dirty Oil and the Future of a Continent*. Vancouver: Greystone, 2008.

———. "The Tar Age." *Alberta Venture* (April 2007): 37–38.

Nixon, Geoff. "Alberta Grizzlies Barely Surviving, Census Shows." *Globe and Mail*. June 11, 2007: A3.

Oil Sands Discovery Centre, "The Basics of Bitumen," Web.

O'Leary, Brendan. "Conservatism." In McLeish, 159–61.

———. "Liberalism." In ibid., 422–24.

Oliver, Frank. *Edmonton Bulletin*. July 1, 1882. In Owram, *The Formation of Alberta*, 55–56.

———. Quoted in Cormack, 65.

O'Neill, Brenda. "Women's Status Across the Canadian Provinces, 1999–2002." In Dunn, 467–86. [Citing *National Survey on Giving, Volunteering and Participating*, 2000]

Ostroff, Joshua. "Hi-Tech Trash a Global Threat." *Trio*. Winter 2004–2005. Web.

Owram, Douglas R. ed. *The Formation of Alberta: A Documentary History*. Calgary: Historical Society of Alberta, 1979.

———. "The Perfect Storm: The National Energy Program and the Failure of Federal-Provincial Relations." In Connors and Law, 391–410.

Pal, Leslie A. "The Political Executive and Political Leadership in Alberta." In *Government and Politics in Alberta*, edited by Allan Tupper and Roger Gibbons. Edmonton: University of Alberta Press, 1992. 1–29.

Palmer, Howard. *Patterns of Prejudice: A History of Nativism in Alberta*. Toronto: McClelland & Stewart, 1982.

Palmer, Howard and Tamara Palmer. *Alberta: A New History*. Edmonton: Hurtig, 1990.

———. "The Alberta Experience." *Journal of Canadian Studies* 17:3 (Fall 1982): 20–34.

Parlby, Irene. Quoted in *Alberta Online Encyclopedia*. "The Famous Five: Heroes for Today: Context." Web.

Pannekoek, Frits. "Interpretation on the New Frontier: The Alberta Experience." *Alberta Museums Review* 20:2 (Fall–Winter 1994): 17–21.

Paulsen, Pat. Quoted in *The Comedy Thesaurus*, edited by Judy Brown. Philadelphia, PA: Quirk Publishing, 2005.

Payne, Michael, Donald G. Wetherell and Catherine Cavanaugh, eds. *Alberta Formed– Alberta Transformed*. Edmonton and Calgary: University of Alberta Press and University of Calgary Press, 2005. 2 vols.

Pembina Institute. "Life Expectancy in Alberta: How Much?" April 2005. Web.

——. Quoted in Brooymans, Hanneke and Jason Makaroff. "Greenhouse Gas Levels Will Climb for 12 Years." *Edmonton Journal*. January 28, 2008: A1.

PRA Inc. *Variation in Turnout by Alberta Electoral Division*. March 2, 2007. Web.

Pratt, Sheila. "Group of 20 Redefines Democracy; Individuals Cut through Provincial Apathy to Mobilize Albertans as Leaders in Climate Change." *Edmonton Journal*. October 4, 2008: A19.

Proudfoot, Shannon. "Albertans Biggest Gamblers Last Year." *Edmonton Journal*. September 27, 2008: A6.

——. "Majority Accepts Mixed Marriages." *Vancouver Sun*. August 29, 2007: A7.

Provincial Archives of Alberta. "Frequently Asked Questions About Our Centennial." Web.

Public Archives of Canada. John A. Macdonald Papers, 510. Macdonald to M.C. Cameron, December 19, 1864. Quoted in Creighton, Donald. *The Road to Confederation*. Toronto: Macmillan, 1964, 165.

R. v. Big M Drug Mart Ltd. [1985] 1 Supreme Court Reports 295.

R. v. Cyr. (1917) 23 Alberta Law Reports 320 (Alta. C.A.).

R. v. Mahé [1990] 1 Supreme Court Reports 342.

Radford, John P. and Deborah C. Park. "The Eugenic Legacy." *Journal on Developmental Disabilities* 4:1 (1995): 73–84.

Radford, Tom [director]. *Tar Sands: The Selling of Alberta*. March 13, 2008. Produced by Peter Raymont. CBC-TV.

Reference re Goods and Services Tax Act [1992] 2 Supreme Court Reports 445.

Reichwein, Baldwin P. "Benchmarks in Alberta's Public Welfare Services: History Rooted in Benevolence, Harshness, Punitiveness and Stinginess." February 2003. Web.

Reilly, James. Letter to the editor. *Calgary Herald*. February 16, 1895. Quoted in Owram, *The Formation of Alberta*, 83–85.

Remington, Robert. "A Calgarian Asks: Why Do They Hate Us?" *Edmonton Journal*. December 6, 2006: A19.

Rennie, Bradford J., ed. *Alberta Premiers of the Twentieth Century*. Regina: Canadian Plains Research Center, 2004.

———. Introduction. In Rennie, vii.

Retson, Don. "Alberta Leads Canada in Most Gay-friendly Churches." *Edmonton Journal*. December 10, 2008: B3.

Richards, John and Larry Pratt. "Oil and Social Class: The Making of the New West." In *Riel to Reform*, 224–44.

———. *Prairie Capitalism: Power and Influence in the New West*. Toronto: McClelland & Stewart, 1979.

Rutherford, A.C. Address to the Canadian Club of Ottawa, October 9, 1906. In *Addresses Delivered before the Canadian Club of Ottawa 1903–1909*, edited by George H. Brown. Toronto: Mortimer, 1910.

———. Quoted in Colombo, 8.

Sadava, Mike. "Taking on the Tyrrell." *Edmonton Journal*. May 24, 2007: A1.

Sandburg, Carl. *Cornhuskers*. New York: Henry Holt, 1918. Quoted in Bartleby.com. Web.

Santayana, George. *The Life of Reason, or, The Phases of Human Progress*. Rev. ed. New York: Charles Scribner's Sons, 1953.

Schultz, Harold J. "Aberhart: The Organization Man." In *The Best of Alberta History*, edited by Hugh A. Dempsey. Saskatoon, SK: Western Producer Prairie Books, 1981. 184–93.

Seiler, Robert M. and Tamara P. Seiler, "Ceremonial Rhetoric and Civic Identity: The Case of the White Hat." *Journal of Canadian Studies* 36 (Spring 2001): 29–49.

Siaroff, Alan. "Provincial Political Data Since 1900." In Dunn, 175–211.

Sierra Club of Canada. *Kyoto Report Card 2007: Stopping Global Warming: Towards a Low-Carbon Canada*. Web.

———. *Rio+14: The Fourteenth Annual Rio. Report on International Obligations. Report Card—2006*. Web. For other years, see ibid., "Rio Report." Web.

Simpson, Jeffrey. "Alberta Remains Canada's Square Peg on Emissions." *Globe and Mail*. March 22, 2008: A21.

Sinclair, Peter R. "Class Structure and Populist Protest: The Case of Western Canada." In Melnyk, *Riel to Reform*, 198–212.

Smith, Roger. "Alberta Fudges its Books to Hide Deficits." *Edmonton Journal*. April 18, 2009: A19.

Solomon, Lawrence. "The 51st and 52nd States." *National Post*. June 5, 2003: FP13.

Staples, David. "Are We World-Class?" *Edmonton Journal.* July 20, 2008: E4.

Statistics Canada. "Aboriginal Peoples in Canada in 2006: Inuit, Métis and First Nations, 2006 Census." *The Daily.* January 15, 2008. Web.

———. "Absence Rates for Full-Time Employees by Sex and Geography." Web.

———. "Age Characteristics." July 24, 2008. Web.

———. "Agriculture Overview, Canada and the Provinces/Tables 1–12. January 7, 2008. Web.

———. "Alberta Weather Winners." Web.

———. "All Data" under "Mobility Status—Place of Residence 1 Year Ago" and "Mobility Status—Place of Residence 5 Years Ago." April 30, 2008. Web.

———. "Average After-tax Income of Families, Canada and Provinces." 2008. Web.

———. "Births and Birth Rate, by Province and Territory." November 29, 2007. Web.

———. "Canadian Internet Use Survey." *The Daily.* June 12, 2008. Web.

———. Cat. No. 91–002 and 71–201. Quoted in Mansell, 26–31.

———. *Cattle Statistics 2007*, Cat. No. 23–012. Web.

———. "Charitable Donors." *The Daily.* November 23, 2006. Web.

———. "Control and Sale of Alcoholic Beverages: Sales of Alcoholic Beverages Per Capita 15 Years or Older." *The Daily.* September 8, 2005. Web.

———. "Cornerstones of Community: Highlights of the National Survey of Nonprofit and Voluntary Organizations, 2003." Revised 2005. Web.

———. "Crime Statistics, 2007." *The Daily.* July 17, 2008. Web.

———. "Deaths 2002." *The Daily.* September 27, 2004. Web.

———. "Deaths and Death Rate, by Province and Territory." June 25 2008. Web.

———. "Disposal and Diversion of Waste, by Province and Territory, 2004 and 2006." July 10, 2008. Web.

———. "Family Violence in Canada: A Statistical Profile 2005." Web.

———. "Government Expenditures on Culture." *The Daily.* October 31, 2005. Web.

———. "Growth Rate for Canada, Provinces and Territories in the Last 50 Years." March 29, 2007. Web.

———. "Hog Inventories." *The Daily.* April 24, 2008. Web.

———. "Hours Worked and Labour Productivity in the Provinces and Territories." *The Daily.* May 14, 2008. Web.

———. "Household Participation Rates for Environmental Behaviours, by Province, 2006." December 16, 2008. Web.

———. "Mid-size Urban Centres with the Fastest Population Growth since 2001." March 29, 2007. Web.

———. "Number of Municipalities. Census Subdivisions and Percentage Distribution by Province, Territory and Type of Region, Canada, 2001." Web.

———. "Population and Dwelling Counts, for Canada and Census Subdivisions (Municipalities), 2006 and 2001 Censuses." March 29, 2007. Web.

———. "Population and Dwelling Counts, for Canada, Provinces and Territories, 2006 and 2001 Censuses." May 11, 2008. Web.

———. "Population by Immigrant Status and Period of Immigration, 2006 Counts, for Canada, Provinces and Territories." December 3, 2007. Web.

———. "Population by Immigrant Status and Period of Immigration, 2006 Counts, for Canada, Provinces and Territories." January 26, 2005. Web.

———. "Population by Religion, by Province and Territory." January 25, 2005. Web.

———. "Population of Canada, Provinces and Territories in the Last 50 Years." March 29, 2007. Web.

———. "Population Urban and Rural, by Province and Territory. Canada. " September 1, 2005. Web.

———. "Portrait of the Canadian Population in 2006: Population of the Provinces and Territories: Alberta: The Engine of Population Growth in the Prairie Provinces." April 13, 2007. Web.

———. "Portrait of the Canadian Population in 2006: Subprovincial Population Dynamics." April 13, 2007. Web.

———. "Prince Edward Island Has the Highest Proportion of Very Active Households, 2006." December 16, 2008. Web.

———. "Residential Telephone Service Survey." *The Daily*. April 23, 2008. Web.

———. "Retail Sales, Canada and Provinces, and Selected Socio-Economic." Web.

———. "Small Towns and Rural Communities with the Fastest Population Decline since 2001." March 29, 2007. Web.

———. "Statistics on Official Languages in Alberta." March 2003. Web.

———. "Study: Canada's Bison Industry." *The Daily*. January 25, 2008. Web.

———. "Study: Christmas Shopping, 2006 in Review." *The Daily*. December 6, 2007. Web.

———. "Study: Firearms and Violent Crime: 2006." February 20, 2008. Web.

———. "Study: The Alberta Economic Juggernaut." *The Daily*. September 14, 2006.

———. "Where We Live? Prairie Provinces." Web.

Stemp, Robert M. *Royal Rebels: Princess Louise and the Marquis of Lorne*. Toronto: Dundurn Press, 1988.

Stenson, Fred. *The Trade*. Vancouver: Douglas & McIntyre, 2000.

———. "The Writer's Life." *Alberta Views* 4:2 (March–April 2001): 34.

Stolte, Elise. "Albertans Spend More for Arts than for their Beloved Sports." *Edmonton Journal*. February 22, 2007: D1.

Stephansson, Stephan G. *Selected Translations from Andvökur*, translated by Watson Kirkconnell. Edmonton: Stephan G. Stephansson Homestead Restoration Committee, 1987.

Stewart, David K. and R. Kenneth Carty. "Many Political Worlds? Provincial Parties and Party Systems." In Dunn, 97–113.

Strom, Harry E. "The Feasibility of One Prairie Province." In *One Prairie Province? A Question for Canada*, edited by David K. Elton. Lethbridge, AB: *Lethbridge Herald*, 1970. 32.

Studin, Irvin, ed. *What Is a Canadian? Forty-Three Thought-Provoking Responses*. Toronto: McClelland & Stewart, 2006.

Swimmer, Gene and Tim Bartkiw. "Provincial Policies Concerning Collective Bargaining." In Dunn, 507–35.

Taft, Kevin. *Shredding the Public Interest*. Edmonton: University of Alberta Press and Parkland Institute, 1997.

Takach, Geo "Ears a Little More Open." *Alberta Views* 4:5 (September–October 2001): 36–40 and *Broadcast Dialogue* (March 2008): 30–36.

———. "How about a Hand for Our Arms?" *Alberta Report*. January 13, 1992: 38.

———. "Rattus Non Gratus." *Alberta Views* 9:6 (July 2006): 40–43.

———, [writer-director]. *Will the Real Alberta Please Stand Up?* Documentary film. Produced by Ava Karvonen and Geo Takach. Broadcast on City TV, June 12, 2009. Edmonton: Stand Up Productions, 2009.

Taras, David. "Alberta in 2004." In Payne et al., 748–65.

Taras, David and Beverly Rasporich, eds. *A Passion for Identity: Canadian Studies for the 21st Century*. Scarborough, ON: Nelson Thomson Learning, 2001.

Tardi, Gregory. "A Nutshell Reminder of the Evolution of Canada's Territories." In Dunn, 337–50.

Taylor, Amy, Chris Severson-Baker, Mark Winfield, Dan Woynillowicz and Mary Griffiths. *When the Government is the Landlord: Economic Rent, Non-Renewable Permanent Funds, and Environmental Impacts related to Oil and Gas Developments in Canada*. n.p.: Pembina Institute, 2004. Web.

Taylor, Brian. Letter to the editor. *Edmonton Journal*. February 8, 2007: A19.

Thomas, L.G. *The Liberal Party in Alberta*. Toronto: University of Toronto Press, 1959.

Thomas, Lewis Robert. *The Struggle for Responsible Government in the North-West Territories 1870–97*. 2nd ed. Toronto: University of Toronto Press, 1978. [Quoting *Regina Journal*, November 10, 1887]

Thomson, Colin A. *The Romance of Alberta Settlements*. Calgary: Detselig, 2004.

Thomson, Graham. "Alberta has Lost its Social Conscience." *Edmonton Journal*. January 11, 2005: A10. [Quoting Lois Hole]

Thorne, Duncan. "Boom Isn't Raising All Family Incomes." *Edmonton Journal*. November 1, 2007: B3.

Thwaite, Leo. *Alberta: An Account of its Wealth and Progress*. New York: Rand McNally, 1912.

Tibbetts, Janice. "Alberta Grade 4 Students Place 3rd out of 45 in International Reading Test." *Edmonton Journal*. November 29, 2007: A1.

Tupper, Allan. "Uncertain Future: Alberta in the Canadian Community." In Connors and Law, 479–96.

Tupper, Charles, M P. *Canada. House of Commons Debates*. May 4, 1883.

Turcotte, Martin. "Life in Metropolitan Areas: Dependence on Cars in Urban Neighbourhoods." *Canadian Social Trends* 85 (Summer 2008): 24. Web.

Turner, Frederick Jackson. *The Frontier in American History*. New York: Henry Holt & Company, 1947 [Orig. pub. 1920].

Tyerman, Marcia, Trudie BonBernard and Phyllis Cardinal, eds. *Our Alberta: Book 1*. Toronto: Thomson Nelson, 2006.

Tyson, Ian. "Four Strong Winds." In *I Outgrew the Wagon*. Vanguard, 1989 [C D, track no. 10].

Tyson, Ian and Colin Escott. *I Never Sold My Saddle*. Vancouver: Greystone Books, 1994.

University of Alberta. "Teaching Excellence." Web.

———. "University of Alberta Facts 2007–08." Web.

Urquhart, Ian. "Alberta's Land, Water and Air: Any Reason Not to Despair?" In Harrison, *Return of the Trojan Horse*, 136–55.

van Herk, Aritha. *Mavericks: An Incorrigible History of Alberta*. Toronto: Penguin Canada, 2001.

———. *The Story of Maverick Alberta*. Toronto: Key Porter, 2007.

———. "Who You Callin' Cultured?" *Alberta Views* 8:8 (December 2005–January 2006): 30–32.

Veno, Kari (Alberta Recycling). "Canada's First." 2006. Web.

Vivequin, Wanda (University of Alberta). "Prof Reveals 'Eugenics Machine.'" *Express News*. July 18, 2003. Web.

Volmers, Eric. "Singer Morphs into Comic-Book Hero." *Edmonton Journal*. March 8, 2007: D1.

Volunteer Alberta. "C S G V P Alberta Statistics Document." Web.

————. "Who are Alberta's Volunteers?" 2004. Web.

Volunteer Canada. "Portrait of Canadian Volunteerism: Highlights and Implications of the *2004 Canada Survey of Giving, Volunteering and Participating*." Web.

Wcpipeline.com. "Hat History Worth Exploring." *The Pipeline*, April 21, 2008. Web.

Wetherell, Donald G. "Making New Identities: Alberta Small Towns Confront the City, 1900–1950." *Journal of Canadian Studies* 39:1 (Winter 2005): 175–97.

————. "Upholding Social Decency and Political Equality: The Lacombe Western Globe and the Ku Klux Klan, 1929–1932." *Alberta History* 51:4 (Autumn 2003): 54–59.

Wetherell, Donald G. and Irene Kmet. *Useful Pleasures: Shaping of Leisure in Alberta 1896–1921*. Regina, SK: Alberta Culture and Multiculturalism and Canadian Plains Research Center, 1990.

White, Graham. "Evaluating Provincial and Territorial Legislatures." In Dunn, 255–78.

Wiebe, Chris. "Unscripted." *Alberta Views* 8:6 (September 2005): 42–47.

Wiebe, Rudy. *The Temptations of Big Bear*. Toronto: McClelland & Stewart, 1973.

Winks, Robin. *The Myth of the American Frontier: Its Relevance to America, Canada and Australia*. Leicester, UK: Leicester University Press, 1971.

Wirth, Louis. "Urbanism as a Way of Life." *The American Journal of Sociology* 44:1 (July 1938): 1–24.

Wiseman, Nelson. "Provincial Political Cultures" in Dunn, 21–56.

Wiseman, Richelle. "Albertans Most Tolerant." *Calgary Herald*. May 09, 2009.

Withey, Elizabeth. "Artists Keen to See Province Pony Up." *Edmonton Journal*. April 15, 2007: B1.

————. "Culture Business a Boon to Alberta Economy." *Edmonton Journal*. March 31, 2007: C1.

Woods, Allan. "Albertans Support Carbon Tax: Poll." *Edmonton Journal*. November 6, 2006: A1.

Yang, Jennifer. "Oilsands Threaten Groundwater." *Edmonton Journal*. July 27, 2008: B1.

Zabjek, Alexandra. "Alberta's Fountain of Youth." *Edmonton Journal*. July 18, 2007: A1.

————. "Alberta's High School Graduation Rate Lowest among Provinces." *Edmonton Journal*. July 29, 2008: B6.

Zabjek, Alexandra and Trish Audette. "Tradition in Transition." *Edmonton Journal*. September 13, 2007: A1.

Zdeb, Chris. "Albertans Keep on Smoking." *Edmonton Journal*. March 17, 2008: D1.

Index

chemistry, 163

constitutional amendment, 170

consumerism, 176–77

creationism, 174

education, 244–46

energy, 175

environmentalism, 300–01

families and young people, 164–66

human rights, 169–70

industry, 175–76

infrastructure, 171–72

Internet access, 172–73

law, 167–68

medicine, 163–64

municipalities and community
organization, 171

ombudsman, 170

paleontology, 173–74

public administration, 170–71

public health, 163–64, 179

retail, 176–77, 273, 281, 286

science and technology, 173

vices, 179–80

wealth, 177–78

women's rights, 168–69

work, 178

young population, 178–79

agriculture, 41–43, 264–65, 270

Airdrie, 312

Alberta Bill of Rights Act, 71, 169–70

Alberta Foundation for the Arts, 227,
229, 230

Alberta Heritage Savings Trust Fund,
277

Alberta, Princess Louise Caroline,
318–28, **319**

achievements, 325–26

legacy, 327, 328

naming province for, 318–21

qualities, 321–27

Alberta Report, 102, 125, 208

Alberta Research Council, 173

Alberta SuperNet, 172–73

Alberta Treasury Branches, 70, 268

Alberta Views, 125, 208

Albertosaurus, 3, 144–47 (interview),
145

Allen, Chris, 215–16, 232

Amber Valley, 87, 234

American

Alberta as oil supplier, 295, 349

Alberta perceived as, 66, 80

frontier thesis of development, 344,
346

immigration encouraged, 234, 342

influence, 8, 64, 66–67, 75–76, 143,
150

manifest destiny, 130, 331

migrations into Alberta, 66–67,
75–76, 85, 140, 233–34

settlement of American West, 40,
342

tariffs on American goods, 139

Wild West vs. Canadian West, 37,
90, 129, 204, 332, 333–34, 347

See also frontier

ambitiousness, 27, 282

anti-Semitism, 98–99

Antoniuk, Tim, 220

apathy, 157–58, 161–62, 301, 337, 351

archaeology, 3

art

Aboriginal, 5, 88, 213, 231

history, 213

See also arts; culture

chinooks, xxi, 19–20, 31, 39, 40, 301

Chrétien, Jean, xxiii, 80, 123, 304

Christianity

    ethos in Alberta, 101–03, 140, 237

    missionaries, 37, 232

    perception of prevalence, 80, 125

    See also Aberhart, William;

        Manning, Ernest; religion

Citadel Theatre, 214, 224

CKUA Radio, **251**

    announcers, 254–55

    cultural contributions, 255–56

    eclecticism, 253

    finances, 252–53, 257

    history, 249–52

    leadership, 248, 256

    uniqueness, 213, 214, 215

Clark, Joe, 76, 123, 162

Clark, Karl, 288

climate, 18–20, **19, 262**–63

coal, 43, 44, 50, 279, 312

coal mining, 16, 68, 235, 285, 332

coat of arms, 8–11

colony, status as, 126, 130, 138–39,

    331, 347

colours, 12, 211

community spirit, 21–22, 28, 31–33,

    95–97

concert halls, 215, 226

Confederation

    Alberta as bad boy, 53, 143

    Alberta contributing to, xxiv, 29,

        115, 352–53

    Alberta joining, 48, 133

    Alberta's place, 349, 352

    as significant event, 114

    See also Canada

conformity, 153–62, 210

conservatism

    and conservation, 302–05

    defined, 54–57

    reputation vs. reality, xxi–xxii, 65,

        338

    symbol of Alberta, 54, 338

Conservative Party (Alberta)

    electoral success, 58, 155–56, 158

    government summarized, 58

    as juggernaut, 155, 158–60

    support base, 33, 150, 160

    See also Getty, Don; Klein, Ralph;

        Lougheed, Peter; Stelmach, Ed

Conservative Party (federal)

    and free trade, 55–56

    as government, 162

    in opposition, 155

consumerism, 92, 176–77, 286

Continental Divide, 9

contradictions

    boom vs. bust, 264, 352

    Christian vs. secular, 103

    concluding remarks, 335–37,

        351–53

    earth-destroyers vs. greens, 302–04,

        307, 309–10, 351

    examples, xxiii, 329–30

    individualist vs. collectivist, 33,

        332–34

    mavericks vs. conformists, 154,

        351–52

    monocultural vs. diverse, 238–39,

        335

    personalities, xvii–xviii

    political labels, 55–56

    rednecks vs. radicals, 57, 111–12,

        351

    rural vs. urban, 32–37, 351

small vs. large government, 74, 110, 154, 208–09

Wild West vs. cultured, 241, 246, 248, 352

contrariness, 136–47

Co-operative Commonwealth Federation, 68, 108, 109, 111

cows. *See* cattle and cattle industry

cowboys, 202–12, 238, 338

   See also Calgary Stampede

creation science, 174–75

Cree, 4, 5, 7, 85, 147, 167, 232, 299, 354

crime rate, 180

Crow Rate, 16

Crowfoot, 8

Crowsnest Pass, 16, 18, 44, 272, 332

culture

   backwater reputation, 208, 226

   economic impact, 227

   entrepreneurial spirit, 216

   government policy, 211–12

   history, 213–14

   private spending, 228

   public funding, 211, 228–30

   See also arts; diversity

Currie, Philip, 2, 23, 174

Cypress Hills, 16

Daley, Doris, 123, 209, 218–19, 279–80, 313–14

Darbasie, Pat, 31, 57, 230

Day, Stockwell, 103, 123

Decoteau, Alex, 166

defensiveness, 136, 282

demographics. *See* population

Depression, **267**

   and Christianity, 103

   and the economy, 265–70

legacy, 266

   and protest, 140–41

   and radicalism, 68–69

   and Social Credit, 58, 63, 70

deviance, 120

Dinosaur Provincial Park, 2, 3, 217

dinosaurs

   in Alberta, 2–3

   Albertosaurus, 3, 144–47 (interview), **145**

   and global warming, 171

discrimination, 86, 91, 97, 101, 240. *See also* tolerance

dissent. *See* protest

distinctiveness, 112–13, 118–20, 122, 126

diversity

   cultural, 236–39

   ecological, 13, 335

   ethnic, 237

   geographic, 14–18

   population, 85, 232–41

   religious, 237–38

   summarized, 335

Donnelly, Andy, 31, 213, 254, 258

doomsday. *See* National Energy Program

Douglas, C.H., 69–70

Douglas, Tommy, 71, 109

Drumheller, 2, 16–**17**, 216–17

Dundas, Joe, 14, 79, 82, 194–95 (interview)

Dundas, Judy Rogers, 194–95 (interview)

Earl Grey. *See* Grey, Albert Henry George

economy

    boom and bust, 28, 262–82

    changing, 310

    and culture of province, 275–76

    forecast, 281

    growth, 272–73

    history in province, 262–74

    and reputation of province, 277–79

    volatility, 276–77

    See also Depression

Edgar, Bud (Bronco Buddy), **280**, 281

Edmonton and Edmontonians

    as capital city, 134, 148–49

    diversity of settlers, 150

    ecological footprint, 286

    economy, 271–72, 274

    environmental efforts, 300–01

    municipal firsts, 171

    perception of, 152

    rivalry with Calgary, 147–53

    self-perception, 151

    spending on arts and culture, 228

Edmonton Eskimos, 88–89, 152

Edmonton Food Bank, 94

Edmonton Grads, xxiii, 143, **169**

Edmonton Heritage Festival, 215, 240

Edmonton Journal

    on party politics, 60

    protesting non-autonomy, 133

Edmonton Oilers, 112, 152, 272

Edmonton Public School Board, 245

education

    achievements, 244–47

    Canadian Composite Learning
        Index, 245–46

    concluding remarks, 352

    history, 244

    public funding, 93, 247

    student performance, 246–47

Edwards, Henrietta Muir, 168

Edwards, Robert Chambers

    foreword by, xiii–xiv

    and Grant MacEwan, 191–92

    introduced, xxii

    populations estimated by, 148

    on truth, 136

egalitarianism, 94, 116, 236–37,
    343–44

elections, federal

    (1911), 55

    (1921), 68

    (1988), 55–56

    (2004), 157–58

    (2006), 299, 303–04

    (2008), 299

elections, provincial

    (1905), 59

    (1917), 61

    (1921), 61–62, 68

    (1926), 68

    (1935), 63

    (1944), 73

    (1948), 73

    (1958), 102

    (1971), 75, 108, 156, 207, 349

    (1982), 89

    (1986), 73

    (1989), 73

    (1993), 57, 76

    (2004), 73

    (2008), 157–58, 159–60

    changes in government, 58, 156

    majority governments, 58

    MLAs, number of, 157

    proportionality of seats to votes, 33,
        73, 156–57, 212, 335

Mackay, Don, 204

Mackenzie King, William Lyon, **49**,
  50, 266

Macoun, John, 38

Manning, Ernest, **53**
  Alberta Bill of Rights Act, 169–70
  and Christianity, 72, 76, 101–02
  and economic growth, 270–71
  ideological shift, 72, 108–09
  isolationism, 207–08
  non-political, 64
  political rise, 64
  politically untouchable, 101–02
  resistance to federal programs, 137,
    138
  Social Credit, 71
  on social services, 73–74
  work ethic, 209

Manning, Preston, **303**
  on business and environmentalism
    (interview), 301–05
  and Christianity, 102–03
  on constitutional inequality, 135
  on democracy, 344
  on Depression finances, 266, 270
  on Ernest Manning, 109, 238–39
  and neo-conservatism, 56
  on north–south split, 149
  on openness, 22
  on pioneering spirit, 282, 341
  and Reform Party, 137

map, xviii

massive roadside attractions, 180–81,
  317

mavericks
  Albertans as, 121–29, 208–09
  Albertans as sheep, 153–62, 210
  in arts and culture, 221–22

concluding remarks, 351–52

defined, 123

mythology, 208–09

McClung, Nellie, 99, 124, 168, 214

McGillivray, Bruce, 14, 20, 152, 238

McKinney, Louise, 61, 168

McLachlin, Beverly, 168

Medicine Hat
  lesson of, 353–54
  library, 242
  naming, 353–54
  natural gas source, 43, 45
  weather, 18–19

medicine wheels, 6

Meikle, Christine, 163

Métis, 8, 84, 166–67, 232, 240, 291

Milk River, 5

Mitchell, W.O., 184, 218

motor vehicles, 287, 289

motto (*fortis et liber*), 12

multiculturalism. *See* diversity

municipal firsts, 171

Murphy, Emily, xxii, 99–100, 124, 168,
  214, 329

museums
  Big Valley Creation Science
    Museum, 174
  Glenbow Museum, 123, 153, 217
  Remington Carriage Museum, 217
  Reynolds-Alberta Museum, 217
  Royal Alberta Museum, 18, 20
  Royal Tyrrell Museum, 22, 145,
    174, 216–17
  Ukrainian Cultural Heritage
    Village, 236
  Whyte Museum of the Canadian
    Rockies, 217

myths
  and Alberta generally, 330–31
  blank slate, 333
  frontier, 79, 333, 341
  reasons for, 334, 348
  wealth for all, 264
  See also contradictions

National Energy Program, 50–51, 79,
      89, 137, 138, 271, 334–35
National Policy, 50, 55, 139, 142, 349
nativism, 83–84
  See also discrimination
natural gas
  use by oil sands industry, 287
  discovery, 45
  and Kipling, 43, 354–55
  royalty regime, 160
  supply, 43
natural resources
  above ground, 41–43, 45–46
  battles for control over, 47–52
  below ground, 43–45
  exploitation, 312, 331
  forests, 43, 285, 289–90
  fur trade, 7, 12, 59, 129, 211, 217,
      310
  jurisdiction over, 46–51, 135
  revenue accounting, 170
  wealth, 47
  See also coal; energy; environment;
      forestry; natural gas; oil; water
New Democratic Party (Alberta), 73
New Democratic Party (federal), 68
non-partisanship, 58–64, 112
  Aberhart's pledge, 63
  Haultain's attempt, 59
  Non-Partisan League, 60

Rutherford's plea, 59
  United Farmers of Alberta, 61
Northern Alberta Institute of
      Technology, 246
North Saskatchewan River, 8, 148
north–south divide in Alberta, 147–53
North West Company, 37
North West Mounted Police, 5, 7, 128,
      130
North-West Territories (Alberta
      1882–1905)
  colonial status, 130, 331
  Haultain's vision, 106
  language pre-1870, 85
  Laurier's vision, 134–35
  Legislature, 59
  Macdonald's vision, 130
  partitioning into districts, 318
  partitioning into provinces, 134–35
  population, 232–35
  provincehood, 130–35
  settlement, 232–35

oil
  and Albertan prime ministers, 162
  and American influx, 75
  Calgary and Edmonton, 151
  demand for friendly oil, 349
  discoveries, 44, 49, 270
  financial dependency on, 160, 271,
      276
  First Law of Petropolitics, 160, 295
  industry, 50–51, 58, 151
  Leduc No. 1, 72, 74, **261, 269**–70
  National Energy Program, 50–51,
      79, 89, 137, 138, 271, 334–35
  National Oil Policy, 50
  OPEC, 50, 177, 271